Egalitarianism

Egalitarianism

New Essays on the Nature and Value of Equality

EDITED BY

Nils Holtug and
Kasper Lippert-Rasmussen

CLARENDON PRESS · OXFORD

OXFORD
UNIVERSITY PRESS

Great Clarendon Street, Oxford ox2 6DP

Oxford University Press is a department of the University of Oxford.
It furthers the University's objective of excellence in research, scholarship,
and education by publishing worldwide in

Oxford New York

Auckland Cape Town Dar es Salaam Hong Kong Karachi
Kuala Lumpur Madrid Melbourne Mexico City Nairobi
New Delhi Shanghai Taipei Toronto

With offices in

Argentina Austria Brazil Chile Czech Republic France Greece
Guatemala Hungary Italy Japan Poland Portugal Singapore
South Korea Switzerland Thailand Turkey Ukraine Vietnam

Oxford is a registered trade mark of Oxford University Press
in the UK and in certain other countries

Published in the United States
by Oxford University Press Inc., New York

British Library Cataloguing in Publication Data

Data available

Library of Congress Cataloging in Publication Data

Data available

Typeset by Laserwords Private Limited, Chennai, India
Printed in Great Britain
on acid-free paper by
Biddles Ltd., King's Lynn, Norfolk

ISBN 978−0−19−929643−9

PREFACE

Virtually everyone believes in some kind of equality. That citizens have an equal right to vote, that people are equals before the law, and/or that public schools and hospitals should serve citizens on an equal basis. Egalitarians, however, believe in equality in a particularly deep sense in that they further believe that, everything else being equal, individuals should have equal shares of resources, or welfare, or equal opportunities to obtain such goods. Nevertheless, a fully developed egalitarian theory will have to say more that this. In fact, as various developments in contemporary political philosophy have revealed, equality is a surprisingly elusive concept.

The chapters in this volume aim to bring greater clarity to the issue and can be seen as contributions to the ongoing project of developing an adequate egalitarian theory. One of the issues dealt with pertains to the *foundations* of equality, in particular, to how this ideal can be defended. Another pertains to the *nature* of equality, where various themes are addressed, including the (allegedly) significant distinction between telic and deontic egalitarianism, prioritarianism, how to define the 'least advantaged group' for the purposes of Rawls's difference principle, equal relations between individuals, and whether egalitarianism applies not just to humans but also to sentient non-human animals (and if so, what the implications are). A third type of issue concerns how equality *relates to other important values* such as desert, responsibility, liberty, and sufficiency. Finally, some specific applications of equality are considered, in particular how equality applies to the issue of health care and whether there are egalitarian reasons—in some cases—to restrict the freedom of suppliers who wish to release products that will confer different levels of risk on consumers, depending on their ability to pay.

Most of the chapters in this book were presented at a conference on egalitarianism at the University of Copenhagen in 2004. We would like to thank the Danish Research Council for the Humanities for financial support, thus making the conference possible. Also, we would like to thank the contributors for their encouragement, cooperative spirit, and, not least, their contributions. Furthermore, we are grateful to Thomas Søbirk Petersen for assistance with organizing the conference. Finally, we would like to thank Claus Hansen for performing the tedious but important task of compiling the index.

N. H. and K. L.-R.

CONTENTS

NOTES ON THE CONTRIBUTORS

Richard J. Arneson is Professor of Philosophy at the University of California, San Diego, and also Director (this really means associate director), Institute for Law and Philosophy, School of Law, University of San Diego. His current research is mainly on two topics: (1) how best to integrate an appropriate concern for personal responsibility in egalitarian theories of social justice, and (2) to what extent one can defend act consequentialism against rival moral doctrines.

Linda Barclay is Lecturer in Philosophy at Aarhus University. Her main area of research is contemporary political philosophy, particularly liberalism. She has published numerous papers concerned with autonomous agency, liberal neutrality, equality, and multiculturalism.

Thomas Christiano is Professor of Philosophy and Law at the University of Arizona and co-director of the Rogers Program in Law and Society in the College of Law at the University of Arizona. He has been a Fellow at the National Humanities Center in Durham, North Carolina, and a Visiting Fellow at All Souls College, Oxford. He is currently finishing a book on the egalitarian foundations of democracy and constitutionalism entitled *The Constitution of Equality*, forthcoming with Oxford University Press. He has published *The Rule of the Many* (Westview Press, 1996) and many articles on the subjects of democratic theory, distributive justice, and moral and political philosophy.

Nils Holtug is Associate Professor of Philosophy at the University of Copenhagen. He has worked on various issues in political philosophy, ethics, bioethics, and metaphysics, and is currently writing a book on welfare and its place in morality and distributive justice. His work is published in various anthologies and in journals such as *Analysis*, *Bioethics*, *Cambridge Quarterly of Healthcare Ethics*, *Economics and Philosophy*, *Ethical Theory and Moral Practice*, *Journal of Agricultural and Environmental Ethics*, *Journal of Applied Philosophy*, *Journal of Ethics*, *Journal of Medical Ethics*, *Theoria*, and *Utilitas*. He can be contacted at nhol@hum.ku.dk

Susan Hurley is Professor of Philosophy at the University of Bristol and a Fellow of All Souls College, Oxford. She is the author of *Natural Reasons* (Oxford University Press, 1989), *Consciousness in Action* (Harvard University Press, 1998), and *Justice, Luck, and Knowledge* (Harvard University Press, 2003), as well as numerous articles for journals and collections, and is editor of *Foundations of Decision Theory* (Basil Blackwell, 1991), *On Human Rights* (Basic Books, 1993), *Perspectives on Imitation* (2 vols., MIT Press, 2005), and *Rational Animals?* (Oxford University Press, 2006).

Kasper Lippert-Rasmussen is Lecturer in Philosophy at the University of Copenhagen. Presently, he is working on the topic of discrimination. His published works fall within the categories of ethics, moral responsibility, political philosophy, and informal logic and have appeared in journals such as *Journal of Political Philosophy*, *Ethics*, *Philosophy and Public Affairs*, *Journal of Ethics*, *Philosophical Books*, *Politics, Philosophy and Economics*, *Philosophical Studies*, and *Journal of Applied Philosophy*. He can be contacted at lippert@hum.ku.dk

Dennis McKerlie is an Associate Professor of Philosophy at the University of Calgary. He has published articles on ancient philosophy and moral philosophy, especially on egalitarianism and justice between age groups.

Ingmar Persson is Professor of Practical Philosophy at Gothenburg University. His interests range over ethics, metaphysics, and the philosophy of mind and action. His principal publication is *The Retreat of Reason: A Dilemma in the Philosophy of Life* (Oxford University Press, 2006). He can be contacted at Ingmar.Persson@phil.gu.se

Bertil Tungodden is Professor in Economics at the Norwegian School of Economics and Business Administration and associated researcher at the Chr. Michelsen Institute in Bergen. His primary research fields are normative economics, political philosophy, and development economics. He co-edited, with Nicholas Stern and Ivar Kolstad, *Toward Pro-Poor Policies: Aid, Institutions, and Globalization* (Oxford University Press, 2004). He can be contacted at bertil.tungodden@nhh.no

Peter Vallentyne is Florence G. Kline Professor of Philosophy at the University of Missouri–Columbia. He writes on issues of liberty and equality—and left libertarianism in particular. He edited *Equality and Justice* (6 vols., Routledge, 2003) and *Contractarianism and Rational Choice: Essays on David Gauthier's 'Morals by Agreement'* (Cambridge University Press, 1991), and he co-edited, with Hillel Steiner, *The Origins of Left Libertarianism: An Anthology of Historical Writings* and *Left Libertarianism and Its Critics: The Contemporary Debate* (Palgrave, 2000). He can be contacted at Vallentynep@missouri.edu

Andrew Williams is a Senior Lecturer in the Department of Philosophy at the University of Reading. As well as publishing articles in journals such as *Ethics* and *Philosophy and Public Affairs*, he is co-editor of *The Ideal of Equality* and *Blackwell Readings in Philosophy: Social Justice*. He is also an Associate Editor of *Politics, Philosophy and Economics*, and *Ratio*.

Jonathan Wolff is Professor and Head of Department of Philosophy, University College London. His recent work tries to connect philosophical analysis with problems in public policy, in the attempt to enrich both fields. He is the author of *Robert Nozick* (Polity Press, 1991), *An Introduction to Political Philosophy* (Oxford University Press, 1996), *Why Read Marx Today?* (Oxford University Press, 2002) and, with Avner de-Shalit, *Disadvantage* (Oxford University Press, forthcoming). He is currently working on a number of issues connected with the ethics of risk. He can be contacted at j.wolff@ucl.ac.uk

1

An Introduction to Contemporary Egalitarianism

Nils Holtug and Kasper Lippert-Rasmussen

1. What Is Equality?

During the 1980s, the number of homeless people in the United States grew rapidly. This was due, among other things, to the Reagan administration's severe cuts to the housing budget. In fact, by the end of the Reagan years the federal government was spending $8 billion annually on housing. The Carter administration had spent $32 billion annually at a time when homelessness was far less common (Singer 1993: 28).[1]

Most egalitarians would think that Reagan's cuts were unjust. This is because these cuts increased inequality. However, egalitarians would not be alone in objecting to Reagan's cuts on the grounds of justice. Most utilitarians would also be troubled, because they would think that the harm the homeless suffered was substantial and not counterbalanced by benefits to taxpayers. These utilitarians would conclude that the Reagan administration produced less total welfare than it could have done with a more generous housing budget and so acted wrongly.

The egalitarian explanation of why Reagan's cuts were unjust refers to equality whereas the utilitarian explanation does not. There is nevertheless a sense in which both egalitarians and utilitarians attach value to equality. In fact, all major normative political theories subscribe to equality in this wide sense. They share what Thomas

---

[1] The editors could easily have found examples of unjust redistribution in favour of the better off, which is closer to home from their perspective. However, they assume the typical reader of this volume will be more familiar with an American example.

Nagel (1979: 111–12) has referred to as 'an assumption of moral equality between persons', according to which equal weight should be given to each person. Thus, utilitarians assign equal weight to persons by taking their interests to be equally important and thus weighing them on the basis of their strength alone. Libertarians hold that everyone has an equal right to him- or herself and to private property. Democrats hold that everyone has an equal right to vote. And conservatives (and almost everyone else) hold that people are equals before the law.

Nevertheless, not everyone is an egalitarian. This is because egalitarians adopt a *particular* interpretation of the assumption of moral equality between persons. They hold that persons should have equal shares of goods such as resources or welfare, or perhaps equal access to, or opportunities to obtain, these goods. This is the kind of equality we shall be concerned with here.

Of course, other theories will assign instrumental value to equality: they will value equality where it promotes other values. Thus utilitarians might claim that, since money has decreasing marginal utility, we should aim for a significant degree of monetary equality (Hare 1981: 164–5). However, egalitarians do not value equality merely because it promotes other values. They value it *intrinsically*, that is, non-instrumentally or for its own sake.

On the face of it, egalitarianism seems a simple political ideal. Perhaps that is part of its attraction. However, as has emerged from the vast literature on egalitarianism since John Rawls published his pioneering work *A Theory of Justice* in 1971, equality is a complex notion that requires considerable elucidation. In this chapter, we shall provide a brief sketch of some of the key issues. We shall characterise egalitarianism by looking at its foundations, nature, value, and applicability. En route, we shall indicate where each contribution in this volume fits into this characterisation, and how, together, the contributions can be seen as part of an ongoing effort to define and defend a plausible egalitarian ideal for our time. Thus, this chapter aims to provide the big picture.

2. Equality of What?

A fully developed egalitarian theory will need to specify *what*, exactly, is to be distributed equally. In *A Theory of Justice*, Rawls suggested that the relevant distributive units are 'social primary goods': rights and liberties, powers and opportunities, income and wealth, and the social bases of self-respect. These are things any rational person is presumed to want, irrespective of her particular plan of life (1971: 62; 1982).

However, what really sparked the 'equality of what?' or 'currency of egalitarian justice' debate was a pair of articles by Ronald Dworkin (1981a, b), published ten years after the appearance of Rawls's *A Theory of Justice*. In these articles, Dworkin distinguishes between *equality of welfare* and *equality of resources*. Equality of welfare initially seems an attractive view. Egalitarians are concerned with how well people fare relative to others. And it seems plausible that the relevant distributive unit should be whatever ultimately matters with respect to how well people fare, i.e. welfare. Resources, by contrast, are important only insofar as they lead to welfare.

Consider income, which is one of the items on Rawls's list of social primary goods. People seek an income, not because they take money to have intrinsic value, but because money can be spent to improve the quality of their lives. It would seem, then, that egalitarians should care about equality of welfare.

Again, to see the appeal of equality of welfare, consider a case in which two people have the same income. One has a disability that requires her to spend most of her money on buying expensive medicine. This means that she has less money to spend on food, housing, and other necessities. Suppose also that, therefore, she has a lower welfare than does the other person. Is that tolerable from an egalitarian perspective? Should we not compensate the disabled person for her extra expenses? Equality of resources fails to explain the disquiet behind these questions, because the two people already *have* the same income. The disquiet is explained by our pre-theoretical leaning towards equality of welfare.

Dworkin nevertheless believes that ultimately equality of welfare should be rejected. One of the reasons he gives is that this theory does not hold people responsible for their choices, including their expensive tastes:

> Imagine that a particular society has managed to achieve equality of welfare ... Now suppose that someone (Louis) sets out deliberately to cultivate some taste or ambition he does not now have, but which will be expensive in the sense that once it has been cultivated he will not have as much welfare ... as he had before unless he acquires more wealth. These new tastes may be tastes in food and drink: Arrow's well-known example of tastes for plovers' eggs and pre-phylloxera claret. (Dworkin 1981a: 229; see also 1985: 206–8)

The point is that to achieve equality of welfare, one would have to devote more resources to Louis than to a person with cheaper tastes, say for beer, sausages, and chips. But surely a plausible ideal of equality would not require us to compensate people for acquiring expensive tastes?

In response to this point, Dworkin develops a theory of equality of resources. Unlike Rawls's theory, this theory compensates people in the sort of case described above, where two people have the same income but one is nevertheless rendered worse off by a disability or some other natural disadvantage. And unlike equality of welfare, this theory holds people responsible for their choices.[2]

---

[2] Incidentally, Rawls's theory does not hold people fully responsible for their choices either. According to Rawls's difference principle, the worst off should be maximally compensated whether or not their being worst off reflects their own choices.

To hold people responsible for their choices, Dworkin devises a hypothetical auction in which people bid for available resources from a platform of equal purchasing power. At the end of the auction, everyone will have a bundle of resources. The resulting distribution should satisfy what Dworkin calls the envy test for equality: No one prefers someone else's bundle of resources to his or her own (Dworkin 1981b: 285). Had someone preferred another bundle, he could have made a bid for it himself. Importantly, this conception of equality holds people responsible for the choices they make, both during and after the auction. If some bidders decide to buy Ferraris rather than to invest, or to buy leisure rather than to work, and so end up with fewer resources than others, that is their choice and they should not be compensated.

However, as Dworkin points out, the auction does not yet accommodate the intuition that people should be compensated for deficits involving 'internal' resources. Consider again the disabled person. She will have to spend a significant portion of her equal initial share on medicine, so she may not have much money left to buy other resources. Dworkin deals with this problem by devising a hypothetical insurance scheme, where people can insure themselves against disadvantages with respect to their internal resources such as disabilities and lack of talent. They are then asked how much of their initial purchasing power they are willing to spend on such insurance. To secure impartiality, they are to insure themselves from behind a veil of ignorance, where they face an equal chance of having the relevant disadvantages. Those who turn out actually to have the disadvantages when the veil is lifted are then compensated on the basis of what people on average have been willing to insure for (Dworkin 1981b: 297–8). Finally, the auction is run on the basis of this new distribution of purchasing power, where those who have natural disadvantages have a higher share than others.

Dworkin's theory has been criticised in various ways. In Chapter 13 in the present volume, Susan Hurley focuses on different accounts of the importance of health for distributive justice. First, she makes the point that equality of welfare does not distinguish between persons whose inefficiency in generating welfare derives from their expensive tastes and those whose inefficiency derives from their ill health. In either case, people may be entitled to compensation. However, she then points out that Dworkin's theory of equality of resources does not assign special significance to health either. Rather, health is on a par with other internal resources such as talents and is in competition with other goods. Equality of resources, then, does not attach special significance to health.

Another worry that has been voiced about Dworkin's account is that, in it, questions of responsibility are confused with the question of whether egalitarianism should take resources or welfare as its currency (Arneson 1989: 88; Cohen 1989b). Thus Richard Arneson has argued for a view he labels 'equality of opportunity for welfare'. This focuses on welfare and yet is intended to accommodate Dworkin's aim to hold people responsible for their choices. For equality of opportunity for welfare to obtain, people must have equally good options in the sense that their options are equivalent in the prospects for welfare they offer. This allows Arneson to argue that people who have deliberately acquired expensive tastes should not be compensated, even if their tastes now render them worse off than others with respect to welfare. What matters is that, at some appropriate time, they had options that were as good as everyone else's, not whether they have in fact made good use of these options.[3]

This issue arises with regard to resources as well. That is, should people have equal shares of resources irrespective of their own responsibility for acquiring, or failing to acquire, those resources, or should their resources be adjusted to reflect responsibility? It can be seen, then, that the issue whether egalitarians should be concerned with welfare or resources, and the separate issue whether (and how) they should accommodate considerations about responsibility, cut across one another. Of course, much more can be said on the relationship between responsibility and equality. We shall give a more detailed account of it in Section 7.

While many egalitarians are attracted to Dworkin's equality of resources and other resource-based theories, many others are sceptical. Indeed it is interesting that seven contributors in the present volume operate either with welfare or opportunity for welfare. Apart from Arneson, this list includes Christiano, Holtug, Lippert-Rasmussen, McKerlie, Persson, and Vallentyne.

In the remainder of this introduction, we shall try not to assume any particular account of the currency of egalitarian justice. We shall speak mostly of 'goods' or of people being 'well' or 'badly' off. However, it will sometimes make a difference what currency is assumed, and where it does we shall be more specific.

3. Equality Between Whom?

Suppose a plausible answer has been given to the 'equality of what?' question. Next, an egalitarian will need to say who should stand in this relation of equality—in the favoured currency—to each other. Several issues need to be addressed here.

First, there is the question whether equality applies to *groups* or to *individuals*. Consider Rawls's difference principle. This principle states that social and economic inequalities are to be arranged so that they are to the greatest benefit of the least advantaged (Rawls 1971: 302). Furthermore, Rawls (1971: 95–100) specifies that by the 'least advantaged', he means the least-advantaged *group* (or the representative member of that group).

---

[3] For other accounts of the currency of egalitarian justice that are broadly speaking in the same ballpark as the welfare-based and resource-based theories mentioned, see e.g. Cohen (1989*b*), Roemer (1996), Sen (1995), and Vallentyne (2002).

Likewise, various issues of equality involving the sexes or ethnicity may seem to be questions about the equality of groups.

However, one may worry that such a focus on groups is unstable. That is, if we are worried about inequalities between groups of individuals, why does this worry not translate into a worry about inequalities between *members* of the group? Suppose that the level of goods for a particular group is its average; and suppose that the worst-off group consists of three members, for whom we can provide either of the following individual levels of goods: (1, 3, 5) or (3, 3, 3). Since both give an average of 3, the difference principle is indifferent. But to many egalitarians (3, 3, 3) is a better distribution.

Since it focuses on groups, Rawls's difference principle should be contrasted with leximin. Leximin is the principle that benefits to the worst-off *person* have priority over benefits to others (and if the worst-off person is indifferent, benefits to the second-worst-off person have priority, and so on). However, in their joint contribution to this volume (Chapter 7), Bertil Tungodden and Peter Vallentyne argue that it may be difficult to obtain a plausible definition of 'least-advantaged group' permitting significant deviations from leximin. This is an interesting result, not least because leximin is generally taken to assign too much weight to the least advantaged. It implies that we should forgo a huge benefit to the second-worst-off person simply to secure a tiny benefit to the very worst-off person even where the latter is only slightly worse off than the former.

Consider now the case of equality between the sexes; and suppose, simply, that all men are well off (and equally so), and that all women are badly off (again, equally so). This situation is represented as A in Figure 1.1. (The columns represent groups of men and women. The width represents the number of people in the group and the height represents how well off they are.) Compare outcomes A and B. The difference between them is that, in B, half the women have joined the better-off group and half the men have joined the worse-off group. And so with respect to equality between the groups of men and women, there is perfect equality in B. On average, women are exactly as well off as men are. Suppose also that in neither A nor B are the individuals involved here responsible for how well off they are. On that assumption, many will

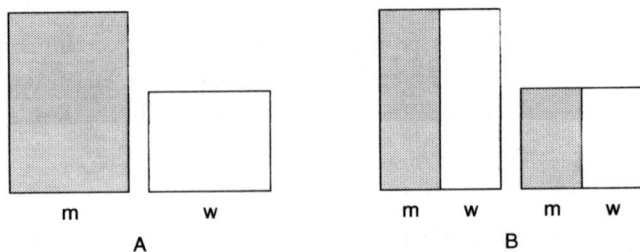

FIG. 1.1

argue that the inequality in B is just as bad as the inequality in A. They will infer that inequality between individuals is what ultimately matters, not inequality between groups: here, it is the fact that in both outcomes half the individuals are worse off than the other half through no fault of their own.[4]

A further question is whether the ideal of equality applies only *within* politically unified societies (such as states) or also *between* them. Of course, the answer to this question will have tremendous practical importance, because some of the greatest inequalities in the world today obtain between rich and poor countries. If we again look to Rawls (1971), he explicitly proposed his theory of justice as a theory for a single society. He did not intend his principles of justice to apply to the relations between states. And he has later argued that international justice does not require anything as strong as the difference principle (1993, 1999).

One could try to argue for 'local' rather than 'global' equality in various ways. One route would be via a contract argument. Along such lines, Rawls imagines that different peoples are represented in an original position in which they are to choose a set of principles of international justice. He argues that they would here agree on a number of fundamental liberty rights but not on any egalitarian ones. However, many have been critical of the idea that a contract in which the parties are genuinely free and equal can be used to rule out equality as a requirement of international justice in a world in which mutually advantageous transactions occur across the globe. In particular, Rawls's idea that the original position can be used to generate egalitarian principles domestically, but only non-egalitarian principles globally, has been subjected to a great deal of criticism (Pogge 1994).

Alternatively, it could be argued that there are other 'special relations' between members of a single society that do not obtain between members of distinct societies. However, it is not clear that there are any such relations. Nevertheless, there is a thesis that may provide a case for a different kind of local equality. This is nationalism. According to many nationalists, special relations obtain between co-nationals, and these relations generate special obligations (Miller 1995: 72). Therefore, it may be suggested that egalitarian concerns are owed exclusively, or at least primarily, to co-nationals. Note, however, that this claim differs in important respects from the claim that egalitarian concerns are owed primarily to members of one's own state. A single state may house different nations and a single nation may be spread out over several states.

Of course, nationalist claims are controversial. It is also worth pointing out that there are powerful resources within the egalitarian framework from which one can

---

[4] Note, incidentally, that even if one aims at equality between individuals rather than between groups, this does not preclude group-oriented measures to implement such equality. For instance, if there are social mechanisms that systematically prevent women from obtaining certain positions or benefits, group-oriented measures (say, affirmative action) may be a way of countering such mechanisms and so of achieving equality between individuals.

argue for *global* equality. Thus, in his defence of the difference principle Rawls himself appeals to the idea that non-deserved inequalities between individuals should be eliminated. We shall consider this eliminative aim—the aim of neutralising luck—in greater detail in Section 6, but let us here merely point out that no one chooses which society they are born in. Therefore, people cannot be said to deserve to be worse off than others as a result of their inherited location or nationality (unless, perhaps, they have had the opportunity to join a different society). Thus, Ethiopians have not chosen to be Ethiopians, and many egalitarians believe that therefore states that are in a position to help have an egalitarian obligation to do so.

Another 'equality between whom?' issue concerns the relationship between generations. Does the present generation have an egalitarian obligation not to pollute the earth because this will harm future generations, perhaps rendering them worse off than we are?

Rawls argues that the difference principle does not apply across generations. He refers to the contractualist view, briefly mentioned above, according to which obligations of justice presuppose mutual advantage. As he puts it: 'We can do something for posterity but it can do nothing for us' (Rawls 1971: 291).

However, this conclusion is in tension with another Rawlsian line of argument, namely, the one that appeals to the idea that people should not end up unequally well off as a result of morally arbitrary factors. Just as people do not choose *where* they are born, they do not choose *when* they are born. So concern about equality does indeed seem to apply to the relationship between generations. At any rate, future victims of pollution cannot be said to deserve to be worse off than the present generation.[5] In truth, the issue of justice between generations is notoriously complex, and we cannot usefully say anything more about it here.[6]

Finally, consider the issue of non-human animals. Do (some) non-human animals fall under the scope of equality or are we dealing with humans only? Peter Singer (1975) has famously argued that 'all animals are equal' and questioned factory farming and animal experiments. However, the doctrine of equality proposed by Singer is not an egalitarian one. He proposes merely that the assumption of moral equality between persons referred to earlier should be extended to non-human animals. More specifically, he proposes a utilitarian doctrine of equal consideration of the interests of all animals, human and non-human.

Egalitarians (proper) have generally had little to say about non-human animals. In the present volume (Chapter 9), Peter Vallentyne aims to rectify this. As he points out, the issue of non-human animals is both important and potentially worrying

[5] The tension between these two Rawlsian lines of thought is a theme in Barry (1989).
[6] For a discussion of some of the complexities specifically pertaining to equality and intergenerational justice, see Temkin (1992).

for egalitarians. Thus, he argues that, given a number of plausible assumptions, egalitarianism implies what he calls the 'problematic conclusion', according to which morality requires a massive shift of resources away from most humans—even most of those with significantly diminished human lives—to most mice (and other sentient non-human animals). This is because, in general, mice have less welfare than humans, and because there seems to be no plausible reason why egalitarianism should not apply to mice. For instance, non-human animals cannot be disregarded on the basis of not possessing self-consciousness, because that would imply that infants and humans with severe cognitive disabilities also fall outside the scope of equality.

Vallentyne considers various possible answers here, including the possibility of simply embracing the problematic conclusion. He ends up offering a solution which, among other things, involves the idea that moral standing comes in degrees, and the further idea that most non-human animals have lower moral standing than most humans. Very roughly, their lower moral standing should be weighed against their having less welfare when we assess their egalitarian claim for resources (in fact, Vallentyne's solution is much more subtle than this). It emerges that even if the claims of non-human animals for resources are sometimes stronger than the claims of humans, often they are not. And so, Vallentyne contends, egalitarianism does not imply the problematic conclusion. Yet it does extend to non-human animals.

4. Equality When?

Egalitarians need to clarify the temporal span of egalitarian justice. What temporal extension, or period, of an individual's life should we focus on when determining how well off she is? Consider two outcomes, C and D, in Tables 1.1 and 1.2. Each outcome contains two individuals, a and b, the numbers refer to their share of goods, and T_1, T_2, ..., T_4 are equally long temporal stages. In C, a enjoys a high level of 9 in the first half of his life and a low level of 1 in the second half; b enjoys the same levels, but the order is reversed. In D, on the other hand, each enjoys a constant level of 5 throughout his life. Is either of these distributions better than the other, in egalitarian terms?

Table 1.1

C	T_1	T_2	T_3	T_4	Total
a	9	9	1	1	20
b	1	1	9	9	20

Table 1.2

D	T_1	T_2	T_3	T_4	Total
a	5	5	5	5	20
b	5	5	5	5	20

Most egalitarians have assumed what may be called 'whole lives egalitarianism', according to which the goods relevant for assessing egalitarian claims are the goods accruing over an entire lifespan.[7] In both C and D, each of a and b have 20 such units. Therefore, whole lives egalitarianism implies that neither C nor D is better than the other with respect to equality: they are equally good. However, in a pioneering article, Dennis McKerlie has challenged this view (1989; see also Temkin 1993: 232–44). He claims that while C is marred by unjust inequality, D is not. At both T_1 and T_2 in C, a has 9 whereas b only has 1. And the fact that their positions are reversed in T_3 and T_4 does not simply nullify the badness of such inequality. In at least one respect, it adds to it.

This suggests that it matters whether people are equally well off at particular times. Furthermore, this intuition can be captured by egalitarian views that focus on stretches of time that are shorter than whole lives. For instance, time-slice egalitarianism implies that, at any point in time, it is bad if some people are worse off than others. And time-stage egalitarianism implies that it is bad if some people are worse off than others over certain stretches of time (where these stretches do not amount to whole lives). Both views imply that since a and b are unequally well off in each of T_1–T_4 in C, and indeed at every point in time, C is worse than D.

Note, incidentally, that whole lives egalitarianism and, for instance, time-slice egalitarianism have importantly different implications with respect to the issue of intergenerational justice raised in the last section. According to whole lives egalitarianism, inequalities between individuals in different generations may well matter. For if the present generation pollutes enough, the entire lives of future individuals may well be worse than our entire lives. However, time-slice egalitarianism is concerned only with inequalities *at* particular time-slices and so does not give us a reason to regret intergenerational inequality.

On the other hand, unlike whole lives egalitarianism, time-slice egalitarianism necessarily creates an objection to simultaneous inequalities between age groups. If the young are now better off than the old, this implies time-slice inequalities. But it does not necessarily imply inequalities over whole lives. Those who are now old were once young, and those who are now young will one day be old (or so one would hope).

---

[7] See e.g. Rawls (1971: 78); Daniels (1996: 259–64); Dworkin (1981*b*: 304–5); Nagel (1991: 69).

Table 1.3

E	T_1	T_2	T_3	T_4	Total
a	9	9	9	9	36
b	1	1	1	1	4

It is doubtful whether time-slice or time-stage egalitarianism can simply replace whole lives egalitarianism. To see this compare C with E (Table 1.3). In respect of time-slice and time-stage inequality, E does not differ from C. However, from an egalitarian point of view, C certainly seems better. This point can be captured by whole lives egalitarianism. Over their entire lives, a and b are equally well off in C, whereas a is much better off than b in E. In view of this, it has been suggested that several theories of the temporal span of egalitarian justice will have to be combined.

In his contribution to this volume (Chapter 6), Dennis McKerlie reconsiders his earlier views about the temporal span of egalitarian justice. He points out that these views relied on certain controversial ideas, including the idea that we must assign moral importance to time itself and the idea that a temporal stage in a life is an appropriate locus of distribution.

Why do egalitarian views that focus on time-slices or time-stages rather than entire lives assign moral importance to time itself or facts about timing? They do so because, while it seems to matter whether people are unequally well off at particular times, it does not similarly seem to matter whether they are unequally well off at different times. If, for instance, two people are born on the same day and lead their equally long lives in tandem, so that at every point in time the welfare of the one equals the welfare of the other, it does not seem to matter that one is worse off in her old age than the other is in her childhood. Thus, what matters is *simultaneous* inequality. However, as McKerlie points out, he did not explain why time itself should have such significance. He simply appealed to our intuitions. Nor did he explain why time-slices or time-stages should be considered appropriate loci of distribution (again here, he appealed to our intuitions).

One turn an egalitarian could take in order to justify time-slice or time-stage egalitarianism involves appeal to Parfit's views about personal identity and what matters in survival (1984). However, McKerlie argues that this is not a plausible option. He suggests instead that perhaps some of the intuitions to which he was appealing are better captured by a different kind of view: prioritarianism. We shall examine prioritarianism in Section 9. For now a brief description will suffice. According to prioritarians, a benefit matters more the worse off the beneficiary is. Unlike equality, priority is not an essentially comparative notion. To assess the moral value of a benefit to an individual, we need only know how well off this individual is, not how well off she is in comparison to others.

McKerlie argues that since priority is, in this sense, not comparative, we can apply it to temporal stages in lives without making an additional case for holding that a temporal stage is an appropriate locus of distribution. Furthermore, we can avoid assigning moral importance to time itself. This is because it is plausible to claim that priority applies to time-slices or time-stages *whenever* they occur, that is, irrespective of their timing. If people have priority at times when they are worse off, it does not, in itself, matter when this is.

5. Measures of Equality

However we answer the questions 'equality of what?', 'equality between whom?', and 'equality when?', we will hardly ever be in a position to choose between a perfectly equal outcome and an unequal one. Rather, we will face choices between different unequal outcomes. To make these decisions, egalitarians need to know which unequal outcomes are worse than others from the point of view of equality.[8] As Larry Temkin has shown, this question turns out to be surprisingly complex (1993: 19–87; see also Rae 1981: 104–28).

We can illustrate the complexity by presenting an extract from Temkin's intricate discussion of the so-called 'sequence'. The sequence consists of 999 different, unequal outcomes in which the same group of 1,000 people exist. In every outcome, each person is either badly off or well off. The well-off people are equally well off across the different outcomes and so are the badly off people. The outcomes differ only in the number of people who are badly off and the number of people who are well off. In the sequence's first outcome, one person is badly off and 999 are well off—the sequence's 'plentiful extreme'. In the second outcome, two persons are badly off while 998 are well off; and so on and so forth, until we reach the sequence's last, dismal outcome in which one person is well off and 999 are badly off—the sequence's 'poor extreme'. This sequence is represented in Figure 1.2. The question now is which of these outcomes are worse than which others from the point of view of equality? Obviously, the plentiful extreme is better, from the point of view of total goods and, very probably, all things considered, but this is not to the point, which is how these outcomes compare from the point of view of *equality*. Two issues seem relevant to this question: who has a complaint about distribution, and how serious is this complaint?

With regard to who has a complaint, there are at least two plausible views. On the first, anyone who is worse off than average has a complaint. If, say, the relevant

---

[8] For a valuable account of different measures of inequality, see Sen (1997).

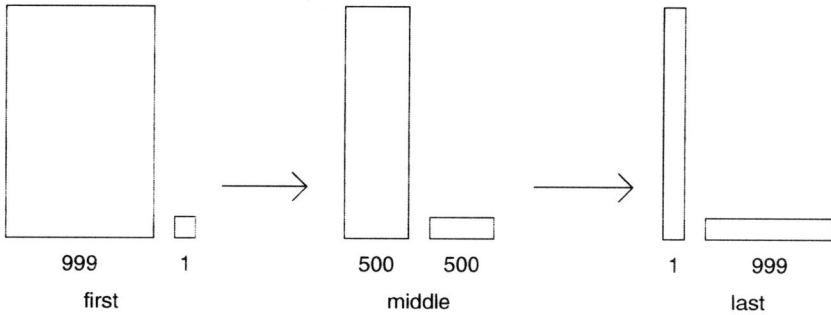

999   1   500   500   1   999

first   middle   last

FIG. 1.2

goods are resources and the sum of resources is constant across different distributions, those who would benefit from an equal distribution would be those who were below the average. On the second view, anyone who is worse off than the best-off has a complaint. Again, there is something to be said for this view, since anyone who is worse off than the best-off person is, we can assume, worse off than this person through no fault or choice of his own.

Moving now to the question of seriousness, at least three views are prima facie attractive. On the first, the greater the difference between a person's level of benefits and the average level, the more serious is this person's complaint. On the second view, the greater the difference between a person's level of benefits and the best-off person's level of benefits, the more serious is this person's complaint. In support of both of these views, it might be observed that, on them, it is only when a person reaches the relevant superior level that he no longer has a complaint regarding inequality. On the third view, to determine the seriousness of a worse-off person's complaint, we should determine how many other people are better off than this person and by how much: the more people who are better off and the greater the gap between them and the person in question, the more serious is this person's complaint. The idea is that the more people who are better off than you through no fault or choice of your own, the worse; and the worse off you are compared to them, again, the worse.

With these suggestions in mind, let us now return to the sequence and assess the equality in the outcomes situated between the plentiful extreme and the poor extreme. One position is that the different outcomes become steadily better (with respect to equality). As the number of badly off people grows, it makes less and less sense for them to see themselves as a group singled out for unfair treatment. A remarkable implication of this view is that if we move from the distribution in which 100 people are badly off to the one in which only one person is badly off, we make things worse—not all things considered, of course, but in respect of equality. (Incidentally, this brings out that descriptive measures of equality are different from the sort of measure that we are after here. For on a typical descriptive measure, for instance the Gini Coefficient, there is very little inequality in the outcome which is worst, according to the present measure of badness of inequality, since only a tiny fraction of the total amount of benefits needs to be redistributed to achieve perfect equality.)

Can this position on the badness of inequality be supported, and if so, how? Suppose we use a maximin principle to assess inequality. This principle says that how bad a given distribution is with regard to equality depends solely on the seriousness of the complaint of those who are worst off. Now the worst-off persons have a still less serious complaint if we accept either the first or the third view about the seriousness of complaints. As we move along the sequence to the poor extreme the gap between the worst-off person and the average person becomes smaller and smaller, and fewer and fewer people are better off than the worst-off person. Hence, on the maximin principle the outcomes of the sequence become steadily better.

Alternatively, it may be submitted that the outcomes become steadily worse. This submission might be underwritten by an additive principle of equality. On this principle, the badness of inequality can be determined simply by adding up the complaints of each worse-off person. On the assumption that the seriousness of a complaint is determined by how much worse off the person in question is relative to the best-off person, it follows that the outcomes of the sequence become worse, from the point of view of equality, as more and more people are badly off.

A third view says that the outcomes at first become worse and worse and then at some point start getting better and better. The reasoning behind this view might be the following. The first outcome is almost equal, except for one badly off person. We then move further and further away from this almost equal distribution until we reach the point where exactly half are badly off and half are well off. After that point it starts getting better, because as more and more become badly off we approach a distribution which is nearly perfectly equal, since everyone except one person is badly off. On this view, the extremes of the sequence are best from the point of view of equality.

We commit ourselves to this line of reasoning if we endorse the additive principle of equality together with the view that the seriousness of a worse-off person's complaint is determined by the distance between his level of benefits and all better-off persons' levels of benefits and by how many persons are better off. Given these assumptions, the first move in the sequence doubles the number of people who have a complaint and does not reduce the seriousness of the complaint of the first person by more than a fraction: the distance between the first worse-off person and the better off is not reduced, but the move reduces the number of persons who are better off from 998 to 997 and thereby the seriousness of his complaint by a fraction. When we have reached the middle of the sequence and move from the distribution in which the number of badly off people equals the number of well-off people to the distribution in which 501 persons are badly off, one more person has a complaint, which makes the inequality worse, but this effect is more than offset by the fact that the seriousness of the very many, already badly off persons' (500) complaints is reduced by a fraction. This countervailing factor grows even stronger as we approach the poor extreme of the sequence.

These remarks by no means do justice to Temkin's rich discussion of measures of the badness of inequality (each of which he shows to have intuitive attractions). However, they well illustrate that the way in which we resolve this matter will have a serious impact on the ranking of unequal outcomes. In practical terms, it is not hard to grasp the importance of the fact that, on some views, we do not improve a situation by bringing some, but not all, of the worst off up to a level enjoyed by the best off, while on others we do.

6. Arguments for Egalitarianism

Much of the work on equality done over the last thirty years involves attempts to articulate cogent, intuitively correct accounts of equality. This work addresses questions like those asked in the last four sections. Egalitarians have tended to *assume* that equality, in one form or another, is desirable. They have thus tended to neglect the, in some ways, more basic question whether equality (in *some* form or other) is desirable.

Clearly, these questions are interpenetrating. One cannot say whether equality is desirable without an understanding of it. Nor can one construct an account of equality without some sense of the desirability that attaches to it, and in the construction process this sense will have to survive critical scrutiny. In this section, however, we want to try to isolate the desirability issue.

There are at least two kinds of argument for the claim that equality is intrinsically just or otherwise intrinsically desirable. One tries to derive equality from more basic moral values, perhaps in conjunction with additional assumptions. The other supports the ideal of equality by demonstrating that this ideal explains many of our considered moral judgments and, more generally, is a component in the most coherent account of our considered moral beliefs—that is, is incorporated in the moral judgments that would survive the auditing process leading to what Rawls calls 'reflective equilibrium'. For instance, when we compare two distributions of the same total amount of welfare, one of which is equal and the other of which is very unequal, many prefer the former to the latter. This might be taken to support the ideal of equality (as against, say, utilitarianism) in that equality explains this preference. This suggests, although by no means establishes, that equality would survive the process leading to reflective equilibrium.

However, even this weak claim has been resisted. First, it has been pointed out that other views explain this preference—for instance, prioritarianism. On this view, an equal distribution of welfare also has greater value than unequal distribution of the same sum. Second, egalitarians are committed to saying that it is in one respect better if everyone is equally badly off than if everyone is better off though not equally so. This claim is implausible, or so many have thought. When we combine these two observations, we see that our preference for the more equal distribution of welfare is better explained by priority than by equality. This may suggest that equality does not survive the auditing process leading to reflective equilibrium. Nevertheless, some observers would urge that it is not implausible to hold that levelling down is in one respect good. We will discuss this so-called 'levelling down objection' in greater detail in Section 8.

Turning now to attempts to derive equality from more fundamental moral principles, one argument that pops up at various places in the literature, although it has never been fully articulated and explicitly endorsed, grounds equality in a deeper aim of neutralising the effects of luck on distribution. One can find this line of thought in Rawls's work. Rawls examines what he calls 'the system of natural liberty'. This is a system in which formal equality of opportunity obtains in so far as 'all have at least the same legal rights to all advantaged social positions' and applicants are assessed on their merits alone (Rawls 1971: 72). He says, 'Intuitively, the most obvious injustice of the system of natural liberty is that it permits distributive shares to be improperly influenced by these factors [i.e. social circumstances and such chance contingencies as accident and good fortune] so arbitrary from a moral point of view' (1971: 71).

This passage may seem to suggest that, under a just distribution, luck—that is, factors that are arbitrary from a moral point of view—will not influence distributive shares (Rawls 1971: 72). G. A. Cohen appears to agree. He writes, for instance, that 'anyone who thinks that initial advantage and inherent capacity are unjust distributors thinks so because he believes that they make a person's fate depend too much on sheer luck' (1989b: 932). This seems to indicate that the aim of neutralizing luck justifies equality and that the realization of equality will eliminate luck.

Let us set aside exegetical questions about the quoted passages and focus on the soundness of the argument itself. Susan Hurley has argued that if the aim of eliminating the influence of luck on the distribution of benefits were to justify equality, it would have to be the case that equality (as opposed, for instance, to utility maximisation, or maximising the position of the worst off) limits the influence of luck on outcomes. Unfortunately, this is not the case (Hurley 2003; compare Parfit 1991: 12). For surely an equal distribution might come about as a matter of sheer luck. If, for instance, we live equally good lives because by some cosmic accident we happen to have a combination of native endowments and environments that ensures that everyone lives equally good lives, luck and equality coexist; and clearly, this does not render the equal distribution less just than it would have been if it had come about through collective social planning (Hurley 2003: 146−80).

In response to Hurley's observation, it might be urged that when luck-egalitarians write about 'neutralising luck' this really is shorthand for something like 'eliminating the differential effects on people's interests of factors which, from their perspective, are a matter of luck' (Arneson 2001; Lippert-Rasmussen 2005). This might indeed be so. However, as Hurley points out, if that is what is meant, it follows that no attempt has been made to justify equality through the luck-neutralising aim, and hence that in so far as we want to justify equality, we still need to do so. The reason is that, on the suggested reading, equality is treated as a default position deviations from which are unjust in so far as they are the result of luck. But then no reason relating to the aim of neutralising luck has been given for holding that equality (and not, say, the distribution that maximises welfare or the position of the worst off) should be the default position.

This criticism of the attempt to ground equality in a luck-neutralising aim might encourage us to look for an alternative basis of justification. Two options here are set out in this volume. Ingmar Persson (Chapter 3) argues in favour of an extreme egalitarian position according to which justice requires everyone to be equally well off (in terms of welfare). He points out that this position follows from the following two claims. First, a formal principle of justice to the effect that a state is just if and only if everyone is equally well off in it unless something makes it just that some are better off than others. Second, the negative claim that nothing makes it just that some are better off than others. The formal principle, Persson conjectures, is true on logical grounds: someone who was to deny it would manifest a misunderstanding of the concept of justice.

The negative claim stands the best chance of being false: it would not be eccentric to suppose that desert or rights can make it just that some are better off than others. However, while Persson does not believe that inequalities are always unjust—in his view, some are neither just nor unjust—he argues that considerations about responsibility and ownership cast doubt on the notion that desert and rights can render inequalities just.

Like Persson, Thomas Christiano (Chapter 2) offers an argument for equality which appeals to a formal principle of justice, in this case the principle that one must treat relevantly similar cases alike and dissimilar cases unalike. He combines this principle with three further claims: that all human beings have equal moral status, that no differences between human beings entail that one person ought to receive more well-being than another, and that well-being has fundamental value of a sort that implies that moral agents have reason to promote the well-being of others (as well as their own).

Christiano suggests that the claim about equal moral status follows from the fact that all human beings have essentially the same capacity to appreciate intrinsic value. He defends his second claim very differently from the way in which Persson defends his negative claim. He simply stipulates that his argument addresses people before the onset of adulthood where, presumably, according to Christiano, but not Persson, relevant differences may derive from considerations about responsibility and desert. Finally, in support of his third claim, Christiano contends that the well-being of any particular person is an intrinsic good that contributes to the good of the world and therefore something anyone has a reason to promote.

Having laid out and defended his four basic claims, Christiano argues that they cohere much better with egalitarian than with sufficientarian or maximising views of distributive justice. Christiano's complex argument can be put very roughly as follows: if one person is justly better off than another, then by the formal principle, there must be some difference between them that renders their cases unalike. However, by the assumption of no relevant differences, there is no such difference. Hence, inequality is incompatible with the formal principle and the assumption of no relevant differences.

7. Equality and Responsibility

In the past, egalitarians held inequality to be bad per se. However, most of today's egalitarians hesitate to say this because they recognise the moral significance of choice and responsibility. Consider representative statements of the basic egalitarian principle, such as: 'It is bad—unjust and unfair—for some to be worse off than others [through no fault or choice of their own]' (Temkin 1993: 13); and '[Egalitarianism's] purpose is to eliminate *involuntary disadvantage*, by which I (stipulatively) mean disadvantage for which the sufferer cannot be held responsible, since it does not appropriately reflect choices that he has made or would make' (Cohen 1989b: 916). For most contemporary egalitarians inequalities need not be bad. They need not be bad because the worse off may be responsible for being worse off.

The modal 'need not' is important here. For statements such as those just quoted do not in themselves tell us whether anyone is ever in fact responsible for being worse off. At this point it is useful to distinguish between three different positions: responsibility-denying egalitarianism, responsibility-affirming egalitarianism, and responsibility-agnostic egalitarianism. Let us examine these positions in turn.

Responsibility-denying egalitarians believe that no one is ever responsible for being worse off. Accordingly, a distribution merits no adverse judgment with respect to equality if, and only if, no one is worse off than another. Though responsibility-denying egalitarianism seems a simple and, for that reason, attractive egalitarian position, it burdens its defenders with the rejection of common-sense beliefs about responsibility. However, as Arneson points out in his contribution to the present volume (Chapter 11), this conflict may be less radical than many have assumed. In most cases where people seem to be responsible for acting in a way that makes them worse off there may be good pragmatic reasons for having them bear the costs of their actions, even if, ultimately speaking, they are not responsible for them.

In their cause, responsibility-denying egalitarians sometimes appeal to a regression principle that says that in order to be responsible for *p* you have to responsible for those facts in virtue of which you are responsible for *p*. Since unwinding, regressive responsibility is impossible—at least if responsibility requires choice or control—it follows that responsibility is impossible. Ingmar Persson, in his defence of extreme egalitarianism, endorses something like the regression principle. In his argument for the proposition that desert and rights never justify inequalities, for instance, he points out that somewhere down the causal chain 'we are bound to arrive at responsibility-giving facts for which we are not responsible; the regress of responsibility cannot be infinite'. While this point is surely correct, it is hard to see why it matters unless we endorse something like the regression principle with regard to responsibility.

Often responsibility and desert are conflated—that is, sometimes when egalitarians argue that inequality is not bad if the worse off are responsible for being worse off, what they really mean is that inequality is not bad if the worse off deserve to be worse off or as badly off as they are. Yet these concepts differ. Suppose, for instance, that some thoroughly virtuous person (in the prudential as well as moral sense) runs a small risk and suffers a rare and very bad outcome. Suppose by contrast that a thoroughly non-virtuous person runs the same risk and enjoys a rare and very good outcome. In this case, we might well say that while the virtuous person is responsible for ending up worse off, he does not deserve to be worse off.

The discussion of desert and equality is in many ways similar to the discussion about the relationship of responsibility and equality. Thus the threefold distinction we made above with regard to responsibility is mirrored by a trio of (denying, affirming, and agnostic) positions on desert; and many desert-denying egalitarians would appeal to something like the regression principle—although, of course, here the claim will be that to deserve something you have to deserve the basis of your desert.

Famously, Rawls's (1971: 103–4) reason for rejecting desert seems to appeal to such a principle:

Perhaps some will think that the person with greater natural endowment deserves those assets and the superior character that make their development possible. Because he is more worthy in this sense, he deserves the greater advantages that he could achieve with them. This view, however, is surely incorrect... [No] one deserves his place in the distribution of native endowments, any more than one deserves one's initial starting place in society ... [His] character depends in large part on fortunate family and social circumstances for which he can claim no credit.

On one interpretation, Rawls denies that individuals with 'superior character' deserve their greater rewards because such individuals do not deserve the cause of their superior character, i.e. their good native endowments and their fortunate 'initial starting point in society'. On this interpretation, Rawls endorses a desert-denying position on the basis of a regression principle (but for a criticism of Rawls's position so construed, see Zaitchick 1977: 370–88).

The second kind of egalitarianism we listed above is *responsibility-affirming egalitarianism*. Responsibility-affirming egalitarians believe that to *some* extent *some* people are responsible for being worse off. A *locus classicus* here is Dworkin's discussion of expensive tastes, to which we referred in Section 2. Recall Louis, who has deliberately cultivated an expensive taste for plovers' eggs and pre-phylloxera claret. As we have seen, Dworkin and other egalitarians—notably Arneson and Cohen (neither of whom qualify as responsibility-affirming egalitarians in our sense)—disagree about the wider implications of this kind of case (Arneson 1989, 1990; Cohen 1989b; Dworkin 1981b). They do agree, however, that the case suggests that it need not be bad from the point of view of equality if some have less welfare than others (compare Rawls 1982: 168–9). Unlike responsibility-denying egalitarianism, responsibility-affirming egalitarianism is consistent with common-sense beliefs about responsibility and desert.

The main worry about responsibility-affirming egalitarianism, of course, is whether it is possible to capture egalitarian intuitions *and* respect common-sense beliefs about responsibility and desert. Another worry is that responsibility-affirming egalitarians have to refute the philosophical arguments against the possibility of responsibility and desert.

Responsibility-agnostic egalitarians take no stand on the question of whether people are ever responsible for being worse off. Arneson's influential (1989) article on equality of opportunity for welfare can be interpreted as a responsibility-agnostic egalitarian tract.[9] He believes that if (and only if) hard determinism is true, equality of *opportunity for* welfare collapses into equality of welfare, extensionally speaking. Yet he does not say whether, in his view, hard determinism is true (Arneson 1989: 86; 1990: 175). Similarly, although Cohen also has non-agnostic things to say in reply to the complaint that in making choice central to distributive justice he subordinates political philosophy to metaphysical questions that may be impossible to answer, he does make the following concession: 'we may indeed be up to our necks in the free will problem, but that is just tough luck' (1989b: 934). By this he presumably means to imply that we have no

[9] For a critique of Arneson's equality of opportunity for welfare, see Lippert-Rasmussen (1999). For a reply, see Arneson (1999).

solution to the free will problem and therefore no justified account of the exact policy implications of egalitarianism.[10]

In his contribution to this volume, Arneson is sympathetic to the idea that equality (or priority) will have to be balanced with desert, although he explicitly allows that in the final analysis there may be no defensible theory of desert (say, because of the truth of hard determinism). He then sets himself the task of articulating the most plausible synthesis of equality and the idea that rewarding desert is in itself valuable. He suggests a principle that is compatible with a control principle, according to which people can be said to deserve only that which they are in a position to control. He then fashions a norm of desert as conscientiousness that is compatible with this principle.

Unlike its denying and affirming counterparts, responsibility-agnostic egalitarianism does not impose a heavy burden on its defenders to provide an account of responsibility. Its main drawback (which may not be a theoretical problem) is that, without some such view, egalitarians must remain agnostic, or undecided, about the exact policy implications of egalitarianism.

Egalitarians who concede that people can be responsible for being worse off may commit themselves to the view that people who end up very badly off through their own fault have no justice-based claim to others' assistance. Thus Marc Fleurbaey (who is otherwise quite sympathetic to egalitarianism) imagines a case where a person, knowing the risks and for no good reason, rides a motorcycle without a helmet. Suppose this person has an accident and is in urgent need of medical assistance as a result of his decision not to wear the helmet. On some egalitarian views, it would be unjust to impose the cost of medical assistance on others (Rakowski 1991). This, Fleurbaey thinks, is implausibly harsh; and this shows that justice has a sufficientarian element according to which everyone should be guaranteed a certain minimum (1995: 40−1). Responding to Fleurbaey's case, Peter Vallentyne defends the view that there is nothing unjust about a system that publicly, and in advance, declares that bad outcome option luck—such as that had by Fleurbaey's unfortunate motorcyclist—will be compensated by means of taxing away good outcome option luck. This, Vallentyne thinks, softens this objection to his favoured left-libertarian theory (2002).[11]

In his contribution to the present volume (Chapter 10), Andrew Williams further considers the issue of how to bring together values such as liberty, responsibility, and equality in a unified account of distributive justice. More precisely, he considers Scanlon's contractualist account of the value of choice and, in particular, its implications

---

[10] We say 'exact' because there are non-free-will-related conditions for responsibility, e.g. knowledge of alternatives, which may not be satisfied independently of whether we have free will. Indeed, one may think that owing to non-free-will-related conditions for responsibility only little inequality will fail to be in itself bad, even if we can be responsible for being worse off.

[11] For a related discussion of the distinction between brute luck and option luck, see Lippert-Rasmussen (2001).

for egalitarianism. According to Scanlon, roughly, there are 'instrumental', 'representative', and 'symbolic' reasons for wanting to have certain powers and opportunities in our lives. That is, such powers and opportunities are likely to make our choices more satisfactory (instrumental value), reflective of our own tastes and affections (representative value), and to signal competence and independence (symbolic value). However, Williams argues that this account needs to be further developed in order to give us a plausible account of permissible restrictions on liberty and of when we may permissibly refuse to compensate individuals for the harmful consequences of their choices. Amongst other things, such an account would need to appeal to the perspectives of agents other than the decision-maker when deciding how liabilities are to be assigned.

8. The Value of Equality

A further question is what sort of value equality is. Various issues arise here. In the egalitarian literature it is sometimes claimed that equality is good. It is also sometimes claimed that inequality is bad. And in some places, both claims are made (in fact, both formulations occur in this introduction). This may simply be due to the belief that it does not matter whether one takes equality to be good or inequality to be bad. Alternatively, it may reflect the thought that if equality has positive intrinsic value, then inequality must be bad because it excludes this positive value. Likewise, if inequality has intrinsic negative value, then equality must be good because it excludes this negative value.

Nevertheless, there is a real issue here. Consider an outcome in which everyone has a life with zero value. If equality has positive intrinsic value, this outcome contains such value. Hence, presumably, we have reason to bring it about, everything else being equal (Persson 2001: 31). If, on the other hand, inequality has negative intrinsic value, the outcome has no positive intrinsic value whatsoever. In that respect, we have no reason to bring it about.

We can also distinguish between impersonal and person-affecting versions of egalitarianism. According to impersonal versions states of affairs or other impersonal entities are the bearers of the value of equality (or disvalue of inequality). According to person-affecting versions, on the other hand, the disvalue of inequality resides in the individuals for whom it is bad (the worse off). The latter view entails that it negatively affects a person's welfare to be worse off than others (and does so irrespective of this person's feelings, preferences, etc.).[12] To appreciate the difference between these

---

[12] Larry Temkin (1993, ch. 9) defends an impersonal version and John Broome (1991, ch. 9) defends a person-affecting version.

versions, consider two populations inhabiting different continents, each unaware of the existence of the other. One day an earthquake reduces the level of welfare enjoyed by one population (the better off) to that of the other (the worse off). Of course, none of the intrinsic properties of the members of the worse-off population are affected. Nonetheless, according to the person-affecting version of egalitarianism, they become better off. At least, this will be so if inequalities between unrelated populations fall within the scope of our egalitarian concern (as we saw in Section 3, and will see again shortly, it is possible to hold that equality has a narrower scope than that).

A further distinction to note is that between what Derek Parfit (1991) has called *telic* and *deontic* egalitarianism. Telic egalitarians think inequality is in itself (or intrinsically) bad. Deontic egalitarians do not. Rather, their objection concerns the way in which many inequalities result from unequal and, thus, unjust treatment of people. Parfit suggests that these forms of egalitarianism can be distinguished in respect of both their scope and their vulnerability to the levelling down objection.

The telic view appears to have the broader scope. For, unlike telic egalitarians, deontic ones would seem to have no objection to natural inequalities or to inequalities between people living in different communities that do not interact with one another. While some egalitarians take this to favour telic over deontic views, others will point out that telic egalitarianism is vulnerable to the levelling down objection. According to this objection, which we briefly mentioned in Section 6, telic egalitarianism implausibly implies that it is in one respect better to increase equality, even if it means lowering the welfare of some and increasing the welfare of none (Parfit 1991: 17).

Consider outcomes F and G in Figure 1.3. Since telic egalitarians claim that inequality is *in itself* bad, it would seem that for them G is *in one respect* better than F. Unlike F, G is perfectly equal. Of course, telic egalitarians need not claim that G is better *all things considered*. If, as seems likely, they are pluralists, they may be in a position to claim that the higher equality in G is outweighed by the higher sum of welfare (or some other value) in F. Thus, they may endorse an all things considered ordering that satisfies the Pareto principle, i.e. the principle that two outcomes are equally

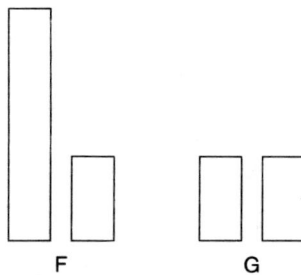

F   G

FIG. 1.3

good if they are equally good for everyone, and one outcome is better if it is better for some and worse for none. Nevertheless, telic egalitarians will still claim that G is *in one respect* better than F. But how can G be *in any respect* better, when there is no respect in which it is better for anyone? Deontic egalitarians need not be embarrassed by this query. They would deny that levelling down makes the outcome better in even one respect—in respect of equality—because they do not think that inequality is in itself bad.

In his contribution to this volume (Chapter 4), Kasper Lippert-Rasmussen unpacks the distinction between telic and deontic egalitarianism into three logically independent distinctions. He then argues that these are largely neutral with respect to scope and that while some, but not all, forms of telic egalitarianism are vulnerable to the levelling down objection, comparable forms of deontic egalitarianism are vulnerable to an analogous objection. In particular, he notices that the principle that 'If an act or omission is *pro tanto* unjust or *pro tanto* wrong, then there is someone for whom it would have been better in some respect had this act or omission not taken place' seems to have no less force than a comparable principle concerning the badness of outcomes that underpins the levelling down objection when directed against telic egalitarian views. Accordingly, Lippert-Rasmussen argues that it is impossible to choose between telic and deontic egalitarianism on the basis of the levelling down objection or on the basis of considerations about scope.

A strategy sometimes used by egalitarians to avoid the levelling down objection is to claim that while equality has intrinsic value (or inequality intrinsic disvalue), it has this value only conditionally. More specifically, one outcome cannot be intrinsically better than another regarding equality unless it is better for some (Mason 2001: 248). On this assumption, the egalitarian can deny the claim that levelling down is in one respect better. Thus, the increase in equality when we move from F to G in Figure 1.3 does not benefit anyone and so does not render G better than F in respect of this value.

Some sort of explanation of *why* equality is valuable only when accompanied by benefits looks necessary, however. Suppose that someone were to claim that equality is intrinsically valuable, but only if it occurs on a Tuesday. We would surely want to know why. Why not on Wednesdays? Likewise, the proposed relation between personal benefits and the value of equality requires explanation (Holtug forthcoming). This is not to suggest that it is somehow prima facie implausible to hold that equality interacts with other values. As we have seen, some responsibility-affirming egalitarians argue that the disvalue of inequality is conditional on the worse off not being responsible for so being. And indeed, they are able to offer an explanation of why this is so.

Alternatively, it may be suggested that one can avoid the levelling down objection by embracing person-affecting egalitarianism. Consider F and G once again. According to person-affecting egalitarianism, the worse off in F benefit if we go from F to G because they are then no longer worse off than the better off. But the fact that they benefit from such a move is not represented in Figure 1.3. More generally, levelling down necessarily benefits some people. But unfortunately person-affecting egalitarianism is no less vulnerable to the levelling down objection than impersonal egalitarianism. Even if the worse off benefit when the better off are reduced to their level, this increase can be counterbalanced by a decrease in the part of their welfare that is unaffected by the welfare of the better off. And if this is so, what we have is a case of levelling down.

A third strategy for avoiding the levelling down objection is proposed in Christiano's contribution to this volume. Christiano argues that egalitarians are not committed to the claim that levelling down is in some respect better. While they need not claim that G is better than F with respect to equality, what they *must* claim is that there is an equal distribution of, say, the sum of welfare in F that is better than that in F in egalitarian terms. More generally, Christiano suggests that egalitarians are committed to the claim that relative to some (Pareto non-comparable) equal outcome (which is to be specified further), an unequal outcome is missing something or is unjust.

Some egalitarians have simply bitten the bullet and accepted that levelling down is in one respect good. Larry Temkin, for instance, sums up his response to the levelling down objection as follows: 'I, for one, believe that inequality is bad. But do I really believe that there is some respect in which a world where only some are blind is worse than one where all are? Yes. Does this mean I think it would be better if we blinded everybody? No. Equality is not all that matters' (1993: 282).

However, Temkin does not simply leave it at that. He challenges the levelling down objection at its very roots. Thus he argues that this objection presupposes a principle he calls 'the Slogan', according to which 'one situation *cannot* be worse (or better) than another *in any respect* if there is *no one* for whom it *is* worse (or better) *in any respect*' (1993: 256). He then argues that the Slogan has implications many will find it difficult to accept. First, it rules out the notion that certain ideals, including autonomy and liberty, contribute to the intrinsic value of outcomes. After all, increases in, say, liberty need not be accompanied by increases in welfare.

Second, the Slogan blocks the intuitively right answer to the so-called 'non-identity problem'. Suppose a woman has toxins in her body. If she gets pregnant now, the child she will have will have a severe disability that will make its life barely worth living. If she waits three months (at which point the toxins will have left her body), she will have a perfectly healthy and much happier child. One's immediate reaction is that it is worse if she gets pregnant now. However, since there is no one *for whom* it is worse, the Slogan rules this reaction out. Perhaps, then, the Slogan should be rejected. If Temkin is right, that would deal a blow to the levelling down objection.

However, in his chapter printed here (Chapter 5), Nils Holtug argues that the levelling down objection does not presuppose the Slogan. It is equally supported by a different person-affecting principle, where a 'person-affecting principle' is a principle that assesses outcomes solely in terms of how they affect individuals for better or worse. Consider again the non-identity problem described above. A woman either has a less happy child sooner or has a happier child later. The principle Holtug proposes enables us to claim that the first outcome is worse because the second outcome is better for the happier child who populates this second outcome. Furthermore, this principle implies that, since no one is affected for the better if we level down, and since no one is affected for the worse if we do not, levelling down cannot be in any respect better. Thus, it supports the levelling down objection.[13]

In the present volume, Hurley, too, offers a distinctive account of the motivation for the levelling down objection. She suggests that what motivates this objection is not a person-affecting principle, but an impersonal perfectionist concern. Suppose we cannot make the sick healthy but we can make the healthy sick. Would there be anything good about doing so? Hurley thinks not. How can equality be better if it wastes excellence? On this approach, the levelling down objection is not just free of reliance on the Slogan or some other person-affecting principle; it is incompatible with any such principle. For increases in perfection need not be accompanied by increases in welfare. So, according to Hurley, perfectionism threatens person-affecting principles.

Finally, perfectionism accommodates something Hurley claims to be missing in both equality of welfare and equality of resources: the fact that health is *special*. Health is not just one good among others to be distributed. It is a distinctive kind of flourishing and good both for people *and* in itself. This means that, when we are assessing the value of distributions, it cannot be traded off against other goods—at least, not on the terms on which other goods are traded.

9. Equality, Priority, and Sufficiency

A great deal of attention has been paid in recent years to the distinction, made by Parfit, between *egalitarianism* and *prioritarianism*. According to prioritarians, benefiting people matters more the worse off these people are. Of course, giving priority to the worse off will often increase equality, but these are distinct values. Parfit writes:

The chief difference can be introduced like this. I have said that, on the Priority View, we do not believe in equality. We do not think it in itself bad, or unjust, that some people are worse off than others. This claim can easily be misunderstood. We do of course think it bad that some people are worse off. But what is bad is not that these people are worse off than *others*. It is rather that they are worse off than *they* might have been. (1991: 22)

---

[13] Holtug (2003) also puts forward this objection to Temkin and Temkin (2003b) responds.

In other words, there is an important sense in which equality is a *relational* value and priority is not. In order to assess the moral value of a benefit to a person in egalitarian terms, we will need to know how well off this person is relative to others. For instance, a further unit to a person who is at level *n* increases equality if everyone else is at *n*+1 but decreases equality if everyone else is at *n*. In order to assess the moral value of such an increase in prioritarian terms, on the other hand, we need only know how well off *this* person is.[14]

Nevertheless, prioritarianism is sometimes referred to as a version of egalitarianism, and some political theorists have even claimed that there really is no distinction to be made (Fleurbaey forthcoming). However that may be, prioritarianism and egalitarianism share an important feature in that both entail that the best possible distribution of a fixed sum of goods is a perfectly equal one. It is therefore no surprise that a number of the contributions to this volume are as concerned with priority as they are with equality (some even more concerned with priority). The affinity of egalitarianism and prioritarianism is also borne out by the practice of some egalitarians of referring to prioritarians as 'decent inegalitarians'!

What sort of priority should the worse off have? There is no consensus on whether leximin should be considered a prioritarian principle, but it does contain a clear conception of what it means to give priority to the worse off. Nevertheless, leximin is rather special in that it rules out trade-offs between the very worst off and others. Another principle, sometimes referred to as 'weighted prioritarianism', involves setting the weights so that benefits to the worse off have greater value than benefits to the better off, but where benefits at higher levels can outweigh benefits at lower levels if only they are sufficiently great or plentiful. Another issue is how to aggregate weighted benefits over persons. Usually, a summative function is assumed, but other functions could be introduced.

Prioritarianism has been thought, by several political philosophers, to be superior to egalitarianism because it is not vulnerable to the levelling down objection. Since levelling down does not benefit anyone, not even the worse off, prioritarians see no value in levelling down.

In his contribution to this volume, Holtug elaborates this defence of prioritarianism. He examines the allegations (*a*) that there is really no distinction to be made between egalitarianism and prioritarianism; (*b*) that even if there is a distinction to be made, this distinction does not separate them vis-à-vis the levelling down objection; and (*c*) that, in any case, this objection presupposes a rather dubious person-affecting principle. He also assesses the claim that prioritarianism fails to capture some common and

---

[14] Arneson (2000), Holtug (1999), Hooker (2000: 55–65), McKerlie (1994), Nagel (1991: 63–74), Parfit (1991), Raz (1986: 217–44), and Scheffler (1982: 31) include discussions that are sympathetic to prioritarianism.

important intuitions about relational justice, and fails to capture the virtue, on which it is based, of compassion.

Furthermore, as we have already pointed out, McKerlie argues in his chapter that prioritarians can provide a better overall account than egalitarians of why it matters how benefits are distributed not only over lives but also over temporal stages. And in his contribution, Arneson simply assumes that prioritarianism is the more adequate distributive principle and then proceeds to ask how it can be combined with a theory of desert.

Sufficientarianism is another alternative to egalitarianism. Sufficientarians agree with prioritarians that the worse off should have priority. However, they argue that there is a level of resources or welfare at which such priority ceases. This is because, at this level, people have *enough*. Along such lines, Roger Crisp defends what he calls the 'sufficiency principle', according to which 'compassion for any being B is appropriate up to the point at which B has a level of welfare such that B can live a life which is sufficiently good' (2003a: 762; see also Frankfurt 1987; Rosenberg 1995). Sufficientarians often defend their view by arguing that, intuitively, we do not care about inequalities above a certain threshold. Thus, inequalities between the rich and the super-rich do not concern us. We have no compassion for the rich even if they have to make do with $200 wines while the super-rich gulp down wines costing $1,000 by the barrel.

Here Fleurbaey's point about securing a decent minimum for everyone is worth recalling. Many egalitarians will instinctively sympathize with the idea that people should be given such minima even if their need is the result of their own choices. This does not sit well with the luck-egalitarian idea that people should be held responsible for their choices. Sufficientarianism represents one way of capturing the need for a decent minimum. However, it has been argued that the sufficientarian lack of concern for inequalities above the threshold is not as plausible as it may initially sound.[15] In this volume, Christiano and Holtug voice their own reservations about sufficientarianism.

10. Critiques of Egalitarianism

Unsurprisingly, egalitarianism has not been met with unanimous approval. Setting aside the various utilitarian, prioritarian, and sufficientarian criticisms we have presented above, we shall end this survey of egalitarianism by sketching three sorts of attack on egalitarianism. These emanate from communitarianism, feminism, and libertarianism.

---

[15] Temkin (2003a). See also Crisp's (2003b) response to Temkin.

As we saw in Section 2, egalitarians tend to assume that there is some overall good, or benefit, in respect of which people should be equally well off, although they differ on whether this good is welfare, or resources, or some other item. Distinguishing these candidate goods, we can see that egalitarians can acknowledge that there are, so to speak, subordinate distributive spheres, such as political influence and citizenship, in which equality can be assessed independently of the equality or inequality attaching to the main, superordinate currency. Thus some egalitarians, including Dworkin, explicitly set aside the issue of political equality for separate treatment.

According to communitarians such as Michael Walzer, however, this acknowledgment of separate distributive spheres does not go far enough. He thinks 'equality of what?' is a misleading question. In what is widely seen as a communitarian criticism of standard, end-result principles of distributive justice, Walzer (1983) claims that there are many distributive spheres, and that this plurality reflects our communal understanding of the differences between goods. In the United States, for instance, it is part of the cultural meaning of medical care that it should be distributed according to need, of higher education that it should be distributed by talent, of political office that it should be distributed according to votes, and of honours that they should be distributed according to desert.

In his contribution to this volume (Chapter 12) Jonathan Wolff explores an interesting application of Walzer's theory.[16] He suggests that the social meaning of safety is such that 'it should be provided equally for all, independently of personal wealth'. This explains why we would be outraged if rail companies were to sell first-class tickets offering better levels of safety than did second-class tickets, even though we do not object to first-class passengers enjoying more comfortable seating, free coffee, and so on. The lesson Walzer draws from such examples is that justice obtains when all goods are distributed according to criteria given by their cultural meanings. Justice is eroded when this is not the case—for example, when power is a means of achieving political office, money is a means of obtaining love, more safety, and better medical treatment, and honours are a means of getting rich.

While Walzer sees his own theory as an egalitarian theory of justice, others have objected to its inegalitarian implications. Richard Arneson (1995), for instance, observes that the fact that criteria of distribution that are allegedly internal to all goods are met would not prevent an elite from deserving all honours, getting all votes, not being in need of medical attention at all, and having talents for higher education. This outcome would hardly qualify as a just society.

Others have argued that Walzer's appeal to shared cultural understandings is either futile, since no such understandings exist, or self-undermining, since insofar as they do exist, one of the strongest such understandings we share is that distributions are

---

[16] Hurley's thought that health is a special good might be construed along similar lines.

not just simply because we think they are—that is, because the distribution conforms to our shared cultural understanding (Dworkin 1985: 214–20; Barry 1995: 75). A final point worth noting is that Walzer's claim about different spheres of justice can to a large extent be accommodated by egalitarians who believe that there is some overall currency in terms of which people should be equally well off. They may simply couple this requirement with the requirement of distribution according to criteria internal to different goods. On this view, a just society satisfies both requirements. A society that fails to satisfy either is unjust.

Communitarians are often criticised by feminists for their blindness to the way in which culture, traditions, and local communities involve various forms of oppression and discrimination. Recently, feminist political philosophers such as Elizabeth Anderson and Iris Marion Young have levelled a related criticism against mainstream egalitarianism, rhetorically suggesting that 'If much recent academic work defending equality had been secretly penned by conservatives' the results would not have been 'any more embarrassing' (Anderson 1999: 87). Mainstream egalitarianism, according to these philosophers, tends to have an obsessive focus on compensating people for bad brute luck. It tends to ignore important inequalities in social relations, such as dominance and oppression (Young 1990: 15–65; Anderson 1999).

According to their feminist critics, egalitarians should focus on the prevention of exploitation and marginalisation. These render people powerless and subject them to cultural imperialism and sometimes violence. In particular, egalitarians should ensure that people can take full part in public life, including democratic decision-making, on an equal standing. This requires people to be adequately fed, housed, and educated. However, it does not require each and every inequality reflecting differential luck to be neutralised; nor does it mean that people should be made to bear the costs of their choices.

Indeed, luck-egalitarianism will often be in conflict with respect for people as equals. Such egalitarianism may involve condescending pity for people who are labelled 'badly off through lack of talents through no fault of their own' (a similar point is made by Jonathan Wolff 1998). And it may involve harsh disregard for people such as Fleurbaey's motorcyclist, mentioned in Section 7, who through a fault of their own are no longer able to participate in public life as equals in the absence of public provision of additional resources.

In the present volume (Chapter 8), Linda Barclay considers Anderson's feminist critique of luck-egalitarianism. She argues that while luck-egalitarians have indeed been insufficiently concerned about social relations, it is not obvious that this reflects a deep problem in their theories. It may be that, while the theories do indeed have important implications vis-à-vis social relations, the luck-egalitarians just do not pay enough attention to them.

Barclay points out that Anderson herself seems to explain the disvalue of unequal social relations in terms of their impact on people's capacities and thus well-being. This suggests, according to Barclay, that social relations are instrumentally valuable only because, and to the extent that, they have an effect on people's capacities. Barclay suggests that we can characterise an oppressive relation as 'one which jeopardises certain important capabilities, that is, opportunities or freedom to do and be certain valuable things'. If social relations only have this derivative sort of importance, they should not be the currency of egalitarian justice.[17]

Robert Nozick, in his now classic libertarian critique of egalitarianism, agreed in effect with feminists that some theories of justice are excessively preoccupied with compensation for bad brute luck. But in Nozick's eyes, this mistake is an expression of the more general misunderstanding that justice involves bringing about certain end-results (e.g. equal distribution or maximisation of the sum of welfare) or certain distributive patterns (e.g. distribution in which rewards fit desert).

Against such views, Nozick put the celebrated Wilt Chamberlain argument. Let us assume, for the sake of argument, that equality of money is the favoured end-result, and that money is distributed accordingly on the first day of the year. On 2 January, Wilt Chamberlain (a basketball player who was famous in the 1960s) offers to play for a certain basketball team for the rest of the year on the condition that anyone who attends this team's games puts 25 cents in a special box with his name on it. Since many people want to see Wilt Chamberlain play, he is rich by the end of the year and equality of money no longer obtains. *Ex hypothesi*, this is unjust. Yet how could the unequal distribution by the end of the year be unjust, Nozick asks? The distribution on 1 January was just, we assumed, and the unequal distribution on 31 December developed from the initial distribution through voluntary 'capitalist acts between consenting adults' (Nozick 1974: 163).

Egalitarians can try to resist Nozick's challenge in two ways. First, they can deny that voluntary agreements made in a just setting necessarily preserve justice. They might do this on the ground that people do not have absolute property rights over their possessions in the initial situation. Specifically, they might say that people do not have the right to give their possessions away or to exchange them for other goods in a way that erodes equal distribution—or, at least, that they do not have the right to do this if the state does not act to restore equality through redistributive taxation. There might well be objections to this move, but simply to assume, as Nozick does, that property rights are absolute is to beg the question against egalitarians who make it (Quest 1977; O'Neill 1981; Ryan 1981).

---

[17] For a similar reply to Anderson, see Arneson (2000). For a discussion of the moral relevance of the distinction between social and natural inequalities, see Lippert-Rasmussen (2004).

Second, egalitarians can argue that we should select an initial distribution other than equality of money. Given this different initial distribution, either inequality in the relevant dimension will not arise, or insofar as it does, this will not be unjust. One response along these lines is to favour initial equality of opportunity for resources instead of equality of money. Obviously, this condition is implicitly assumed not to obtain in Nozick's example, because Wilt Chamberlain has superior basketball skills. However, if we were to assume an initial equality of opportunity for resources and take everyone to have Wilt's talents, then either Wilt would not end up with more resources than others on 31 December, or he would, but that would not be unjust according to initial equality of opportunity for resources because others could have done exactly what he did. The latter possibility reflects the fact that initial equality of opportunity for resources (or welfare, for that matter) is not an end-result principle in Nozick's sense: whether a certain distribution of resource is just on this view depends on 'how it came about' (1974: 153).

Setting aside Nozick's critique of competing theories of justice, let us look briefly at the essentials of his own libertarian theory. According to Nozick, we own our own bodies and minds. One way to support this assumption of moral self-ownership is to imagine what might be just if we reject it. Suppose, for instance, that half of us have no eyes while the other half have two eyes. Suppose, moreover, that eyes can, without cost, difficulty, or suffering, be moved from one person to another. Without moral self-ownership, there would seem to be no injustice involved in the non-voluntary removal and transplantation (to the eyeless) of single eyes from those who have two. Many recoil at this implication.

Moral self-ownership tells us nothing about how we acquire property rights over things that are external to our bodies and minds. Here Nozick offers two 'historical' principles of justice.[18] All external resources were once unowned. In that situation, a person could acquire private ownership of a certain external resource in so far as his or her appropriation of it did not worsen the situation of others. This condition, the so-called 'Lockean proviso', can be interpreted in various ways. Nozick assumes that it is rather easily satisfied, since everyone benefits from the creation of incentives that result from permission to appropriate (1974: 181).

To this principle of just initial appropriation, Nozick adds a principle of just transfer (to which it seems his Wilt Chamberlain argument implicitly appeals). On this principle, if a rightful owner of something voluntarily transfers the object to

---

[18] In fact, he offers three. For simplicity, however, we leave out the third principle, which deals with how to make up for violations of the first two, and thus more basic, principles of justice. Moreover, Nozick's presentation of his three favoured principles of justice is explorative in nature and offers no clear statement of them. Here we disregard various complications and assume one plausible and common interpretation of Nozick's entitlement theory.

another for any reason whatsoever—for instance, to obtain some other good, to benefit the other person in an unselfish way, to promote a worthy cause, or to reduce inequality—the other person is the rightful owner of the object.

Nozick believes that the principle of just transfer applies to bodies and minds too. Being the rightful owner of my own body and mind, I am entitled to transfer my right to them—or perhaps better, to their use—to someone else. Obviously, there is little reason to think that many people would turn themselves into slaves. However, if all but one does so, the extremely unequal outcome that results will be just, provided self-ownership and the principles of just initial appropriation and just transfer have not been violated. On Nozick's view, *any* outcome will be just, provided it is brought about in a way that does not violate either historical principle.

There are two main egalitarian responses to Nozick's libertarianism. One is to reject the idea of self-ownership; the other is to accept the idea of self-ownership, but deny its inegalitarian implications. The latter has recently attracted a number of able defenders.[19] While the present survey cannot do justice to the richness of the growing body of left-libertarian literature, we shall briefly indicate a way in which self-ownership can be reconciled with distributive implications that are more congenial to egalitarians than Nozick's. Nozick assumes that the world, excluding people's minds and bodies, was initially unowned and could be privately appropriated as long as this worsened no one's position—that is, as long as the Lockean proviso was satisfied. But the Lockean proviso needs to be fleshed out. Thus, in determining whether someone's situation is worsened by private appropriation, it makes a huge difference whether we are comparing this situation with one in which the appropriated object continued to be unowned or with one in which the affected person instead appropriated the object himself.

Nozick nowhere provides a thorough defence of the assumption that the world was initially unowned; nor does he properly explain the Lockean proviso. And by disputing either of these assumptions—that is, by in effect rejecting Nozick's principle of just initial appropriation—it is possible to defend egalitarian redistributive schemes, especially in view of the fact that any effective use of one's body requires external resources such as air or the physical space one's body occupies (Cohen 1986a, b, 1989a).

Of course, not all egalitarians have become left libertarians. Some simply reject self-ownership. Persson, in this volume, argues that the idea that one owns one's body because one was the first to occupy it or make use of it must be rejected. According to Persson, 'it is just that everyone gets equally good bodies (i.e. bodies that enable them to be equally well off) unless there is something to make it just that some get better bodies than others'. Thus it will be just that some have better bodies than others only if those who do are responsible for getting better bodies and those who do not are

---

[19] Van Parijs (1991, 1995); Otsuka (1998, 2003); Steiner (1994, 1998); Steiner and Vallentyne (2000).

responsible for getting worse bodies. But surely no one is responsible for either. It is hard to see how it could be possible for someone to be responsible for 'getting' a good or a bad body.

Christiano also rejects self-ownership, but for rather different reasons. His main argument is that such ownership is inconsistent with our honouring of the value of humanity. As we have seen, Nozick's theory allows one to sell oneself justly into slavery for no particular reason. It also allows one to kill oneself for no particular reason. But Christiano argues that one has a duty 'to value and respect one's own humanity', and that this 'implies that one is not permitted to destroy it or damage it or waste it or even sell it in perpetuity (unless on the basis of very weighty considerations)'. These restrictions on what one may do to oneself, deriving from a Kantian duty to promote and honour the humanity in oneself, are incompatible with Nozickean self-ownership. Accordingly, so Christiano thinks, we must reject the latter, thus paving the way for a more substantial egalitarianism.

References

ANDERSON, E. (1999), 'What Is the Point of Equality?', *Ethics*, 99/2: 287–337.

ARNESON, R. J. (1989), 'Equality and Equal Opportunity for Welfare', *Philosophical Studies*, 56: 77–93.

_____ (1990), 'Liberalism, Distributive Subjectivism, and Equal Opportunity for Welfare', *Philosophy and Public Affairs*, 19/2: 158–94.

_____ (1995), 'Against "Complex Equality" ', in D. Miller and M. Walzer (eds.), *Pluralism, Justice, and Equality* (Oxford: Oxford University Press), 226–52.

_____ (1999), 'Equality and Equal Opportunity for Welfare Defended and Recanted', *Journal of Political Philosophy*, 7: 488–97.

_____ (2000), 'Luck Egalitarianism and Prioritarianism', *Ethics*, 110/2: 339–49.

_____ (2001), 'Luck and Equality', *Proceedings of the Aristotelian Society*, 75/1: 73–90.

BARRY, B. (1989), *Theories of Justice* (Berkeley: University of California Press).

_____ (1995), 'Spherical Justice and Global Injustice', in D. Miller and M. Walzer (eds.), *Pluralism, Justice, and Equality* (Oxford: Oxford University Press), 67–80.

BROOME, J. (1991), *Weighing Goods* (Oxford: Basil Blackwell).

COHEN, G. A. (1986a), 'Self-Ownership, World-Ownership, and Equality', in F. Lucash (ed.), *Justice and Equality Here and Now*, (Ithaca, NY: Cornell University Press), 108–35.

_____ (1986b), 'Self-Ownership, World-Ownership, and Equality: Part II', *Social Philosophy and Policy*, 3/2: 77–96.

_____ (1989a), 'Are Freedom and Equality Compatible?', in J. Elster and K. O. Moene (eds.), *Alternatives to Capitalism* (Cambridge: Cambridge University Press), 113–26.

_____ (1989b), 'On the Currency of Egalitarian Justice', *Ethics*, 99/4: 906–44.

CRISP, R. (2003a), 'Equality, Priority, and Compassion', *Ethics*, 113/4: 745–63.

_____ (2003b), 'Egalitarianism and Compassion', *Ethics*, 114/1: 119–26.

DANIELS, N. (1996), 'The Prudential Life-Span Account of Justice Across Generations', in Daniels, *Justice and Justification: Reflective Equilibrium in Theory and Practice* (Cambridge: Cambridge University Press), 257–83.

DWORKIN, R. (1981a), 'What Is Equality? Part 1: Equality of Welfare', *Philosophy and Public Affairs*, 10/3: 185–246.

_____ (1981b), 'What Is Equality? Part 2: Equality of Resources', *Philosophy and Public Affairs*, 10/4: 283–345.

_____ (1985), *A Matter of Principle* (Oxford: Oxford University Press).

FLEURBAEY, M. (1995), 'Equal Opportunity for Equal Social Outcome', *Economics and Philosophy*, 11: 22–55.

_____ (forthcoming), 'Equality Versus Priority: How Relevant Is the Distinction?', in D. Wickler and C. J. L. Murray (eds.), *'Goodness' and 'Fairness': Ethical Issues in Health Resource Allocation* (World Health Organization).

FRANKFURT, H. (1987), 'Equality as a Moral Ideal', *Ethics*, 98/1: 21–43.

HARE, R. M. (1981), *Moral Thinking* (Oxford: Clarendon Press).

HOLTUG, N. (1999), 'Utility, Priority and Possible People', *Utilitas*, 11/1: 16–36.

_____ (2003), 'Good for Whom?', *Theoria*, 69/1–2: 4–20.

_____ (forthcoming), 'A Note on Conditional Egalitarianism, *Economics and Philosophy*.

HOOKER, B. (2000), *Ideal Code, Real World* (Oxford: Clarendon Press).

HURLEY, S. (2003), *Justice, Luck, and Knowledge*, (Cambridge, Mass.: Harvard University Press).

LIPPERT-RASMUSSEN, K. (1999), 'Arneson on Equality of Opportunity for Welfare', *Journal of Political Philosophy*, 7/4: 478–87.

_____ (2001), 'Equality, Option Luck, and Responsibility', *Ethics*, 111/3: 548–79.

_____ (2004), 'Are Some Inequalities More Unequal Than Others? Nature, Nurture, and Equality', *Utilitas*, 16/2: 193–219.

_____ (2005), 'Hurley on Egalitarianism and the Luck-Neutralizing Aim', *Politics, Philosophy, and Economics*, 4/2: 249–265.

McKERLIE, D. (1989), 'Equality and Time', *Ethics*, 99/2: 475–91.

_____ (1994), 'Equality and Priority', *Utilitas*, 6/1: 25–42.

MASON, A. (2001), 'Egalitarianism and the Levelling Down Objection', *Analysis*, 61/3: 246–54.

MILLER, D. (1995), *On Nationality* (Oxford: Clarendon Press).

_____ and Walzer, M. (eds.) (1995), *Pluralism, Justice, and Equality* (Oxford: Oxford University Press).

NAGEL, T. (1979), 'Equality', in Nagel, *Mortal Questions* (Cambridge: Cambridge University Press), 106–27.

_____ (1991), *Equality and Priority* (New York: Oxford University Press).

NOZICK, R. (1974), *Anarchy, State, and Utopia* (New York: Basic Books).

O'NEILL, O. (1981), 'Nozick's Entitlements', in J. Paul (ed.), *Reading Nozick* (Totowa, NJ: Rowman & Allanheld), 305–22.

OTSUKA, M. (1998), 'Self-Ownership and Equality: A Lockean Reconciliation', *Philosophy and Public Affairs*, 27/1: 65–92.

_____ (2003), *Libertarianism Without Inequality* (Oxford: Oxford University Press).

PARFIT, D. (1984), *Reasons and Persons* (Oxford: Clarendon Press).

PARFIT, D. (1991), *Equality or Priority?* The Lindley Lecture, (Lawrence: University of Kansas).

PERSSON, I. (1997), 'Person-Affecting Principles and Beyond', in N. Fotion and J. C. Heller (eds.), *Contingent Future Persons* (Dordrecht: Kluwer Academic Publishers), 41–56.

—— (2001), 'Equality, Priority and Person-Affecting Value', *Ethical Theory and Moral Practice*, 4/1: 23–39.

POGGE, T. (1994), 'An Egalitarian Law of Peoples', *Philosophy and Public Affairs*, 23/3: 195–224.

QUEST, E. (1977), 'Whatever Arises from a Just Distribution by Just Steps Is Itself Just', *Analysis*, 37: 204–8.

RAE, D. (1981), *Equalities* (Cambridge, Mass.: Harvard University Press).

RAKOWSKI, E. (1991), *Equal Justice* (Oxford: Clarendon Press).

RAWLS, J. (1971), *A Theory of Justice* (Oxford: Oxford University Press).

—— (1982), 'Social Unity and Primary Goods', in A. Sen and B. Williams (eds.), *Utilitarianism and Beyond* (Cambridge: Cambridge University Press), 159–85.

—— (1993), 'The Law of Peoples', in S. Shute and S. Hurley (eds.), *On Human Rights* (New York: Basic Books), 41–82.

—— (1999), *The Law of Peoples* (Cambridge, Mass.: Harvard University Press).

RAZ, J. (1986), *The Morality of Freedom* (Oxford: Oxford University Press).

ROEMER, J. E. (1996), *Theories of Distributive Justice* (Cambridge, Mass.: Harvard University Press).

ROSENBERG, A. (1995), 'Equality, Sufficiency, and Opportunity in the Just Society', *Social Philosophy and Policy*, 12/2: 54–71.

RYAN, C. (1981), 'Yours, Mine and Ours: Property Rights and Individual Liberty', in J. Paul (ed.), *Reading Nozick* (Totowa, NJ: Rowman & Allanheld), 323–43.

SCHEFFLER, S. (1982), *The Rejection of Consequentialism* (Oxford: Clarendon Press).

SEN, A. (1995), 'Capability and Well-Being', in M. C. Nussbaum and A. Sen (eds.), *The Quality of Life*, (Oxford: Clarendon Press), 30–53.

—— (1997), *On Economic Inequality*, rev. ed. (Oxford: Clarendon Press).

SINGER, P. (1975), *Animal Liberation* (New York: Random House).

—— (1993), *How Are We to Live? Ethics in an Age of Self-Interest* (Melbourne: Text Publishing Company).

STEINER, H. (1994), *An Essay on Rights* (Oxford: Basil Blackwell).

—— (1998), 'Choice and Circumstance', in A. Mason (ed.), *Ideals of Equality* (Oxford: Basil Blackwell), 95–111.

—— and VALLENTYNE, P. (eds.) (2000), *Left Libertarianism and Its Critics: The Contemporary Debate*, (New York: Palgrave).

TEMKIN, L. S. (1992), 'Intergenerational Inequality', in P. Laslett and J. S. Fishkin (eds.), *Justice Between Age Groups and Generations* (New Haven: Yale University Press), 169–205.

—— (1993), *Inequality* (New York: Oxford University Press).

—— (2003a), 'Egalitarianism Defended', *Ethics*, 113/4: 764–82.

—— (2003b), 'Personal Versus Impersonal Principles: Reconsidering the Slogan', *Theoria*, 69/1–2: 21–31.

VALLENTYNE, P. (2002), 'Brute Luck, Option Luck, and Equality of Initial Opportunities', *Ethics*, 112/3: 529–57.

van Parijs, P. (1991), 'Why Surfers Should Be Fed: The Liberal Case for an Unconditional Basic Income', *Philosophy and Public Affairs*, 20/2: 101−31.

―― (1995), *Real Freedom for All* (Oxford: Oxford University Press).

Walzer, M. (1983), *Spheres of Justice* (Oxford: Basil Blackwell).

Wolff, J. (1998), 'Fairness, Respect, and the Egalitarian Ethos', *Philosophy and Public Affairs*, 27/2: 97−122.

Young, I. M. (1990), *Justice and the Politics of Difference* (Princeton: Princeton University Press).

Zaitchick, A. (1977), 'On Deserving to Deserve', *Philosophy and Public Affairs*, 6/4: 370−88.

Part I

Foundations for Equality

2

A Foundation for Egalitarianism

Thomas Christiano

1. Introduction

My aim in this chapter is to provide an argument for the claim that egalitarianism is the fundamental principle of distributive justice. I do not argue here that it is the only such principle but I do argue that if there are other principles of distributive justice, they must be secondary to the principle of egalitarian justice. The point of giving a fundamental argument for equality is twofold. One, it is an attempt to show that the principle of equality can be defended on the basis of relatively uncontentious premises. Hence the argument is meant to show that we have good reason to give our allegiance to the principle of equality. Two, the argument is designed to show how one of the most serious objections to equality can be defeated. I argue that the leveling down objection to the principle of equality can be defeated. This is shown by the fact that equality does not require leveling down.

This chapter is a distant descendant of a paper I wrote entitled 'An Argument for Equality and Against the Levelling Down Objection,' in *Law and Social Justice* Joseph Campbell, David Shier, and Michael O'Rourke (eds.), (Cambridge, Mass.: MIT Press, 2005). It was started with the help of a fellowship at the National Humanities Center in 2000 and it was finished with the help of a visiting fellowship at All Souls College, Oxford, in 2004. I would like to thank Paul Abu Habib, Chris Bertram, Paula Casal, John Christman, Jerry Cohen, Marc Fleurbaey, Craig Duncan, Nils Holtug, Kasper Lippert-Rasmussen, Serena Olsaretti, Houston Smit, and Andrew Williams for their helpful comments on previous drafts of this chapter. I also want to thank audiences in the Philosophy Departments at the University of Arizona, the University of Bristol, and the University of Reading, and the Political Thought and Intellectual History Seminar at Cambridge University, for stimulating and instructive discussions, as well as participants in a splendid session at All Souls College.

What I will do in this chapter is give an account of egalitarian justice as I understand it. Then I will say why an argument for equality is desirable. I will lay out and defend the principles of generic justice and propriety from which I proceed and a number of subsidiary principles. Then I will give the basic argument for egalitarian justice, along the way criticizing sufficiency theories. I also give some reasons why we ought to prefer the approach I take to the historical entitlement approach. I will then go on to show how the traditional leveling down objection to egalitarian justice fails to impugn the justice of equality and I will outline the ways in which the principle of equality has priority over other principles of distributive justice, if there are any other such principles.

2. What Is Egalitarian Justice?

The principle of equality that I will defend states that justice is fully realized only in the establishment of a Pareto optimal and equal distribution of substantial good among persons. All inequalities are unjust on this view, but not all equalities are fully just. For instance, a Pareto optimal equal distribution of substantial good is more just than a Pareto sub-optimal equal distribution of that substantial good. On this principle, equality in the distribution of substantial good is more just normally than Pareto noncomparable inequalities, though there may be some cases in which this is not true. But it will also be the case that Pareto superior inequalities are more just than the Pareto inferior equalities. What marks the principle out as egalitarian is that it states that only equality can be fully just and that for any inequality there is a Pareto noncomparable equality that is more just.

To explain this principle, I will need to make some distinctions. First, I will distinguish the concept of equality in use in this principle from other related concepts. Second, I will explain the notion of a fundamental substantial good. Third, I will explain the presence of the idea of Pareto optimality in the principle; and finally, I will distinguish the principle from the Priority View.

We need to distinguish different concepts of equality here. First, we might think of equality as a merely *good making property* of states of affairs say in the way that Larry Temkin conceives of it. Temkin seems to think of equality as a kind of intrinsic good along with other intrinsic goods such as well-being and that we should try to bring about as much of it as possible, other things being equal. On this view, equality of well-being among persons is a good to be promoted.[1] We can also think of equality in a purely *generic* sense as understood by Aristotle when he says that justice is equality. This

---

[1] See Temkin (1993).

principle states that one must treat relevantly like cases alike and unlike cases unlike. This is distinct from the principle of equality that I will defend but it is a premise that I will use in the defense of egalitarian justice. In addition, we can understand equality as fundamental equality in the sense that all human beings have the same *fundamental moral status*. This too is a premise that is required for defending egalitarian justice.

None of the above principles are the same as egalitarian justice. As I understand egalitarian justice, it is a principle of distributive justice. It states that individual persons are *due* equal shares in some fundamental substantial good. This principle is a comparative principle of justice: it makes the share that each person is due a comparative function of what others are due. Distributive justice, as I understand it, is a *condition* among persons wherein each person's good is advanced in a way that is due to him or her. Saying that distributive justice is a condition among persons implies that it is not merely a property of actions. Actions are just to the extent that they ensure that each person receives what is due to him or her. That is why, at the limit, we can think that it is just that a person receives his just reward, even if no actions are at the basis of this distribution. It is why, traditionally, it has been thought just that the virtuous are happy and the vicious unhappy. It is also why it is thought unjust when a person is convicted for a crime he did not commit even though the conviction was obtained through the completely conscientious use of an excellent criminal trial procedure and no one is at fault for having made this mistake.

Distributive justice is a condition under which the advantages and disadvantages among persons are distributed in a way that is responsive to relevant inherent qualities of those persons. The distribution of advantages and disadvantages ought not to be arbitrary or based on considerations that do not reflect the relevant qualities of each person. As a principle of justice, the principle of equality states more than that equality is a good thing to bring about; it states a condition on what human beings are due.

The concept of *fundamental substantial good* that I employ here has three basic components. First, it is the concept of an object that all rational beings must pursue for themselves and others. Second, it is the concept of a good in terms of which an overall assessment of the quality of life of a person can be given. Third, it is a concept of a good in terms of which at least rough interpersonal comparisons can be made. The good is substantial in that it is a good any rational being must pursue in order to lead a good life. The clearest examples of such a fundamental substantial good are well-being and capability in the sense that Sen has characterized.[2] These are things that are valued for their own sakes by people. But the argument that I provide does not require that the substantial good that is equalized be good for its own sake. The argument might work as well for those who think that resources, in the sense that Dworkin has in mind, ought to be distributed equally. What is

---

[2] See Sen (1992).

crucial about fundamental substantial goods is that they play a kind of unifying role in the assessment of a person's life. A fundamental substantial good is not merely one good among others; it can provide us with an overall assessment of the quality of a person's life. It is even possible that we have some combined metric of equality such as advantage or access to advantage, which includes well-being, resources, and capabilities, as long as there is some important sense in which we can give an overall evaluation of the quality of a person's life by means of this metric and we can make at least rough comparisons between the qualities of different persons' lives by means of the account of fundamental substantial good.

Furthermore, what is crucial for the argument that follows is that fundamental substantial goods are indeterminate goods in the sense that on the one hand, more of these goods are better than less for any particular person, but on the other hand, when it comes to balancing the good of one person against those of others what each person *ought* to have is not settled merely by reference to the nature of the good. Another principle must come in to determine how much of the good a person ought to have or ought to pursue.

No doubt a number of difficult issues arise in trying to determine what the good that ought to be distributed should be, and there has been an extremely illuminating and useful discussion of this question over the last thirty years. My hope is that this question can, to some significant degree, be put to the side in trying to assess whether equality as a distributive principle matters at all. And in order to put the question to the side, I introduce the idea of a fundamental substantial good as a kind of place holder that can be filled by a number of different objects to be distributed. Probably some accounts of the fundamental substantial good for persons will not be compatible with the argument I provide, but I do think that many of them will be and so my argument relies on weaker premises than would be required if we had to rely on a particular account of fundamental substantial good. My argument in what follows actually uses well-being in the place of the fundamental substantial good. But I believe that other accounts of substantial good could fit the bill as well. In the end, only one of these accounts of fundamental substantial good will be correct, and so the principle of equality will be one that includes an account of this basic good. As a consequence, the principle of equality will vary a bit depending on the nature of the good that is to be equally distributed. But in order to have an argument for equality, it is not necessary to decide which account of fundamental substantial good is the right one.

The principle of equality I defend is opposed to the idea that a Pareto inferior equality can be more just than a Pareto superior inequality with respect to the principle of equality. The principle of equality I defend has two inseparable dimensions: it implies that justice is concerned with the common good and it implies that the common good is ideally just only to the extent that it is egalitarian. The common good and distributive dimensions are both essential to the principle of equality I defend. This is what makes the principle avoid the brunt of the leveling down objection. Once I give the argument for the principle and for how it avoids the leveling down objection, I will say why I think that it should be accepted by egalitarians who might have been inclined to say that any equality is better with respect to the principle of equality than any inequality.

While the view that I am defending has some similarities to the Priority View, it is not the same. For this view says that there is always something unjust in inequality, while the Priority View has no such implication. The view has a very different moral character as a consequence. This is what makes the Priority View more of a consequentialist position. There is no loss as long as the total amount of value is maximized. In the case of the egalitarian principle, there is loss as long as there is inequality even though not every equality can make up for that loss. Furthermore, in contrast to the Priority View, the egalitarian principle does not always recommend that state which maximizes the total amount of good. There are likely to be states that maximize the total amount of good that are unjust even when the fully just equality does not maximize the total amount. So, even if the egalitarian principle does not require leveling down, it will sometimes imply that a state wherein there is less total good is a more just state.

In this chapter, I will argue that the principles of equality in the generic and moral senses in conjunction with some principle of a good life imply a principle of equality of the fundamental substantial good. This principle is not a principle for assessing the goodness of states of affairs *simpliciter*. It is meant to be a principle of justice.

3. Why Do We Need an Argument for Equality?

Some might say that we already have adequate reason for thinking that equality is a principle of justice. They may say, for example, that the principle of equality is self-evident. Or they may say that some presumption in favor of equality is self-evident. But this seems to be false or in any case unjustified. It seems false because so many people have thought about the question and have rejected the idea that equality of condition in any form is a principle of justice. And contemporary opponents of equality have been exposed to the idea in its most desirable forms as presented by its most thoughtful and devoted exponents. At the very least, this suggests that the idea that equality is self-evidently a principle of justice is as yet undefended.

A common way of defending equality in recent years has been to say that justice forbids that some people's lives should go worse than others through no fault of their own. These thinkers argue that departures from equality can be justified only by pointing to facts that show that the worse-off people are somehow responsible for their situations. Equality is a way of eliminating the effects of brute luck on the distribution of advantages.[3] But this idea, while quite illuminating, does not give us an argument for equality. It presupposes the idea that we ought to start with equality and only allows departures from it when people are responsible for them. But the question we need to ask is, why ought we to think of equality as a starting point from which departures need to be justified? Surely most nonegalitarian thinkers would reject this starting point. Indeed, for most nonegalitarians, this starting point is precisely the principle that they reject.[4] And it is this principle that I wish to defend in this chapter.

In addition, an argument for equality as a principle of justice can illuminate the nature of the value of equality. In the argument I give below I show how, and in what circumstances, equality can be intrinsically just. But, in addition, one advantage that my argument for, and conception of, the principle of equality has is that it allows for departures from equality when this works to everyone's advantage. Hence, the conception of equality defended here is not subject to the leveling down objection. In other words, when we see what reason there is for thinking that equality is just, we will have a clearer idea of the limits and qualifications on egalitarian justice.

4. Two Basic Ideas of Justice

There are two fundamental ideas about justice that will play key roles in my argument. The first is that justice consists in each person receiving his or her due. We might call this the *principle of propriety*. The idea behind this is that justice is concerned with ensuring that each person has what is due him or what it is fitting that that person have. What is due a person is grounded in some quality of the person that gives the person a certain status or merit. The idea is that inasmuch as the person possesses a certain status or merit, it is fitting that the person have a certain thing. This is what the person is due. The idea is close to the ideas of rights and desert, though it is more abstract than either of these notions. On the one hand, the idea of what a person is due establishes something like a claim that person has on the things that are due him. On the other hand, the ideas of rights and desert are notions that flesh out and articulate what a person is due in particular moral theories. But the basic idea is that justice is concerned with persons having those things that it is fitting that they should have.

---

[3] See Arneson (1989) and Cohen (1989) generally for excellent accounts of this approach to equality. It is not clear that these authors endorse the argument I briefly described above but it is often attributed to them and merits some response.

[4] Two other efforts to defend equality should be mentioned here. John Rawls (1971) provides a defense of a principle of equality with his original position argument. This is a powerful and illuminating argument but it has been subject to a great deal of persuasive criticism starting with Barry (1973). Also Thomas Nagel has defended equality in an important paper (1979). The principle he actually ends up defending is closer to the principle of priority than a principle of equality.

There is a kind of bond between the features of the person and the treatment justice requires, which is characterized as what the person is due.

For example, many have thought that it is fitting that a virtuous person be happy or that a vicious person not be happy. Here the idea is that happiness is the virtuous person's due and unhappiness is the vicious person's due. Virtue and vice are relevant qualities of persons, many have thought, in virtue of which a person ought to be happy or unhappy. Happiness has been thought by many to be a fitting response to virtue and unhappiness a fitting response to viciousness, on these accounts.

The second principle is the commonly accepted principle that one ought to treat relevantly like cases alike and relevantly unlike cases unlike. This principle, called the *generic principle of justice*, is sometimes taken as directly supporting a principle of egalitarian justice. Many authors infer a principle of egalitarian justice once they have shown that there are no relevant differences between persons (Persson, Chapter 3 in this volume). I want to show that this inference, in the form that it usually takes, is mistaken but that there is a good version of the inference.

The generic principle regulates those reasons that accord specifically with the principle of propriety. First, as a regulator of reasons, it requires that one act in accordance with the relevant reasons relating to a particular situation and it requires that one's treatment of different situations be consistent with the same set of reasons. It requires that one's treatment of situations be in accord with the reasons that apply and not with irrelevant considerations. And since the reasons are general, when two situations are relevantly alike, the reasons that apply are the same.

Second, the generic principle regulates reasons that accord specifically with the principle of propriety. So it tells us to treat persons who are relevantly similar alike. And it requires that the relevant similarities and distinctions among persons that justify similar or different treatment be ones that are connected with what is due to a person. The properties of persons in virtue of which they are to be treated similarly or differently from others may not be incidental or merely relational properties of those persons. They must be qualities or features that display a distinctive worth or status in the persons. What is due to a person is what ought to be done or ought to be had by a person by virtue of meritorious features or features that display the worth or status of the person that are relevant to the ownership. What the person is due is a fitting response to the worth of the person in question.

Let me illustrate the way relevant meritorious qualities function in reasoning about justice by way of a contrast with utilitarian reasoning. Utilitarianism at least logically permits that one do something harmful to one person merely in order to advance the interests of others. One might suppose that there are circumstances where a harm to one person will benefit others while the very same harm to another, who is similar in other respects, will not benefit others. E. F. Carritt's example of a utilitarian judge who convicts an innocent person of a crime in order to stop a crowd from rioting comes to mind here.[5] On a utilitarian principle, this could be quite consistent with insisting on not convicting an innocent person under other less dangerous circumstances. Now the mere principle of reason that says treat like cases alike, with no restriction on the nature of the likeness, would not rule out that one harm the one and not the other.

But this action would not be just, whatever else one might think of its justification.[6] And the reason it would not be just is that it predicates the difference in treatment between the two people on the basis of something that is not a difference of merit or status between the two. It predicates the treatment of the one on the basis of something that somehow does not have to do with his distinctive worth. Justice, in contrast, requires that what we do to people should depend on morally relevant facts about their status or merit. And the generic principle, to the extent that it includes the principle of propriety, requires that the differences and similarities among people that ground different or similar treatments ought to be a fitting response to the worth or status of those people.

The reason this principle is a generic principle is because it is a schema into which any consideration of justice can fit. But it is a principle of justice because it requires that the features that determine relevant likeness and unlikeness among persons in virtue of which the same or differential treatment of them is justified are features that ground what is due to a person. So it is not a mere principle of consistency. One way in which it is different from a mere principle of consistency is that it requires us to ensure that the actions which are due to people are the same or different depending on the sameness or difference of the relevant qualities. One may think that it is perfectly consistent to love one person and not another person, even though they are the same in the relevant respects. One has only so much love to go around. There would be nothing irrational in this. But one cannot do this when considerations of justice are at issue. This is because considerations of justice are grounded in qualities of persons that make certain treatments due to those persons. It is not a relevant reason, as far as justice is concerned, for treating one person one way and another a different way that one does not care about the other person, or that one does not have any more time. The reasons that justice deals with have their sources in the persons who are being dealt with. In this respect, justice is, as Allen Buchanan has put it, subject centered and not agent centered.[7] So the reasons are grounded in the persons and, as

---

[5] See Carritt (1947: 65).

[6] This is not a criticism of utilitarianism. I take it that most utilitarians would accept the point and then go on to say that utilitarianism is the underlying principle behind the principle of justice and that it gives considerations that ought to override justice under some circumstances. See e.g. Mill (1979, ch. 5). I do think that justice is a deeper value than utilitarianism can allow, but I will sketch an argument for this below.

[7] See Buchanan (1990) in general for this.

a consequence, the relevant likeness and unlikeness must be qualities of the persons who are the subjects of justice.

I will say more in this chapter about the features that determine the worth or status of a person as opposed to incidental features of persons. Suffice it to say for the moment that only those features of persons that make their lives better or worse whether morally or prudentially can be relevant features of persons to which justice must be responsive. A partial list of these things would be the moral goodness of a person, the moral quality of a person's actions, the capacity of a person for living a flourishing life, the interests a person has in life, liberty, and property. Here the crucial idea is that there is something about that person in virtue of which one *owes it to that person* to treat them in a certain way.

Of course, utilitarianism requires that one take each person into account or into consideration. Each person is to count for one and no more than one. The utilitarian takes each person's well-being into account when deciding what to do. But the decision itself does not require that one suit the action or the event to the person. The result of the utilitarian calculus is such that the action or event that is decided on for a particular person may be justified because of its effects on another person. So even if a person's well-being has been taken into account, the utilitarian decision may be to sacrifice that person for the sake of another's well-being or for the sake of many other persons' well-being. The actual treatment of that person is not suited to that person. And it is precisely this that the principle of propriety forbids. It says that the treatment of a person or the event that occurs to a person must be somehow fitting for that person.

The generic principle is a *second order principle*. That is, it is a principle that regulates the operation of other principles. And in some cases the principle merely requires a second order equality. It functions in a merely second order way when *determinate* normative considerations already apply to the cases at hand. Determinate normative considerations are ones that yield determinate requirements on action in a way on their own. An example of a determinate normative consideration is the consideration that one ought to comply with one's contractual obligations. Here, what one is required to do is specified exactly by the contract. And this requirement is dependent only on the conditions for a valid promise and not otherwise on the context in which it is found. Of course, determinate normative considerations are only *pro tanto* considerations so they may be overridden by other considerations.

The generic principle of justice does have some bite even in the case of determinate normative considerations. For in the case of considerations of justice, the principle imposes a constraint of *generalization* over what is due to persons on the agent's reasoning. For example, if one believes that each person is owed the complete product of the things that he or she helps produce, then one will not be able to satisfy everyone's claim and the principle is self-defeating. Or a principle of justice that required that each person has unlimited liberty would also be self-defeating. So the generic principle of justice imposes a constraint of generalization on determinate normative considerations, which may, in effect, defeat certain such considerations.

5. Why Does Justice Matter?

In this chapter, my concern is mainly to show that the principle of egalitarian justice can be defended as a principle of distributive justice. In principle this is compatible with justice being merely an instrumental good, which may promote overall utility. It is even compatible with the idea that justice is of no importance in moral considerations. These would, I think, be implausible claims but the main thrust of this chapter will not undermine these claims. Here I will merely sketch an argument for why these claims are implausible and for why we ought to see justice as a fundamental moral value.

The importance of justice or the importance of giving each person his or her due is grounded in the special significance of persons. The importance of justice is grounded on a value that cannot be fully grasped if we attend only to the values of pleasure or other forms of utility as utilitarians do. In addition to the values of pleasure, happiness, beauty, and others that can be promoted, I believe we must acknowledge another kind of value that is not primarily to be promoted and that is the value of *humanity*. The fact of humanity confers a special status on most human beings, which ought to be honored.[8]

The humanity of a person is that person's capacity to recognize, appreciate, engage with, harmonize with, and produce intrinsic goods.[9] It is in virtue of this feature of human beings that they bring something unique and distinctive to the world. They are capable of seeing the value in the world. They see the values of life, beauty, and pleasure among other things. They are also capable of appreciating these values. They enjoy them; they celebrate and affirm these values. And, the appreciation, enjoyment, and love of valuable things are in themselves of great value. Human beings are also capable of engaging with these values and harmonizing with these values. They can make their lives be in harmony with the values of life and beauty and they do this because they appreciate and love these values and want to be part of a world that includes them. They are also capable of producing valuable things. They produce

---

[8] See Pettit (1990) generally for the helpful distinction between promoting and honoring.

[9] The notion of humanity I sketch here owes much to Immanuel Kant's conception of humanity in his *Foundations of the Metaphysics of Morals* (1985: 46−7). It is also quite different in that the value of humanity, in my view, connects human beings with the realm of value in the world and is not the ground of all value, as many Kantians would have it.

justice, beauty, culture, and happiness in others. They do this once again because they appreciate and love these values.

Humans do not merely cause these things to come about as, say, a river causes the conditions of life to come about; they bring about these things self-consciously and through their own activity because they appreciate them. And it is the fact that they bring them about self-consciously, and as a result of their appreciation, which gives the values their special quality. Consider the difference between looking at a particular formation of stone as merely a natural object and looking at that same formation as the product of a self-conscious attempt to realize beauty and express something about the values of life by a human being. We can appreciate the beauty of the natural rock formation, but when we look at it as the product of self-conscious human activity and as displaying an appreciation of value, it takes on a whole new dimension of value.

This new dimension of value derives from the fact that we are thinking of the human being as a kind of authority in the realm of value. They are authorities in the realm of value to the extent that they are uniquely capable of recognizing and appreciating value as well as self-consciously producing it and to the extent that their exercise of this authority is itself intrinsically valuable. By analogy, we value the love that someone has for us because it derives from an independent being who does it self-consciously and in a way authoritatively. In the same way, the value that human beings bring to the world in their appreciation of the world is partly constituted by the fact that it comes from independent beings that are authorities in the realm of value.

It is the fact that human beings have this highly significant authority in the realm of value that gives them a special status in the world. We can see this from the following two observations. To fail to acknowledge the special authority of human beings in the realm of value is to cut oneself off from all the values that are realized in this way. Think again of the stone sculpture. If we were to think of this as merely the product of natural forces, we would recognize and appreciate beauty but we would fail to see something fundamental about its value. It is only once we see it as the product of a human being, and we think of this human as not merely being a set of causal forces but in addition being a kind of authority in the realm of value, that we come to see the full value of it.

Moreover, to treat human beings as mere means for bringing about more of the goods they produce (such as appreciation of intrinsic good, creation of intrinsic good) is to fail to acknowledge their special status. It is a status that may not be sacrificed merely for the sake of these goods because it is more important than they are. It is more important than they are because it is the ground of their value. It is because the appreciation of the values in the world comes from a being with the kind of authority human beings have that the appreciation is so important. Indeed, the appreciation, harmonization with, and production of value by human beings derives its distinctive character and value from the fact that it is an activity engaged in by a being that has the kind of authority human beings have.

There are two different aspects of this value that are worth emphasizing here. One is that human beings have a special worth as substances. Hence, their worth goes beyond the mere valuing of events and states of affairs that is characteristic of consequentialist reasoning. It is in virtue of certain essential properties of these substances that they are due a certain kind of treatment. This idea of what is due or owed to something does not work with events or states of affairs. We do not owe states of affairs or events anything; these are not the sorts of things to which something can be owed or due.

The second feature that is important is that the nature of the worth of persons is not primarily expressed by talk of the promotion of this value. The primary form of valuation of these kinds of beings is honoring or respecting or acknowledging the dignity of these kinds of beings. Of course, this is consistent with saying that it is important that human beings continue to inhabit the earth and that their survival be promoted.

The only way to acknowledge the special status of human beings as authorities in the realm of value is to make sure that what happens to them and what we do to them be responsive to their special worth when we deal with them. In other words, it is the status in virtue of which we must make sure that we give each his or her due. And what is due to this kind of being is that it be enabled to exercise its enormously valuable authority.[10] In my view, the happy exercise of this authority is the distinctive form of well-being of human beings.

6. The Principle of Egalitarian Justice

The principle of egalitarian justice is itself a first order principle. It says that how much one person ought to receive of some important good can only be ascertained relative to what others can receive. Egalitarian justice is not the only such comparative principle; some desert principles are comparative as well. I want to argue in what follows that egalitarian justice follows from the generic principle, the equal status of

---

[10] The notion of the status of humanity that I have sketched here bears some resemblance to the idea of the status of inviolability that has been discussed by Francis Kamm (1992: 385). It is also similar to that discussed by Thomas Nagel (1995: 91). The status of humanity, in my view, supports a distributive principle. Whether it supports constraints on how we may treat persons in particular cases cannot be addressed here. It may be that the status of humanity constrains what we may do to bring about justice. In that case, it would play a role in the process of establishing justice among persons in actions, practices, and institutions. I discuss the establishment of justice in detail in my book *The Constitution of Equality* (forthcoming *a*).

persons, and the absence of relevant differences in conjunction with what I call the principle of well-being.

The *principle of well-being* states that to the extent that it is feasible and other things being equal, it is better that individuals have more well-being rather than less. The principle of well-being is an *indeterminate* requirement. What does it mean to say that the principle is indeterminate? It means that, at least under certain circumstances, the principle states that *more well-being is better than less*, but it does not specify a definite amount of well-being that the person *ought* to have when there is a conflict with the well-being of others. What the person ought to receive is to be determined partly by reference to the context the person is in and by some other principle.

In contrast, the principle of need states each person ought to have a definite amount of good. And some think that the principle of retribution requires that the commission of a crime be followed by a definite amount of hard treatment. Furthermore, some say that the activity of production implies that the producer ought to receive a definite amount of the good produced. And some say that a contract implies that each person ought to receive some definite amount of some good, that amount specified by the contract. In these cases, the principle specifies some particular quantity of good or evil that is to be assigned to the individual by virtue of some action or character trait of the person and that quantity is specified independently of the contingent circumstances.

The indeterminacy of the principles of opportunity, capability, and well-being implies that the principle must be supplemented by another principle in order to determine what a person ought to have. And for different kinds of questions, the indeterminacy might be resolved in different ways. For instance, a person might think that he ought to pursue as much well-being as possible. But we might also think that individuals ought to be equally well off. Some other theorists might think that well-being ought to be maximized as in utilitarianism.

The argument I want to lay out is that, when applied to indeterminate principles, the generic principle of justice actually does generate a first order requirement that is not already present in the indeterminate principles. Indeed the idea is that the generic principle actually determines what justice requires regarding realization of indeterminate principles.

7. The Basic Argument

The basic argument for the idea that equality in the distribution of fundamental goods is required by justice employs four main premises. First, the argument requires the truth of the generic principle of justice elaborated above. Second, the argument requires a conception of the basic respect in which individuals are equals. Third, the argument requires that there are no relevant differences between human beings that can determine that one person ought to receive more well-being than others (compare Persson, Chapter 3 in this volume). Fourth, it requires that well-being has fundamental value that gives reason for moral agents to promote it in other beings. Here the idea is that more well-being is better than less and that the worth of well-being is not derived from any other value. And this value of well-being gives each person a reason, albeit indeterminate, to enhance other people's well-being.

One additional feature of the argument is that it occurs in different stages. In the first stage it is concerned only with a fixed stock of divisible goods. In the second stage of the argument we will give up this restriction.

8. Equal Status

To start with, human beings have *equal moral status*. Since the status of humanity derives from the fact that humanity is a kind of authority in the realm of values, equal status is based on the fact that human beings all have essentially the same basic capacities to be authorities in the realm of value. This does not mean that they appreciate the same values. The realm of value is an extremely pluralistic world. No one can experience and appreciate more than a small proportion of that realm of values. Indeed, to be able to appreciate many of the values of the world requires the kind of discipline and focus that rules out appreciating many other values.

The question of how to establish the truth of the equal moral status of persons is one of the most profound problems of moral philosophy and, to my knowledge, has not been answered completely. In the context of the view that I am defending here, the problem is made difficult by the fact that people are obviously differently capable of appreciating intrinsic values. Some, it would seem, are more capable than others in this respect. One might ask, Since the status of persons is based on the possession of the distinctive capacity to appreciate value, why can't difference in status be based on difference in capacities?[11] I cannot say that I have more than a few remarks that might help build an answer to this question. The first observation is that the worth of persons far outstrips in importance any of the values that any particular person can produce, hence it cannot be gauged merely in terms of the amount and quality of the values a person is capable of producing. The second observation is that the world of value is so pluralistic that it is hard to compare the values of the products of different people or at least the capacities to produce value. This of course is primarily an epistemic and practical difficulty, but the difficulty may be so deep for us human beings that we cannot do better than fall back on equality of status.

[11] See generally Arneson (1999); and Waldron (2002) for incisive discussions of this issue.

The third observation is that the inequalities in abilities we see in the world around us are often the result of difference not in capacity but in external circumstances. The development of these capacities can be suppressed in particular persons as a result of poor education and other highly adverse circumstances, but this speaks not to the worth of the capacity but of the external circumstances.

These remarks do no more than gesture at a possible argument and they are unsatisfactory as they stand, but I will have to leave the issue and proceed as if the idea that persons have equal moral status is a well-established premise.

9. No Relevant Differences

What kinds of differences are relevant reasons for treating people differently in particular with respect to their well-being? The usual relevant reasons are connected with considerations of desert, reciprocity, productivity, and need. A relevant difference between two persons with regard to how they ought to be treated will include whether one person deserves more than another or one person is more productive than another or one person is needier than another. These are the traditional bases of differential treatment.

In order to establish no relevant differences, I propose to narrow the scope of the argument. The argument is to be applied to people before the age of adulthood. At this stage in life, it is normally thought that individuals are not deserving of greater fundamental goods than others, nor are people's relative productivities thought to be such that they entitle them to greater shares of fundamental goods.[12]

To determine the exact age at which we think that a person becomes capable of deserving more than others or not is not essential here as long as the persons beneath the age of maturity are still capable of appreciating intrinsic value. My inclination is to say that the ages of 16 to 18 are the right ones for this transition, but it is compatible with this argument that the ages are 12 or 14. Furthermore, that I am defending equality beneath one of these ages should not be taken to imply that I think we should accept a principle of desert or a principle of productivity above these ages. I have grave doubts about either of these principles at any age.[13] And, in any case, my

---

[12] One relevant difference that merits discussion but that I that will discuss later in this chapter is inheritance. For those who regard private property as a basic component of justice and who assert that that right includes a full right of bequest, one child might have a right to greater resources than another because someone has given those greater resources to him. See Nozick (1974) for a view of this sort. See Christman (1994: 47–66) and Cohen (1995) generally for some quite persuasive criticism of this whole approach.

[13] See Ingmar Persson's contribution to this volume (ch. 3) for an attempt to refute principles of desert generally.

suspicion is that, once the egalitarian argument I am making has been accepted, the only principles of desert or productivity that can be accepted are ones that are very close to a principle of equality for whole lives. I will have more to say about this at the end of this chapter.

10. Well-Being

People beneath these ages are nevertheless capable of well-being to a significant extent, and this is the quality that is relevantly similar among them when the other considerations do not differentiate them. That well-being is a fundamental good can be seen from the fact that societies are devoted to realizing the common good and that the common good is to be understood in terms of well-being.

Well-being can also be seen to be a fundamental good once I say a bit about what I take to be well-being. I understand by well-being that quality of a person's life that involves an appreciative and active engagement with intrinsic goods. In addition, well-being requires that a person enjoy or take pleasure in or be happy with the appreciation and active engagement with intrinsic good. Hence a person's well-being is enhanced when that person is enjoying the experience of a work of art. Or a person's well-being is enhanced when that person happily acts morally. The account of well-being presupposed here is neither entirely subjectivist nor objectivist strictly speaking. It includes an objective factor and the subjective appreciation of the objective good as it is realized in the person.[14]

In terms of the conception of the status of humanity I sketched earlier, the well-being of a person is, broadly speaking, the happy exercise of the distinctive authority of persons. We can see why well-being ought to be promoted. It is an intrinsic good that contributes to the good of the world. And we can see why it is the case that a person is due well-being. The happy exercise of the distinctive authority of a human being is the most complete realization of good in a person's life.

This idea of well-being attempts to bring together two quite distinct aspects of our thought about the good of a person. On the one hand, it attempts to grasp the fact that well-being is a good that is good for a person. In this respect to say that a person's life is a good life is not sufficient for saying that that person has well-being. For it may be that the person does many good things and does so self-consciously but is miserable in doing so. So, the man on the rack may be doing what he knows to be the right thing but to the extent that he suffers in doing so and does not enjoy the doing of the right, he does not thereby have well-being. This is because, though his life may

---

[14] For an account of well-being that is very similar to the one here, see Darwall (2002, ch. 5).

be good, it is not good for him. This goodness for him can only be had if that person enjoys the good.

This account of well-being, though it is grounded in intrinsic good, can explain the conceptual distinction between acting well and acting for one's self-interest. A person may sacrifice his well-being on this account for the sake of a greater good.[15]

The second thought this idea of well-being is meant to bring out is that well-being is a special kind of intrinsic value. First, to the extent that there are intrinsic goods, the appreciation of intrinsic goods is itself valuable. Second, to the extent that enjoyment of intrinsic goods is a fuller way in which we, as embodied human beings, can appreciate intrinsic goods, the enjoyment of intrinsic goods is not only intrinsically good in itself, it constitutes an essential part of the fullest realization of our natures as authorities in the realm of value. It gives us an account of the flourishing of persons.

So the account of well-being on offer, then, brings together two central thoughts about well-being: the fact that it is good for the person and the fact that it constitutes the flourishing of the person.

In addition, this account of well-being explains why the principle of well-being is important to justice. To honor the distinctive authority of the person is to ensure that it happily exercises that authority in its life. Ensuring the happy exercise of its distinctive authority is a fitting response to the fact that a person has that distinctive authority. To the extent that well-being consists in the happy exercise of the distinctive authority of human beings and each person is due the exercise of that distinctive authority, well-being is due each person.

The more a person has well-being, in general, the better. Each person has an overall good that is an unattainable maximum at least for practical purposes. But how much well-being ought we to try to ensure that a person has? This is not immediately determined by the fact that more well-being is better than less for each person. That is why well-being is an indeterminate principle. The nature of well-being does imply that a person ought to have his or her well-being advanced. But the principle of well-being does not specify exactly how much for most circumstances.

Now that we have these four principles in mind, let us consider some principles of distribution that might still apply when the distribution of good is at stake but that do not require desert or productivity as a relevant difference. I think there are two classes of principle in addition to equality. The first is a set of principles of maximization. The second is a set of sufficiency principles. Let us consider each in turn.

---

[15] The same cannot be said, I think, for Joseph Raz's account, which asserts that a person's well-being consists in the successful and wholehearted pursuit of rational aims. Raz's account seems to me to suggest the paradoxical assertion that the man on the rack has well-being (on the rack). On the other hand, Raz separates a person's well-being from a person's self-interest, which does require contentment. See Raz (1986: 294–8).

11. Maximization

We would say that if a person's well-being is the one and only moral basis for treating a person and that person is the only person under consideration, that person ought to be made as well off as possible. If more well-being is better than less and well-being is the only consideration that ought to inform our moral duty to a particular person, then we ought, other things being equal, to make that person as well off as possible.

This is where the generic principle of justice comes in. Once we take into account the fact that there are many individuals, we can see that if one person ought to be made as well off as possible, then every other like situated person ought to be made as well off as possible. If we apply the principle of maximum well-being to one person, then we must apply it to everyone when there are no relevant differences and there is a fundamental and morally relevant likeness between them.

But here the application of the generic principle to the maximization of well-being leads to a problem. The idea that one ought to maximize each person's well-being cannot be satisfied even in principle. This principle cannot be satisfied since it requires maximization of more than one independent variable. Hence, when we apply the generic principle to the principle of the maximization of well-being we run into a problem. The problem is a kind of generalization problem. When generalized, the maximization of one person's well-being implies that we ought to maximize each and every person's well-being separately. But this is impossible.

Notice that *maximization of the total well-being* of all persons is not a way of maximizing the well-being of each and every person independently. Total maximization cannot maximize the well-being of each and every person because the latter is impossible. Furthermore, the generic principle of justice is one that requires us to take each person separately and maximize his well-being separately, but that cannot be done by total maximization.

Another possibility is a kind of *sequential maximization* of each person's well-being. Here what we do is maximize the well-being of one person and then, given what is left over, maximize the well-being of another and we apply this procedure over again until we have gotten to every person. The consequence of this in many cases will be that the persons at the end of the procedure will get very little or nothing. But is this a conceivable application of the generic principle with no relevant differences to the principle of maximization of well-being?

This proposal suffers from violating the generic principle itself. It does not treat each relevantly like person alike. First of all, one must choose a sequence of persons as recipients of the maximization procedure. The first are likely to do very well and the later are likely to do very badly. Are there reasons, grounded in the persons themselves, why some should come first and others should come later? By hypothesis, there are none. The sequential maximization procedure seems to be an arbitrary procedure if any is.

This conclusion is interesting since it displays the way in which the generic principle can have some bite. The requirement to maximize a person's well-being cannot be conjoined with the generic principle of justice if one thinks that each person's well-being is important. To treat everyone alike in the way specified by the principle of maximization is impossible. But this implies that there is injustice when one maximizes the well-being of any arbitrary person.

I think that these arguments apply to any notion of maximization. So not only do they apply to maximization of well-being, they also apply to the Priority View. For the Priority View says that we ought to maximize the total amount of moral good where that good is a weighted function of the well-being of each person. The Priority View says that there is a diminishing marginal goodness of increases of well-being. The well-being of a person who is better off is worth less than the well-being of that same person or some other person who is worse off. The Priority View simply says that we want to maximize the total good when understood as this kind of weighted function of well-being. Hence, the Priority View will have the same problems as utilitarianism on this argument.

The conclusion shows us that we ought to pursue for each person some level below what is the best for each in order to satisfy the principle of generic justice while advancing the well-being of persons. This is what leads to the interesting result in the subsequent stretch of argument. It enjoins us to find a level that is consistent with the generic principle.

12. Sufficiency

One level of well-being that would be consistent with the generic principle is *sufficiency*. We might think that there is a level of well-being that we can bring about for people, which is enough for each person. This is, in other words, an adequate level of well-being. And to the extent that this is not a maximum of well-being, we might think that this principle can be made consistent with the generic principle at least under certain circumstances. There may be circumstances in which everyone has enough and then the generic principle conjoined with the principle of sufficiency can yield a determinate and plausible answer.

Sufficiency is a complex notion and it is important to be clear about it.[16] Let us distinguish between three different levels of sufficiency that might be thought to fit

---

[16] See Frankfurt (1997) generally for this kind of view.

the bill here. The first notion of sufficiency is the level of *subsistence*. This is a very natural notion of sufficiency because it is a relatively clear way of specifying what is enough. A person has an adequate share on this account when she can survive and live an average length life on the share she has. The second notion of sufficiency is the level of a *decent minimum*. This is the share of goods a person needs to live a decent life. Of course, how much a person needs for a decent life all depends on what the conception of a decent life is. One can imagine a number of different criteria here. I do not want to get into the details here. It is generally thought to be above the level of mere subsistence, but it is also thought to be beneath the level that would make a person as well off as possible. The idea is that there is some adequate level of well-being that can be improved upon but that does not really matter morally. A third level of sufficiency is a kind of *maximal sufficiency*. This level is the level at which a person has enough so that one can no longer contribute to that person's well-being by giving that person more.

We need to specify the currency of sufficiency as well. To make the discussion consistent with our argument here, let us suppose that the sufficiency is spelled out in terms of well-being. So the subsistence level is a level of well-being such that the person can survive an average lifespan. Having enough in this sense is compatible with many different levels of well-being above the survival level. So two people have enough when they can both survive even though one person is very well off and the other is very badly off. The decent minimum level is also a level of well-being. A person is living a reasonably good life with what he has. Again, people can have very different levels of well-being above this level. And the maximal notion is that level of well-being at which a person's life cannot be substantially improved. If we are dealing with a subjectivist standard, it is the level at which a fully informed person no longer cares if he has more than what he has. If it is an objective level of well-being, then it is a level beyond which improvements cannot be made, except perhaps trivial improvements.[17]

There are some clear problems with the subsistence and the decency standards of sufficiency. If we accept the importance of sufficiency as part of a conception of justice, does justice have nothing to say when there are conflicts of interests above the level of sufficiency? Surely this cannot be right. And I think, if we can show this for the decency standard, then we will have shown it for the subsistence standard as well. An example of this might be the division of office space in an academic building. Let us suppose that each person thinks that a single office is quite enough for performing the tasks of doing work, receiving students, relaxing by listening to music or reading a novel, etc. Surely no one will quarrel with this. Now suppose that there are four separable and similar rooms to be divided between two people. The chairman gives

---

[17] See Raz (1986: 241–3) for this kind of account.

one to one of them and gives three to another. He does not ground this difference on differential need or on greater merit. He reasons that one is sufficient for the one and three is more than sufficient for the other and there is no reason to be concerned about the inequality. The person with three offices will now have separate offices in which to receive students, work, and relax or read. Let us suppose that both can get along with only one office but that they also both like the idea of having separate rooms for separate activities. Is there no injustice here? Surely there is, and one of these people will complain loudly about the unequal treatment over and above the adequate. Indeed, short of arguments connected with the common good or perhaps of greater need or merit, the idea is that a less than equal division is unjust. Obviously if this criticism is right about the decency standard, then it will also be on target concerning the subsistence standard.

Furthermore, since the decent level of sufficiency is greater than the level of biological need satisfaction, it is important to know what one must do when there are conflicts of interests between those who do not reach this level of sufficiency. The solutions to such conflicts require that one invoke a principle in addition to that of sufficiency. And this is, at least for most of human history, a large set of cases.

Now if we take the maximal notion of sufficiency, then I think the sufficiency theorist has a powerful idea with which to criticize this argument. If there were a maximal level of well-being at which nearly everyone could be, then there may well be no further reason to be concerned with equality or any kind of distribution above the level. Such a state of the world may be described as beyond the circumstances of egalitarian justice. The circumstances of egalitarian justice, I claim, are the circumstances in which people can be made substantially better off than they are. The aspiration to equality relies on the thought that the things we want to equalize are such that more of them are better than less. If some thing, of which the just distribution was in question, was not such that more is better than less, then who would care about equality? Justice may still be possible in such a world, because we might at least want to be sure that everyone does actually have the maximally sufficient amount, but equality would no longer matter once we were talking about the distribution of good over and above the level of sufficiency. So this notion of sufficiency does offer a substantial challenge to the argument for equality.

It is important to see what premise in the argument is called into question by the thought that everyone can reach the level of maximal sufficiency. The premise that is challenged by this thought is the thesis that more well-being is better than less. The relevant aspect of the premise that is inconsistent with the maximal sufficiency notion is the fact that the premise asserts that persons are capable of an unlimited amount of well-being at least when we consider the circumstances of human life as we know them and as they are likely to be for the long term future.

The trouble with the maximal notion is that it does not seem that for now or ever in the past or for the long term future, this level will be reached by many people, if any. Perhaps some can reach this level, but the vast majority of people will always be able to improve their well-being in substantial and important ways. There are always new ways in which we can improve our well-being. We know this because we have conceptions of worlds in which our well-being is vastly greater than it presently is. The idea of heaven in the world's monotheistic religions and the idea of enlightenment in other religions point to our capacity to grasp greatly improved states of well-being. Furthermore, we find that with every new technological invention and every new medical advance as well as with every new advance in our understanding of the sources of and forms of treatment of mental illness, that we can see new ways of improving our well-being. And this is a very large set of cases. Human beings tend to have capacities for well-being that far outstretch what they have available to them. It is hard to see how, for most people, the maximal level of sufficiency can be met.

As a consequence, though the maximal level of sufficiency would imply a serious criticism of the argument for equality if it could be met for most people, that maximal level simply cannot be met.

In general, then, the idea that there is an attainable level of sufficiency above which moral concern does not extend is implausible. So the idea that distributive concerns ought actually to be limited to a principle of sufficiency is also quite implausible since, on the decency standard, there are important questions of how to distribute good above and beneath the level of sufficiency. And since no one or nearly no one can satisfy the maximal standard, the distributive question of how to distribute below that level is always the live issue. For the moment, let us put aside this answer.[18]

13. Equality

Once we put aside the sufficiency principle of justice, we are not left with any suitable alternative principle that can be used to assign well-being to each individual on his or her own. But this need not mean that there is no principle. The only principles that can help us are the generic principle of justice coupled with the equal status of persons and the no relevant differences thesis and the principle of well-being.

The key idea is that if there is a reason for any person to be brought to a certain level of well-being, then the same reason holds for every person to be brought to that level of well-being. Once we have ruled out relevant differences, only equal status comes in

[18] See Paula Casal (2004) generally for a lucid and much more detailed criticism of the principle of sufficiency. See also the contributions in this volume of Nils Holtug (Ch. 5) and Andrew Williams (Ch. 10). Holtug argues against sufficiency while Williams offers a qualified defense.

to determine how much well-being each person ought to have. The generic principle ruled out maximization of everyone's well-being because it failed to generalize. And the principle of well-being rules out sufficiency, at least for the cases that arise in the world as we know it. The question is, Does the generic principle determine the level we ought to bring about when we are dealing with the principle of well-being or any analogous principle?

What we need to do is select levels of well-being until we come to the point that is consistent with the generic principle of justice and the absence of relevant differences and equality of status, and the only such point is equality of well-being. Hence, there is a reason for a person to be made as well off as possible consistently with everyone else being that well off. Any other distribution of well-being would violate either the generic principle of justice or the fundamental value of well-being or the equal status of persons coupled with the no relevant differences thesis.

Therefore, only equality of well-being is compatible with the fundamental value of well-being, the generic principle of justice, equality of persons, and the absence of relevant differences between persons. Notice that without equality of status the generic principle coupled with the no relevant differences thesis does not imply equality. This is because the absence of relevant differences is not a sufficient basis for saying that the cases are alike. If there were no remaining equality when the relevant differences are ruled out, the generic principle would simply be indeterminate. Furthermore, it is essential that, for each person, more well-being is better than less, otherwise the concern with equality of well-being would be without point.

Here is a way of making this argument intuitive. If there are two people and we believe that one person ought to be better off than the other, it follows that we think that there is a reason for the better-off person to be better off than the other and justice requires that this reason be a relevant difference between them. But, by hypothesis, there are no relevant differences and the persons have equal status, so it follows that the same reason holds for the other person to be that well off. So, if the other person is not as well off, then that person is being treated in violation of the generic principle of justice or of his equal status. Hence, either the better-off person does not have reason to be treated that way or there is a relevant difference or the generic principle is false. By hypothesis there is no relevant difference between these persons of equal status, and the generic principle of justice is true. Therefore, the better-off person does not have reason to be treated better than the worse-off person. There is only one level of well-being that can satisfy the generic principle of justice, the fundamental value of well-being, and the fact of no relevant differences among equals, and that is the level at which there is equality of well-being.

Here we have derived the principle of equality of condition from the generic principle of justice, equality of status, no relevant differences, and the fundamental value of well-being.

14. The Rejection of the Historical Entitlement View on Justice

What I want to do in this section is defeat the arguments for an important alternative approach to justice to the one I am defending. I will start by showing that the arguments for the entitlement view are not cogent arguments. And I will then proceed to show that the fundamental consideration that is meant to support the entitlement view in fact supports the approach that I am defending here.

15. The Challenge of the Historical Entitlement

It is at this point that we should discuss a major alternative to the view that I have been defending. The historical entitlement view elaborated by Robert Nozick says that the proper response to humanity is to respect each person's ownership of things in the world including ownership of himself. The idea is to give full liberal rights to each person to engage in voluntary transactions with others concerning the things that they legitimately own. Each person legitimately owns himself and the things he has acquired among previously unowned objects in the world (as long as enough is left for others) and all those things he has acquired by voluntary transfer from others (as long as those others previously legitimately owned the transferred object). And furthermore, no one has any fundamental rights to anything else. This is the classical liberal view of the rights of persons. It essentially defends a completely unfettered market economy among persons (except of course in cases where everyone consents to another form of social organization).

This view constitutes a challenge to the position I am defending here in a number of ways. First, it pays little attention to well-being. Its major historical predecessor, Locke's conception of property, does ground both property rights and the proviso on acquisition of property rights in a concern for the satisfaction of human needs. But Nozick pays little attention to human needs except in the formulation of the Lockean proviso. Second, the view I have been defending articulates a kind of pattern conception of justice in terms of which rules of behavior (including rules of ownership) are to be evaluated; in contrast this view sets out a set of rules for the guidance of individual behavior (which Nozick calls side constraints on action) that are to be followed nearly absolutely such that if everyone follows them, the results are just. Partly as a consequence of this position, a third difference is that the view allows that some may become much better off than others merely as a result of voluntary gifts from others. This would be, as it were, a relevant difference among persons, although the justice of this kind of inequality is grounded primarily in the right of the person who gives. As long as side constraints have been observed, one child may grow up in miserable circumstances that make it highly likely that he will not flourish while another may grow up in circumstances that make it much more likely that he will flourish. This difference could be deemed just, on this view, because it arose from a series of transactions, which violated no one's liberal property rights, culminating in the bountiful inheritance of one and the wretched inheritance of the other. Fourth, the view allows persons to become much better or worse off than others as a result of the cumulative effects of voluntary transfers and acquisitions of previously unowned objects.

Why would such a package of rights seem to be the proper response to the humanity of persons? There are a couple of arguments suggested by Nozick's treatment of the issue. One argument is that this package of rights seems to be the only one consistent with self-ownership.[19] A second argument is that only such a package of rights respects the liberty of each person.[20] A third argument is that only by respecting these rights of persons can we treat them as ends-in-themselves.[21] In my view, the third argument undergirds the other two and it is a rival approach to mine concerning the value of humanity, so I shall discuss the other two first and then proceed to this more fundamental consideration.

In my view, none of the above suggested arguments are cogent. The argument from self-ownership to the possibility of ownership of parts of the world seems to depend not only on self-ownership but also on contentious claims about the prior susceptibility of the external world to be owned. If, for example, we think that the external world is owned in common by human beings, then mere self-ownership will not be sufficient to move from acquisitive actions over objects to ownership of those objects. The consent of all will be required, or at least a principle that all could reasonably consent to would have to govern acquisition and transfer. Or if we think that the external world is there for the meeting of human needs, we will not be able to infer from self-ownership to ownership over external objects except through a principle that guarantees the satisfaction of human needs.

The argument from liberty to this package of rights is also quite weak. If we think of liberty as essentially the noninterference of persons with other persons' activities, then the property rights that arise from the historical entitlement view will clearly constitute severe restrictions on liberty. The property right of one person implies that others are not free to use that part of the world for their own ends without the consent of that person. The question might be whether such a view implies more or less restriction on liberty than a view that says that property rules should be set up so as to advance the well-being of persons. It is hard to say in advance one way or another. Of course, it is true that more egalitarian property rights will restrict actions

---

[19] See Nozick (1974: 172).   [20] See Nozick (1974: 163).   [21] See Nozick (1974: 31–2).

that are not restricted in libertarian property rights schemes. But the same can be said for libertarian property rights schemes. What these schemes do primarily is distribute liberty in different ways. Which scheme produces the most liberty is quite uncertain. Of course, if we understand liberty in a more moralized way, then we face the danger that the whole argument is circular. For instance, if we think of liberty as what one is permitted to do under the correct system of rights,[22] then the correct system of rights will not be something that can be defended by reference to a concern with liberty.[23]

16. Humanity and Self-Ownership

The fundamental argument is that only in a scheme of full liberal property rights do we treat persons as ends-in-themselves. This argument is a direct challenge to the argument I have given. And it seems to me to be the crucial argument. For only this argument can provide the basis for the premises of the first two arguments anyway. So my concern with this argument is to see whether the classical liberal approach gives a superior account of how we ought to treat persons as ends-in-themselves or out of respect for their humanity or whether the egalitarian account that I am giving does a better job at this.

Let us consider first whether the value of humanity provides a basis for the value either of self-ownership or of liberty as noninterference. It is hard to see how the value of humanity as I have elaborated it can provide a basis for a doctrine of self-ownership in the strong sense that libertarians would have it. This strong sense is, one, that one may do anything to oneself that one pleases (as long as it does not violate the rights of others) and, two, that the requirement of respecting people's property rights in themselves and their objects is always stronger than the requirement to help others when they are in need (unless one has contracted with them to help them).

It would seem that both of these two elements of the right of self-ownership are inconsistent with the value of humanity. The thought that one has a right to kill oneself for no particular reason or that one has a right to do damage to oneself in this way seems incompatible with the value of humanity to the extent that one must honor the value of humanity in oneself just as one must honor it in others. To kill oneself for no particular reason or to do damage to oneself for no good reason or even to waste one's life on valueless projects seems in conflict with the requirements that stem from the value of one's own humanity. And selling oneself into slavery seems equally inconsistent with a proper respect for one's own humanity. To value and

---

[22] As Nozick (1974: 169) seems to think.

[23] The arguments of these last two paragraphs have been developed by G. A. Cohen in a series of papers culminating in his powerful critique (1995) of Nozick. See also Kymlicka (2002, ch. 4).

respect one's own humanity, in my view, implies that one is not permitted to destroy it or damage it or waste it or even sell it in perpetuity (unless on the basis of very weighty considerations). These are very strong restrictions on ownership such that it no longer seems reasonable to say that one does own oneself in Nozick's strong sense once these restrictions are in place.

Second, it seems inconsistent with the value of humanity to say that one is not required to come to the help of someone in need. To value humanity is not only to think that it ought not to be damaged, it is also to think that it ought not to be allowed to be destroyed or damaged when these can be avoided. But it also seems clear that to value humanity is also to think that the conditions for its flourishing must be assured as much as possible. This is peculiarly so on the account of humanity that I have given. For this account says that our humanity consists in our capacities to recognize, pursue, appreciate, harmonize with, and create intrinsic value. To respect humanity is inextricably tied to valuing its flourishing. To respect and value humanity but think that one is not required to do what enables it to flourish is a very strange combination of principles.[24]

Now if the duty to advance the flourishing of humanity is an implication of the valuing and respect owed to humanity, then this duty can compete with the duty to respect the liberal property rights of a person. It is hard to see, once this competition is permitted, how the duty to enable persons to flourish must always be weaker than the duty to respect property rights. And of course, the capacity for the duty of aid to defeat the duty of respect for property seems greater the more external to the person the property is. So, the duty to respect a person's right to external property that is solely used for the purpose of reaping monetary profit seems to be more easily defeated by the duty to come to the aid of others than the duty not to torture persons or the duty not to remove the bodily parts of a person. The duty to respect external property that is necessary to pursue personal projects seems less easy to defeat than the duty to respect profitable property but easier to defeat than the duty not to torture or not to remove a person's body parts. And in general we can see that there are gradations of strength of duty with respect to the things that people own. It is reasonable to infer that the correlative rights are similarly graded in this way. The right that one's body be unmolested is much stronger than rights to external property, and the right not to be mentally tormented is stronger than the right not to be physically tormented.

It strains credulity in the extreme to think that the duty not to interfere with a person's property right in some investment property is generally stronger than the duty to help another in serious danger of losing his life or other essential means to well-being. It also strains credulity in the extreme to suppose that the duty to respect such property rights is stronger than the duty to come to the aid of someone who is

---

[24] The arguments of these last two paragraphs are made by Kant (1985: 47–9).

in danger of being tortured. In each of these cases, it seems clear that if the only way to help the potential victim is to take some of the property of an unwilling potential donor, no one can reasonably disagree that this is the right thing to do. Compare this with the case where it is suggested that we kill one person or torture a person or remove a body part from that person for the sake of stopping another from being tortured or even seriously set back in his capacity to pursue well-being. Here we would clearly have serious reservations about doing any one of these things, though fewer reservations for the later elements of the list than the earlier. But the fact that there is some serious gradation in the strength of the rights is very clear.[25] And the associated claims that there may be good enough reason to take some investment property away from a person to help another, but not good enough reason to take a person's life in order to help another in serious need, seem much more consistent with a valuation of and honoring of humanity than the absolute side constraints that Nozick has to offer.

So if we survey the intuitive evidence and the relation to the value of humanity, it seems clear that the value of humanity will not support the strong thesis of self-ownership that Nozick claims to be at the basis of full liberal property rights. The rights one has over oneself are limited in many ways that are inconsistent with the strong self-ownership thesis. And the duties to respect the property of others are clearly weaker in many ways than the duties to help others. Both of these limitations on self-ownership are clearly called for by the value of humanity. So the Nozickian argument from the principle of humanity to the principle of self-ownership must be rejected.

17. Why Self-Ownership Is Not Central to Rights

But let us explore some possible implications of this gradation. Suppose that someone accepts this graded system of rights over oneself and other things. What could account for it? I want to say that what accounts for it is the greater centrality of the more protected objects to a person's well-being. So the health of the mind is more important to well-being than the health of the body, and the health of the body is more important than external objects, to a person's well-being. But this is presumably not the way someone still friendly to classical liberalism would see it. Someone who is still friendly to the classical liberal program might try to account for this gradation in strengths of right to a kind of gradation in strengths of ownership. It would be because I own my mind more than I own my body and I own my body more than I own external things that there are lesser strengths in rights to the protection of these things. So the gradation in rights is derived from a gradation in ownership.

[25] See Nagel (1980: 196) for a statement of this argument.

But this seems like an unpromising way to explain matters, at least if one wishes not to depart too far from intuitive evidence. The reason for this is that there are important ways in which one's ownership of one's mind and body are much more limited than one's ownership of external things, as we have seen above. For instance, one does not have the right to destroy one's mind or body (at least without very strong reasons) but one does have the right to destroy many of the physical objects one owns. Furthermore, it seems quite intuitive to me that one does not have the right to sell one's mind or body to others, at least in perpetuity. Voluntary slavery seems clearly wrong. But it also seems clearly right to say that we have rights to sell external objects in perpetuity. And we have rights to destroy some external objects. Furthermore, one does not have the right to waste one's humanity entirely on valueless things or damage it without good reason. But one does have the right to do these things to the external objects one owns at least for the most part. So in that respect our ownership over external things is more extensive than our rights over our bodies and minds.

These observations are consistent I think with how our rights to do things to ourselves and external objects are related to the value of humanity. It is precisely because of the great importance of the value of humanity that we do not have rights to destroy or damage or sell our bodies or our minds or even to waste them entirely on valueless projects. It is because our minds are more central to our humanity than our bodies that the duty to protect our minds is greater than the duty to protect our bodies. And given the greater distance of the value of external objects from our humanity than the value of our minds, we seem to have more extensive property rights over the external objects. So an intuitive rendering of the value of humanity suggests that we have fewer property rights over our bodies and minds than we have over external objects, at least in some important respects. And so, at least in some important respects, the centrality to the value of humanity seems inversely proportional to the strength of ownership rights.

It is still the case that the strength of the rights not to be molested in mind and body is greater than the strength not to be molested in external property. But it doesn't seem that this can be accounted for on the idea that rights of self-ownership are at the core of all of our rights. For the rights that are strongest in one respect are quite limited in another respect. And the rights that are quite weak tend to be less limited. What we have is just a complex array of rights and duties that cannot be unified under the rubric of self-ownership. So the point that I want to make here is that the whole idea of ownership over one's body or mind seems quite misplaced except in the minimal sense that is derivable from the fact that one has limited but strong rights to do some things with one's body or mind. How they can be accounted for in a unified fashion is part of a larger task that cannot be undertaken here.

18. Humanity and Well-Being

This complexity in the rights we have to be unmolested in body and mind and the rights in external property suggests that these rights are not connected to self-ownership at all. The gradations in strength of rights are more plausibly connected with the centrality of these rights to the promotion of the well-being of the person. And the importance to well-being of these rights also accounts for the limitations on the rights to body and mind as well as the strength of the so limited rights. Both the gradations in strength of rights and the limitations seem grounded in the importance of these rights to well-being and the duties it generates in human beings both to themselves and to others. The rest of this argument cannot be undertaken here.[26]

So my thesis here is that the rights we associate with liberalism are best understood as grounded in and derivative from a concern with the well-being of persons and the requirement of justice that the well-being of persons be equally advanced.

19. Humanity and Self-Determination

Some might think that the value of humanity is best honored by allowing the person to engage in self-determination. And they might think that this is achieved only by giving the person alternative options. In a way, this is the thought behind Sen's capacity view. Each person, on this account, ought to have the capacity to engage in valuable functionings. But having the capacity, Sen seems to think, involves having the options not to engage in the valuable functionings. And we should value each person's capacity to turn away from the good to something valueless or even evil.

How does this relate to the notion of humanity that I have laid out? The first thing to note is that the value of humanity as I have laid it out does not require options. All that is needed for a human being to flourish is that the person enjoys or takes pleasure in the genuine appreciation of and engagement with intrinsic value. It needn't be the case that the person had alternatives to do lesser things in order for that person's genuine valuation of intrinsic value to be genuine. So to the extent that self-determination involves alternative possibilities to do otherwise, the view I have defended does not require this. But to the extent that self-determination involves a person endorsing and appreciating the value of what she does, the account does involve self-determination. The idea of self-determination in this limited sense is

---

[26] I undertake the larger tasks mentioned in the last few paragraphs in Christiano (forthcoming *a*, ch. 4).

implicit in the idea of the well-being of the person, but the idea of having options to do otherwise is not implicit in this account.

It is hard to see why we would want any further kind of self-determination at the ground of the view of the person. Why should we value in some fundamental way the options to do things that are worthless or bad? Of course, we think it is important in the ordinary run of things for people to have these options because, first of all, the alternative is to have fallible and biased others determining what is valuable for them. In general, we think it best for a person to find their own way through the realm of value because they are more likely to live decent lives in this way than when others try to impose the good on them. Second, we value options because we think people learn best when they are able to learn from their mistakes. In general, the presence of options becomes important in politics. This is because the imposition of a particular form of life by one person over another is, under the normal circumstances of politics, a subordination of the interests of the latter person to the interests of the former. And in any case, the imposition of a way of life by one person over another is highly likely to set back the interests of that other. So given a set of weighty interests that people have in making choices for themselves, under the normal circumstances of politics, the limitation of a person's liberty is highly likely to amount to a treatment of that person as an inferior. But this account of the importance of certain liberties is not grounded in any fundamental value of being able to do otherwise; it is grounded in certain basic interests people have and the requirement that people be treated as equals in society.

At the level of fundamental value, we honor and respect the humanity in a person by enabling that person to exercise her distinctive authority in the realm of value and to do so in a way that integrates the whole person in the process. In my view, the exercise of the distinctive authority in the realm of value in an integrated way is the well-being of the person. Self-determination is important to the extent that it is an integral part of this exercise of authority, but it is not of fundamental importance that a person has the possibility to do otherwise than exercise the distinctive authority.

20. The Leveling Down Objection

It has been said by some that the principle of egalitarian justice is subject to a fatal intuitive objection. The objection is that the principle of equality defended has an extremely implausible implication. Suppose two alternative states S_1 and S_2 such that in S_1 everyone is equally well off and in S_2 everyone is better off than in S_1 but some are better off than others. Some have argued that the principle of equality has an important but implausible implication. The principle appears to say that S_2 is worse than S_1 at least in the respect relevant to the principle of equality. This is because S_1 is egalitarian while S_2 is not. So S_2 represents a departure from equality while S_1 does not. Thus the principle of equality implies that, at least as far as equality is concerned, we ought to make everyone worse off. Of course, other principles may contend with equality and override its recommendation in this case. But the worry is that to the extent that the principle of egalitarian justice makes the recommendation that everyone be made worse off, that is a strike against the principle.[27]

Not everyone agrees that this is a strike against the principle of egalitarian justice. Temkin argues that there are other principles that may have strongly Pareto inefficient implications. Temkin cites principles of retributive desert that imply in some circumstances that everyone ought to be worse off than they could be because they deserve to be worse off. He argues that many accept such a view despite its welfare diminishing character.[28]

Temkin is right to point out that not every principle is likely to be tarnished by the implication that it sometimes implies that states can be better than others in certain respects even though everyone is worse off in them. But it is not clear to me that most egalitarians can do this. For most egalitarians seem to hold both to the idea that equality is important and to the idea that well-being is important (or at least opportunity for well-being or capacities for functioning). And these two judgments seem to come together in their egalitarianisms. For one thing, many egalitarians think that the promotion of well-being, or at least the opportunities or access to well-being, is important. The principles are principles of equal opportunity for or access to welfare, and the reasons given for this idea is that welfare is intrinsically important. This suggests to me that these egalitarians cannot be indifferent between two equal states S_1 and S_3, which are such that everyone is better off (or has more opportunities or access to being better off) in S_3 than in S_1. Egalitarians must prefer the Pareto superior equality to the Pareto inferior equality, and that preference derives from the correct understanding of the principle of equality that I have defended, or so I shall argue.

There is an internal connection between the idea of equality and the value of the relevant fundamental good that is equalized. We discussed this a bit in the argument about sufficiency. There we noted that if it was not true that more well-being was better than less, then there would be no point to equality. There would be no reason to care about equality. Since the importance of well-being or opportunity for well-being seems to be built into the principle of equality—it is the reason for the principle taking the shape that it does—they cannot be indifferent between these two states.

---

[27] See Parfit (1991: 23) for an account of the objection. See also Narveson (1983) and Frankfurt (1997: 266) for other sympathetic accounts of this objection.

[28] See Temkin (2000: 138). See the Nils Holtug's contribution to this volume (Ch. 5) for criticisms of Temkin.

To take an example, suppose that we are concerned with distributing bread among persons and we have much more than is needed. In this context there is a definite level at which each person has enough and beyond which more does not matter. In this context we would only be concerned that each receive enough of the bread and beyond that we would not care how much each gets. Whether we distribute equal amounts of bread or not would be, in and of itself, a matter of indifference.

Of course, if we did not have enough for everyone, we might be concerned with equal distribution. So if we had enough for everyone to survive but not enough to satisfy everyone, we would be concerned with the correct distribution of bread. But in this case, it is precisely because the amount of bread we have is such that more is better than less for everyone that we concern ourselves with its distribution.

Another example is a concern over how many letters people have in their last names. For the most part people are indifferent to how many letters they have in their names. As a consequence, they will be indifferent to quantitative distribution of letters in each person's name. Equality could not be important in this context.

So a necessary condition for equality mattering is that the thing being equalized is such that more is better than less. I want to argue that since the truth of the proposition that more substantial good is better than less substantial good is a necessary condition for the truth of the principle of equality in the substantial good, the right account of the principle of equality must somehow include the idea that equalities in which everyone is better off are better than equalities in which everyone is worse off.

Clearly this proposition is not a conceptual one. One can imagine a principle of equality of shares in substantial good that does not concern itself with whether people have more of that substantial good. But the question is, Does such a principle make sense? The things of which we care about egalitarian distribution are things that we want more of rather than less for everyone. And it is because we want more of rather than less of these things for everyone that we think that egalitarian distribution of these things matters.

Moreover, unlike a retributive desert principle, the principle of equality does not have any component that justifies lowering the welfare of a person (or the opportunity for welfare). It makes sense for some desert principles to favor a Pareto inefficient outcome in those circumstances where everyone deserves to be worse off. But this is part of the value theory of these conceptions of desert. On these views, it is better that a person who deserves it is worse off. We may reject this value theory, but it makes some sense. But there is no analogous feature in egalitarian principles.

One possible analogy is that if a person is responsible for having less welfare than someone else, then that person's being worse off may not be unjust. But now consider a situation in which every person is responsible for having less welfare than they might have had. Each decided not to make the extra effort that would have brought him or her more well-being overall. Then, unexpectedly, a new set of resources becomes available such that each can bring him or her to the higher level of well-being without any extra effort. Most egalitarians would say that this increase in good for everyone was an improvement.

But the same would not hold for all kinds of desert. If every person in a society turned out to be vicious, then each might deserve to be badly off. And the introduction of a new set of resources that could make everyone better off would not be an improvement; indeed, on the desert theory if everyone were to be made better off than they deserved to be, that would be worse. So the desert theorist would be within her rights to respond to the objection that her theory endorsed Pareto inferior states that that is not an objection to her theory but a statement of it.

Notice that this implication holds primarily for noncomparative desert theories. It holds for views that say that bad people should suffer and good people should do well. On such a view, justice will demand that everyone be badly off in the case in which everyone is bad. It will demand that everyone be well off in the case in which everyone is good.

It isn't clear that this kind of implication will hold for a comparative desert theory. Such a theory will appear to work very much like the opportunity theory I described above. Suppose that some people have made greater efforts towards the production of the common good than others and that our desert theory says that they deserve more than those who made the lesser efforts. Now suppose that, suddenly, it is realized that the group finds a large new supply of resources for personal consumption. These resources will be distributed either equally or in accordance with desert. There is no pressure to throw the resources away.[29] The egalitarian theorists are not in the position of the noncomparative desert theorist. There is nothing in the value theory that says that it is better for a person to be worse off.

Because there is an internal connection between the importance of equality and the idea that it is better to have more rather than less of the thing being equalized, the leveling down objection is an objection that ought to be taken seriously by egalitarians,

---

[29] There may be some question about whether leveling down applies to comparative desert theories. Suppose that two people produce two things. One of these things is very valuable and the other is only a little bit and the things cannot be divided up. Now we must distribute these things between the two of them. Now suppose that one of them is a bit more deserving than the other but the two objects are very different in value so that their distribution cannot fit the differential merits. Indeed, the only way to fit the merits would be to give the small object to the more deserving person and destroy the large object. This is because the more deserving person is only a little more deserving and the smaller object has only a little value. Would such a desert theory require the destruction of the larger, more valuable object? Here we can see pressures in the direction of distributing the more valuable object as well as pressures in the direction of destroying the more valuable object. After all, some will say, the less deserving person deserves something. And if we distribute in accordance with the exact merits, the less deserving will not get anything. But if we make sure the less deserving gets something, the less deserving will get much less than he deserves at least by comparison with the more deserving.

if it works. But I do not think that it works. And the fact that it does not work can be seen in a number of ways.

21. A Gap in the Leveling Down Objection

The leveling down objection derives its apparent strength from the claim that an egalitarian must think that something is lost when there is some inequality. This claim follows from the central egalitarian claim that all inequalities are unjust. And from this it is inferred that any egalitarian state must be better than any nonegalitarian state, at least in one respect. And from this it is inferred that there is one important respect in which an egalitarian state is better than a strongly Pareto superior state (one in which everyone is better off).

But the first inference is not valid. From the fact that there is loss from inequality it does not follow that any egalitarian state is better in respect of equality than any nonegalitarian state. What the egalitarian does need to say is that for every nonegalitarian state there is some (Pareto noncomparable) egalitarian state that is superior to the nonegalitarian state (even if it does not maximize utility or total good).

Consider three states: S_1, S_2, and S_3. S_1 and S_3 are egalitarian and S_2 is nonegalitarian. S_3 and S_2 are both strongly Pareto superior to S_1. S_2 and S_3 are Pareto noncomparable. But S_3 is egalitarian and S_2 is not. The difference is that in S_2 at least one person is better off and another is worse off than in S_3. All the egalitarian is committed to asserting is that there is something lost in S_2 because all the people in S_2 are not equally well off. This may merely imply that S_3 is better or more just than S_2. It is compatible with this to say that S_2 is better or more just than S_1 just as S_3 is. And this set of claims is sufficient to ground the claim that, for every inequality, there is something lost with respect to equality.

Of course, S_3 may not be feasible, but this is not a reason to think that failure to be S_3 is not the defect in S_2. All that is needed for the egalitarian is to say that relative to some nearby possible equality that is set at a level of well-being in between that of the persons in the unequal state (perhaps at the average of the well-being of the two persons), the unequal state is missing something or is unjust because it is not equal. This is still an importantly egalitarian theory, but it does not say that any equality is better in some respect to any inequality. It says merely that every inequality is unjust because there is an equality relative to which it is unjust.

What my argument so far has shown is that there is a significant gap in the leveling down objection against equality. It has shown that a crucial inference is unsupported by the objector and that alternatives to that inference are logically possible. What I want to show in the next section is that the logically possible alternative missed by the proponents of the leveling down objection is in fact the one that the argument for equality I have provided supports.

What I argue for in the following is not a complete principle but a strategy for constructing such a principle. We do not have the time to construct a complete principle and I am not sure I can do it at the moment anyway. But it is a defensible strategy, which implies that there is some principle that satisfies the strategy, which is the correct principle of equality. It is sufficient to defeat the leveling down objection that this is a legitimate strategy.

22. An Argument for the Least Unequal Pareto Optimal Inequalities

The first important extension of the argument for equality of condition generates an account of justice in the cases of Pareto improvements over equality of condition. I have in mind *weak* Pareto improvements in which less than everyone is better off under inequality than under equality and no one is worse off. Let us consider cases of Pareto improvements where some are better off and none are worse off under inequality than under equality. There are a number of cases of this sort. In one sort of case, some goods are lumpy, so we cannot achieve a completely egalitarian distribution. The second case involves production. In such a case, the complexities and uncertainties of production require that incentives be offered to those who are most suited to the tasks to be performed. In this kind of case, inequalities arise as a kind of by-product of the process of production.[30] My thesis is that if some person can be made better off than under the best feasible equality, then we should choose that state in which some are better off and none are worse off than under the best feasible equality.

In the case I shall consider here, I shall consider whether it is just to bring about a Pareto improvement over equality given the argument I have just made above. I will discuss a case of lumpy goods where if one insisted on equality one would have to throw away some of the lumpy goods in order to achieve equality. And I shall just consider this for two persons: A and B. This is a narrow idealization but it is hard enough to grasp it properly. The argument proceeds by comparing two states: S_1 in which A and B are equally well off and S_2 in which one is better off than in S_1 and one is at the same level of well-being as in S_1; A is better off than B.

Let us suppose that A is better off under an unequal distribution of well-being than under an egalitarian distribution. Hence it looks like the Pareto improvement in S_2 pushes us beyond the equality of S_1. It pushes us in a direction that does not allow us

---

[30] See my (forthcoming *b*).

fully to satisfy the constraint on reasons stated by generic equality. Someone is not being treated fully in accordance with the reasons that apply to him. Either someone is being treated better than the reasons applying to him allow, or someone is being treated worse than the reasons applying to him allow, or both of these are true. So there is some kind of failure of justice in cases of unequal distribution. In our example, either A is being treated better than the reasons allow in his case, or B is being treated worse that the reasons allow in his case, or both of these claims are true.

If we compare S_1 (equality) and S_2 (Pareto improvement) the generic principle of justice says that there is something wrong in S_2 because it is not equal. But I want to say that there is something even worse in S_1 with regard to justice. And so we have reason to prefer S_2 to S_1, from the point of view of justice. What is my reason for this?

Let us start by considering a small variation on the above example. Let us think of S_1 and another state S_2^*, in which both A and B are better off than in S_1 but A is better off than B. S_2^* is a strong Pareto improvement over S_1. The argument starts from the observation that in S_2^* either A is better off than he ought to be, or B is worse off than he ought to be, or both of these are true. But if we look at S_1, we notice that both A and B are worse off in S_1 than in S_2^*. A is worse off in S_1 than B is in S_2^*. The principle of well-being and the generic principle pick out the level of well-being of B in S_2^* as the one that everyone ought to have because there is a sense in which this is a level of well-being which everyone can be at or better. So ideal justice seems to require that everyone be at least at the level B is at in S_2^*. The egalitarian level in S_1 is worse for both A and B. So to the extent that A and B ought to be at the level of B in S_2^*, there are two failures from the point of view of justice in S_1. Two people are worse off than justice says they ought to be. It seems to me, then, that we can see that from the point of view of justice, S_1 is worse than S_2^* even though S_1 is egalitarian and S_2^* is not.

It seems to me that this reasoning can help us see why S_2 is more just than S_1 even though only one person is better off in S_2 than in S_1 and no one is worse off. For in S_2, one person is better off than in S_1 and no one is worse off, which implies that there is a gain in well-being in S_2. Now S_2 is still unjust because it is not equal. But the equality relative to which we can say that S_2 is unjust is some equality that is set at the level of well-being somewhere between A's and B's in S_2. This equal state is Pareto noncomparable to S_2 because B would be better off and A would be worse off than under S_2. This state, call it S_3, is egalitarian. And it is because S_2 is not this state that we think that S_2 is unjust. S_2 could not be made more just in any respect if it were brought down to S_1. But we can see how one can be an egalitarian without saying that S_1 is better in some respect. S_2 is unjust because there is some Pareto noncomparable S_3 that is ideally just and relative to which S_2 is defective.

This seems to me to give exactly the right result. The idea is that there *is* in-justice in an unequal condition when there are no relevant differences between the persons between whom the inequality holds. But, there is *less* injustice in such an unequal condition than in an equal condition that is strongly or even weakly Pareto inferior to the unequal condition. So though there is something wrong with the Pareto improving inequality, it is less problematic than the Pareto inferior equality.

But this shows how one can think that though there is something lost and problematic in efficient inequality, it does not follow that egalitarians are committed to the proposition attributed to them in the leveling down objection. For that objection to work against an egalitarian principle of justice it is not enough that the egalitarian is committed to the injustice of inequality. The leveling down objection applies to equality only if the egalitarian is also committed to the claim that inequality is worse from the point of view of the principle of equality than a Pareto inferior equality. But it is this last claim that the egalitarian need not be committed to, as I have argued.

Now we can see a strategy for the construction of a principle of equality that avoids the leveling down objection. The principle states that for any situation there is some Pareto optimal equality that is fully just. Relative to this equality, inequalities are unjust. But it is also true that relative to this equality, Pareto inferior equalities are unjust. This equality may be specified in a variety of ways. One way it could be specified is by taking the average level of good for persons and saying that equality at that level is ideally just. But this needn't be the only way to specify the principle.

One way that I would argue we should not specify the principle is to say that the principle asserts that equality at the highest level of well-being is the only fully just arrangement. The reason for this rejection is that such a principle would not be distinctively egalitarian. This is because it would say what nonegalitarians could readily agree to, which is that Pareto improvements are to be pursued. I doubt if many want to disagree with that. What makes the principle of equality distinctive is that it recommends making some people worse off if that will make others better off and it recommends this up to the point of equality.

Have I simply changed the question? I have responded to the leveling down objection by defending a principle that seems to avoid it. But is this really what egalitarians are after? Or is it a new principle? I want to defend the claim that it is the right principle of equality. Remember that the rationale for the principle of equality involves the claim that more substantial good is better than less. The argument I have given for equality involves this essential premise. What would be the point of equality if this were not so? Given the internal connection between equality and the idea that more is better than less when it comes to the thing equalized, and given the argument for equality that I have given, it seems reasonable to hold that this is the proper conception of equality.

23. Equality, Productivity, and Desert

Does this principle extend beyond youth? It would appear that at least it extends to the point where considerations of desert and productivity arise. But does it extend to them as well? Here is a way in which it might. Each person's well-being matters equally and so conditions for well-being ought to be equal. Productivity and desert, if they are legitimate concerns of justice, are principles that require the modification of the well-being of each person. Therefore, each ought to have equal conditions for being productive and deserving *if* differential rewards to productivity and desert are legitimate principles by which the society ought to organized.

Is this an arbitrary claim about productivity and desert? I don't think so. Each of these principles requires that prior conditions be in place in order for them to be legitimate. In order for a person to be productive, a person must have those things that are necessary tools for productivity. The right to these tools cannot itself be given by the principle of productivity. The right must be given by a prior principle. To the extent that we have argued for the great and universal importance of equality of well-being, a right in each person to the conditions of productivity is implied by the principle of equal conditions for well-being. Should the right to the conditions of well-being also determine the shape of the principle of productivity as well? It is hard to see why not in the light of the previous considerations.

The same kind of consideration goes for comparative positive desert claims but for different reasons. Comparative positive desert claims can only be justified when there is a prior baseline that specifies that each person had some chance to engage in the deserving action. One person cannot deserve more in the comparative sense than another for an action he performed and the other did not, if the other person did not have the opportunity to engage in the action. That itself is not sufficient to show that equality is the necessary baseline. But desert does require a baseline, and the principle of egalitarian justice determines justice in the absence of considerations of desert. It would appear that complete justice would require that at least at the start each have a chance to engage in deserving actions that is consistent with equal conditions for well-being.

What these remarks imply is that to the extent that the principle of equal advancement of well-being applies to youth, it also applies at least to the initial conditions for the operation of the principles of desert and productivity. If the principles of desert or productivity are legitimate principles, and I am not arguing here that they are, they must be constructed in such a way that each person has an equal opportunity to become more deserving of greater well-being or productive of greater well-being. Suppose that at the moment at which desert can begin to play a role in determining how well a person's life goes, some persons have greater chances than others to become deserving of more well-being than others. That seems to imply that the well-being of those favored persons is in some sense more favored than the well-being of the less favored persons. But, by hypothesis, there is no relevant difference between them such that one ought to be more favored with respect to well-being than the others. This is because we are considering them, as it were, at the moment at which desert will be able to come into play. That moment is not one in which it has come into play, and so it is regulated by the same principle as regulated distribution of well-being in youth.

It stands to reason that a theory that asserts that through youth well-being must be distributed equally among persons because there are no relevant differences between them will also assert that justice requires that the conditions under which desert of unequal shares can occur must also be distributed equally. Suppose that one person has had a thriving life as a consequence of having received a good education and a decent set of resources in youth with which to realize his talents while another has had a miserable life as a consequence of having received no education and little or no resources in youth with which to realize his talents. Their differing fortunes are due in significant part to differences in conditions in youth that favored one person's thriving and disfavored another's. Again, by hypothesis, there is no relevant difference between them that could justify these differing conditions for the achievement of well-being. And so this must be considered an injustice.

So the principle of equal advancement of well-being, even if it is to be supplemented by some principle of desert, has a reach that goes beyond youth. It is what we might call a fundamental principle because it places constraints on all other principles that might come into play. It sets initial conditions on the operation of the other principles and it constrains them. For, the other principles cannot generate inequalities that are inconsistent with the demand that the inequalities be ones that anyone could have benefited from. My sense is that this constrains principles of desert to remain close to effort based principles, because principles of desert that favored persons with a lot of natural talent are ones that do not seem to provide people with equal initial conditions with which to lead thriving lives. They seem to favor some right from youth over others even though there is no relevant difference between them.

Of course differential abilities and circumstances that arise from effort and that subsequently benefit a person would be compatible with this constraint. And so significant differences in well-being that result from differential deserts are still compatible with the constraints the principle of equality places on other principles, should those other principles ever be defensible.

The other main aspect of this principle that I want to emphasize is its function as a kind of baseline principle of justice. That is to say, when other principles such as desert are not in play to help justify inequalities, justice requires equality. This proposition is a necessary consequence of the argument that I have given since when other principles do not come into play, there are no relevant differences that can justify inequalities. And since there is always the fundamental equality of status that requires equality when there are no relevant differences, equality is the fallback position.

This idea that equality is the fundamental principle that serves as initial condition, constraint, and baseline for other principles will loom large in what follows when we move from the impersonal and abstract principle of equality to the public principles that must regulate the establishment of justice in actual societies. For when we look to the establishment of justice in society as a whole, we will be first concerned to make sure that the institutions of society are structured fundamentally to advance the well-being of all persons equally. For the institutions of society frame the different possible life courses for persons. They frame the opportunities people face as well as the contours of the lives people can live. Even if we accept some inequality generating principles such as desert principles, the institutions must in some fundamental way give each person equal prospects for success. Hence the institutions must be set up in such a way that the well-being of each person can be equally advanced.

24. Conclusion

So far, I have argued that egalitarianism is the principle of justice that ought to regulate the distributions of goods during the pre-adult phase of life. I have also argued that equality of condition is the basis for a kind of equality of opportunity for well-being at the onset of adulthood. And this equality of condition can only be suspended if there are defensible principles of desert or productivity that can justify inequalities. I have also argued that equality can be abridged (in a way that is consistent with its underlying rationale) when all can be made better off as a consequence. So we avoid the leveling down objection.

One last remark: this chapter only defends a very abstract principle of justice. I do not claim that this principle is all there is to be said about justice. I think that justice is something that must be established in the world through social practices and institutions as well as the actions of persons. But for this to be, justice must be seen to be done in addition to being done. So justice requires publicity as well as fair distribution. A full account of just institutions would require, therefore, a much fuller treatment than the one I have given here.

References

ARNESON, R. (1989), 'Equality and Equal Opportunity for Welfare', *Philosophical Studies*, 56: 77–93.

——— (1999), 'What, If Anything, Renders All Humans Equal?', in D. Jamieson (ed.), *Singer and His Critics* (Oxford: Basil Blackwell), 103–28.

BARRY, B. (1973), *The Liberal Theory of Justice* (Oxford: Oxford University Press).

BUCHANAN, A. (1990), 'Justice as Reciprocity Versus Subject Centered Conceptions of Justice', *Philosophy and Public Affairs*, 19/3: 227–50.

CARRITT, E. F. (1947), *Ethical and Political Thinking* (Oxford: Clarendon Press).

CASAL, P. (2004), 'Why Sufficiency Is Not Enough', unpubl. MS.

CHRISTMAN, J. (1994), *The Myth of Property*, (Oxford: Oxford University Press).

CHRISTIANO, T. (forthcoming a), *The Constitution of Equality* (Oxford: Oxford University Press).

—— (forthcoming b), 'Cohen on Incentives and Inequality', in C. Favor, G. Gaus, and J. Lamont (eds.), *Ethics and Economics* (Amsterdam: Rodopi Press).

COHEN, G. A. (1989), 'The Currency of Egalitarian Justice', *Ethics*, 99/4: 906–44.

—— (1995), *Self-Ownership, Freedom and Equality* (Cambridge: Cambridge University Press).

DARWALL, S. (2002), *Welfare and Rational Care* (Princeton: Princeton University Press).

FRANKFURT, H. (1997), 'Equality as a Moral Ideal', in L. Pojman and R. Westmoreland (eds.), *Equality: Selected Readings* (Oxford: Oxford University Press), 261–73.

KAMM, F. (1992), 'Non-Consequentialism, the Person as an End-in-Itself, and the Significance of Status', *Philosophy and Public Affairs*, 21/4: 354–99.

KANT, I. (1985), *Foundations of the Metaphysics of Morals*, ed. and trans. L. W. Beck (New York: MacMillan).

KYMLICKA, W. (2002), *Contemporary Political Philosophy*, 2nd edn. (Oxford: Oxford University Press).

MILL, J. S. (1979), *Utilitarianism*, ed. G. Sher (Indianapolis: Hackett).

NAGEL, T. (1979), 'Equality', *Mortal Questions* (Cambridge: Cambridge University Press), 106–27.

—— (1980), 'Libertarianism Without Foundations', in J. Paul (ed.), *Reading Nozick* (Totowa, NJ: Rowman & Allanheld), 191–205.

—— (1995), 'Personal Rights and Public Space', *Philosophy and Public Affairs*, 24/2: 83–107.

NARVESON, J. (1983), 'On Dworkinian Equality', *Social Philosophy and Policy*, 1/1: 1–22.

NOZICK, R. (1974), *Anarchy, State and Utopia* (New York: Basic Books).

PARFIT, D. (1991), 'Equality or Priority?', The Lindley Lecture (Lawrence: University of Kansas).

PETTIT, P. (1990), 'Consequentialism', in P. Singer (ed.), *A Companion to Ethics* (Oxford: Basil Blackwell), 230–40.

RAWLS, J. (1971), *A Theory of Justice* (Cambridge, Mass.: Harvard University Press).

RAZ, J. (1986), *The Morality of Freedom* (Oxford: Oxford University Press).

SEN, A. (1992), *Inequality Reexamined* (Cambridge, Mass.: Harvard University Press).

TEMKIN, L. (1993), *Inequality* (Oxford: Oxford University Press).

—— (2000), 'Equality, Priority and the Leveling Down Objection', in M. Clayton and A. Williams (eds.), *The Ideal of Equality* (New York: St Martin's Press), 126–61.

WALDRON, J. (2002), *God, Locke and Equality* (Cambridge: Cambridge University Press).

3

A Defence of Extreme Egalitarianism

Ingmar Persson

1. What Is Not Distinctive of Extreme Egalitarianism

Extreme egalitarianism[1] is the claim:

   (EE) A state is just if and only if everyone (capable of being well or badly off) is equally well off in it.

Extreme egalitarians make this claim because they believe in a formal principle of justice to the effect (compare Christiano, Chapter 2 in this volume):

   (F) A state is just if and only if everyone (capable of being well or badly off) is equally well off in it unless there is something to make it just that some are better (or worse) off than others,

and they make this negative claim:

   (N) There is nothing to make it just that some are better (or worse) off than others.

For valuable comments, I would like to thank participants in the conference on egalitarianism at the University of Copenhagen, 2004, and participants at a seminar at Stockholm University. I am, however, especially grateful to Jerry Cohen, Susan Hurley, Kasper Lippert-Rasmussen, and Andy Williams for their detailed and penetrating comments.

   [1] I might have preferred the label 'radical egalitarianism' were it not for the fact that it has already been appropriated by others for different kinds of egalitarianism; see e.g. Nielsen (1985).

Of the two premises, it is (N) that is distinctive of extreme egalitarianism and that I shall therefore be concerned with defending here. *Moderate* or *restricted* egalitarians could agree with (F), which seems to be true on logical grounds (as an instance of the general principle that there can be no difference in degree of value unless there is something that makes one thing more (or less) valuable something else). They would then differ from extreme egalitarians by denying (N), claiming that there sometimes *is* something—for instance, differing deserts and rights—that makes it just that some are better off than others. Consequently, they would hold that the scope of equality is restricted to those domains in which these just-making features do not apply to compose differences between individuals. How much moderate egalitarians differ from extreme egalitarians in practice will depend upon the size of the area outside the operation of these variables.

There are controversial aspects of the premises which extreme and moderate egalitarianism could have in common. They are not of prime importance here, since they do not concern what distinguishes extreme egalitarianism from modest egalitarianism. Yet, they are worth mentioning on account of their general significance.

First, there is the much discussed problem of the *equalisandum* of equality, of what it is that egalitarians should make individuals equal as regards. Equality between individuals matters only if it is equality in respect of something that *matters to them*. For instance, it does not matter whether individuals are equal in respect of distance to a certain twig because their distance to this twig is likely to be a matter of indifference to them. Furthermore, in the end equality between individuals must be in respect of something that matters to them *for its own sake* or *in itself*. I think this must be specified in terms of the fulfilment of certain intrinsic desires, but this is no position I shall try to vindicate now. It is still what I have in mind when I speak of the *equalisandum* as being the *well-being* of individuals or how well off they are, but my arguments do not require this interpretation.

Second, we have the problem of the range of equality of well-being, the extension of the class of beings whose relative well-being levels can be just or unjust. I have parenthetically specified it to be beings who are 'capable of being well or badly off'. I take it that these are beings who have, or are capable of developing, consciousness. So, it is not unjust that cars and carrots are worse off than a lot of human beings because existence can be neither good nor bad for cars and carrots while it is good for the humans. This is not unjust, it might be said, because there is no possibility of cars and carrots being better off than they actually are. For, as they are incapable of consciousness (and thus of the possession of desires), existence for them can only be of neutral value. However, it might also seem true of anencephalic infants that there is no possibility of their being better off than they are since, like cars and carrots, they appear to lack not only consciousness, but even the potential to develop it. Yet, it is less clear that it is not a tragic instance of natural injustice that anencephalic infants, like other handicapped humans, are in general worse off than normal humans.[2] If this is unjust, it may be because these infants belong to a kind for which consciousness is normal. But I shall not pursue this problem about the range of equality of well-being.

Third, there are also problems about the relation between the ideal of justice as equality and other considerations that are morally justificatory, though they are not considerations of justice. For instance, there are considerations of *beneficence*, laying down, roughly, that it is in itself morally better if individuals are better off rather than worse off (cf. Parfit 1995: 4). If egalitarians could not appeal to considerations of beneficence, they could not say that it is morally better if beings are equally well off at a higher level of well-being rather than at a lower level. Now egalitarians could—and should—agree that considerations of beneficence could morally justify that some are better off than others, although this is unjust. This could be because, were a small inequality to reign, everyone would be much better off than they would be were they all equally well off (e.g. for the reason that everyone benefits from the gifted being rewarded). But to say that this outcome would be morally justified is neither to say that it would be *just* (or fair), nor to say that it is morally justified because it is just. It is instead morally justified because it contains so much more well-being that this outweighs its injustice. I shall not say anything more about such weighings between considerations of just equality and beneficence. The point is only that when extreme egalitarians claim that a state is just if and only if everyone is equally well off in it, this should not be taken to imply that the state is *morally right* if and only if everyone in it is equally well off.

There is another reason why (EE) does not imply that a state is morally right if and only if everyone in it is equally well off. This has to do with the tricky relation between just equality and exercises of *autonomy* by informed, voluntary choices. Like considerations of beneficence, considerations of autonomy can make it morally permissible to bring about an unequal outcome, although it is not just.[3] Suppose that, in a state in which, justly, everyone is equally well off, some individuals out of love, generosity, etc. autonomously choose to transfer some of their well-being to others, friends or beloved ones. They effect this transfer because they are concerned about the well-being of the others for its own sake, and more concerned about it than they are concerned about their own well-being (without this being due to their being misinformed or deceived about their relations to the others). The result would then

---

[2] For someone who thinks anencephalic infants fall outside the sphere of justice, see McMahan (2002: 147).

[3] Contrast Nozick, who writes: 'Patterned distributional principles . . . do not give the right to choose what to do with what one has; they do not give the right to choose to pursue an end involving (intrinsically, or as a means) the enhancement of another's position' (1974: 167).

be a state in which some are worse off than others. This state of inequality cannot be made just by the fact that it arises through an autonomous transfer, for this is nothing that can make a state just. To show this more clearly, it may be helpful to introduce one of the factors that is designed to make it just that some are better off than others, namely desert. Suppose A is deservedly worse off. If an autonomous transfer of benefits to him then makes him better off, this does not make it just that he is better off.

On the other hand, a state of inequality which arises out of just equality through autonomous transfer cannot be said to be unjust either, for this would imply that there is something morally wrong about bringing it about in itself. It may be morally wrong because it has bad consequences, such as giving rise to envy that stokes up violent conflicts. But, from the point of view of justice, individuals are morally permitted to autonomously give away to others what is justly theirs.[4] Hence, I think that this state of inequality is neither just nor unjust.

In this respect, considerations of autonomy differ from considerations of benefi-cence. Considerations of beneficence can *outweigh* those of justice, so that it may be morally permissible, and even required, to bring about a state, though it is unjust. Considerations of autonomy rather render considerations of justice *inapplicable*, so that an unequal outcome which arises out of exercises of autonomy may be morally permissible because it is not unjust, without it following that it is just.

Autonomy has a partly similar relation to beneficence. It does not seem to be morally wrong to benefit another, although the benefit to this person is smaller than the damage to yourself. For instance, it does not seem to be morally wrong to sacrifice your own life to save the leg of another. If this decision is criticisable, it is because it fails to be autonomous (through being misinformed, say), not because it is morally wrong. Common-sense morality does not forbid you to favour others at your own expense. It rather sets lowest levels of self-sacrifice below which you are not allowed to fall (exactly where is moot), but no highest levels. Such a highest level could easily be counter-productive from the point of view of beneficence, since people often get less well-being out of things they want to give away.

Egalitarians must provide some room for autonomy. Employees cannot be paid for their work at every moment. They must be paid at longer intervals, such as every day, week, or month. It is up to the employees to autonomously distribute their money within these periods, since it is assumed that they are equally concerned about themselves at every point of time. In contexts in which it can be assumed that people care at least as much about others, such as, for example, the context of parents

---

[4] Compare the custom, which exists in some countries, of giving victims, or relatives of the victims, the power to pardon criminals from the penalty to which they have been sentenced, though the punishment is presumably thought to be just and deserved.

and their children, the goods may similarly be given to a representative, with the expectation that they be spread over the group in a morally justifiable way.[5]

If, in a state of equality, A transfers some of her well-being to B, B might become better off not only than A, but also than a third individual C. C cannot then claim that it is unjust that B is better off than him if A and B together do not possess more than twice as much well-being as him, and B has more than C only because A out of love or charity has autonomously transferred some of her well-being to B. This is analogous to the situation in which the lives of two individuals, D and E, contain an equal amount of well-being, but D is better off than E *at the present moment* because D has autonomously chosen to distribute his well-being over his life so that he is better off than E at some times and worse off at other times. Just as such unequal intrapersonal distributions of justly possessed well-being are morally permitted, so are unequal interpersonal distributions of justly possessed well-being between lovers and friends who sympathise or identify with each other.[6]

For similar reasons individuals in a state of just equality are morally permitted to redistribute their well-being by autonomously engaging in a *gamble* which will result in some being better off than others. The resulting inequality, that some are better off than others, is not unjust because it is autonomously chosen—or, rather, one autonomously chooses to accept the chance or risk that it will result. Note that the situation would be different were individuals offered a lottery which would not, like this one, merely redistribute the *same* sum of well-being, but which would increase it as well as distribute it unequally.[7] This case raises the further question of whether justice does not demand that the larger sum be distributed in a different way and, in the absence of such a way, that it not be distributed at all.

Note also that there are foreseen consequences of things autonomously done that are not chosen in the relevant sense. Suppose, for instance, that one autonomously decides to try to save someone, though one realizes that one risks being injured. Sure enough, one is injured, although one is successful in the rescue operation. If one's injury leaves one worse off than others, this is unjust, and one should be compensated for the injury, even though one autonomously accepted the risk of it just as gamblers autonomously accept a risk of losing. For there is a relevant difference between the rescuer and the gamblers: facing the risk of losing is an *integral* part of

---

[5] Like the aim of just equality, the aim of maximizing well-being within a single life also conflicts with autonomy.

[6] I believe this contention could be supported by arguments such as the ones Parfit gives for the view that 'identity is not what matters' (1984, pt. III).

[7] Lippert-Rasmussen discusses a case in which a lottery distributes a larger sum than an equal distribution in such a way that the gamble is made one that 'it would be unreasonable to decline'. But he seems to assume that his conclusion can be generalised to a case in which the lottery would merely redistribute the same sum, so that it would not be unreasonable to decline the gamble (2001: 572–5).

gambling—there can be no gambling without the possibility of losing alongside the possibility of winning—but running the risk of being injured is not an integral part of saving. It is rather an unfortunate side-effect which could be absent.

To summarize, in defending (N), the claim that there is nothing to make it just that some are better off than others, I shall not be claiming that there is nothing that could make it morally right that some are better off than others. On the contrary, I believe that considerations of beneficence can outweigh considerations of justice and make something morally right, though it is unjust. I also believe that considerations of autonomy can make an unequal outcome morally permissible by rendering considerations of justice inapplicable. So, the formal principle of justice, (F), does not imply that

> (X) If there is nothing to make it just that some are better off than others, it is *unjust* if some are better off than others.

All that follows from (F) is that, under the mentioned circumstances, it is *not just* if some are better off than others. These implications are different because it does not follow from the fact that a state is not just that it is unjust. This can be seen by considering a wholly inanimate universe in which nothing can be good or bad for anything. The fact that this state cannot be called just does not imply that it is unjust. It is neither just nor unjust. Since (F) does not imply (X), (EE) does not imply that a state in which some are better off than others, though there is nothing to make this just, is perforce unjust and that there is to this extent something wrong with it. I have argued that the state in which benefits have been autonomously transferred could exemplify such an unequal state beyond the pale of justice. Thus, what egalitarians should strive for is strictly speaking not just equality, but the absence of unjust inequality.[8]

The recognition of considerations of beneficence and autonomy is not distinctive of extreme egalitarianism. Moderate egalitarians have to acknowledge, for example, that autonomy plays something like the role outlined (at least) within the restricted sphere in which they take the ideal of equality to rule. True, moderate egalitarians could differ from extreme egalitarians, as I conceive them, by holding that exercises of autonomy could make outcomes just (since they are not committed to (EE)). But, as I have argued, that is as implausible as holding that these exercises could make outcomes unjust. We should now turn to factors that *are* designed to make it just that some are better off than others.

---

[8] This squares with a claim that I have made elsewhere, namely that the intrinsic value of justice is not positive, but is merely the absence of the negative value of injustice (2003: 111–3).

2. Two Just-Making Conditions

I suggest that there are two candidates for such factors: *deserts* and *rights*. What someone deserves is clearly a consideration of justice: if some deserve to be better off than others, it follows that it could be just that they are better off. Likewise, if some are better off than others owing to the fact that they have rights to healthier bodies or more property, it follows that it could be just that they are better off. Furthermore, it would be unjust if somebody capable of recognising rights were to rob them of their property even if this were the only means by which some who have less than they deserve could be made better off. Thus, common-sense morality takes rights to 'trump' desert as, in Ronald Dworkin's famous phrase, they trump considerations of utility. That rights—more precisely, 'claim' rights, not 'liberty' rights which are mere permissions—have this property follows from the fact that they are correlated with duties. Every right is had against other individuals capable of recognising rights. To make intelligible this relation to others, we have to interpret a right to something, such as life or property, as having a reference to others. If, as is reasonable, A's right to this is construed as negative, it will presumably come out as a right against others that they do *not* interfere with A's life or property. The correlative duty is obviously the duty of others not to interfere with A's life or property.[9] It is wrong to fail to discharge this duty in order to rectify an injustice (by giving some what they deserve), just as it is wrong to fail to discharge it in order to maximise well-being (at least if the gain in well-being is not very great).

Although I cannot prove that there is no further factor, alongside deserts and rights, which could make it just that somebody is better off than somebody else, I shall now attempt to show that deserts and rights fit together in a way that leaves no space for any further just-making factor. The task I then set myself in Section 3 is to argue that (N) is true because differences neither in respect of what individuals deserve nor in respect of what they have rights to can make it just that some are better off than others.

When individuals deserve something, they do so in virtue of some features that they have. This has been called *the basis* of desert by Feinberg (1970: 59). A basis of desert is that which is supposed to make it just that individuals get that which they are said to deserve. I call the latter *the return* (deserved). The return consists in a benefit or burden or, in other words, something that is good or bad for the recipient. An obvious example of a basis of someone's desert is the responsible actions they have

---

[9] A liberty right to X is equivalent to one's not being under any duty not to use X. The ground of such a right is simply that nobody (else) has legitimately occupied X.

performed. Thus, the fact that individuals have responsibly performed good deeds is thought to make it just that they receive something that is good for them in return, and the fact that they have responsibly performed bad deeds is thought to make it just that they receive something that is bad for them. Presumably, there has to be a certain balance or equivalence between the value of the desert basis and the value of the return (where the value of the latter is a value for the recipient, but the value of the former is not). This balance is another complicated matter which I shall here have to set aside. It will not be of great importance, though, if I am right in my argument that the concept of desert has no application.

It might be thought that in order for a desert basis to make the receipt of a return just, the basis must itself be something that the subject *deserves*.[10] For if the basis is not deserved, but is due to fortuitous circumstances or luck, it would seem that an appeal to the (undeserved) basis could make a distribution just as little as a direct appeal to lucky circumstances. If the premise of this argument were correct, advocates of desert would be caught up in a regress which has all the appearance of being vicious. Robert Nozick, however, replies to this worry by claiming that the basis of desert could be something to which you have a *right* (or are entitled) instead of being something deserved. It could consist in things you 'just may *have*, not illegitimately. It needn't be that the foundations underlying desert are themselves deserved, *all the way down*' (1974: 225).

Your own body and its psychological and physical capacities are something to which you could credibly be believed to have a right. John Locke famously writes: 'every man has a "property" in his own "person". This nobody has any right to but himself. The "labour" of his body and the "work" of his hands, we may say, are properly his' (1924/1690: II. v. 27).[11] It has been suggested by some rights theorists that each of us has a right to their own body by being the first one to 'occupy' or make use of it (see e.g. Kamm 1992: 101). As a consequence of this right to our bodies and their capacities, we may be thought to have a right to what, thanks to these factors, we make out of unowned natural resources. In Locke's own words: 'Whatsoever, then, he removes out of the state that Nature hath provided and left it in, he hath mixed his labour with it, and joined to it something that is his own, and thereby makes it his property' (1924/1690: II. v. 27). We can now see the difference between the basis of rights, consisting in this first occupancy or appropriation, and the basis of desert. The basis of rights is supposed to make it just that you continue to enjoy or make use of something that you have put yourself in a position to enjoy or make use of.

---

[10] Rawls (1971: 103–4) opposes such a view.

[11] Locke does not here seem to think it necessary to treat the person and the body separately—he switches from claiming that we have a 'property' in the *person* to implying that the *body* is ours—though he is celebrated for his distinction between them in *An Essay Concerning Human Understanding*.

In contrast, the basis of desert is supposed to make it just that you be in a position to enjoy or make use of something that you may not already be in a position to enjoy or make use of, but that you have to be given by others. To illustrate, suppose a farmer single-handedly cultivates his own land. Then he has a right to the crop he in fact gets. But it may be smaller or greater than the crop he deserves—smaller, if, despite his great efforts, the crop is rather small owing to circumstances beyond his control, such as bad weather. In the light of this, we can understand why deserts and rights could be the only just-making features, for if it is just that you have something that is good for you, it must either be just that you remain in possession of it or that you receive it.

This comparison of deserts and rights also makes it comprehensible why it is tempting to adopt Nozick's strategy of appealing to rights to stop the regress of desert. If you deserve a return R in virtue of the basis B, R and B are distinct in the sense that you may possess B without possessing R. So, if your possession of B is to be justified as deserved, this must be in terms of something distinct from B, the basis B*. But this is not so if your possession of B is justified as something to which you have a right. The basis of your right to B consists in your being the first to come into possession of B.

3. The Argument Against Ultimate Responsibility

The appeal to rights with respect to desert bases is, however, of no avail, for the regress argument can be restated in terms of *responsibility* instead of desert. While the basis in virtue of which you deserve a return need not be deserved, it must be something for which you are responsible. Otherwise, your getting the return cannot in the end be just. For example, it would not be deserved and just to punish some infants because they cause their mothers a lot of pain while being born, and reward other infants who cause their mothers little pain. This is surely because these infants are not responsible for the amount of pain they cause their mothers while being born. Therefore, if it is claimed that it is just that some are better off than others because they deserve more on account of something to which they have a right, they must have this right in virtue of something for which they are responsible.

Imagine, for instance, it is claimed that it is just because deserved that some are better off because of the good deeds they have responsibly performed by making use of psychophysical capacities to which they have a right in virtue of their being the first occupants of their bodies. Then this can be just only if they are responsible for being the first occupants of these bodies rather than of other bodies or no bodies at all. If it is a matter of circumstances beyond one's responsibility whether one finds oneself in a well-equipped or poorly equipped body, it cannot be just to reward one if one is bodily well equipped and consequently performs good deeds and punish one if one is poorly bodily equipped and consequently performs bad deeds. For this is to reward and punish on the basis of features which are in the end a matter of luck.

It might be objected that the natural distribution of psychophysical resources can be held to be just if it is viewed as the upshot as a sort of lottery. But this requires that the lottery itself can regarded as just. The natural lottery cannot, however, be regarded as just because everyone has an equal chance of getting good resources and runs an equal risk of having bad ones. For this presupposes that individuals are 'bare selves' who could be identified independently of all their empirical features and assigned equal chances of acquiring any possible set of these features.

Another possible objection is to the effect that the distribution of bodies and their psychophysical capacities, because they are the upshot of non-moral, natural processes, cannot be said to be either just or unjust. It is of course true that this distribution cannot be motivated by considerations of justice. But even though a distribution cannot be *motivated* by justice, it can still be just or in accordance with justice in the sense that it *coincides* with a distribution that would be thus motivated. Now, the formal principle (F) tells us that it is just that everyone gets equally good bodies (i.e. bodies that enable them to be equally well off) unless there is something to make it just that some get better bodies than others. But we have seen that there can be no such just-making difference in the absence of responsibility. So we arrive at the following claim:

(1) It can be just that some are better off than others only if this is proportionate to differences in respect of something for which they are responsible.

For instance, it is just that some are better or worse off than others only if this is proportionate to the greater goodness or badness of deeds for which they are responsible. As the example of the newborns illustrates, it is not just to make individuals better or worse off, to reward or punish them, because they benefit or harm others without being responsible for it.

But when you are responsible for a fact F, you must be so in virtue of certain facts—call them 'responsibility-giving facts'. These facts may not include every fact that is causally necessary for your being responsible for F, through being necessary for your very existence—e.g. such general conditions as the occurrence of the Big Bang or the presence of oxygen—but could include only facts causally necessary and sufficient to determine whether, given your existence, the properties you possess comprise the particular property of being responsible for F.

Suppose you are responsible for F because this is something that you have intentionally brought about. To intentionally bring it about that F, you must have a certain body of information, a character which inclines you to intend to bring it about that F in the light of this information, and abilities that allow you to execute this intention, and so on. It is possible that you are responsible also for these particular responsibility-giving facts, G. But if so, this must be in virtue of certain other responsibility-giving facts, H, which make you responsible for G. Evidently, this regress of responsibility cannot be infinite, as we are temporally finite beings. Instead,

(2) The responsibility-giving facts in virtue of which individuals are responsible are ultimately ones for which they are not responsible.

In other words, suppose you are—*directly*, as we may put it—responsible for F, in virtue of your intentions, abilities, and so forth. Then you still cannot be *ultimately* responsible for F, since when we trace backwards the responsibility-giving facts in virtue of which you are responsible for F, we ultimately arrive at facts for which you are not (directly) responsible.

It should be noted that ultimate responsibility cannot be saved by the introduction of indeterminism. For suppose, for instance, that the responsibility-giving facts G do not fully determine the state of your being responsible for F, but that this state is partially undetermined, a matter of chance. Then to that extent you are not responsible for being responsible for F, since you cannot control what is a matter of chance. On the other hand, to the extent that your being responsible for F is determined, it will in the end be determined by facts for which you are not responsible. Again, you would not be ultimately responsible.[12]

Susan Hurley, however, claims: 'If responsibility for X requires A's hypothetical choice rather than A's choice or control of X, then regressive responsibility is not impossible' (2003: 29). In other words, Hurley claims that if it were sufficient for one's being responsible for responsibility-giving facts that one would choose them to hold, if one had a choice in the matter, then regressive—or, in my terminology, ultimate—responsibility would be possible. But, as she realises (2003: 28–30), hypothetical choice cannot be sufficient for responsibility. For instance, the fact that you would choose to be born in the country in which you in fact happen to be born does not show that you are responsible for being born in it. It follows that Hurley does not after all succeed in showing regressive or ultimate responsibility to be possible (though she claims to have shown it to be possible in a sense I do not understand).

Hurley makes a related claim about luck. Suppose

an agent did not choose and does not control the religious beliefs he was brought up with, and their associated burden of guilt. He would, however, have chosen them had he been able to, and would not choose to be without them. Thus, they are not plausibly regarded as matters of luck for him. (2003: 26; cf. p. 92)

---

[12] An analogous argument is advanced by Strawson (1999). See also Nagel (1979).

If, through circumstances beyond his control, the agent in this respect turns out to be the way he would choose to be, though he could easily have turned out a way he would choose not to be, I think, *pace* Hurley, he could count himself lucky (for this is something for which he is not responsible), even if he is worse off than others through his feelings of guilt. This indicates that his hypothetical choice might make it the case that it is not unjust that he is worse off than others. If so, it shows that we could construe the justice-excluding condition of the autonomous choice we talked about in Section 1 hypothetically.[13]

Now, it follows from (1) and (2) that

(3) It cannot be just that some are better off than others because this is proportionate to differences in respect of these ultimate responsibility-giving facts (in virtue of which these individuals have (direct) responsibility).

Surely, this can be just as little as it can be just that some infants are made better off than others because they cause their mothers little pain while being born. In neither case can this be just because that which is supposed to make just the differences in well-being is differences that are due to forces beyond the subject's responsibility.

However,

(4) If it cannot be just that some are better off than others because this is proportionate to differences in respect of these ultimate responsibility-giving facts, it cannot be just that they are better off because this is proportionate to differences in respect of something for which they are (directly) responsible, i.e. differences in respect of something which is ultimately due to responsibility-giving facts for which they are not responsible.

For this means that they are in the end better off because of the ultimate responsibility-giving properties on the basis of which it is agreed that it cannot be just that they are better off. It cannot be just that some are better off than others, on the basis of properties that they are guaranteed to have by properties they are not responsible for having and that the others are prevented from having through lacking properties beyond their responsibility.

---

[13] This is Cohen's view (1989: 935–9). There is much I find congenial in Cohen's claim that the purpose of egalitarianism 'is to eliminate *involuntary disadvantage*, by which I (stipulatively) mean disadvantage for which the sufferer cannot be held responsible, since it does not appropriately reflect choices that he has made or is making or would make' (1989: 916). But if the condition of (autonomous) choice is widened to actual *or* hypothetical choice then, as I have argued, it is no longer sufficient for responsibility for the chosen object. That Cohen overlooks this is indicated also when he maintains, falsely, that hypothetical choice 'is strictly inconsistent with luck' (1989: 938). It seems that he mistakenly assumes that hypothetical choice is inconsistent with luck because it implies responsibility. However, even if the widened choice condition does not rule out luck (by ensuring responsibility), it could still rule out injustice, for reasons implied by my argument in Section 1.

Imagine that a return R is held to be just in terms of your being directly responsible for F, and it turns out that you are directly responsible for F in virtue of certain responsibility-giving facts, G, for which you are directly responsible in virtue of H, for which you are not directly responsible. Then, since you are not ultimately responsible for F, it is after all not just that you receive R on the basis of your (direct) responsibility for F. The rationale of the idea that it is just to give you R, whose value for you is equivalent to the value of F, only if you are responsible for F is that the value of F then is due to what flows from your responsibility and from nothing else. But this rationale is undercut if F in the end turns out to flow from something external to your responsibility. There is no plausibility in the idea that justice consists in an equivalence between the value of the return for *you* and the value of a contribution to the world which is only mediately within your responsibility. For then the value of this contribution in the end comes from something other than from what you are responsible for, and this does not make it just that you enjoy the value of the return.

From (3) and (4) it follows that

(5) It cannot be just that some are better off than others because this corresponds to differences in respect of something for which they are (directly) responsible.

Finally, (1) and (5) yields:

(6) It cannot be just that some are better off than others.[14]

That is, as (N) puts it, there is nothing to make it just that some are better off than others. But (N) in conjunction with the formal principle (F) establishes the extreme egalitarian view (EE), that a just state is one in which everyone is equally well off.

This argument is consistent with—indeed, it presupposes—responsibility in the direct sense. Now, direct responsibility is sufficient for a 'forward-looking' moral justification of the practice of rewarding and punishing, in terms of considerations of beneficence, that is, in terms of the future beneficial consequences of this practice. For if you are directly responsible for your actions in virtue of acting on the basis of certain intentions you have, rewards and punishments can change your future behaviour—to the benefit of all—by providing you with reasons to form different intentions in the future.

In the present context, it is important for at least two reasons to realize that we *are* responsible in some sense. First, if we were not responsible for anything, it would seem that there could not be anything that we (morally or rationally) *ought* to do, such as reducing unjust inequality. For if we ought to do something, we must be responsible

[14] My argument for this conclusion is presaged by Sidgwick, though he remarks that this argument leads to 'such a precipice of paradox that Common Sense is likely to abandon it' (1981/1907: 284).

for whether or not we do it.[15] Second, it follows from the fact that we autonomously choose something that we are responsible for choosing it. But the responsibility here involved is direct, not ultimate, responsibility. So, autonomy as here conceived does not require impossible ultimate or total self-determination.

Ultimate responsibility is, however, required by the 'backward-looking' justification of responsibility which is in play when it is held that to reward or punish you is just, because deserved, in view of what you have done or are, i.e. your contribution to the value of the world. Here the claim is that the fact that there is an equivalence or proportion between the value of this return for you and the value of a contribution that you are ultimately responsible for makes the return just. If there is nothing for which you are ultimately responsible, but everything that is valuable about you stems from factors outside your responsibility—as surely must be the case since you are a finite being—it cannot be just that you receive something which for you is equivalent to the value of any of your contributions, which in the end do not flow from you. We do not have, then, the ultimate responsibility that could prevent inequality in respect of well-being from being unjust, by making it just, whereas we do have the direct responsibility that could prevent this inequality from being unjust (by making it autonomously chosen), without, however, making it just.

To sum up. The state in which some individuals are better off than others can be just only if there is some fact F concerning them (e.g. their having done certain good deeds) for which they are responsible. But since we are always responsible for something, such as F, in virtue of other facts, G (e.g. the formation of a certain intention and the possession of certain abilities), the question arises why G is a fact. If we are not responsible for G, it seems that it cannot after all be more just to be better (or worse) off on the basis of F, for which we are in fact responsible, than it would be if we were not responsible for F. For indirectly this is to be better off on the ground of properties for which we are not responsible, properties which guarantee that we shall be responsible for F and exclude those who lack them from this sort of responsibility. If we are responsible for G owing to some other fact about us, H, the same question of responsibility arises as regards H. But eventually, since we are temporally finite beings, we are bound to arrive at responsibility-giving facts for which we are not responsible; the regress of responsibility cannot be infinite. So, we cannot possess the ultimate responsibility which is requisite to make it just that some are better off than others. Such an unequal distribution of well-being can be morally justified only in

[15] In this respect, I agree with Hurley, who argues that egalitarianism cannot survive the rejection of all responsibility (2003: 175). Nevertheless, by its rejection of deserts and rights as well as of ultimate responsibility, my brand of egalitarianism probably takes a more 'deflationist' view of human beings than egalitarians commonly do.

other terms, in terms of considerations of beneficence or autonomy, for these forms of justification require only direct responsibility.

This constitutes my defence of (N), which along with (F) yields extreme egalitarianism, (EE). (EE) must then be a part of a sound morality, although for reasons chiefly given in Section 1, it cannot be the whole of it. The rejection of desert and rights is a common feature of my position and the utilitarian tradition. But utilitarians reject the notion of justice along with the notions of desert and rights. This is, however, a further move which demands justification. It amounts to holding, to my mind implausibly, that it is sufficient to reject the prima facie self-evident principle (F) to show that there is nothing that could make it just that some are better off than others.

References

COHEN, G. A. (1989), 'On the Currency of Egalitarian Justice', *Ethics*, 99/4: 906—44.

FEINBERG, J. (1970), 'Justice and Personal Desert', in Feinberg, *Doing and Deserving* (Princeton: Princeton University Press), 55—94.

HURLEY, S. (2003), *Justice, Luck, and Knowledge* (Cambridge, Mass.: Harvard University Press).

KAMM, F. M. (1992), *Creation and Abortion* (New York: Oxford University Press).

LIPPERT-RASMUSSEN, K. (2001), 'Egalitarianism, Option Luck and Responsibility', *Ethics*, 111/3: 548—79.

LOCKE, J. (1924/1690), *Two Treatises of Government* (London: Everyman).

MCMAHAN, J. (2002), *The Ethics of Killing* (New York: Oxford University Press).

NAGEL, T. (1979), 'Moral Luck', repr. in Nagel, *Mortal Questions* (Cambridge: Cambridge University Press), 24—38.

NIELSEN, K. (1985), *Equality and Liberty: A Defense of Radical Egalitarianism* (Totowa, NJ: Rowman & Allanheld).

NOZICK, R. (1974), *Anarchy, State, and Utopia* (New York: Basic Books).

PARFIT, D. (1984), *Reasons and Persons* (Oxford: Clarendon Press).

—— (1995), *Equality or Priority?*, The Lindley Lecture (Lawrence: University of Kansas).

PERSSON, I. (2003), 'The Badness of Unjust Inequality', *Theoria*, 69/1—2: 109—24.

RAWLS, J. (1971), *A Theory of Justice* (Cambridge, Mass.: Harvard University Press).

SIDGWICK, H. (1981/1907), *Methods of Ethics*, 7th edn. (Indianapolis: Hackett).

STRAWSON, G. (1999), 'The Impossibility of Moral Responsibility', repr. in L. Pojman and O. McLeod (eds.), *What Do We Deserve?* (New York: Oxford University Press), 114—24.

Part II
The Nature of Equality

4

The Insignificance of the Distinction Between Telic and Deontic Egalitarianism

Kasper Lippert-Rasmussen

1. Introduction

Slightly more than a decade ago, Derek Parfit introduced a distinction between teleo-logical and deontological egalitarianism or, for short, telic and deontic egalitarianism. In his influential presentation of the distinction, Parfit suggests that whereas the concern for equality has, in a way that is attractive, a wider scope on the telic view, deontic egalitarianism has the advantage of being invulnerable to the levelling down objection. Both of these suggestions are widely accepted in some form or another (McKerlie 1996: 280; Nagel 1997; Temkin 1993: 247–8).[1]

In this chapter, I want, first, to unpack the distinction between telic and deontic egalitarianism into three logically independent distinctions. These, I claim, better capture the logical space of possible egalitarian positions. This claim is not intended as a criticism of Parfit. As I understand him, his aim in introducing the distinction between telic and deontic egalitarianism was not to provide an exhaustive map of

I am grateful to Richard Arneson, Roger Crisp, Nils Holtug, Karsten Klint Jensen, Dennis McKerlie, Ingmar Persson, Thomas Petersen, Robert Pulvertaft, Jesper Ryberg, Andrew Williams, and two OUP referees for helpful comments on an earlier version of this piece.

[1] Like Parfit, neither McKerlie, nor Temkin, believes that the levelling down objection is decisive. Nagel sees the narrower scope of deontic egalitarianism as an attractive feature.

the sort I would like to present, but to sort typical egalitarians into two types, which offer a helpful way of thinking about a number of those egalitarians who have been most influential. For this purpose, the definitions of the two forms of egalitarianism may well tie together several logically independent distinctions. While this project is valuable, the widespread use of the distinction now makes the other sort of project worthwhile too. Having disentangled the different distinctions embodied in Parfit's account of telic and deontic egalitarianism, I argue, first, that these dimensions are largely neutral with respect to scope. Second, while some, but not all, forms of telic egalitarianism are vulnerable to the levelling down objection, comparable forms of deontic egalitarianism are vulnerable to an analogous objection. My main claim, then, is that in so far as we want to choose between telic and deontic egalitarianism, we cannot make that choice on the basis of the levelling down objection or on the basis of considerations about scope.

2. Some Distinctions

With an important qualification, to be introduced shortly, Parfit's telic egalitarians claim that

> (1) It is in itself bad if some people are worse off than others. (1998: 4)

As defined by Parfit, telic egalitarians may, in addition to thinking that inequality is in itself bad, object to the way in which an unequal outcome was produced. It is less clear what deontic egalitarians claim, but clearly their position is inconsistent with telic egalitarianism. For deontic egalitarians hold that 'it is not in itself bad if some people are worse off than others' (1998: 6). While it is often unjust, according to deontic egalitarians, that some people are worse off than others, '[their] objection is not really to the inequality itself. What is unjust, and therefore bad, is not strictly the state of affairs, but the way in which it was produced' (Parfit 1991: 9). While these claims separate deontic from telic egalitarians, they do not separate deontic egalitarians from non-egalitarians. Nozick, for instance, does not think that inequality is in itself bad, and he finds certain ways in which inequality may arise unjust because these involve violations of people's property rights. Yet, he is not in any helpful sense a deontic egalitarian. Accordingly, I take it that deontic egalitarians differ from non-egalitarians in virtue of the distinctive account they give of what makes the genesis of a particular outcome objectionable, e.g. that it involves not treating people with equal respect or concern where that involves something else than simply respecting people's Nozickean entitlements. Nowhere does Parfit state what such an account must look like.

When Parfit says that deontic egalitarians object 'to the way in which [inequality] was produced', there are two ways to understand this claim. On one reading, it is necessary for the genesis's being unjust, in a way deontic egalitarians care about, that it led to inequality. Hence, deontic egalitarians do not object to an otherwise comparable genesis of an outcome that for some reason resulted in equality. Suppose that I divide some good between two persons on the basis of my throwing of some deliberately skewed dice (or dice that I falsely believe to be skewed) intending to favour one of them. On the present reading, if this leads to inequality, then the outcome has been produced in an unjust way. However, if this leads to an equal division, because I improbably (or so I think) end up throwing the same dice for both of the two persons involved, then the genesis of the outcome was not unjust. Call this view *genesis-and-outcome-focused deontic egalitarianism*.

On the second reading, it is not necessary for the inequality-producing process's being unjust that it led to inequality. Hence, if an otherwise comparable process led to equality, then this process would be unjust as well and the equal state of affairs would be bad in that the way in which it was produced was unjust. Call this view *pure genesis-focused deontic egalitarianism*. Since Parfit writes that it is *often* unjust that some are worse off than others, it is reasonable to understand him as implying that, according to deontic egalitarians, it is *sometimes* not unjust that some are worse off than others. Accordingly, we might take it that on pure genesis-focused deontic egalitarianism, an equal outcome does not imply a just genesis and an unequal outcome does not imply an unjust genesis. This form of deontic egalitarianism is a theory of pure procedural justice (in so far as equality is a component in or constitutes justice).

I now want to suggest that there is logical space for a third deontic position, according to which certain outcomes are unjust, not because they have been brought about in a way that is unjust, nor because the unequal outcome is in itself unjust, but for some other reason. First, at one point Parfit describes deontic egalitarianism as the view that 'we should aim for equality, not to make the outcome better, but for some other moral reason. We may believe, for example, that people have rights to equal shares' (Parfit 1991: 4). This example of a deontic position clearly is outcome-focused: the content of the right is not a right to be treated in a certain way, but a right to a certain outcome. Second, an outcome may be unjust because it matches people's unjust desires or values. So, by way of illustration, suppose that men are much better off than women, that all men desire and value that women are worse off, but that the reason that men are better off has nothing to do with this. Some might say that in this case the inequality is not in itself bad, nor need it have been produced in a way that is unjust. It is unjust because there is a propositional match between men's unjust desires and values and the inequality. We have a reason to eliminate this inequality, if we can, that we would not have had, had men not had such sexist desires.[2] This view would surely qualify as egalitarian. Yet, it would qualify neither as telic egalitarianism, since it does not imply that inequality is in itself bad, nor as deontic egalitarianism, since it does not object to the genesis of the outcome. Let us nevertheless call views such as the one sketched here *outcome-focused deontic egalitarianism*. This view comes in two versions. According to the narrow version, only unequal states can be unjust given, say, people's unjust desires for inequality. According to the broader version, equal as well as unequal states can be unjust. The former case is due to the fact that people may, say, unjustly desire equality, when equality is unjust owing to differential exercise of responsibility.

The distinction between outcome-, genesis-and-outcome-, and pure genesis-focused can also be applied to telic egalitarianism. It is clear that there is such a view as *pure outcome-focused telic egalitarianism*. (1) states such a view. It is significant, however, that Parfit also writes: 'We might add [to (1)], "through no fault or choice of theirs" ' (1998: 3 n. 5). Egalitarians who add this qualification—and most do—care about, but do not only care about, outcomes. Like deontic egalitarians, they care about the way in which unequal outcomes are brought about, e.g. whether someone is worse off now as a result of what he chose in the past.[3] Hence, to accommodate Parfit's remarks about fault and choice, we should allow for *genesis-and-outcome-focused telic egalitarianism*. It follows that (1) is a particular species of telic egalitarianism and not a statement of telic egalitarianism as such.

---

[2] In a discussion of racially discriminatory laws Dworkin rejects these because 'it is unacceptable to count prejudice as among the interests or preferences government should seek to satisfy . . . We concede that laws having exactly the same economic results might be justified in different circumstances. Suppose there were no racial prejudice, but it just fell out that laws whose effect was especially disadvantageous to blacks benefited the community as a whole. These laws would then be no more unjust than laws that cause special disadvantage to foreign car importers or Americans living abroad, but benefit the community as a whole' (1985: 66). I think it is testimony to the intuitive appeal of the deontic view entertained here that Dworkin makes his point by imagining a situation where there is no racial prejudice, rather than one in which there is racial prejudice but everyone correctly believes that it played no causal role in the enactment of the law.

[3] Some egalitarians prefer to state their view as a matter not of whether the worse off are worse off through no choice or fault of their own, but of whether they are worse off through no responsibility of their own. On most accounts of responsibility for an outcome, responsibility depends on what one did or omitted to do in the past. Hence, on most accounts of responsibility, egalitarians who prefer this responsibility-clause to Parfit's likewise do not only care about outcomes. However, on some accounts of responsibility, responsibility depends on what I would now choose hypothetically. On such accounts, egalitarians who are concerned with responsibility need not be interested in how a certain outcome came about (Hurley 2003: 15–53). For further discussion of the relations between responsibility, desert, and the value of equality, see Arneson's and Persson's contributions to this volume (Chs. 11 and 3 respectively).

If we allow that past choices and faults can be relevant to whether an unequal state of affairs is bad, presumably, there could be other historical factors that influence the badness of inequality. For instance, inequality that results from what human agents did or failed to prevent from happening in the past may be thought worse than inequality that is the result of natural causes. Given this, there seems logical space for a pure genesis-focused telic egalitarianism, i.e. the view that it is in itself bad that an outcome, whether unequal or not, is brought about in a certain way. Call such a view *pure genesis-focused telic egalitarianism*.

So far I have distinguished between three focuses of evaluations, outcomes, geneses, and a combination thereof, and between whether these are evaluated in terms of injustice or badness. I have argued that even if telic egalitarians are concerned with badness and deontic egalitarians are concerned with injustice, both of them can adopt each of these three focuses. Unlike what Parfit's text sometimes suggests, deontic egalitarians are not restricted to care about geneses and telic egalitarians are not restricted to care about outcomes.

Some might challenge the use of the distinction between justice and badness to distinguish between telic and deontic egalitarians. After all, to say that something is unjust is to say that it is in one way bad and this is what telic egalitarians say. In response, it might be conceded that nothing substantial hangs on whether we say that something is bad or whether it is unjust. We might then decide to reserve the label 'deontic egalitarians' for those egalitarians whose focus is exclusively on geneses and use 'telic egalitarians' to refer to those egalitarians whose evaluative focus is also on outcomes or geneses-and-outcomes. Another, and in my view more attractive, response consists in saying that justice concerns a particular way in which outcomes or geneses of outcomes can be bad, namely one that essentially involves agency or representations. (Except for the representation bit, Parfit might have had something like this in mind when writing, 'Deontic Egalitarians are concerned only with what we ought to do'; 1998: 7 n. 11.) On this account, deontic as well as telic egalitarians may say, for example, that unequal outcomes are bad. However, they will give different accounts of what makes the unequal outcome bad. Hence, we might then say that telic egalitarians are those who think outcomes or geneses can be in themselves bad even if they do not involve agency or representations, while deontic egalitarians are those who affirm this necessary condition for badness. However, telic as well as deontic egalitarians can adopt each of the three focuses that I have distinguished between.[4]

---

[4] A third possibility, which may allow us to distinguish genesis-and-outcome-focused telic egalitarianism from genesis-and-outcome-focused deontic egalitarianism, is to say that according to the former view it is the unequal state of affairs that is non-instrumentally bad provided that it has a certain genesis, while according to the latter view it is the genesis which is unjust and, thus, bad provided that it results in an unequal outcome. I leave open here whether this is more than a mere verbal difference.

Whether we evaluate in terms of badness or injustice, or whether we are outcome- or genesis-focused egalitarians, we may differ on whether the badness or injustice of inequality or unequal treatment is simply a matter of what actually happens or whether it is also a matter of what could have happened. *Actuality-focused egalitarians* think that what could have happened is irrelevant, whereas *alternatives-focused egalitarians* think that this is relevant.[5]

In saying that deontic egalitarians may hold an actuality-focused view, I understand the view differently from how one passage suggests Parfit understands it. Quoting Rawls, he writes that the kind of case that most clearly separates deontic from telic egalitarians is that 'in which some inequality cannot be avoided. For deontic Egalitarians, if nothing can be done, there can be no injustice' (Parfit 1998: 7) and, hence, there is no deontic egalitarian objection to the inequality-producing process. I am reluctant, however, to read this passage as implying that on Parfit's view deontic egalitarians have no objections to inequalities that result from the unavoidable and inequality-producing exercise of human agency (which may or may not be rare, but which surely is conceptually possible).

First, the passage from John Rawls, to which he refers, as well as the example involving inequalities in natural talents, which he uses to illustrate his point, both involve unavoidable inequalities that do not result from the exercise of human agency. The Rawls passage concerns the unalterability of the fact that while present generations can do something for future generations, future generations cannot do anything for past generations. Rawls continues: 'What is just or unjust is how institutions deal with natural limitations and the way they are set up to take advantage of historical possibilities' (1971: 291). The pertinent fact about intergenerational relations is not only unavoidable; it is also something that does not result from the exercise of human agency. Hence, it leaves it open that if the fact resulted from the unalterable exercise of human agency, Rawls might consider the question of justice relevant.

Second, consider a Frankfurt-type set-up. A sexist employer wholeheartedly discriminates against a female applicant, thereby making her worse off. Surely, the

---

Note that, even if it is more than a mere verbal difference, the two views are extensionally equivalent in the sense that for any genesis-and-outcome-focused telic egalitarian view there is a comparable genesis-and-outcome-focused deontic view that will judge any genesis-cum-outcome unjust, if, and only if, it is bad on the telic view. In any case, this particularistic interpretation does not allow us to distinguish outcome-focused or genesis-focused telic views from outcome-focused or genesis-focused deontic views. Accordingly, I shall ignore it henceforth.

[5] In relation to the Mere Addition Paradox, Parfit defended what Larry Temkin has seen as a 'person-affecting version of egalitarianism ... [which is] essentially pair wise comparative' (Parfit 1984: 425; Temkin 1987: 171). On this view, it is not bad that some people are worse off in an outcome, A+, if the alternative to this outcome, A, is one which is identical in all respects except that the worse off in A+ do not exist in A.

employer treats her unjustly. The discriminatory treatment, however, was unavoidable in the sense that, had the employer been inclined not to discriminate, someone or something would have intervened and made him do what he in fact did. Surely, some might think that in order to tell whether the discriminatory treatment was unjust, we do not need to know whether the counterfactual intervener could have been absent. Yet, their objection need not be to the resulting inequality in itself. So if they are not deontic egalitarians, we need to introduce a third kind of egalitarian. Hence, given the nature of the present sort of enquiry, it is better to untie the distinction between avoidable and unavoidable inequalities from the distinction between deontic and telic egalitarianism. (In saying this, I assume that the issue is whether deontic egalitarians care about unavoidable as well as avoidable inequalities. Hence, if deontic egalitarians care about both, then symmetry between deontic and telic egalitarians is established, i.e. there is no real issue as to whether telic, or for that matter deontic, egalitarians care about unavoidable inequalities only.)

Alternatives-focused egalitarians may differ on when a state of affairs is an alternative and on which alternatives matter. With regard the latter issue, alternatives-focused telic egalitarians may hold that if there are no alternative distributions, where those who are worse off in the alternative are better off than those who are actually worse off, it is not bad that they are worse off. Similarly, alternatives-focused deontic egalitarians may claim that if there are no alternative ways of treating those who suffer unequal treatment (but, for perverse reasons, may end up better off), then their being treated unequally is not unfair. These, however, are not the only positions available to alternatives-focused egalitarians. For instance, they may think that what matters is whether there are alternatives available where those who are actually worse off are worse off or alternatives where those who are better off are better off to a lesser degree than those who are worse off, etc.

With regard to when a state of affairs is an alternative, one issue is whether we should adopt a tracing approach to alternatives. On this approach it might be that although we cannot now act differently such that worse-off people become better off, distributions in which the worse-off are better off is still in the relevant sense a feasible alternative. This is so if in the past, people might have acted differently such that either we could now have made the worse off better off or the worse off would have been better off. On a *global tracing approach*, something is an alternative if the world history from the dawn of mankind could have taken a course such that this alternative would have been realized. On a *local tracing approach*, something is an alternative if it could have been realized holding varying past stretches of the world history of humanity constant. Another issue is whether something is an alternative if it could have been realized had either someone or everyone acted differently, or whether something is an alternative only if it could have been realized given that some, but not all, e.g. people living within a certain community but not people outside, had acted differently. Call the former view the *global agency approach* and the latter, less inclusive, view of alternatives the *local agency approach*. If we adopt the global approach in both dimensions, then inequalities that we have brought about are likely to be inequalities to which, barring fundamental doubts about determinism and the ability to act otherwise, alternative and more equal distributions exist. However, it is still conceptually possible, although perhaps rare, for a certain inequality that has been created by human beings to be one that human beings could not have avoided creating.

To conclude this section: deontic egalitarians differ from telic egalitarians in that they think that outcomes or geneses of outcomes can be bad only when they involve agency or representations. Deontic and telic egalitarians do not differ in respect of whether they adopt a genesis or an outcome focus or whether they adopt an alternatives or an actuality focus. Hence, it is better to keep these three distinctions separate. I now turn to the issue of what significance the distinction so construed has, as well to how the two latter dimensions, which, as we saw, were sown into Parfit's distinction between telic and deontic egalitarianism, relate to the issues of scope and levelling down.

3. Telic Versus Deontic and the Scope of Equality

There are countless dimensions in which one may distinguish between narrow- and broad-scope egalitarianism, e.g. time, space, states involving different people, and different kinds of individuals. Call a view according to which equality has the broadest scope possible in all dimensions *unrestricted-scope egalitarianism* and the rest *restricted-scope egalitarianism*. On a telic version of the former view, it is bad if two individuals are unequally well off whether or not they live at different times, in different communities, or belong to different species, e.g. it is bad if one is a contemporary, happy fellow citizen and the other a dolphin suffering constant pain in 400 BC (Parfit 1998: 9).[6] As this example reminds us, almost all forms of egalitarianism that have actually been defended are forms of restricted-scope egalitarianism, and, to my knowledge, no one has explicitly endorsed unrestricted-scope egalitarianism.

Parfit holds that the choice between deontic and telic egalitarianism is likely to affect the scope of equality. Whereas deontic egalitarians may, for instance, plausibly restrict the scope of equality to people living within the same community, telic egalitarians cannot plausibly do so. Moreover, since there are cases where such restrictions seem counter-intuitive, considerations about scope favour telic egalitarianism. Before discussing these claims in more detail, I want to make two general remarks.

---

[6] There are more issues of scope than those mentioned here; see Temkin (1995: 72–3 n. 2).

First, suppose that we believe that the ideal of equality is sound and has the widest possible scope. Suppose, moreover, that injustice requires human agency or representations. Finally, for the purpose of illustration, suppose that Europeans were better off than Americans prior to the crossing of the Atlantic. Given these assumptions (and ignoring complications about the global tracing approach), it follows that this inequality is bad but not unjust. Given this, and given the construal of deontic and telic egalitarianism proposed in the last section, this does, indeed, favour the telic over the deontic view, since only the telic view allows us to make this claim. However, this is due simply to the way in which we, and Parfit, have defined the two positions, i.e. that telic egalitarians *may* think that inequalities and geneses of outcomes not reflecting human agency or unjust representations are bad, whereas deontic egalitarians deny this. If our definition allowed deontic egalitarians to hold that, say, inequality, in addition to being unjust when involving human agency and representations, *may* be bad even when not involving any of these, and said that telic egalitarians deny that inequalities are unjust, then examples of bad inequalities between communities that are not aware of each other's existence have no tendency to favour telic over deontic egalitarianism as such, although they show that impure deontic positions are preferable to pure deontic positions.

Second, if we build into the distinction that telic egalitarians are concerned with outcomes and deontic egalitarians are concerned with the way in which outcomes are generated, as some of Parfit's formulations suggest, then we cannot helpfully say that telic egalitarianism has a broader, as opposed to different, scope than deontic egalitarianism: the former view is concerned with outcomes, whereas the latter is concerned with geneses of outcomes. Accordingly, we must make sure that there are no ways in which an outcome, possibly an equal one, may be generated in ways that involve unjust, unequal treatment, before we conclude that cases such as the divided unequal world is a scope-related, all-things-considered good reason to favour telic over deontic egalitarianism. For if cases of the former sort exist, e.g. wrongful discrimination that unpredictably leads to equality, then these cases counterbalance whatever *pro tanto* reason cases such as the divided unequal world give us to be telic egalitarians. Considerations about scope, then, would not provide us with a reason to favour pure telic over pure deontic egalitarianism; rather it would favour combining the two views.

Now I turn to Parfit's specific claims concerning the natural scope of telic and deontic egalitarianism. Consider first the claim that telic egalitarianism is most plausibly seen as having the broadest possible scope. Parfit writes: 'If we believe that inequality is in itself bad, we may think it bad whoever the people are between whom it holds' (1998: 8). Accordingly, he thinks that it would be odd for telic egalitarians to hold that inequality is bad only when it obtains between people in the same community: 'If it is in itself bad if some people are worse off than others, why should it matter where or when these people live?' (Parfit 1998: 7).

Unfortunately, this rhetorical question has force only for people attracted to pure outcome-focused telic egalitarianism. Genesis-and-outcome-focused telic egalitarians do not think that inequality is in itself bad. Consider telic egalitarians who endorse the responsibility-clause mentioned by Parfit. They think that an unequal state of affairs is bad only if the worse off are not worse off through their own fault or choice, and this implies that inequalities with certain geneses are not in themselves bad.[7] Presumably, telic egalitarians may think that the genesis of a state of inequality may matter in other ways as well. For instance, they may say:

(2) It is in itself bad if some people are worse off than others provided that (i) the worse off are so through no fault or choice of theirs and (ii) the better off contributed causally to making or allowing these people to be worse off.

Both (i) and (ii) will in practice imply derivative restrictions in scope, by which I mean restrictions in which inequalities matter from an egalitarian point of view that derive from the genesis of the inequalities. Suppose that, prior to the crossing of the Atlantic, people in America were worse off than people living in Europe through a fault of their own. In that case this would not in itself be bad, because the unequal state of affairs fails to satisfy either of the two requirements concerning geneses.

It might be replied that from the fact that genesis-and-outcome-focused egalitarians endorse restrictions in scope that derive from conditions pertaining to the genesis of unequal states, it does not follow that they must accept restrictions in scope not derived from a concern with the proper genesis. This is indeed true. But note, first, that the focus of almost all egalitarians would suggest either that they think that the scope of equality is restricted to human beings, or that while they think that human beings fall within the scope of equality they have no view on whether non-human animals fall within that scope as well. Hence, almost all egalitarians that Parfit would classify as telic egalitarians do, as a matter of fact, accept non-derived restrictions in scope. This reminds us that Parfit's appeal to the fact that telic egalitarians think that inequality is in itself bad can do no work. For even if we say that, i.e. that inequality is in itself bad, we still need to say whom we think of when we say that it is bad if some are worse off than others. Moreover, if it could do real work here, presumably it would also follow that telic egalitarians cannot restrict the scope of equality to people who are not responsible for being worse off. If inequality is bad in itself, why should it matter whether the worse off are responsible for so being? This leaves us with Parfit's claim that it seems a 'strange coincidence' if inequality is bad only if it obtains between members of the same community (1991: 7). However, in itself this

---

[7] Unlike the suggestion in Parfit (1991: 13).

hardly provides a reason for rejecting the view (although it may point to the fact that its subscribers can offer no reason to accept it). I conclude that while there is a form of telic egalitarianism, which is unrestricted in scope, it has not been shown to be the only reasonable telic view.

Consider next the plausible scope of deontic egalitarianism. Deontic egalitarians object to inequalities with a certain history or to geneses of a certain sort whether they lead to inequalities or not. It is natural to assume that the history of a certain outcome can be objectionable only if it involves some human agent conducting himself in an objectionable manner. As Parfit seems to imply: on the deontic view, inequality is unjust and 'injustice is a special kind of badness, one that necessarily involves wrong-doing . . . Deontic Egalitarians are concerned only with what we ought to do' (1998: 7).[8] So far, I have largely followed Parfit in assuming this.[9] It is, however, logically possible and not utterly implausible, as I shall now argue, to think that a certain genesis is unjust even if it involves no wrongdoing, i.e. no people acting in a way that they ought not to act.

On many people's view, including Parfit's own, it is possible for an outcome to be unjust or unfair even if it does not result from, nor could have been prevented by, the exercise of human agency (Parfit 1998: 7 n. 11). But if so, why could not a genesis of a certain outcome be unjust even if it did not result from human agency, nor was under the control of human agency? In reply, it might be conceded that this is, indeed, possible albeit not plausible. However, I am inclined to think that this is too hasty given that natural injustice in outcomes is possible. Suppose two persons, each living on a deserted island, are busy tending to their scarce crops. For strange reasons the occurrence of hurricanes on the islands is influenced by two naturally formed, indeterministic, quantum-mechanical devices, the effects of which are magnified such that there is a great probability of hurricanes sweeping the first person's island and a slight probability of hurricanes sweeping the second person's island. Just prior to harvest time a hurricane destroys the first person's crops. However, it also washes ashore several barrels of corn, thereby compensating the loss caused by the storm, an event that, even given the occurrence of a hurricane, is very improbable. Might we not say here that although there is no natural injustice in outcome, the genesis of the outcome is naturally unjust, i.e. that it was naturally unjust that the two persons

---

[8] See also McKerlie (1996: 280–1). Note that I can be concerned with what we ought to do from the point of view of equality and yet not be concerned with the genesis of the present state of affairs. For instance, I may think that we should always act in such a way that we maximise future equality. On that view, it is irrelevant how it came about that some are worse off than others. Accordingly, the concern for how a certain state of affairs was (or will be) produced is different from a concern for what we ought to do (or ought to have done).

[9] I insert the qualification 'largely', because I allowed for injustice due to a propositional match between unjust desires and values, on the one hand, and an outcome or genesis, on the other.

ended up equally well off through a series of improbable events and that one of them had so much better prospects than the other?

We might deny this, because we think justice concerns outcomes only; because no agency, whether human or non-human, was involved in the genesis of the outcome; or because we think that what the example shows is simply that a particular kind of outcome is bad, i.e. inequalities in prospects. The first objection is beside the point, because the present issue is whether, on the assumption that genesis matters, we can meaningfully speak of natural injustice in the genesis of an outcome. The second objection is beside the point, because it does not establish a difference between deontic and telic egalitarianism. If injustice requires human agency, then there can be natural injustice neither in outcome, nor in genesis, and for present purposes we have already granted natural injustice in outcomes. In response to the third objection, we might say that although this is one interpretation of the example, it is also possible to insist that what matters is how well off people actually end up being and the justice of the way in which their levels of well-being are produced. In support of these replies consider that, according to Temkin, a state of affairs is naturally unjust if it is such that 'if someone *had* deliberately brought it about she would have been perpetrating an injustice' (1995: 76). If one accepts this view about the injustice of outcomes, then it is hard to see how one could deny that a genesis of an outcome, even an equal one, could not be unjust, too. Surely, if someone had deliberately made the fate of the two individuals in my previous example depend on the imagined indeterministic devices, this would be seen by many as unjust even if no unequal outcome resulted.

Suppose that, despite what has been said so far, we reject natural injustice in geneses (despite accepting the possibility of natural injustice in outcomes). In that case, a genesis can be unjust only if it somehow involves human agency or representations. On a broad deontic account, any genesis that results from or could have been relevantly different through the exercise of human agency may be unjust.[10] On a narrow deontic account, only geneses that result in a certain way from, or that could have been relevantly different through, a particular kind of exercise of human agency, e.g. the inequality was intended and not merely foreseen or brought about and not merely allowed to arise, may be unjust. It may be the case that any inequality that is bad on a telic account and that is avoidable is unjust on a broad deontic account. Hence, whenever an unequal outcome is bad on a telic account and not unjust on the deontic account, then the inequality is unavoidable, in which case the difference

[10] Nagel seems to adopt this position when he denies that there is any morally relevant distinction between inequalities that the state produces and those that the state merely allows, i.e. the state is negatively responsible for inequalities; see Nagel (1991: 84, 99–102, 107–8).

between the two positions is merely nominal in the sense that it never gives rise to conflicting recommendations.[11]

Parfit writes that deontic egalitarianism may connect with the traditional deonto-logical doctrines of doing and allowing and the doctrine of the double effect: '[deontic egalitarianism] may cover only inequalities that result from acts, or only those that are intentionally produced' (1998: 8). Since Parfit writes that deontic egalitarianism *may* cover only such inequalities, this is not contrary to the view taken here. At least, this is so unless it is implied that telic egalitarians may not consider inequalities that are brought about rather than simply allowed to exist or inequalities that are countenanced intentionally rather than merely countenanced as a foreseen side-effect as worse. However, given that telic egalitarians endorse a responsibility clause, it is hard to see how they can simply dismiss that other facts about the way in which an unequal outcome was brought about may be relevant for its badness.

In conclusion, the distinction between deontic and telic egalitarianism is much more loosely connected with the choice of scope than is commonly assumed, and considerations of scope have not been shown to favour one view over the other.

4. Telic Egalitarianism and Levelling Down

Influenced by Parfit's Lindley Lecture, many believe that, unlike deontic egalitarianism, telic egalitarianism is vulnerable to the so-called levelling down objection: telic egalitarians think that inequality is in itself bad. But if so, then levelling down from a state of inequality to a state where everyone is worse off and equally well off makes the outcome better in one respect. However, given that no one is made better off in any respect by levelling down, it is implausible that the latter state of affairs is in any respect better.[12] Since deontic egalitarians deny that inequality is in itself bad, they are immune to this objection. In response, I shall now challenge, first, the view that all forms of telic egalitarianisms are vulnerable to the levelling down objection and, then in Section 5, the view that no form of deontic egalitarianism is vulnerable to a comparable objection. Together these claims amount to the claim that telic and deontic egalitarianism are symmetrically positioned relative to levelling down objections.

Telic egalitarians believe that it is in itself bad if some are worse off than others. Does this imply that inequality is always bad? In an excellent article, Andrew Mason

---

[11] I assume here that if something is bad, then there is a reason to avoid it (if one can).

[12] But see Temkin (1993: 245–82).

points to the relevance of two different distinctions.[13] The first distinction is between instrumental and non-instrumental value. Something has non-instrumental value if it has value for its own sake, whereas something has instrumental value if it has value as a means to something else. The second distinction is between intrinsic and extrinsic value: 'The intrinsic value of a thing is any value it possesses that is grounded entirely in its intrinsic properties, where its intrinsic properties are those which do not depend, even in part, on the existence or nature of something else' (Mason 2000: 247–8). These two distinctions diverge. Something may have non-instrumental value in virtue of its extrinsic properties. When this distinction is clearly set out, it seems that, although telic egalitarians say that inequality is in itself bad, what they really mean is that inequality is non-instrumentally bad (Parfit 1998: 5).

Mason exploits the difference between these two distinctions to propose two forms of telic egalitarianism that are immune to the levelling down objection. Although both of them hold inequality to be non-instrumentally bad, none of them implies that it is in one way better to level down. According to the first form of conditional egalitarianism:

(3) Inequality is extrinsically and non-instrumentally bad provided that it harms some.[14]

This position qualifies as egalitarian because it holds inequality to have non-instrumental disvalue. Moreover, it accommodates the levelling down objection because inequality has no disvalue on this view when no one is harmed by it, and exactly this is the case when the only alternative to, say, half at 50 and half at 75 is everyone at 25.

To this form of conditional egalitarianism Mason adds another form of telic egalitarianism, which appeals to a particularist conception of intrinsic value:

---

[13] McKerlie (1996: 287–8) suggests a possible egalitarian position that resembles Mason's conditional egalitarianisms. However, McKerlie believes that the real view underlying such a position may well be the priority view. Temkin considered similar 'person-affecting' versions of egalitarianism (1987; 1993: 248). In Section 2, in connection with my discussion of alternatives-focused egalitarianism, I mentioned some forms of conditional egalitarianism that are comparable to Mason's two forms.

[14] Unlike me, Mason states conditional egalitarianism in terms of a claim about the value of equality and not in terms of a claim about the badness of inequality. Thus, the relevant counterpart to (3) is: equality is extrinsically and non-instrumentally good only when at least some people benefit from it. It seems reasonable to hold that equality is valuable only if no one is harmed by it rather than only if some benefit from it. For suppose there are two possible states of affairs. In both states people are equally well off and they are equally well off across these states. The two states differ in terms of properties that do not affect people's levels of well-being. Surely, egalitarians would want to say that these states of equality are valuable even if no one benefits from, or is harmed by, the equality.

(4) Inequality is intrinsically and non-instrumentally bad provided that it harms some.[15]

The idea here is that the disvalue of inequality depends on the context. This is no different from (3). But unlike (3), defenders of (4) will not say that a state of inequality is disvaluable in virtue of the fact that people are unequally well off and that some are harmed by it. Instead, they will say that a state of inequality is bad in virtue of the fact that people are unequally well off. However, in their view inequality does not always possess intrinsic disvalue. It does so only when it harms someone. The general idea here is that something may be necessary for something's being good or bad and yet not be something in virtue of which the latter is good or bad. Some, of course, would argue that the difference between saying that the fact that inequality harms some is something that enables inequality to be in itself productive of disvalue and saying that this fact together with the fact of inequality is productive of disvalue is merely verbal. Even if this is right, it remains a fact that a form of conditional egalitarianism is invulnerable to the levelling down objection.

It may seem odd that the disvalue of inequality is conditional. However, in reality, Mason's conditional egalitarianism differs from standard telic egalitarian views not in being conditional, but in virtue of the content of the condition invoked, i.e. that inequality harms some and not that the worse off are not responsible for so being. I have several things to say about Mason's conditional forms of egalitarianism. First, I want to make a taxonomical observation. Conditional egalitarianism raises the question of where exactly to draw the line between egalitarian and non-egalitarian positions. Consider the following position:

(5) Welfare is non-instrumentally good provided that people are equally well off. Nothing else is non-instrumentally good.

On the one hand, this seems an (implausibly) extreme egalitarian position. Nothing is good if people are unequally well off. On the other hand, this position does not claim that equality has non-instrumental value (or that inequality has non-instrumental disvalue). It is just that equality is a necessary condition of anything having non-instrumental value. In view of this, the fact that this position does not claim that equality has non-instrumental value is by no means a decisive argument for disqualifying it as egalitarian. Note also that this position is (extremely) vulnerable to the levelling down objection: if half is at 75, the other half at 74, then there is nothing good about this outcome. However, if we were to level down to 1, then not only

---

[15] The positive counterpart to (4) is: equality is intrinsically and non-instrumentally good provided that it benefits at least some.

would this state be in one respect better, presumably it would be all-things-considered better! Hence, if we refuse to call (5) an egalitarian position on the ground that it does not take inequality to be non-instrumentally bad, then we must concede that some telic non-egalitarian positions are vulnerable to the levelling down objection. This is significant because many are inclined to see vulnerability to the levelling down objection as a reliable test, if not a criterion, for a view's constituting telic egalitarianism.

Whereas Mason's line of argument suggests that it is not clear that egalitarians need even claim that equality has non-instrumental value, it is also not clear that one qualifies as an egalitarian simply because one accepts (3) or (4). Endorsing either of these positions is consistent with believing that inequality has intrinsic, non-instrumental value given a particular type of context. For instance, the view that inequality is intrinsically valuable provided that it matches people's differential, libertarian entitlements seems an anti-egalitarian view. Accordingly, I suppose that at least in some contexts it would be counter-intuitive to call someone who endorses this view in addition to (3) or (4) an egalitarian.[16] While conditional egalitarianism is an egalitarian *view*, holding an egalitarian view does not make *you* an egalitarian, for you may, consistently with so doing, hold an anti-egalitarian view. What is at stake here is not simply a matter of the well-known fact that egalitarians may be pluralists and subscribe to non-egalitarian values, but that inequality may be both non-instrumentally bad and non-instrumentally good given different features of the situation in which it obtains. In sum, Mason's considerations complicate considerably the business of distinguishing egalitarians from non-egalitarians at a theoretical level at least.

It might be replied, to the claim that not all forms of telic egalitarianism are vulnerable to the levelling down objection, that this point is, although true, rather insignificant, since those forms that are not are either utterly implausible for different reasons, or not egalitarian views at all. While for the purpose of establishing my main claim, i.e. that there is no relevant asymmetry between telic and deontic egalitarianism as far as the levelling down objection is concerned, I could concede this point, I want to respond to it by addressing two reasons why one may be attracted to this reply.

First, suppose we have a state of inequality. There is an empirically possible alternative state of affairs in which people are equally well off and some are better off than they are in the actual state of affairs. In this case, the actual, unequal state of affairs is bad from the point of view of conditional egalitarianism. But now suppose that anti-egalitarians render the alternative state of affairs impossible. In that case,

---

[16] I say 'some contexts' because in some contexts it may not, e.g. a context in which people are differentially responsible.

the actual and unequal state of affairs is no longer bad from the point of view of conditional egalitarianism. This seems implausible. If egalitarians were to try to render the alternative state of equality possible again, it would seem reasonable for them to say that they do so in order to improve the situation from the point of view of equality. Suppose they can make the alternative state of equality possible without cooperation, but cannot make it actual without cooperation from some they know will not cooperate. Conditional egalitarianism implies that they should not render the equal state possible, for in so doing they would make the world worse. Most will reject this implication. While I concede that this implication is unattractive, I believe that conditional egalitarianism can accommodate it by adopting a suitable version of the tracing approach to the identification of alternatives. On such a version, the mere fact that we cannot realize a certain state of affairs now does not imply that it is not an alternative in the relevant sense, since it may be the case that we could have acted differently in the past such that this state of affairs would have been realized.

Second, it might be objected that while standard forms of telic egalitarianism are, indeed, forms of conditional egalitarianism owing to the common responsibility-clause, and while the forms of telic egalitarianism that meet the levelling down objection are concerned with relativities, the latter cannot be defended in terms of the underlying rationale for egalitarianism, i.e. that it is unfair that some are worse off owing to bad luck. Hence, when we consider the underlying rationale for conditional egalitarianism, we see that it is not an egalitarian view after all.[17] While I am sympathetic to this account of the underlying rationale for egalitarianism, it is not uncontroversial, and other views that are commonly regarded as egalitarian cannot be motivated by this rationale, e.g. that social inequalities are worse than natural ones. Hence, I do not think that appeals to underlying rationale are decisive in the present context.[18] Moreover, appealing to underlying rationales in the present context seems inappropriate in any case. These are at a different level from the level at which we distinguish between forms of egalitarianism according to which inequality is non-instrumentally bad and those forms of egalitarianism according to which it is not. For present purposes, I concentrate on this distinction and ask if at this level there is any relevant asymmetry between these two views as regards the levelling down objection.

I conclude that not all forms of telic egalitarianism are vulnerable to the levelling down objection and that those that are not cannot be immediately dismissed as extremely implausible versions of telic egalitarianism or as non-egalitarian views.

[17] McKerlie suggests that rendering the badness of inequality conditional on disadvantages to the worse off reflects a non-egalitarian commitment to benefiting the worse off rather a commitment to equality (1996: 288).

[18] See Susan Hurley's bias-neutralizing account of egalitarianism (2003: 256–80).

5. Deontic Egalitarianism and Levelling Down

I shall now argue that some, but not all, forms of deontic egalitarianism are vulnerable to an objection comparable to that of the levelling down objection. Consider, first, a deontic egalitarian position according to which it is unjust to treat people unequally, where that means treating one more favourably than another without there being any good reason for treating this person more favourably than the other. Suppose that I can either give A or B, but not both, 70 where the other will then have 25, or alternatively that I can give both 10. Since I have no good reason to give A instead of B or B instead of A 70, I shall be treating them unequally if I go for the first option. The mere fact that I have a good reason to give one of them 70 does not imply that there is a good reason for me to give one rather than the other 70. Hence, I shall be acting unjustly on the proposed deontic view. However, were I instead to treat them equally, then both of them would end up worse off. This might prompt one to ask: How can it be unjust to treat people unequally, when treating them equally requires treating everyone worse and benefits no one in any respect? In fact, it seems to me that this question has exactly the same force as the similar one asked about the goodness of outcomes in situations involving levelling down.

One initial reaction to this deontic version of the levelling down objection is that most people who think about the goodness of outcomes are inclined to accept what Larry Temkin has called the Slogan:

(6) If one outcome is worse than another in any respect, then it is worse for someone in some respect.[19]

Yet, many are inclined to think that the justice and wrongness of actions are not similarly constrained. Indeed, many see the goodness of outcomes to be explained in terms of benefits to people, see justice as a deontological constraint, and, hence, accept that in some cases justice requires acting in a way that prevents us from bringing about the best outcome. Hence, many would, one might think, reject the following parallel to the Slogan as having no comparable intuitive appeal:

---

[19] Some argue that it is not the Slogan that underlies the levelling down objection, but a wide person-affecting principle; see Holtug (2003: 65–85; Ch. 5 in this volume, Sect. 5). Others argue that the examples offered by Temkin in support of his claim that the Slogan is often invoked in arguments in moral philosophy rely on some version of the Pareto principle and not the Slogan; see Tungodden (2003: 6–10). Since both the wide person-affecting principle and Tungodden's version of the Pareto principle have deontic versions comparable to that of the deontic version of the Slogan presented below, I can sidestep these objections to Temkin's discussion. For Temkin's replies, see (2003a: 71–8; 2003b). For further discussion of the levelling down objection, see Christiano's, Holtug's, and Hurley's contributions to this volume (Chs. 2, 5, and 13 respectively).

(7) If an act or omission is *pro tanto* unjust or *pro tanto* wrong, then there is someone for whom it would have been better in some respect had this act or omission not taken place.[20]

To distinguish this slogan from the Slogan discussed by Temkin, I shall call the former slogan the Deontic Slogan. I now want to argue that the Deontic Slogan may be no less attractive than the Slogan, i.e. the Telic Slogan. Since my aim is to defend this comparative thesis and not to defend the Deontic Slogan as such, my line of argument is not threatened by putative counter-examples to the Deontic Slogan, e.g. the view that it would be unjust to benefit sinners thereby making them better off than saints even if there is no one for whom not doing so would be better in any respect.[21]

Temkin believes that the levelling down objection is forceful. He believes that 'It is the Slogan that gives the [levelling down objection its] powerful rhetorical force.' While the Slogan along with the levelling down objection ultimately must be rejected in Temkin's view, he carefully shows how the Slogan is 'implicitly involved' in a number of influential arguments in moral philosophy (Temkin 1993: 249). However, of the seven examples he gives, six of them are best seen as implicitly involving the Deontic rather than the Telic Slogan.[22] These examples are: (i) it would be 'wrong, not to' turn a non-Pareto optimal situation into one that is; (ii) *pace* some formulations of Rawls's difference principle, gains to the better off might be 'permissible' even if they do not benefit the worse off; (iii) Nozick's celebrated Wilt Chamberlain argument for why no one can 'complain on grounds of justice' against voluntary exchanges draws force from the assumption that there is no one for whom such exchanges are worse; (iv) on Locke's theory of appropriation one can justly acquire an unowned, external thing only when one does not worsen the situation of others; (v) Scanlon implies that rights can only be justified 'by appeal to the human interests their recognition promotes and protects'; and, (vi) standard objections to rule-utilitarianism, virtue ethics, and deontological theories often appeal to cases 'where no one benefits and

---

[20] However, as Temkin notes, the Telic Slogan may be used against those deontic egalitarians who think that 'other things equal an outcome where one has acted wrongly will be worse than an outcome where one has acted rightly' (1993: 254 n. 17). A similar consideration applies to those deontic egalitarians who think that equality produced through treating people equally is just and, thus, good. The Deontic Slogan may be used not only against these egalitarians, but also against those who deny that an outcome is bad in one respect, if someone has acted wrongly or good if someone has acted justly.

[21] Incidentally, Temkin appeals to proportional justice to raise an analogous objection to the Telic Slogan (1993: 262).

[22] The one example that is not best so construed is Parfit's claim that if an outcome, A+, differs from another, A, only in that A+ contains additional people who are worse off than the people who exist in A, then A+ cannot be worse than A even though A+, unlike A, contains inequality (Temkin 1993: 252–3). The Deontic Slogan also explains why, as Rawls thinks, inequality that benefits the worst-off group is not unjust (although bad), see Parfit (1991: 35).

some are harmed, or where some benefit and no one is harmed, if only one does or doesn't (a) follow the rule, (b) act virtuously, or (c) do one's duty' (Temkin 1993: 249–55). In all of these cases what is directly at stake is not the comparative goodness of different outcomes, but whether a piece of conduct that harms no one really can be said, for example, to be impermissible or wrong, or to violate someone's rights. Hence, to the extent that some deeper principle underlying the views mentioned by Temkin constitutes our underlying reason for finding the levelling down objection forceful, and I certainly think that he does identify some crucial considerations in this respect, we should find the Deontic Slogan, thus, and the analogous levelling down objection to deontic egalitarianism, at least as forceful as the Telic Slogan and the levelling down objection to telic egalitarianism. While this is by no means a compelling argument in favour of the equivalence of the Telic and the Deontic Slogan, it is striking that Temkin's discussion of the Slogan offers no reason to think that while the Slogan with regard to the goodness of outcomes is intuitively very attractive, no such thing can be said for a comparable Slogan with regard to the rightness or justice of actions.[23] If anything, it is the reverse. And since this Slogan commits us to an objection to deontic egalitarianism, which is comparable to the levelling down objection to telic egalitarianism, it suggests that telic and deontic egalitarianism are symmetrically vulnerable to considerations about levelling down.

In response to this some might simply say that Temkin's examples are misleading. They might insist that treating people unequally when the alternative is to treat everyone worse is not unjust, and for that reason deontic egalitarians do not object to unequal treatment in such cases. Deontic egalitarians object to unequal treatment when and only in so far as this involves unjust treatment.

This response is flawed. First, while deontic egalitarians might say that treating people unequally is unjust only when treating them equally does not harm everyone, this establishes no asymmetry between telic and deontic egalitarianism. This position would simply represent the deontic counterpart to the forms of conditional telic egalitarianism discussed in Section 4.

Second, if we disregard conditional telic egalitarianisms and allow deontic egalitarians to endorse unequal treatment in some cases and do not allow telic egalitarians to

---

[23] There is a further reason why the Deontic Slogan may actually appear in Temkin's reasoning. Suppose we have a choice between two states, A and A+. In A everyone is at 100. In A+, twice as many people exist, half of them those who would otherwise exist in A and the other half some who would not exist otherwise. Suppose, moreover, that the former would still be at 100 in A+, while the latter would be at 50. Temkin seems to think that the inequality in A+ is objectionable (although A+ would not, all things considered, be worse than A) and that this supports telic egalitarianism, because, as I understand Temkin, the worse-off people cannot claim to have been treated unjustly by being caused to exist, when the alternative for them were not to exist at all (Temkin 1993: 253–4 n. 15). If that claim could not be made, it would be less clear that Temkin's finding the inequality in A+ objectionable could not be construed deontically.

endorse inequality in comparable ones, we compare logically heterogeneous positions. While we insist that telic egalitarians are concerned with relativities, we allow that deontic egalitarians, to a certain extent, are not. But then the resulting asymmetry of telic and deontic egalitarianisms with regard to levelling down is due not to the structural differences between telic and deontic egalitarianism, but to certain idiosyncratic additional clauses built into our definition of these two positions, as I shall now explain more fully.

We need to distinguish between egalitarian and non-egalitarian accounts of just treatment. On the one extreme, accounts that say that treating people justly (and, for that matter, equally) is to respect their Nozickean entitlements or to maximise the sum of welfare are clearly non-egalitarian accounts (Kymlicka 2002: 37–45, 121–7). On the other extreme, an account that says that treating people justly is to make sure that they are equally well off is clearly an egalitarian account. In between these two extremes are views such as the view that treating people equally is to act in such a way that people have equal prospects for well-being or, if doing so implies giving no one better prospects, to act in such a way that the worse off have prospects for well-being that are as good as possible. A similar intermediate view, modelled on the priority view, says that to treat people equally is to maximise (or aim at maximising) the weighted sum of individual prospects where the weighting is such that increases in prospects at lower levels count for more. We might call such intermediate views forms of deontic egalitarianism just as the telic version of the priority view is often called an egalitarian position. However, if we do the former and if we at the same time insist on a more restrictive definition of telic egalitarianism, according to which, for example, the priority view is not an egalitarian view, then it is hardly very interesting to conclude that whereas telic egalitarianism is vulnerable to the levelling down objection, deontic egalitarianism is not vulnerable to any comparable challenge. This asymmetry is not due to the fact that, say, the focus of deontic egalitarians is on unjust geneses and not on the badness of unequal outcomes, but due to the fact that to count as a telic egalitarian you must be concerned with relativities, whereas to qualify as a deontic egalitarian you need not.

A similar reply is available to counter those who would like to press the objection that Dworkin distinguishes between treating people as equals and treating them equally, where, in his view, neither implies the other and the former is what he thinks governments are obligated to do (1985: 190). While Dworkin's requirement is in one way concerned with relativities, clearly it is so in a way that is different from standard telic views. For one thing, being treated as unequals is a moralised notion—we need to know how it is befitting for equals and unequals to be treated to tell if some are not treated as equals—where being unequally well off in the way that telic egalitarians are concerned with is not. A telic view, which is comparable to Dworkin's, says that it is bad if through no fault of their own some people have less than what is befitting given that all are equals. Presumably, if Dworkin can avoid the deontic levelling down objection by saying that giving some more when the only alternative is to leave some worse off and no one better off is compatible with treating these people as equals, then so could the proposed telic view avoid the corresponding telic levelling down objection.

Third, at least some deontic egalitarians subscribe to views that would suggest that they are vulnerable to the deontic version of the levelling down objection. Consider, for instance, Dworkin's diachronic envy test. According to Dworkin, a test of whether a certain distribution has treated everyone with equal respect and concern is whether anyone prefers anyone else's bundle of resources, because he lacks unchosen endowments that the other person has (van der Veen 2002: 55—67). If, in my deontic levelling down objection, I choose to give A the prospect of gaining 70 rather than giving everyone 10, then B may reasonably envy A's prospects for A's prospects are indisputably better. Hence, insofar as the diachronic envy test is seen as a reliable indicator about the nature of Dworkin's view about what constitutes equal treatment, then at least one paradigmatic deontic egalitarian has a view that is vulnerable to the deontic levelling down objection.[24]

What lurks in the background of the present discussion is probably the thought that the deontic concern for equality takes the form of a deontological side-constraint, e.g. that we cannot treat people unequally even if that brings about a better outcome. However, nothing in the discussion above implies that it must take this form. Deontic egalitarians may be consequentialists. They may think that it is bad from an agent-neutral point of view if persons are treated unjustly and think that we should maximize the sum of moral value (which in some cases may require treating someone unjustly to prevent more cases of people being treated unjustly). Moreover, telic egalitarianism is simply a claim about what is in itself bad. As such it is consistent with consequentialist as well as deontological moral views. For instance, one could be a telic egalitarian and hold that it is impermissible for us to bring about an unequal outcome even if it is the best outcome. Such a deontological constraint would operate not on the genesis of the unequal outcome, but on the outcome in itself.

This, of course, is not to deny that it might be useful to draw a distinction between deontological and consequentialist egalitarians (in the standard sense). Deontological egalitarians, on this view, think that there is at least one moral restriction on our conduct such that there could be circumstances under which bringing about the best

---

[24] In a reply to van der Veen's article, Dworkin insists that treating people with equal concern is best understood as implying equality of resources *ex ante* (2002: 120—5). This suggests a rejection on Dworkin's part of the diachronic envy test. However, in my view this test does form part of his earlier view at least; see Dworkin (2000: 85, 89, 91). Also, other deontic egalitarians have adopted this view from Dworkin even if he does not hold it now and may never have; see Kymlicka (2002: 81).

outcome (-cum-genesis) would be morally impermissible, because it would require treating someone in a way that violates egalitarian justice. Moreover, this constraint either might be agent-relative, e.g. it would forbid members of a given society not to bring about the best outcome because doing so requires their not treating someone unequally, or it might be agent-neutral, e.g. because it forbids all of us to treat someone unequally or allows someone to be treated unequally even if doing so would bring about a better outcome. Consequentialist egalitarians think that inequality is in itself bad or that it is bad if people are treated unjustly and that we should maximise overall moral value. Since it would be implausible to claim that only equality has intrinsic value, they would have to admit that in some cases bringing about the best outcome would require bringing about an unequal outcome or treating someone unjustly.[25]

While I have not shown that it might not turn out, say, that deontic egalitarians are better equipped, at the end of the day, to meet the deontic levelling down objection than are telic egalitarians vis-à-vis the telic levelling down objection, at least I have shown that there is a prima facie case to be made for symmetry in this respect. Not only do the examples invoked by Temkin in favour of the Telic Slogan in fact better support the Deontic Slogan, but the assumption that deontic egalitarians are invulnerable to the levelling down objection may stem from irrelevant features, e.g. that we stipulate that telic egalitarians necessarily are concerned with relativities and make no similar stipulation in the case of deontic egalitarians. I conclude then that in so far as we want to be either deontic or telic egalitarians (and cannot be both), we cannot base that choice on considerations of scope or levelling down.

References

DWORKIN, R. (1985), *A Matter of Principle* (Oxford: Clarendon Press).
——— (2000), *Sovereign Virtue* (Cambridge, Mass.: Harvard University Press).
——— (2002), '*Sovereign Virtue* Revisited', *Ethics*, 113: 106–43.
HOLTUG, N. (2003), 'Good for Whom?', *Theoria*, 69: 65–85.
HURLEY, S. (2003), *Justice, Luck, and Knowledge* (Oxford: Oxford University Press).
KYMLICKA, W. (2002), *Contemporary Political Philosophy*, 2nd edn. (Oxford: Oxford University Press).
McKERLIE, D. (1996), 'Equality', *Ethics*, 106: 274–96.
MASON, A. (2000). 'Egalitarianism and the Levelling Down Objection', *Analysis*, 61/3: 246–54.
NAGEL, T. (1991), *Equality and Partiality* (Oxford: Oxford University Press).
——— (1997), 'Justice and Nature', *Oxford Journal of Legal Studies*, 17: 303–21.

---

[25] 'Teleology', unlike 'consequentialism', is not taken to imply an agent-neutral ranking of states of affairs. But if teleological egalitarians think that inequality is in itself bad, then inequality is bad for anyone and for everyone there is a reason to eliminate it.

PARFIT, D. (1984), *Reasons and Persons*, (Oxford: Oxford University Press).

_____ (1991), 'Equality or Priority?', The Lindley Lecture (Lawrence: University of Kansas).

_____ (1998), 'Equality and Priority', in A. Mason (ed.), *Ideals of Equality* (Oxford: Basil Blackwell), 1–20.

RAWLS, J. (1971), *A Theory of Justice* (Oxford: Oxford University Press).

TEMKIN, L. (1987), 'Intransitivity and the Mere Addition Paradox', *Philosophy and Public Affairs*, 16: 138–87.

_____ (1993), *Inequality* (Oxford: Oxford University Press).

_____ (1995), 'Justice and Equality: Some Questions About Scope', in E. F. Paul, F. D. Miller, Jr., and J. Paul (eds.), *The Just Society* (Cambridge: Cambridge University Press), 72–104.

_____ (2003a), 'Equality, Priority, or What?', *Economics and Philosophy*, 19: 61–87.

_____ (2003b), 'Personal Versus Impersonal Principles: Reconsidering the Slogan', *Theoria*, 69: 21–31.

TUNGODDEN, B. (2003), 'The Value of Equality'. *Economics and Philosophy*, 19: 1–44.

VAN DER VEEN, R. (2002), 'Equality of Talent Resources: Procedures or Outcomes', *Ethics*, 113: 55–81.

5

Prioritarianism

Nils Holtug

1. Introduction

Prioritarianism is the view that, roughly, a benefit has greater moral value the worse
the situation of the individual to whom it accrues. This view has received a great deal
of attention in recent years.[1] In part, this is due to the fact that prioritarianism has only
recently been distinguished from egalitarianism, at least by political philosophers.
Thus, it has been suggested that perhaps some political theorists who have thought
of themselves as egalitarians are in fact better described as prioritarians (Parfit 1991:
19–22). A second, more important reason is that it has recently been argued that,
unlike egalitarianism, prioritarianism is not vulnerable to the so-called Levelling
Down Objection. According to this objection, it cannot, in any respect, be better to
increase equality when this means lowering the welfare of some and increasing the
welfare of none (Parfit 1991: 23). Since egalitarians are committed to the claim that it
is in at least one respect better to increase equality, even if by levelling down, they
are subject to the Levelling Down Objection. Prioritarians, on the other hand, do not

Thanks to Roger Crisp, Karsten Klint Jensen, Kasper Lippert-Rasmussen, Dennis McKerlie, Larry
Temkin, Peter Vallentyne, participants at the Seventh Conference of the International Society for
Utilitarian Studies in Lisbon 2003, and participants at the conference on egalitarianism at the University
of Copenhagen, 2004, for comments on this chapter and my work on prioritarianism that preceded it.

[1] Arneson (2000; Ch. 11 in this volume); Broome (forthcoming); Brown (2003); Crisp (2003); Fleurbaey
(forthcoming); Hausman (forthcoming); Holtug (1999, forthcoming); Hooker (2000: 55–65); Hurley
(Ch. 13 in this volume); Jensen (2003); McKerlie (1994, 1997, 2003; Ch. 6 in this volume); Nagel (1991);
Parfit (1991); Persson (2001); Raz (1986: 217–44); Scanlon (1982: 123); Scheffler (1982: 31); Temkin (1993a, b,
2000, 2003a, b); Tungodden (2003); Weirich (1983).

value equality but are simply concerned with the fate of the worse off and so see no value in levelling down. Several political philosophers have therefore considered prioritarianism superior to egalitarianism (Arneson 2000; Crisp 2003; Holtug 1999, forthcoming; Parfit 1991).

These claims about prioritarianism and its relative merits have been challenged in various ways. Thus, some have argued that there really is no distinction to be made between egalitarianism and prioritarianism (Fleurbaey forthcoming; Hausman forthcoming). Others have argued that even if there is a distinction to be made, it does not serve to distinguish them with respect to the Levelling Down Objection (Broome forthcoming; Fleurbaey forthcoming). Furthermore, some have raised doubts with respect to the person-affecting basis of prioritarianism (Temkin 1993*a*: 245–82; 2000: 151–3). Finally, it has been argued that prioritarianism fails to capture some common and important intuitions about relational justice and is in this respect inferior to egalitarianism (Temkin 2003*b*: 12–19), and fails to appropriately capture the virtue on which it is based, namely that of compassion (Crisp 2003: 755–63).

In the following, I shall first make a suggestion as to how the distinction between egalitarianism and prioritarianism should be drawn. I shall then argue that, according to this distinction, the Levelling Down Objection does serve to distinguish between these two distributive views. Furthermore, I shall argue that while prioritarianism includes an impersonal element, it is quite compatible with the person-affecting basis of the Levelling Down Objection. Finally, I shall argue that prioritarianism may well accommodate our intuitions about relational justice and the virtue of compassion. Thus, my argument will amount to a defence of prioritarianism against a number of objections.

Before I begin my defence, I need to say something about the framework I shall employ. I am concerned with axiology. More precisely, my concern is with principles that order outcomes in terms of welfare. In fact, I shall assume a welfarist axiological doctrine according to which outcome value is a function only of the welfare of individuals.[2] This means that the versions of prioritarianism and egalitarianism I shall consider are welfarist axiological versions.[3]

Obviously, the welfarist doctrine I shall assume is highly controversial, but it allows me to focus on some particular aspects of distributive justice and to leave out others. And even if one is not a welfarist, my discussion may be of interest because even non-welfarists may want to attach some importance to the distribution of welfare.

---

[2] For similar characterisations of welfarism, see Blackorby *et al.* (1984: 328–32); Ng (1990: 171); Sen (1987: 39). In Holtug (2003*b*), I point to some problems with this characterisation, but argue that different characterizations may be appropriate in different contexts. And in the present context, this characterization will serve us just fine.

[3] Sometimes axiological versions of such principles are called 'teleological'; see Parfit (1991: 3–4).

I need to be a bit more precise about my claim that egalitarianism is vulnerable to the Levelling Down Objection. Strictly speaking, I shall only be concerned with axiological welfare egalitarianism and so I shall not consider how this objection applies to other egalitarian views.[4] And since axiological welfare egalitarianism is the only kind of egalitarianism I shall be concerned with, I shall simply refer to it as 'egalitarianism'.

2. Egalitarianism

In this section and the next, I consider the issue of how to distinguish prioritarianism from egalitarianism. Consider first egalitarianism. Egalitarians value equality, and equality is a *relation*.[5] But what does it mean that egalitarians *value* this relation? First, they value it *intrinsically*. That is, egalitarians value equality because they take it to be *good in itself* and not (merely) good because it tends to further some other goal, say, fraternity, political stability, or the general welfare. Thus, a utilitarian may have reasons to prefer some degree of equality, but surely that does not make her an egalitarian. To be an egalitarian, a person must value equality *for its own sake*.

Second, to qualify as an egalitarian, a person must value equality in the sense that she considers more equal outcomes *in one respect better* than less equal outcomes.[6] However, she need not consider more equal outcomes better all things considered. After all, clearly she may have other concerns, say, for liberty, autonomy, or the general welfare. Combining these two claims, what we get is

Outcome Welfare Egalitarianism. An outcome is in one respect intrinsically better, the more equal a distribution of individual welfare it includes.

Of course, different measures of equality will rank outcomes differently and so there may be genuine disagreements about which outcomes are better than others with respect to this value. Nevertheless, I want to suggest that in order for a measure to be a measure of *equality,* it must imply

---

[4] But for the suggestion that the Levelling Down Objection applies to many other forms of egalitarianism as well, see Lippert-Rasmussen (Ch. 4 in this volume).

[5] Thus, it is common to stress the *relational* nature of egalitarianism. For instance, Parfit writes: 'Egalitarians are concerned with *relativities*: with how each person's level compares with the level of other people' (1991: 23). And Temkin states: 'The egalitarian has no intrinsic concern with how much people have, her concern is with how much people have *relative to others*' (1993a: 200). Others, however, use the term 'egalitarianism' in a wider sense, where it includes at least one view that does not attach intrinsic value to relations between people, namely prioritarianism (see e.g. McKerlie 1996: 277).

[6] For a similar principle and the suggestion that it is central to egalitarianism, see Tungodden (2003: 6).

The Perfect Equality Claim. An outcome in which everyone has the same share of welfare is more equal than an outcome in which individuals have different shares.

Like the claim that, according to egalitarians, more equal outcomes are in one respect intrinsically better than less equal outcomes, the Perfect Equality Claim seems to me to be a part of our ordinary conception of what (welfare) equality is (see also Vallentyne 2000: 4).

While Outcome Welfare Egalitarianism and the Perfect Equality Claim each seem innocent enough, together they imply

The Egalitarian Relational Claim. An outcome in which everyone has the same share of welfare is in one respect intrinsically better than an outcome in which individuals have different shares.

The Egalitarian Relational Claim, it seems to me, nicely captures an important relational aspect of egalitarianism. A principle that satisfies it will imply that an increase in an individual's welfare from n to $n+1$ intrinsically improves an outcome in one respect if everyone else is at $n+1$, but makes it intrinsically worse in one respect if everyone else is at n. Thus, the value of such an increase depends on the recipient's welfare level relative to that of others. However, as we shall see in Section 4, the Egalitarian Relational Claim renders egalitarianism vulnerable to the Levelling Down Objection.

In the following, then, I shall assume that egalitarians are committed to Outcome Welfare Egalitarianism, the Perfect Equality Claim, and (hence) the Egalitarian Relational Claim. Of course, these three principles amount only to a very limited characterization of egalitarianism. Thus, they only tell us how to rank equal outcomes against unequal ones and only in one respect. Let me address these two limitations separately.

The proposed egalitarian principles do not tell us anything about how to rank various patterns of inequality. However, they are of course compatible with a number of further restrictions. For simplicity, let us momentarily assume that we hold an all things considered version of Outcome Welfare Egalitarianism (such a version is obtained by deleting 'in one respect' from the original formulation). This version may satisfy, for instance, the Pigou–Dalton Principle of transfer. According to this principle, if the sum of welfare remains constant, equality is increased by a transfer of welfare from a better-off person to a worse-off person, as long as their relative positions are not reversed. What this principle captures is the intuition that *equalizing* transfers between two individuals that do not affect the total sum of welfare improve an outcome. However, I do not intend to specify the egalitarian ordering of different patterns of inequality here because, as I shall argue in the next section, the characterization I have already provided suffices to distinguish egalitarianism from prioritarianism.

My characterization is also limited in the sense that it does not tell us anything about how to order outcomes *all things considered*. Consider again Outcome Welfare Egalitarianism. Egalitarians will not want to claim that equality is all that matters and so will not simply hold this principle; they will want to combine the concern for equality with certain other distributive concerns. After all, Outcome Welfare Egalitarianism does not even imply that welfare equality at high welfare levels is better than welfare equality at low welfare levels. Furthermore, if we combine the concern for equality with certain other distributive concerns, there is no guarantee that the resulting principle will imply that an equal distribution is better than an unequal one, all things considered.

Some such principles that combine egalitarian and non-egalitarian concerns will satisfy the Pareto Principle, according to which two outcomes are equally good if they are equally good for everyone, and one is better than the other if it is better for some and worse for none.[7] Let us call such versions Pareto Outcome Welfare Egalitarianism.[8] Because it satisfies the Pareto Principle, Pareto Outcome Welfare Egalitarianism implies that an increase in an individual's welfare (holding the welfare of others constant) improves an outcome even if it changes it from a situation of equality to one of inequality. Furthermore, since Pareto Outcome Welfare Egalitarianism is supposed to capture not just the concern for equality but also other relevant moral concerns, I shall take it to be a principle that orders outcomes all things considered.

Note that while Pareto Outcome Welfare Egalitarianism implies that some unequal outcomes are better than some equal outcomes, it nevertheless satisfies the Egalitarian Relational Claim. This is because I have defined Pareto Outcome Welfare Egalitarianism as a principle that combines egalitarian and non-egalitarian concerns such as to satisfy the Pareto Principle, and I have characterised egalitarian concerns in terms of this relational claim. Thus, Pareto Outcome Welfare Egalitarianism implies that an outcome in which everyone has the same share of welfare is *in one respect* intrinsically better than an outcome in which individuals have different shares.

---

[7] This version differs from standard versions of the Pareto Principle, since standard versions are formulated in terms of preferences rather than welfare; see e.g. Broome (1991: 152). It corresponds to Broome's principle of personal good; see (1991: 165).

[8] While many egalitarians seem to accept the Pareto Principle, not all do. Brian Barry reconstructs (and endorses) an argument of Rawls's, according to which equality is unjust when it is Pareto—inferior and, in particular, when there is a Pareto—superior outcome in which the worst off are better off; see Barry (1989: 213–54). Furthermore, Broome defends the Pareto Principle and combines it with egalitarian concerns in Broome (1991: 165–201). Also, Tungodden endorses the Pareto Principle from within an egalitarian framework; Tungodden (2003: 10). Incidentally, both Broome and Tungodden seem to consider the Pareto Principle a plausible restriction on egalitarianism in its own right, rather than an implication of a plausible weighing of egalitarian and non-egalitarian (e.g. utilitarian) concerns. On the other side of this egalitarian divide, McKerlie suggests that there is no particular reason why egalitarians should weight equality and welfare such that the Pareto Principle is always satisfied; McKerlie (1996: 287). Temkin holds a similar view (2003b: 80).

To put it differently, we might say that egalitarians are committed to a particular *reason* for holding the particular all things considered ordering that they hold. Of course, egalitarians do not share all their reasons (then they would hold the same orderings all things considered), but they have at least *one* reason in common. And this reason is itself an axiological ordering, albeit a partial ordering of outcomes in one respect only.[9]

However, Marc Fleurbaey rejects the idea that egalitarianism should be characterized in terms of reasons. He considers what he calls the minimal egalitarian statement that 'unequal distributions have something bad that equal distributions do not have', but claims that this statement has almost no implications for the social ranking (Fleurbaey forthcoming). Obviously, what Fleurbaey calls the minimal egalitarian statement is very similar to the Egalitarian Relational Claim. So what, exactly, is the problem with this statement supposed to be? Fleurbaey stresses that 'it is important to distinguish disagreements about the social ranking from disagreements about the *reasons* supporting the social ranking. Only the former have practical implications and are directly relevant for the policy-maker' (Fleurbaey forthcoming). In other words, what is important for the policy-maker is the social ranking, and the minimal egalitarian statement says almost nothing about that.

Let me make two brief points. First, the Egalitarian Relational Claim *is* defined in terms of a ranking of outcomes, although a partial ordering in one respect only. Nevertheless, I am sure that Fleurbaey will insist that what is important for the policy-maker is the all things considered ordering. This brings me to my second point. There is of course a sense in which it is true that what has practical implications for individuals is the all things considered ordering. What should be implemented is the all things considered ordering and, in its implementation, the implications of each separate reason that supports this ordering are not felt by anyone.

But how is this supposed to show that the distinctions between distributive principles should be drawn (only) in terms of such orderings? The policy-maker, or anyone else for that matter, may want to know why she should implement a particular ordering, or whether an ordering that is already implemented is justified, and to answer these questions, she will need to invoke reasons. So distinctions in terms of reasons certainly have real importance.

Another implication of accounting for egalitarianism in terms of reasons is that we may find egalitarians and non-egalitarians endorsing identical orderings all things considered. In fact, as we shall see in the next section, we may even find egalitarians

---

[9] This ordering is partial because the Egalitarian Relational Claim implies only that *equal* outcomes are in one respect intrinsically better than *unequal* outcomes. Thus, it does not tell us how to rank equal outcomes against other equal outcomes and nor does it tell us how to rank unequal outcomes against other unequal outcomes.

and prioritarians in agreement here (for a similar point, see Fleurbaey forthcoming; Jensen 2003: 101–3; Tungodden 2003: 30–1). The difference, of course, will consist in their reasons for endorsing a particular ordering.

But note that this talk of different reasons for accepting a particular ordering all things considered is in no way mysterious. For instance, several reasons have been given for accepting Rawls's difference principle. One of these reasons appeals to Rawls's contract argument, whereas another appeals only to the 'intuitive' case for giving priority to the worst off in cases where they are not themselves responsible for so being (Barry 1989: 213–14; Kymlicka 1990: 55). So do two people who both hold the difference principle, but each for their own reason, hold the same view? In a sense yes, and in another sense no. In order to bring out the full extent of their commitments, we shall have to refer to their reasons for holding the difference principle. Likewise, in order to describe the difference between egalitarians and other theorists, we shall have to refer to *their* reasons for ordering outcomes in the manner they do.[10]

On this account of egalitarianism, then, it may not always be possible to determine whether an ordering that a particular person holds is egalitarian or not. Furthermore, turning from the person who holds this ordering to the ordering itself, there may be no determinate answer to the question of whether it is egalitarian or not. This may seem to be a rather impractical implication.

However, first, there is nothing that this characterisation of egalitarianism prevents us from saying. Even if we cannot always determine whether a particular ordering is egalitarian, we can explain exactly why this is so and what the implications of this ordering are. We can, for instance, say that it is *compatible* with egalitarianism.

Second, as I have stressed, it seems to me that to be worthy of the predicate 'egalitarian', a principle must involve a commitment to Outcome Welfare Egalitarianism, the Perfect Equality Claim, and so the Egalitarian Relational Claim. Therefore, in order to be justified in calling a certain distributive view egalitarian, we must understand it as including a particular (egalitarian) reason for accepting it.

Finally, as I have already mentioned, the feature I have called the Egalitarian Relational Claim is what invites the Levelling Down Objection, and so drawing the distinction between egalitarianism and prioritarianism in terms of it ensures that this distinction has real theoretical interest.

My characterisation of egalitarianism, then, is limited both in that it does not enable us to order various patterns of inequality and in that it does not enable us to order

[10] Incidentally, Fleurbaey seems to acknowledge that egalitarianism and prioritarianism rely on different normative reasons even if these reasons do not translate into any difference in the all things considered ordering (forthcoming). Broome also acknowledges that these two principles rely on different reasons, but claims that this difference *does* translate into a difference in the ordering (forthcoming).

outcomes all things considered. Nevertheless, as we shall now see, it does suffice to distinguish egalitarianism from prioritarianism.

3. Prioritarianism

According to prioritarians, roughly, a benefit morally matters more the worse off the individual to whom it accrues. How does this view differ from egalitarianism? Egalitarians value equality, and equality is a relation. Prioritarians, on the other hand, do not value a relation. Rather, what they are concerned with is *absolute* levels of individual welfare (Parfit 1991: 22–4). A benefit that falls at a particular level of welfare has the same moral value no matter what levels other individuals are at. And the lower this particular level, the greater the value of the benefit.

This description of the value commitments of the prioritarian needs to be made more precise. Like the egalitarian, we should characterise the prioritarian in terms of her commitments with respect to intrinsic value. We should require that she favours giving priority to the worse off not (only) because doing so will tend to further some other goal of hers, say, fraternity or political stability, but (at least in part) because she holds that, everything else being equal, an outcome in which a benefit falls at a lower level is *intrinsically* better than an outcome in which an equal benefit falls at a higher level.

I suggest that the best account of these value commitments is that the prioritarian ascribes intrinsic value to compound states of affairs, each consisting of the state that a benefit of a certain size befalls an individual and the state that the individual is at a particular welfare level, where this value increases when the size of the benefit increases but decreases when the level of welfare increases. Thus, the (compound) state that a benefit befalls an individual at a lower level is intrinsically better than the (compound) state that an equal benefit befalls an individual at a higher level.

Furthermore, like the egalitarian, a prioritarian may be a pluralist. That is, she may have concerns other than priority. But, *qua* prioritarian, she will hold that an outcome in which a benefit falls at a lower level is *in one respect* better than an outcome in which an equal benefit falls at a higher level. Combining these claims (and introducing an additive function) we get:

> *Outcome Welfare Prioritarianism.* An outcome is in one respect intrinsically better, the larger a sum of weighted individual benefits it contains, where benefits are weighted such that they gain a greater value, the worse off the individual to whom they accrue.

I have suggested that egalitarianism satisfies the Egalitarian Relational Claim. Outcome Welfare Prioritarianism, on the other hand, does not let the value of a benefit to an individual depend on the welfare levels of others. The moral value of a further unit of welfare to any individual depends only on the welfare level of that individual and the weight function. Therefore, prioritarianism does not satisfy the Egalitarian Relational Claim.

Furthermore, whereas Outcome Welfare Egalitarianism cannot reasonably be claimed to exhaust our axiological concerns, Outcome Welfare Prioritarianism may be claimed to do just that. For instance, unlike Outcome Welfare Egalitarianism, it favours equality at higher levels over equality at lower levels. After all, additional benefits increase the value of an outcome whatever the level at which they fall. So from now on and for simplicity, unless otherwise indicated, I shall simply assume that prioritarianism implies an all things considered ordering of outcomes equivalent to the ordering with respect to priority generated by Outcome Welfare Prioritarianism (although, strictly speaking, prioritarians are only committed to the latter principle *qua* prioritarians). That is, from now on I shall take 'prioritarianism' to imply

> *Overall Outcome Welfare Prioritarianism.* An outcome is intrinsically better, the larger a sum of weighted individual benefits it contains, where benefits are weighted such that they gain a greater value, the worse off the individual to whom they accrue.

On this assumption, we can bring out the structure of prioritarianism and so the structural difference between egalitarianism and prioritarianism to which I referred above in greater detail. As John Broome has pointed out, prioritarianism can be formally represented by an additively separable function of the following form:

$$G = f(w_1) + f(w_2) + \cdots + f(w_n),$$

where f is an increasing and strictly concave function of individual welfare, w_i (Broome 1991: 179). Thus, as I pointed out above, the contribution each individual makes to the value of an outcome depends only on her own welfare, not on the welfare of others.

Importantly, it is here assumed that individuals have identical weight functions in the sense that the moral value of a further unit of welfare is the same for *all* individuals who are at identical welfare levels. In a sense, the claim that individuals have identical weight functions can be said to express an ideal of the moral equality of individuals. A benefit to an individual at a given welfare level is exactly as important as a similar benefit to any other individual at the same level.[11] But of course, the claim that individuals are moral equals does not commit the prioritarian to *egalitarianism*, which encompasses the view that it is in one respect intrinsically better if individuals have more equal shares of welfare.

Furthermore, according to prioritarianism, moral outcome value is a strictly concave function of welfare, as illustrated in Figure 5.1. Thus, benefits *gradually* decrease in moral value, the higher the level at which they fall.

---

[11] More technically, the equal weight assumption is captured by the requirement of anonymity.

Moral outcome value

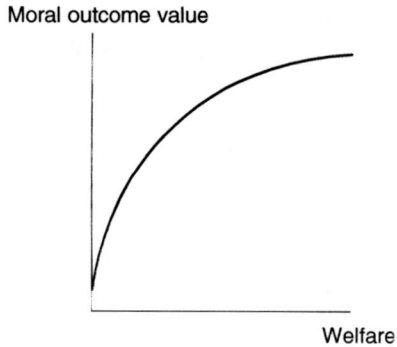

Welfare

FIG. 5.1

Also, prioritarianism is an *aggregative* (indeed additive) principle, and I shall assume that it implies that for any finite sum of benefits that fall at a lower level, it can be outweighed by a sufficiently large sum of benefits that fall at a—indeed any—higher level. In this respect, it differs from a principle that would give absolute priority to the very worst off.[12]

Finally, note that prioritarianism satisfies the Pareto Principle. Since all increases in individual welfare, holding others constant, increase outcome value, it satisfies the Pareto Principle. And since it responds to transfers of a fixed sum of welfare from a better-off individual to a worse-off individual (that does not reverse their relative positions) by giving greater weight to this sum, there is a sense in which it satisfies the Pigou Dalton Principle (although it does not assign value to equality).

Let us now return to the distinction between egalitarianism and prioritarianism. Note that my characterisation of the difference between these two principles is in terms of *reasons*.[13] Whatever particular all things considered ordering an egalitarian accepts, she will do so at least in part because she accepts the Egalitarian Relational Claim. Prioritarianism, on the other hand, does not involve a commitment to the Egalitarian Relational Claim. Of course, as I pointed out above, some may want to combine prioritarian and other concerns, and so the acceptance of Outcome Welfare Prioritarianism is *compatible* with a commitment to this claim. But it is not something to which one is committed in virtue of one's *prioritarian* concerns.

Note also that, as I pointed out in the last section, this way of construing the difference between egalitarianism and prioritarianism does not rule out that egalitarians may in fact endorse a prioritarian ordering of outcomes all things considered. But since

---

[12] Thus, neither maximin nor leximin are versions of prioritarianism.

[13] For the suggestion that the difference is to be explained in terms of reasons or justifications, see also Tungodden (2003: 24).

only egalitarians will endorse this particular ordering in part because they endorse the Egalitarian Relational Claim, egalitarianism and prioritarianism are *distinct* views.

Nevertheless, Fleurbaey denies that egalitarianism and prioritarianism are fundamentally different views. Thus, he argues that not only egalitarians, but also prioritarians, attach value to equality (Fleurbaey forthcoming). More precisely, assuming that the resulting ranking of outcomes is continuous, a prioritarian view can be represented by a function of the form

$$W = T(1 - IN),$$

where T is the total sum of welfare, and IN is an inequality index that satisfies the Pigou–Dalton Principle. Fleurbaey provides the following proof. We choose W as a function that represents the prioritarian ordering of outcomes and implies that whenever an outcome holds an equal distribution of welfare, W equals T. According to Fleurbaey, it can be shown that such a function exists. We then adopt the following inequality index:

$$IN = 1 - (W/T).$$

This is held to be a reasonable inequality index because, first, $IN = 0$ when the distribution is equal. And second, IN satisfies the Pigou–Dalton Principle. After all, a prioritarian view satisfies this principle and so any Pigou–Dalton transfer increases W (while T is held constant) and so decreases IN. The point, of course, is that by reversing IN, we get $W = T(1 - IN)$, which is what had to be proved.

In other words, just as Pareto Outcome Welfare Egalitarianism can be divided into parts some of which are egalitarian and others are not, so can prioritarianism. However, the egalitarian value to which Fleurbaey thinks the prioritarian is committed is instrumental, not intrinsic (Fleurbaey forthcoming). More precisely, Fleurbaey thinks the prioritarian is committed to the instrumental value of equality in a logical sense of 'instrumental value'. Prioritarians hold equality to be instrumentally good in that an equal distribution of welfare is held to be intrinsically better than an unequal distribution of the same sum. This logical sense of 'instrumental value' should be distinguished from its more ordinary causal sense, where an entity has instrumental value in so far as it causally produces some (intrinsic) value.

In fact, prioritarians hold that equality has instrumental value not only in the logical sense, but also in the causal sense. Equality has instrumental value in the causal sense because at least certain ways of increasing equality—giving to the worse off rather than the better off—will promote intrinsic prioritarian value.

But even if prioritarians are committed to the instrumental value of equality in both these senses, this does not make them *egalitarians*. Egalitarians hold that equality has *intrinsic* value. And as we shall see, this implies (amongst other things) that egalitarians consider levelling down to be in one respect intrinsically good. Prioritarianism has no such implication.

Nevertheless, even if prioritarians are not *committed* to egalitarianism, some may well be egalitarians. I have already conceded this much in the case of *pluralist* prioritarians, who combine Outcome Welfare Prioritarianism and egalitarian concerns. But the point here is that even proponents of Overall Outcome Welfare Prioritarianism may in fact be egalitarians. This much seems to follow from the availability of Fleurbaey's inequality index, IN. According to IN, inequality reduces to zero when individuals have the same shares, in accordance with the Perfect Equality Claim. And so if an overall outcome welfare prioritarian holds Outcome Welfare Egalitarianism with respect to IN, she will indeed be an egalitarian. But, of course, she *need not* hold Outcome Welfare Egalitarianism with respect to IN. So once again, we reach the verdict that prioritarians are not committed to egalitarianism *qua* prioritarians.

While some prioritarians may be egalitarians, unless otherwise indicated, I shall assume that prioritarians hold their prioritarian views simply because they take benefits to have greater intrinsic value at lower levels and so not partly because they consider more equal outcomes in one respect intrinsically better than less equal outcomes.

4. The Levelling Down Objection

Outcome Welfare Egalitarianism and the Perfect Equality Claim imply that it is in one respect intrinsically better if inequality is eliminated, even if it does not involve making the worse off better off, but only involves making the better off worse off. After all, together, these two principles imply the Egalitarian Relational Claim, according to which an outcome in which everyone has the same share of welfare is in one respect intrinsically better than an outcome in which people have unequal shares. (For the claim that egalitarianism does in fact *not* have this implication, see Christiano, Chapter 2 in this volume, Sections 20–2.)

Of course, egalitarians need not claim that it is better *all things considered* to increase equality by harming some and benefiting none. Obviously, Pareto Outcome Welfare Egalitarianism implies that this would in fact be a change for the worse. Nevertheless, since Pareto Outcome Welfare Egalitarianism incorporates the three egalitarian principles mentioned above, it implies that an elimination of inequality that harms some and benefits none is *in one respect* intrinsically better. It is intrinsically better regarding equality. But how could this in any respect be better? It would benefit no one, not even the worse off. This constitutes the gist of the Levelling Down Objection (Parfit 1991: 17).

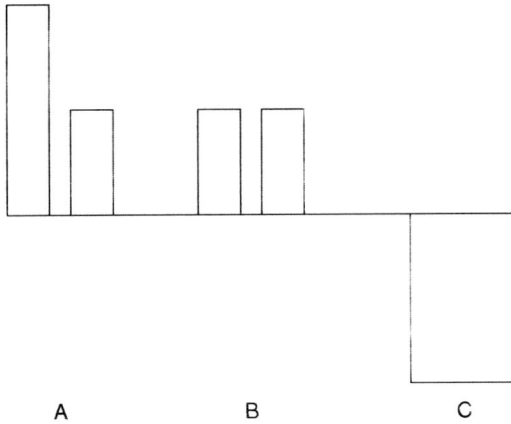

Fɪɢ. 5.2 Levelling down.

To illustrate the objection, consider the outcomes in Figure 5.2 (where the width of the columns represents the number of individuals in a group, the height of the columns represents their welfare, and the horizontal line connecting the columns represents the level where life ceases to be worth living). For egalitarians, B must in one respect be intrinsically better than A, namely regarding equality, although it is better for no one. Furthermore, C must in one respect be intrinsically better than A, although everyone suffers terribly in C. These judgements illustrate the force of the Levelling Down Objection.

Prioritarianism, on the other hand, is not vulnerable to the Levelling Down Objection. The feature of egalitarianism that invites this objection is the Egalitarian Relational Claim and, as I have argued, prioritarianism does not satisfy this claim. Prioritarians value increases in welfare, especially to the worse off, and when we level down there are no increases.[14] Therefore, the Levelling Down Objection serves to distinguish egalitarianism and prioritarianism.

Unsurprisingly, Fleurbaey disagrees. Consider again the prioritarian function W. Fleurbaey argues that when a distributional change implies that W is reduced in spite of a decrease in IN, the prioritarian must hold that the change worsens things *in spite* of the fact that something good happens on the IN side. Thus, Fleurbaey concludes that 'insofar as prioritarians give instrumental value to equality, as shown above, they should also be subject to *a similar kind of criticism* [the Levelling Down Objection]' (Fleurbaey forthcoming; my emphasis).

[14] Remember that I am assuming that prioritarians do not hold this view (in part) because they are egalitarians. If they are *egalitarian* prioritarians, they will of course be vulnerable to the Levelling Down Objection.

Presumably, the sort of case Fleurbaey has in mind here is a case of levelling down. So let us assume that the welfare level of the better off is reduced to the level of the worst off, resulting in decreases in W, T, and IN. T is reduced because there is a decrease in the sum of welfare and W is reduced because there is a decrease in the sum of *weighted* welfare. And since there is now perfect equality, IN reduces to zero. In other words, levelling down improves an outcome in one respect, namely regarding IN.

However, the *mere fact* that prioritarianism can be split into separate components such as to give rise to an extensionally equivalent ordering does not show that prioritarianism, or anyone who holds it, attaches any relevant kind of value to these separate components. And so the fact that IN decreases in the case described above does not imply that prioritarians are committed to the claim that there is, in any interesting sense, something good about levelling down.

It may be helpful to consider the following analogy. Total utilitarianism can be represented by:

$$U = w_1 + w_2 + \cdots + w_n.$$

Furthermore, U is equivalent to the following function of average welfare:

$$V = n \times \text{AVE},$$

where

$$\text{AVE} = (w_1 + w_2 + \cdots + w_n)/n.$$

Does this mean that total utilitarians are committed to the claim that an outcome that has a higher average welfare than another is in one respect better? Obviously not. Consider the following two outcomes (where the numbers represent individual welfare levels):

D : (−10, *)
E : (−10, −9).

In D, there is only one individual and he has a horrible life (the asterisk represents the non-existence of a second individual). In fact, he has a negative welfare level. In E, there is also another individual, and she has a life just slightly less horrible, but still clearly on the negative side.[15] Importantly, the move from D to E decreases V in spite of the fact that AVE increases (people are, on average, slightly better off in E). So on Fleurbaey's line of reasoning, total utilitarians must admit that while V decreases, something good is happening on the AVE side.

But obviously, total utilitarians do not consider E to be in any respect better than D. They will hold that E is not intrinsically better in any respect. Furthermore, in

---

[15] This case is inspired by a very similar case described by Parfit (1984: 393).

such cases, AVE does not have instrumental value in the causal sense. While certain ways of increasing AVE will also increase total welfare, the move from D to E does not do that. What about instrumental value in the logical sense, then? Admittedly, total utilitarians will take AVE to have instrumental value in the sense that, holding n constant, an increase in AVE increases the value of V. But this just means that if we held the number of individuals in D constant, any increase in AVE would intrinsically improve the outcome. And surely, the mere fact that there are such *other* outcomes that are intrinsically better than D does not imply that, in any interesting sense at least, E is better than D.

Likewise, prioritarians do not consider B to be in any respect better than A in Figure 5.2 (where B results from levelling down A). As we have seen, they will hold that B is not intrinsically better in any respect. Furthermore, in levelling down cases, decreases in IN do not even have instrumental value in the causal sense. While certain ways of decreasing IN will also increase prioritarian intrinsic value, the move from A to B does not do that. Of course, prioritarians will take decreases in IN to have instrumental value in the (logical) sense that, holding T constant, such a decrease increases the value of W. But this just means that if we held T constant, any decrease in IN would intrinsically improve the outcome. And again, the mere fact that there are such *other* outcomes that are intrinsically better than A does not imply that, in any interesting sense, B is better than A. A prioritarian will happily admit that there are such better outcomes, but surely this does not weaken her position. In any case, it is a far cry from claiming that B is in one respect intrinsically better than A, which is what the egalitarian claims. And so the 'similar criticism' Fleurbaey believes prioritarianism to be vulnerable to is really not similar at all.

Let us therefore now assess the Levelling Down Objection (only) in relation to egalitarianism. I believe that there are two distinct concerns from which this objection derives its force. The first is a somewhat general moral concern. There is a strong tendency to think that the value of outcomes must be tied to value for individuals. Roughly, an outcome cannot be better (worse) than another in any respect unless there is someone *for whom* it is better (worse). A problem that levelling down poses for the egalitarian, then, is that levelling down renders no one better off and yet it may involve an improvement in equality.

Therefore, part of the intuitive force of the Levelling Down Objection derives from the fact that the link between equality and improvements in welfare is purely contingent. Equality can come about in different ways, and some of these ways do not involve benefits to anyone. I shall discuss the basis of this intuition and the precise relation between outcome value and benefits it expresses in the next section.

The other concern from which the Levelling Down Objection derives its force is this. Cases of levelling down suggest that the concerns that motivate many of us to be egalitarians may not really be captured by egalitarianism. Part of what motivates our concern for equality may be a concern for how those who are worse off—or worse off than others—fare. Our concern for equality, then, may in one way or another reflect a concern for the worse off. But we may wonder whether egalitarianism adequately captures this concern. Consider, for instance, a move from A to C in Figure 5.2 (where C is perfectly equal but everyone has a life worth not living). Equality is supposed to capture our concern for the worse off but, with respect to equality, C is better than A. The problem, of course, is that the move from A to C does not seem in any way to respond to our concern for the worse off. In fact, the worse off in A are much worse off in C.

Prioritarianism, on the other hand, nicely accommodates this second concern. In fact, it is simply designed to express a concern for the worse off. And while it does not assess the value of a change in the situation of a worse-off individual in terms of how her welfare level compares with that of others, it will tend to favour benefits to those who are worse off than others. If we can confer a benefit of a fixed size on one of two individuals and one of them is worse off than the other, then, everything else being equal, it is better to confer it on the one who is worse off.

5. The Strong Wide Person-Affecting Principle

I have suggested that one of the reasons why the Levelling Down Objection seems so persuasive is that we have a strong tendency to think that the value of outcomes must be tied to value for individuals. Roughly, an outcome cannot be better (worse) than another in any respect unless there is someone for whom it is better (worse). And since levelling down benefits no one, it cannot truly in any respect make an outcome better.

Outcome values, then, do not enter the scene out of nowhere; they crucially depend on how individuals are affected for better or worse. And the problem with egalitarianism is that the link between equality and benefits is purely contingent. However, in order for the idea that outcome values are tied to values for individuals to support the Levelling Down Objection, clearly this idea must be spelled out in greater detail. It is fine to say that outcome values depend *crucially* on values for individuals, but unless we are able to specify the nature of the relation with greater precision, we will not be able to tell just how supportive of the Levelling Down Objection this idea is.

Clearly, this is a point the egalitarian may want to press. He may argue that the sort of relation between outcome values and benefits we must assume does not stand up to closer scrutiny. In fact, this is exactly the strategy employed by Larry Temkin. Temkin suggests that the Levelling Down Objection presupposes a principle he calls the 'Slogan'. According to the Slogan: 'One situation *cannot* be worse (or better) than another *in any respect* if there is *no one* for whom it *is* worse (or better) *in any respect*' (Temkin 1993*a*: 256). Or, to put it slightly differently, the objection presupposes

> *The Strong Narrow Person-Affecting Principle.* An outcome, O_1, cannot *in any respect* be better (worse) than another outcome, O_2, if there is no one for whom O_1 is *in any respect* better (worse) than O_2.

Obviously, this principle implies that there is no value to be found in levelling down. Since, in Figure 5.2, B is not better than A for anyone in any respect, it cannot be better in any respect.[16] So, equality cannot be a value that renders an outcome better than another in even one respect.

However, Temkin believes that the Strong Narrow Person-Affecting Principle is implausible. One of his reasons is that he takes it to be incompatible with various moral ideals such as autonomy, freedom, and proportional justice (1993*a*: 258–77). But in the present context of axiological welfarism, we need not worry about this. After all, none of these ideals is a function merely of welfare.[17] Another of his reasons for considering the Strong Narrow Person-Affecting Principle implausible is, however, highly relevant. This principle gets us into trouble when applied to the Non-Identity Problem. Consider Figure 5.3. *p*, we may suppose, is a group of people who presently exist. The people in this group may adopt the 'live for today policy', which involves having their children immediately and depleting natural resources for current uses.

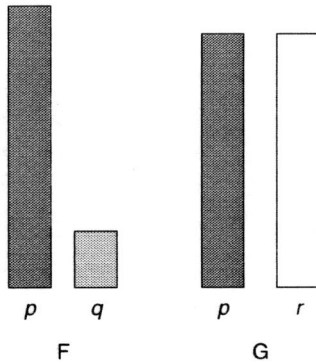

FIG. 5.3 The Non-Identity Problem.

---

[16] Strictly speaking, the people who are worse off in A might be in some respect better off in B than in A but not better off all things considered. For simplicity, however, let us assume that whenever a group is not better off in one outcome than in another, all things considered, then it is not in any respect better off.

[17] In Holtug (2003*a*), I consider this reason of Temkin's in greater detail. And Temkin responds in Temkin (2003*c*).

In that case, F would occur: they would enjoy a great many benefits, but their children would enjoy far less. Or they may adopt the 'take care of tomorrow policy', which involves waiting a few years before they have children, thus conserving some of the resources. The children they would then have are numerically different from those they would have in F. Furthermore, with the 'take care of tomorrow policy', these presently existing people would be slightly worse off, but their children would be much better off than their children would be in F. In other words, G would result (for this particular version of the Non-Identity Problem, see Temkin 1993a: 255–6).

Clearly, F is worse than G. However, Temkin argues that according to the Strong Narrow Person-Affecting Principle it cannot be.[18] According to this principle, in order for F to be worse in even one respect, there must be someone for whom it is worse in at least one respect. And, according to Temkin, there is none. Clearly, F is not worse for *p*. Nor is it worse for *q*. This group has lives worth living and would not exist if G came about. Finally, Temkin argues that F is not worse for *r*, since if F obtains, *r* does not exist and so cannot be worse off. As he puts it: 'one cannot harm or act against the interests of someone who will never exist and, more particularly, one does not harm someone by failing to conceive her' (Temkin 1993a: 255).

Nevertheless, since it seems fairly clear that F *is* worse than G, we should reject the Strong Narrow Person-Affecting Principle. And then this principle cannot support the Levelling Down Objection. Thus far, I agree with Temkin. However, it seems to me that the proper response to the Non-Identity Problem is not to abandon a person-affecting account of the value of outcomes, but to opt for a *wide* person-affecting account. Thus, I propose

> *The Strong Wide Person-Affecting Principle.* An outcome, O_1, cannot *in any respect* be better (worse) than another outcome, O_2, if there is no one for whom, were O_1 to obtain, O_1 would be *in any respect* better (worse) than O_2 and no one for whom, were O_2 to obtain, O_2 would be *in any respect* worse (better) than O_1.[19]

This principle allows us to claim that F is worse than G if G would be better for some, were it to obtain. And it may be argued that, if G were to obtain, then this would be better for *r*. This does not contradict Temkin's claim that 'one cannot harm or act against the interests of someone who will never exist'. Rather, since *r* exists in G, these individuals can have properties there, including the property of being

[18] Strictly speaking, what Temkin says is this: 'Most believe that the "take care of tomorrow policy" should be adopted. But this is incompatible with [the Narrow Person-Affecting Principle] . . . ' (Temkin 1993a: 255). However, this principle is in fact quite compatible with the claim that the 'take care of tomorrow policy' should be adopted. After all, there is more to morality than axiology. Thus, perhaps the 'live for today policy' would be wrong, even if it would be worse for no one.

[19] See also Holtug (1998: 17; 2003a: 8). My wording of a principle similar to this in Holtug (1998) was unfortunate, as Glen Newey has pointed out.

better off than in F. More precisely, if G obtains, the triadic relation—G is better for *r* than F—may also obtain. Obviously, if G obtains, then the first two relata obtain and while the third relatum does not obtain, the non-obtaining of an outcome does not prevent it from figuring in a betterness relation (if it did, then the relation 'the outcome that the allies win the war is better than the outcome that the Nazis win the war' could not obtain either).[20] Therefore, G can be better for *r* than F, and so the Strong Wide Person-Affecting Principle is compatible with the claim that F is worse than G.[21]

Furthermore, the Strong Wide Person-Affecting Principle implies that it cannot be in any respect better to level down. Consider Figure 5.2 once more. B cannot in any respect be better than A since, were B to obtain, there would be no one for whom, in any respect, this outcome would be better than A and, were A to obtain, there would be no one for whom this outcome, in any respect, would be worse than B.

Since, then, the Strong Wide Person-Affecting Principle implies that there is no value to be found in levelling down, Temkin's claim that the Levelling Down Objection presupposes the Strong Narrow Person-Affecting Principle cannot be correct. Since, furthermore, the Strong Wide Person-Affecting Principle does not get us into trouble with the Non-Identity Problem, it seems to be just the principle needed to meet Temkin's objection (see also Holtug 1998, 2003*a*). Incidentally, Temkin has recently acknowledged both that the Strong Wide Person-Affecting Principle can be invoked to support the Levelling Down Objection and that it handles the Non-Identity Problem (Temkin 2003*b*: 74).

Furthermore, prioritarianism does not contradict the Strong Wide Person-Affecting Principle. In order for prioritarianism to imply that an outcome is intrinsically better than another, in any respect or all things considered, it would have to be better for someone, were it to obtain, or the other outcome would have to be worse for someone, were that outcome to obtain. Therefore, the Strong Wide Person-Affecting Principle enables the prioritarian to provide support for the Levelling Down Objection in a manner that is quite consistent with her own commitments.[22]

[20] For a much more elaborate argument to the effect that existence can be better for an individual than never existing, see Holtug (2001).

[21] Unlike the Strong Narrow Person-Affecting Principle, the Strong Wide Person-Affecting Principle also allows us to avoid what I call the Problem of Suffering; see Holtug (1998: 170).

[22] Note, however, that since some prioritarians may hold prioritarianism partly in virtue of egalitarian concerns, some prioritarians may hold views that do not satisfy the Strong Wide Person-Affecting Principle. Furthermore, while Outcome Welfare Prioritarianism satisfies the Strong Wide Person-Affecting Principle, if we combine this principle and other concerns, the resulting principle *need* not satisfy it. For instance, someone may want to combine prioritarian and egalitarian concerns, and such a combined principle will, obviously, not satisfy the Strong Wide Person-Affecting Principle. (Temkin and Tungodden both seem to accept such a combined view, see Temkin 1993*a*: 24 and Tungodden 2003: 26.)

6. Impersonal and Person-Affecting Values

While prioritarianism is thus compatible with the Strong Wide Person-Affecting Principle, there is nevertheless a sense in which it is not a person-affecting principle. It implies that a benefit of a fixed size has a higher moral value if it falls at a low level of welfare than if it falls at a high level. But this extra value that is realised at the low level is not a value *for anyone*. Thus, prioritarians seem committed to the existence of impersonal values (see also Persson 2001: 28−9; Temkin 2000: 151−3).

What I have suggested is that what prioritarians ascribe intrinsic value to is compound states of affairs, each consisting in the state that a benefit of a certain size befalls an individual and the state that she is at a particular welfare level. Obviously, both these constituent states concern individual welfare.[23] But when we focus on the *size* of the intrinsic value ascribed to the compound state, we realise that it includes an impersonal element. The difference in value between a compound state that includes a lower welfare level, at which a benefit falls, and a compound state that includes a higher welfare level, at which an equal benefit falls, is not a difference in value for anyone. And, of course, it is the fact that equal benefits can give rise to unequal values that makes it possible for the prioritarian to give priority to the worse off.[24]

While prioritarians are thus committed to the existence of an impersonal element in intrinsic value, they are not committed to the existence of intrinsic values that contain *only* impersonal elements. In fact, they are committed to the claim that if an outcome is intrinsically better than another, then, compared to this other outcome, the better outcome *necessarily* includes improvements in individual welfare. In this respect, prioritarians differ from egalitarians. Egalitarians are committed to the intrinsic value of states of affairs that are only contingently linked to welfare improvements, namely states of equality.

---

[23] I do not mean to suggest that prioritarians cannot ascribe intrinsic value to anything but the compound states of affairs under consideration. For instance, they may hold that besides such compound states, one of the constituents, namely the state that a benefit of a certain size befalls an individual, has intrinsic value. This would explain why they are concerned with the *welfare* of the worse off. My point here is merely that, *qua* prioritarians, they ascribe intrinsic value only to the compound state of affairs.

[24] However, Dennis McKerlie has suggested a different account of prioritarianism that does not assign impersonal value to benefits (personal communication). He suggests that an equal gain in the lives of two individuals may have an unequal impact on the value of their lives and that this is what is reflected in the judgement that benefits at lower levels have more value than benefits at higher levels. This account relies on a distinction between a gain in welfare and its contribution to the value of the life in which it occurs and I am not quite sure how this distinction should be made. Also, it is incompatible with the claim that increases in life-value that fall at lower levels should have priority and this is a claim that some prioritarians will want to make.

Nevertheless, does the impersonal element in prioritarianism somehow compromise this position? Prioritarianism, as Ingmar Persson points out, is incompatible with the following principle (2001: 28):

The Person-Affecting Improvement Principle. If an outcome, O_1, is in some respect better (worse) than another outcome, O_2, then the betterness (worseness) of O_1 for some (collective) is greater than the betterness (worseness) of O_2 is for any (collective).

This principle provides a much stronger link between outcome values and individual welfare than does the Strong Wide Person-Affecting Principle. It links the value of outcomes to the *size* of benefits. Consider the two outcomes in Figure 5.4 (where the slashed line represents the average level of welfare in both H and I). Prioritarians and egalitarians will hold that I is better than H, but this judgement is ruled out by the Person-Affecting Improvement Principle. There is no individual or group of individuals for whom I is better to a greater extent than H is better for any individual or group. Thus, while I is better for q, H is to the same extent better for p. More precisely, the sum of benefits that accrues to q when we go from H to I equals the sum of benefits that accrues to p when we go from I to H.

In fact, the Person-Affecting Improvement Principle implies that just as I cannot be better than H, H cannot be better than I. More generally, while it does not directly imply axiological utilitarianism, it is closely related to this principle.

Now, Persson's point is that since prioritarianism is incompatible with the Person-Affecting Improvement Principle, the prioritarian cannot invoke this principle in defence of the Strong Wide Person-Affecting Principle. Thus, the prioritarian will have to reject what is a conclusive reason for accepting the latter principle.[25] And the

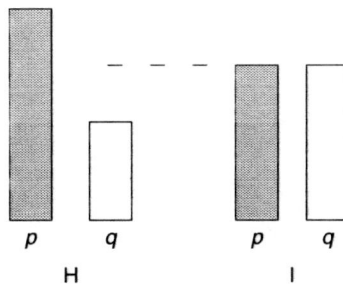

FIG. 5.4

[25] Persson (2001: 29). Strictly speaking, Persson does not consider the Strong Wide Person-Affecting Principle, but a principle similar to the Slogan. As we have seen, the Strong Wide Person-Affecting Principle is a revised version of the Slogan that allows us to reach the right answer when applied to the Non-Identity Problem. Furthermore, while the Person-Affecting Improvement Principle does imply the Strong Wide Person-Affecting Principle, the former principle gets us into trouble with the Non-Identity

Strong Wide Person-Affecting Principle, of course, is what is supposed to explain at least part of the force of the Levelling Down Objection.

However, it seems to me that the Strong Wide Person-Affecting Principle is quite capable of standing on its own when explicating the force of the Levelling Down Objection. I have suggested that this objection trades on the fact that, in egalitarianism, the link between outcome value and improvements in welfare is entirely *contingent*. In other words, one problem with egalitarianism is that equality can be improved in the absence of increases in welfare. And as I have pointed out, this is exactly the feature that is ruled out by the Strong Wide Person-Affecting Principle. This principle claims that an outcome cannot be improved in any respect in the absence of increases in welfare. Therefore, the Strong Wide Person-Affecting Principle provides a plausible diagnosis of (at least part of) what is troubling about levelling down. And so prioritarians do not need to invoke the Person-Affecting Improvement Principle to defend their commitment to the Strong Wide Person-Affecting Principle.

Now, Temkin suggests that there is in fact a stronger relation to be found between the Strong Wide Person-Affecting Principle and the Person-Affecting Improvement Principle—a relation that I have so far ignored. He claims that reflections on these two principles suggest that those who are attracted to the former should also be attracted to the latter, and that those who reject the latter should also reject the former (Temkin 2000: 152). Hence, since prioritarians reject the Person-Affecting Improvement Principle, they should also reject the Strong Wide Person-Affecting Principle.

However, I have argued that the relation between these two principles is not as strong as suggested by Temkin. A prioritarian may have reasons to hold the Strong Wide Person-Affecting Principle that are quite independent of the Person-Affecting Improvement Principle. For instance, she may hold the former principle because it nicely explains her worries about levelling down as well as about various values that can be realised in the absence of increases in welfare. For instance, it nicely explains the view that there is no value to be found in, say, respecting people's rights or the flourishing of ecological systems in cases where it benefits no one.[26] And worries about such values need not hinge on the Person-Affecting Improvement Principle.

In conclusion, prioritarianism not only avoids the Levelling Down Objection, it fully accommodates both the concerns from which this objection derives its force.

Problem and does so for the same reason as does the Slogan. Nevertheless, although I shall not elaborate on this point here, the Person-Affecting Improvement Principle can be revised along the lines of the Strong Wide Person-Affecting Principle, such as to avoid these problems *and* imply this principle.

[26] For an extensive list of arguments in which a principle such as the Strong Wide Person-Affecting Principle seems to be implicitly invoked, see Temkin (1993a: 249–55).

7. Relational Justice

I have now argued that prioritarianism handles levelling down cases better than does egalitarianism. This, I believe, gives us a reason to prefer the former view to the latter, although this reason is not conclusive. Nevertheless, it may be suggested that there are also important aspects of our moral thinking that would be lost if we were to abandon egalitarianism in favour of prioritarianism. Thus, Temkin invites us to consider the following case of a 'typical' poor person in the United States:

Ruth is not wretched, but she is a single parent of four, works at two jobs, drives an old car, wonders how she will meet the payments on her two bedroom apartment, and has no idea how her children will afford college on her $20,000 income. Many are deeply moved by the plight of people like Ruth in a land where *so* many others live in half million dollar homes, own fancy new cars, send their children to private schools, take expensive vacations, and have annual household incomes well over $100,000. Is it not clear that the extent to which many are moved by Ruth's situation is heavily influenced not merely by how she fares in *absolute* terms, but by how she fares *relative to the other members of her extraordinarily well-off society*? (Temkin 2003*b*: 70)

If I understand him correctly, Temkin's point is that the motivational pull Ruth exercises on us is so strong in part because she lives in a society where so many people are much better off than she is. Had her circumstances been the same, but everyone else been much worse off than she is, then we would not have been equally motivated to help her (Temkin 2003*b*: 70−1).

I am inclined to think that Temkin is right about this. But the question is whether it really shows that, in our moral thinking, we are committed to the value of equality. Let me point to two other features that may help explain our motivational patterns in this sort of case. First, since we are told that there are people (indeed, many of them) who are much better off than Ruth, we tend to focus on how grand it must be for them to be this well off. Being presented with the further details of such lives (half million dollar homes, fancy new cars, etc.), we imagine this rather vividly! We then think of poor old Ruth, worried sick about how to make ends meet, and imagine how grand it would be if *she* were this well off.

If, on the other hand, we are presented with a case in which Ruth is better off than everyone else, we are not as inclined to focus on the sort of life the rich lead, and thus not as inclined to imagine what it would be like for Ruth to lead such a life. Nevertheless, if someone were to prompt us to vividly imagine how nice such a life would be for Ruth (not having to worry about house and car payments, education for her kids, etc.), arguably, the thought of helping Ruth would start to exercise a greater pull on us. The point, of course, is that this explanation of the difference in motivational pull in the two cases does not rely on the thought that *equality* matters.

Second, and more importantly, motivational pulls may have a tendency to weaken when they are confronted with stronger motivational pulls. By way of illustration, suppose that I feel like having a drink and happen to remember that there is an ice-cold beer in the fridge. Strongly motivated, I open the fridge. I then notice that sitting on the shelf just next to the beer is a delicious bottle of Chardonnay. Realising that I would much rather have the wine, my motivation to have the beer instantly drops. However, it then hits me that the wine is for the guests I am having over. Slightly annoyed, I grab the beer. I know that I shall not enjoy *the beer* any less just because I cannot have the wine, but my motivation to have it has nevertheless dropped. I cannot help thinking of the wine I could have had instead.

Now consider the situation of Ruth. Since Ruth is worse off than most others, she is, if not first in line, then at least in the front part of the queue with respect to whom we most want to help. As prioritarians, we have a stronger urge to help her than we have to help all those who are better off than she is. So, in terms of our motivation in this case, she does not face much superior competition. If, instead, we imagine that Ruth is better off than everyone else, she is no longer in the front part of the queue. Rather, she is now at the very back. And so, in terms of our motivation to help, she does indeed face superior competition, and lots of it. Therefore, even if she is the only person we *can* help, we may be less motivated to do so. Not because we believe that it is morally less important to help her than it was in the former case, but because we cannot help thinking of how much *better* it would be if we could help some of those people who are much more unfortunate than she is. Importantly, this explanation of our motivational structure does not rely on the thought that *equality* matters, but merely on the thought that priority does.

I do not mean to suggest that the account of our motivational patterns I have just sketched is clearly right and that Temkin's is clearly wrong. In fact, it seems to me that it would be difficult to determine which explanation is best. Nevertheless, I believe that I have provided a somewhat plausible alternative explanation. And the fact that such an explanation can be given weakens Temkin's case for claiming that, in our moral thinking, we are committed to the value of equality.[27]

---

[27] However, perhaps Temkin is not appealing to our *motivations* but to our *reasons* to help Ruth. Perhaps he takes us to believe that there is a stronger reason to help Ruth if she is worse off than most others than if she is better off than most others. But it is not clear to me that this is what we (or most of us) believe. Alternatively, we may believe that whereas the reason to help Ruth does not change, this reason's relative position in our total pattern of reasons *does* change. That is, it may go from being one of our strongest moral reasons to being one of our weakest. Again, I do not want to claim that this account is superior to Temkin's; merely that it does not seem inferior.

8. Compassion

Let me now turn to a final objection to prioritarianism. According to this view, the worse off always have a higher priority than the better off, no matter how well off the worse off are. Roger Crisp has recently complained that this is implausible. He suggests that our concern for the worse off is based on the virtue of *compassion*. Furthermore, he suggests that our compassion is limited to individuals who are, in absolute terms, poorly off. Once an individual reaches a certain level of welfare, compassion runs out (Crisp 2003: 757).

To accommodate this point about compassion, Crisp proposes a principle with the following structure:

Outcome Welfare Sufficientarianism. An outcome is in one respect intrinsically better, the larger a sum of weighted individual benefits it contains, where benefits are weighted such that they (*a*) have zero-value when they fall at or above a specific threshold of individual welfare, *l*, and (*b*) have positive value when they fall below *l*, where this value decreases the closer to *l* they fall.

Outcome Welfare Sufficientarianism expresses the idea that benefits become increasingly less important, morally speaking, the better off an individual is, and that there is in fact some level of welfare where further benefits simply have no moral value at all. Of course, a benefit of a fixed size has the same value for the individual to whom it accrues no matter what level of welfare she is at, but its moral value decreases the better off she is. At some point, our compassion ceases and this is where the threshold is.[28] Graphically, this view can be represented as in Figure 5.5 (where the slashed line represents the welfare threshold). Note that this graph is similar to that of prioritarianism in Figure 5.1, up to the point where the threshold is reached (this first part of the curve is strictly concave). Thus, Outcome Welfare Sufficientarianism is in a sense prioritarianism, but with a narrower scope. But while intimately related to prioritarianism, Outcome Welfare Sufficientarianism nevertheless is not a version of prioritarianism as I have defined it. I have claimed that, in prioritarianism, priority has maximal scope.

It seems to me dubious that compassion runs out above a certain level of welfare.[29] Suppose that a given individual is at the threshold level. Let us assume, for the sake

---

[28] There are other proponents of the principle of Outcome Welfare Sufficientarianism, besides Crisp; see Frankfurt (1987); Rosenberg (1995); Tungodden (2003: 37–40). Frankfurt, it should be noted, is concerned with monetary rather than welfare priority.

[29] Perhaps I should qualify this claim. In the dictionary sense of 'compassion', compassion is a feeling directed at the *suffering* of others (see e.g. *The Oxford Advanced Learner's Dictionary of Current English*). If this is what we mean by 'compassion', clearly there are increases in welfare that cannot be objects of this virtue.

Moral outcome value

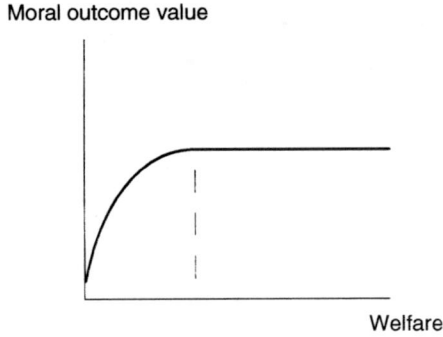

Welfare

Fig. 5.5

of argument, that this level is quite high. So she is quite well off. Suppose also that, owing to some (very fortunate) changes in the world economy, everyone else becomes much better off than she is. So everyone but her now has a life of extreme luxury and happiness. It seems to me that, in such a case, we would not only regret the fact that she was 'left behind', and so attach value to further benefits to her. We would in fact attach greater value to benefits to her than to (further) benefits to others. If we were in a position to redistribute, we would want to favour her, everything else being equal.[30]

Even, then, if we were to grant Crisp that compassion is at the heart of priority, we need not agree that there is a level at which compassion sets out. It seems to me more plausible to claim that our compassion is simply greater, the worse off an individual is. Given this, the virtue of compassion is better captured by prioritarianism.

Admittedly, when individuals are very well off, we may *feel* no compassion for them at all, but I suggest that this is because two potentially misleading features affect our emotions. One is that when some people are much worse off than others, we are inclined to focus only on *their* misfortune. However, when there are no such others to 'steal' our attention, we realise that our compassion reaches out even to those who are very well off. The other relevant feature is that what I am suggesting is that compassion is relative to welfare levels; we should thus not expect to feel a *great deal* of compassion for individuals who are doing very well with respect to welfare. In fact,

---

However, this conception of compassion cannot be what Crisp has in mind. After all, an individual need not actually *suffer* in order to have a low welfare level. Perhaps her life just consists of a few simple joys and nothing else.

[30] It may be objected that, in this example, it is the fact that she is now worse off *than others* that is doing the intuitive work. Therefore, I am appealing to egalitarian rather than prioritarian concerns. However, the fact of the matter is that both egalitarians and prioritarians can provide an explanation of why we should redistribute in this case, albeit different such explanations. What the presence of others who are *better* off does, for the prioritarian, is to push forward the worse-off individual in the queue with respect to whom it is most urgent to help.

when individuals are very well off, our compassion may be so reduced that it almost *seems* as if we have none. And when both of these two features are at work at once, we may *feel* no compassion at all.

Let me note a further worry about Crisp's account of distributive justice. Outcome Welfare Sufficientarianism does not assign any weight to benefits above the threshold. Therefore, it does not satisfy the Pareto Principle. In fact, it does not even satisfy the *Weak* Pareto Principle, according to which an outcome is better than another if it is better for everyone. After all, if everyone is at or above the threshold, Outcome Welfare Sufficientarianism does not assign any value to increases to anyone. So even if we could increase everyone's welfare level immensely, it would not make for a better outcome. Surely, this cannot be right.[31]

However, Outcome Welfare Sufficientarianism orders outcomes in one respect only and so may be combined with one or more other principles that do assign value to increases in welfare above the threshold. Along such lines, Crisp suggests that it should be combined with a version of axiological utilitarianism. On the resulting view, priority is given to increases in welfare below the threshold, whereas equal increases have equal value from the threshold up (Crisp 2003: 758). This view satisfies the (Strong *and* Weak) Pareto Principle.

Now, there are different ways in which the two principles can be combined. Crisp's suggestion is that non-trivial benefits below the threshold have absolute priority over benefits above the threshold (2003: 758–9). Presumably, the purpose of the requirement that benefits below the threshold should be *non-trivial* to have absolute priority is to rule out that even the *tiniest* benefits below outweigh even the *greatest* benefits above. And indeed, such an implication would be implausible. However, if one is troubled by the claim that trivial benefits below have absolute priority over huge benefits above, then why think that it completely changes the picture if we substitute 'non-trivial' for 'trivial' benefits in this claim? The difference between a trivial and a non-trivial benefit may be very slight indeed.

In reply to this objection, perhaps it may be suggested that the notions of 'trivial' and 'non-trivial' benefits appealed to here are vague. Thus, if we have a spectrum that covers all the possible sizes a benefit may have, there is a range in which it is neither determinately true that the benefits are trivial, nor determinately true that they are non-trivial. And so, between the largest (determinately) trivial and the smallest (determinately) non-trivial benefit there is a range of indeterminacy. Owing

---

[31] Nevertheless, perhaps Frankfurt endorses such a view. He claims that 'We tend to be quite unmoved, after all, by inequalities between the well-to-do and the rich; our awareness that the former are substantially worse off than the latter does not disturb us morally at all' (Frankfurt 1987: 32). While, in this passage, Frankfurt addresses only *inequalities* above the threshold, perhaps his concern (or the lack thereof) for the well off can be generalised. At least, he does not in any way suggest that benefits above the threshold matter morally.

to this range of indeterminacy the difference between the two benefits in question cannot be too slight. Accordingly, it may seem less awkward that although a trivial benefit below the threshold does not have absolute priority over even the greatest benefit above, a non-trivial benefit below still does have just that.

However, this reply introduces a new problem, namely what to say about trade-offs between benefits in the indeterminacy range that fall below the threshold and benefits above the threshold. Do indeterminate benefits below have absolute priority over benefits above? If we answer yes, then our original problem reappears at another level: while the largest possible trivial benefit below the threshold does not have absolute priority over benefits above, a slightly bigger benefit in the indeterminacy range does. If, on the other hand, we answer no, then the original problem again reappears. The largest possible benefit in the indeterminacy range that falls below the threshold does not have absolute priority over benefits above, even though a slightly greater non-trivial benefit below the threshold does have such priority.

Perhaps, then, it is better to say that it is neither determinately true nor determinately false that benefits in the indeterminacy range that fall below the threshold have absolute priority over benefits above. However, this leaves us with the problem that Crisp's combined principle does not always provide us with determinate answers, not because the empirical reality to which it is applied is complex, but for purely theoretical reasons. Of course, if the indeterminacy range is rather narrow, so is the range of cases in which the principle does not yield determinate answers. But if the indeterminacy range is narrow, then the difference between (determinately) trivial and (determinately) non-trivial benefits is correspondingly slight. Thus, again, it may seem strange that while a non-trivial benefit below the threshold has absolute priority over benefits above, a trivial benefit below does not.

I also have another worry about Crisp's suggestion. Consider the following outcomes (the numbers represent individual welfare levels):

J: (8, 100) L: (8, 8, 8, 8, 8, 100)

K: (10, 10) M: (9.9, 9.9, 9.9, 9.9, 9.9, 10)

Assume that the threshold level is 10 and that an increase in welfare has to contain at least two units in order to amount to a non-trivial benefit. Clearly, then, Crisp's principle implies that K is better than J. After all, in the move from J to K, there is a (non-trivial) gain of two welfare units for the first individual, which falls below the threshold. Therefore, it has absolute priority over the loss of 90 units by the second individual above the threshold. Now consider L and M. Intuitively, it would seem that if K is better than J, then M is better than L. After all, in the move from L to M *five* people each gain *almost* as much as *one* person does in the move from J to K, whereas one person loses 90 units in both moves. However, Crisp's principle does not entail that M is better than L. In fact, it says nothing about how to compare them.

Crisp may of course invoke the utilitarian element in his principle to deal with trivial benefits below the threshold, but note that L has a higher total of welfare than M does, entailing that this utilitarian element cannot explain why M should be better.

Finally, since it implies that equal benefits above the threshold have equal value, Crisp's account remains at variance with at least my intuitions about conflicts above the threshold. Consider Figure 5.6 (where the slashed line represents the average level of welfare in N and O, and the continuous line represents the welfare threshold). Suppose that the differences between the two groups do not in any way correspond to differences in desert or responsibility. In N, the first group just happens to be much luckier than the second group, although the second group is itself quite well off. In their forests, the first group has discovered some very special fruit trees. The fruits contain vitamins that not only vastly increase people's health, but also allow them to live, say, 200 years. Having heard the good news, the second group has searched their forests but only to find that they have not been blessed with any of those marvellous trees.

Nevertheless, the first group could decide to share their fruits with the second group. Unfortunately, there are not enough fruits such that both groups can obtain the maximal effect of the vitamins. But even so, if the fruits were shared equally, both groups would experience a significant increase in welfare (perhaps the individuals in both groups would experience some improvements in their health and live, say, 120 years). In fact, the increase that would be experienced by the second group would exactly equal the loss that would be experienced by the first group. In other words, if the fruits were shared equally, O would result.

Now, according to Crisp's account, N and O are equally good. This is because, above the threshold, an extra unit of welfare always counts the same. However, intuitively, O seems to be better than N. Indeed, I suggest that O is better for the same reason that an equal distribution of a particular sum is better below the threshold. Welfare matters more at lower levels. All in all, then, it seems to me that prioritarianism will handle cases of conflict both across and above the threshold better than Crisp's account.

Crisp has, in response to my fruit tree scenario, argued that if we are inclined to prefer O to N, then it just shows that the threshold has been set too low (personal communication). Thus, had the more unfortunate group in N been at a suitably *high*

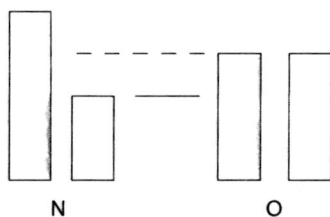

N   O

FIG. 5.6

level of welfare, we would no longer be inclined to believe that it would be better to distribute the fruits equally. In fact, no matter where we place the threshold, Crisp may reply that if we take an equal distribution above the threshold to be better, this is because the threshold is still too low.

I have some worries about this line of argument. First, the proponent of sufficient-arianism cannot just dismiss cases in which this principle seems to have implausible implications by saying that the threshold has been set too low. Surely it is up to him to point to a threshold and tell us why it is plausible.

Second, it seems to me that the fruit tree scenario contradicts Crisp's suggestion even at very high levels. Suppose that everyone in N lives for at least 10,000 years but that the lucky first group gets an additional 10,000 years. In O, on the other hand, the welfare is more evenly spread out, since each group gets an equal share of the fruits. Suppose also that N is the actual outcome. It seems to me that, standing at the end of their lives and yearning for more excellent years to live, the second group may reasonably claim that it would be fairer and better if the first group had shared their fruits with them. Why should *they* (the second group) have to die when there is an alternative outcome in which *everyone* has, say, 3,000 happy years ahead of them (with no loss in total welfare)?

Finally, it is worth pointing out that if the threshold is set at a sufficiently high level, sufficientarianism will have no distinct practical significance whatsoever. If, say, the threshold is reached only after 200 years of pure ecstasy, no one will ever be above the threshold and so, for all practical purposes, sufficientarianism will coincide with prioritarianism. It may be replied that, for practical purposes, prioritarianism does not differ much from utilitarianism either, and that a prioritarian would therefore be ill advised to push this point too far. However, it is hardly obvious that prioritarianism and utilitarianism do not differ much on a practical level. Furthermore, if they do not, this will primarily be because it is very difficult to assess welfare precisely and so to know where utilitarianism and prioritarianism come apart in their practical recommendations. The practical implications of sufficientarianism, on the other hand, would coincide with the practical implications of prioritarianism even if we had full knowledge of the possible welfare distributions.

9. Conclusion

I have provided an account of the distinction between egalitarianism and prioritari-anism and argued that it renders the former but not the latter principle vulnerable to the Levelling Down Objection. I have also suggested that there are two distinct concerns from which this objection derives its force and that prioritarianism, unlike egalitarianism, is compatible with both of them. This, I have suggested, gives us a reason to consider prioritarianism superior to egalitarianism, albeit not a conclusive reason.

Nevertheless, it has been suggested that there are important aspects of our moral thinking concerning relational justice that would be lost if we were to abandon egalitarianism in favour of prioritarianism. However, I have suggested that these aspects are in fact explained equally well in prioritarian terms. Finally, I have considered the suggestion that priority is based on the virtue of compassion, and that we only have compassion for individuals who are, in absolute terms, poorly off. Against this I have argued that there is no such limit to compassion and pointed to some further problems with this suggestion.

Thus, I have defended prioritarianism against various objections. And in the process of doing so, I have suggested that prioritarianism is superior to egalitarianism. However, I have not provided anything like a positive case for prioritarianism. So, for all I have said, prioritarianism may be more plausible than egalitarianism and yet not plausible enough to be justifiable. Nevertheless, many political theorists are attracted to views that favour redistributing welfare from the better off to the worse off and, if my arguments are sound, perhaps these theorists should go for priority rather than equality.

References

ARNESON, R. J. (2000), 'Luck Egalitarianism and Prioritarianism', *Ethics*, 110/2: 339–49.

BARRY, B. (1989), *Theories of Justice* (Berkeley: University of California Press).

BLACKORBY, C., DONALDSON, D., and WEYMARK, J. A. (1984), 'Social Choice with Interpersonal Utility Comparisons: A Diagrammatic Introduction', *International Economic Review*, 25/2: 327–56.

BROOME, J. (1991), *Weighing Goods* (Oxford: Basil Blackwell).

—— (forthcoming), 'Equality Versus Priority: A Useful Distinction', in D. Wickler and C. J. L. Murray (eds.), *'Goodness' and 'Fairness': Ethical Issues in Health Resource Allocation* (World Health Organization).

BROWN, C. (2003), 'Giving Up Levelling Down', *Economics and Philosophy*, 19/1: 111–34.

CRISP, R. (2003), 'Equality, Priority, and Compassion', *Ethics*, 113/4: 745–63.

FLEURBAEY, M. (forthcoming), 'Equality Versus Priority: How Relevant Is the Distinction?', in D. Wickler and C. J. L. Murray (eds.), *'Goodness' and 'Fairness': Ethical Issues in Health Resource Allocation* (World Health Organization).

FRANKFURT, H. (1987), 'Equality as a Moral Ideal', *Ethics*, 98/1: 21–43.

HAUSMAN, D. M. (forthcoming), 'Equality Versus Priority: A Badly Misleading Distinction', in D. Wickler and C. J. L. Murray (eds.), *'Goodness' and 'Fairness': Ethical Issues in Health Resource Allocation* (World Health Organization).

HOLTUG, N. (1998), 'Egalitarianism and the Levelling Down Objection', *Analysis*, 58/2: 166–74.

HOLTUG, N. (1999), 'Utility, Priority and Possible People', *Utilitas*, 11/1: 16–36.

_____ (2001), 'On the Value of Coming into Existence', *Journal of Ethics*. 5/4: 361–84.

_____ (2003a), 'Good for Whom?', *Theoria*, 69/1–2: 4–20.

_____ (2003b), 'Welfarism—the Very Idea', *Utilitas*, 15/2: 151–74.

_____ (forthcoming), 'Equality, Priority and Levelling Down', *International Journal of Ethics*.

HOOKER, B. (2000), *Ideal Code, Real World* (Oxford: Clarendon Press).

JENSEN, K. K. (2003), 'What Is the Difference Between (Moderate) Egalitarianism and Prioritarianism?', *Economics and Philosophy*, 19/1: 89–109.

KYMLICKA, W. (1990), *Contemporary Political Philosophy* (Oxford: Clarendon Press).

McKERLIE, D. (1994), 'Equality and Priority', *Utilitas*, 6/1: 25–42.

_____ (1996), 'Equality', *Ethics*, 106/2: 274–96.

_____ (1997), 'Priority and Time', *Canadian Journal of Philosophy*, 27/3: 287–309.

_____ (2003), 'Understanding Egalitarianism', *Economics and Philosophy*, 19/1: 45–60.

NAGEL, T. (1991), *Equality and Priority* (New York: Oxford University Press).

NG, Y.-K. (1990), 'Welfarism and Utilitarianism: A Rehabilitation', *Utilitas*, 2/2: 171–93.

PARFIT, D. (1984), *Reasons and Persons* (Oxford: Clarendon Press).

_____ (1991), *Equality or Priority?* The Lindley Lecture (Lawrence: University of Kansas).

PERSSON, I. (2001), 'Equality, Priority and Person-Affecting Value', *Ethical Theory and Moral Practice*, 4/1: 23–39.

RAZ, J. (1986), *The Morality of Freedom* (Oxford: Oxford University Press).

ROSENBERG, A. (1995), 'Equality, Sufficiency, and Opportunity in the Just Society', *Social Philosophy and Policy*, 12/2: 54–71.

SCANLON, T. M. (1982), 'Contractualism and Utilitarianism', in A. Sen and B. Williams (eds.), *Utilitarianism and Beyond* (Cambridge: Cambridge University Press), 103–28.

SCHEFFLER, S. (1982), *The Rejection of Consequentialism* (Oxford: Clarendon Press).

SEN, A. (1987), *On Ethics and Economics* (Oxford: Basil Blackwell).

TEMKIN, L. S. (1993a), *Inequality* (New York: Oxford University Press).

_____ (1993b), 'Harmful Goods, Harmless Bads', in R. G. Frey and C. W. Morris (eds.), *Value, Welfare, and Morality* (Cambridge: Cambridge University Press), 290–324.

_____ (2000), 'Equality, Priority, and the Levelling Down Objection', in M. Clayton and A. Williams (eds.), *The Ideal of Equality* (London: Macmillan), 126–61.

_____ (2003a), 'Egalitarianism Defended', *Ethics*, 113/4: 764–82.

_____ (2003b), 'Equality, Priority or What?', *Economics and Philosophy*, 19/1: 61–87.

_____ (2003c), 'Personal Versus Impersonal Principles: Reconsidering the Slogan', *Theoria*, 69/1–2: 21–31.

TUNGODDEN, B. (2003), 'The Value of Equality', *Economics and Philosophy*, 19/1: 1–44.

VALLENTYNE, P. (2000), 'Equality, Efficiency, and the Priority of the Worse Off', *Economics and Philosophy*, 16/1: 1–19.

WEIRICH, P. (1983), 'Utility Tempered with Equality', *Noûs*, 17/3: 423–39.

6

Egalitarianism and the Difference Between Interpersonal and Intrapersonal Judgments

Dennis McKerlie

1. Introduction

Egalitarianism came into its own as a moral theory during the 1970s. The most important factor was the publication of John Rawls's *A Theory of Justice* (1971), but writers like Thomas Nagel (1970, 1979), Ronald Dworkin (1977), and Thomas Scanlon (1976, 1982) also made valuable contributions. This school of writers produced worked-out egalitarian moral theories, theories that sometimes differed significantly in their content. But apart from the differences, these writers tended to share certain ideas about the source or the starting point of egalitarianism. At the deepest level, they tended to say the same things about egalitarian distributional constraints.

One shared idea was that egalitarianism involves, and perhaps depends on, there being a fundamental difference between interpersonal judgments and intrapersonal judgments. Interpersonal judgments distribute benefits and harms (for the sake of simplicity I will assume that benefits and harms, or increases and decreases in well-being, are the currency of egalitarianism, not resources or opportunities or capacities) between different people and so across different lives. Intrapersonal judgments distribute benefits and harms inside one life, a life led by a single self-identical person.

I would like to thank Nils Holtug and Kasper Lippert-Rasmussen for helpful comments on earlier versions of this chapter.

The shared thought held that intrapersonal judgments are governed by a maximizing principle. When we are dealing with a single person, we should only be concerned with achieving the greatest possible surplus of benefits over harms, regardless of how those benefits and harms would be distributed inside the person's life from its beginning to its end. Prudential rationality on the part of the person whose life it is, and benevolent moral concern on the part of someone else acting in that person's best interest, agree in pursuing this goal.

By contrast, interpersonal judgments are not governed by a maximizing principle. We should not simply aim at bringing about the greatest possible surplus of benefits over harms when the benefits and harms in question will be experienced by different people. Just because we are dealing with different lives, distributional constraints apply to this choice. These constraints will be expressed by the principle of equality itself, which might of course be interpreted in different ways and might be assigned different degrees of strength when it is weighed against other moral values.

The writers tended to offer the same further explanation of this shared thought. They suggested that if a benefit and harm occur in the same life, and the benefit is greater than the harm, then the benefit morally outweighs the harm. It is better for the person to experience both than to experience neither. However, if the harm and benefit will be received by different people, the greater benefit might not morally outweigh the lesser harm. It is not necessarily better for one person to experience the harm and the other person to experience the benefit than for neither person to be benefited or harmed. The writers said that it is the moral importance of the so-called 'separateness of persons' that can prevent the benefit from outweighing the harm.[1] In the interpersonal case the two individuals are separate persons with separate lives, while in the intrapersonal case there is only a single person and one life, so nothing prevents the benefit from outweighing the harm.[2]

---

[1] Some egalitarians believed that the separateness of persons led initially to a moral position that was distinct from the egalitarian distributive principle itself, for example the view that benefits or harms in one life could never morally outweigh benefits or harms in a different life. They suggested that the egalitarian distributive principle could be derived from this moral position. This is to suppose that the moral importance of the separateness of persons can be used as a premise in an argument for the value of equality. For criticisms of such an argument, see Brink (1993) and McKerlie (1988).

[2] Thomas Nagel comments that the fact that benefits can outweigh harms inside a life does not by itself give us a reason to think that benefits do not outweigh harms across lives—that is, maximizing in intrapersonal cases does not positively support accepting egalitarianism in interpersonal cases (1979: 120). I agree. The contrast between intrapersonal judgments and interpersonal judgments is central to egalitarianism because, once we have agreed that intrapersonal judgments are governed by a maximizing principle, we must think that interpersonal judgments are fundamentally different from intrapersonal judgments if we are to be egalitarians.

I will call these ideas the 'standard egalitarian view'. Offering these ideas as an explanation of egalitarian moral concern has certain consequences. The price of defending the existence of egalitarian distributional constraints between lives is conceding that there are no such distributional constraints inside lives. Of course this is a price that the egalitarians of the 1970s were not at all reluctant to pay. In addition—although people did not remark on this consequence at the time—the ideas will restrict the application of egalitarian principles to people's complete lifetimes. The concern for equality will turn out to be a concern for equality between people's complete lives when those lives are assessed from the cradle to the grave.

2. Equality Between Lifetimes

To see why this follows, suppose that there is a deep inequality at a particular time T_1 between A's life and B's life, an inequality that favours A. Can this inequality between two simultaneous temporal parts or temporal stages in two different lives itself generate a reason for trying to create equality between the two lives at T_1? Remember that we are supposing that benefits can outweigh harms over time inside lives if not across lives. It is possible that at some other time T_2 B's life might be better than A's life to exactly the same degree that A's life is better than B's at T_1. If that were the case then B's advantage or benefit at T_2 would outweigh or balance out B's disadvantage or harm at T_1. If there is such outweighing inside B's life it seems that B's harm or disadvantage at T_1 does not give us a reason to make B better off at T_1. After all, B's disadvantage at that time is already compensated for by his advantage at T_2, so B does not deserve extra compensation at T_1. So to decide whether to redistribute between A and B at T_1 we must check the rest of their lives for this kind of compensation. Essentially we have to compare the complete lives of A and B before we can decide whether to make an interpersonal judgment that there should be redistribution between them. This means that the concern for equality is a concern that their complete lives should be equally good. The temporal scope of egalitarian principles will be complete lifetimes.

Nevertheless, some have felt that there can be a case for a more equal distribution between temporal parts of lives. I was one of them, and I relied on intuitive judgments about particular examples to make this case (McKerlie 1989). In particular it seemed to me that there was something objectionable about allowing people who were old to live miserable lives while younger people were much better off. I thought this would remain objectionable even if this deep inequality in the present was compatible with their lives as temporal wholes being roughly equal. So I thought that there was a case for redistributing between the young and the old to reduce the current misery of the elderly, and I assumed that the case would be expressed by some principle concerned with equality. My aim was to state explicitly the most persuasive version of such a principle, so that its reasonableness could be assessed.

However, I did not want to abandon the ideas about the source of egalitarianism that I have already described. I continued to suppose that there were no distributional constraints applying inside lives—that is, in the case of the different temporal parts or stages of the same life there was no claim to equality between those parts. I thought that my task was to explain how there could nevertheless be distributional constraints applying between the temporal parts of different lives.

3. Equality Between Parts of Lives

The nature of the positive view I wanted to defend led naturally to a criticism of the most influential theory about justice between the young and the old or justice between age-groups, the prudential lifespan account developed by Norman Daniels (1988). This theory claims (roughly) that the social distribution between people of different ages or age-groups, if it is to be just or fair, should match the distribution that prudential rationality would choose when distributing over the different temporal stages inside a single life. If we divide people's lives into the three temporal stages of youth, middle age, and old age, the theory says that the fair distribution at a particular time between people who are young, people who are middle-aged, and people who are elderly should match the distribution prudence would prefer over the three temporal stages of youth, middle age, and old age. This theory uses a prudential diachronic judgment made about a single life as the criterion for a just synchronic distribution between different people, where the later distribution is essentially a distribution between the temporal parts of different lives.

I hope my criticism of this view will be obvious. The prudential judgment made about a single life will be a maximizing judgment. This is appropriate given that we agree that equality does not apply inside lives. But we are investigating the possibility that a requirement of equality might apply between the temporal parts of different lives. If we take that possibility seriously, the prudential judgment about a single life will be a dubious criterion of justice just because it is a maximizing judgment. Daniels regards the conclusions reached by the prudential lifespan account as judgments about fairness in distribution between temporal parts in lives that are independent of fairness between complete lives. If we think that distributional constraints applying to temporal stages in different lives do exist, why should we suppose that the constraints are expressed by a judgment that simply maximizes?

I have already explained the reasons why the standard egalitarian view seems to restrict us to caring about equality between lifetimes. I needed to answer these reasons to defend my positive view.

My attempt began by conceding that outweighing inside lives does indeed take place. As a result, from the point of view of the individuals concerned there was no reason—at least no reason concerned with the quality of their lives—to prefer a distribution under which person A and person B have a level of well-being of 3 at both time T_1 and time T_2 to a distribution under which at T_1 A's level is 1 and B's is 5 while at T_2 A's level is 5 and B's is 1. Nevertheless, I claimed that we could still think that the first alternative was better with respect to equality. In considering the second distribution we could find the inequality between their lives at T_1 and at T_2 objectionable for its own sake, even though the harms which constituted that inequality were balanced out by compensating benefits at another time for the people who experienced the harms. We could think this if we thought that inequality was bad because the difference between two lives that inequality involves was in itself a bad thing. There is such a difference between the lives of A and B at T_1. The fact that their respective positions are reversed at T_2 does not erase the difference between their lives that existed at T_1 (indeed, it creates another significant difference between their lives at T_2), even if it does mean that the disadvantage for B at T_1 is compensated for at T_2.

In other words, I suggested that we can agree that benefits outweigh harms across time inside lives and still object to inequality between the temporal parts of different lives if we care about equality in a particular way. It is not the only way to care about equality, but some egalitarians do care about equality in that way even apart from the judgments about temporal parts of lives that I was trying to defend. They would be willing to say, thinking about the complete lifetimes of A and B, that A at a level of 6 and B at 9 is worse in terms of inequality than A at 5 and B at 5. They must be objecting to the difference between the lives of A and B in the first alternative. If we just think in terms of harms and benefits for A and B the first alternative is clearly better than the second alternative.

Although some egalitarians do care about equality in this way, others will see the need for this commitment as a disadvantage of my view. I believed that the view involved another commitment. It seemed to me that in the examples where we are inclined to object to inequality between parts of lives, it is only inequality between simultaneous temporal parts of different lives that we find objectionable. If Alex and Betty are born on the same day and live their lives in tandem, so that their levels of well-being are equal during youth, middle age, and old age, with the result that they are also perfectly equal in terms of lifetime well-being, we would not object because there was non-simultaneous inequality between Alex's youth and Betty's middle age. So I felt we had to be willing to make this claim as well in order to think that inequality between the temporal parts of different lives can matter for its own sake. But restricting the view in this way seems to mean giving a certain kind of moral importance to time itself or to facts about timing. It is in effect to say that simultaneous inequality is morally important while non-simultaneous inequality is not. If our intuitive judgments push us in that direction, some would be willing to accept that claim as well. But it is another commitment that we must be willing to assume in order to hold the view I defended.[3]

As I have said, my case for this view depended on our intuitive judgments about examples. I did not argue that if we care about differences between lives for their own sake when we consider lifetimes we are also required to care about differences in simultaneous temporal parts of lives for their own sake when we think about temporal stages of lives. Someone might grant that I have shown that we could care in this way about inequality between temporal stages in lives—in the sense that I have shown that the basic ideas in egalitarianism do not rule out such a concern—but still hold that there actually is no reason to care about this kind of equality.

To put the concern more simply, my view requires that we think of a temporal stage in a life as an appropriate locus of distribution, as a morally significant unit that may have distributional constraints applying to it. But I did not give an argument for thinking of a temporal stage in a life in that way (apart from the appeal to examples). Someone may think that a lifetime—the complete life of a single self-identical person considered from its beginning to its end—is such a locus of distribution, but not be inclined to think that the same is true of a temporal stage. So the view that a temporal stage in a life is itself an appropriate locus for distribution is a third claim that we must be willing to accept to hold the view.[4]

When I explained this view, I thought that we could hold it compatibly with also accepting an egalitarian principle concerned with equality between lifetimes. It seemed to me that believing that inequality between temporal parts of lives could matter for its own sake did not rule out thinking that inequality between people's complete lifetimes also mattered for its own sake. And I also thought that by defending the view, given the account of its basic ideas that I have just provided, I was not committing myself to any specific conclusion about the respective importance of inequality between temporal parts of lives and inequality between lifetimes. A person who accepted that view might find extra reasons for thinking that it was more important to eliminate inequality between lifetimes than to end inequality between

---

[3] If we do agree that it is inequality between simultaneous temporal stages in lives that matters, this will connect with another feature of the view. If we were to apply equality inside a life, it obviously could not be to different simultaneous temporal stages of that life. It would have to be to non-simultaneous stages. The restriction of egalitarian constraints to simultaneous stages is in line with the rejection of intrapersonal egalitarian judgments, although that was not my reason for refusing to apply equality inside a life.

[4] Temkin defends a similar view about equality between temporal parts of lives (1993, ch. 8).

temporal parts of lives, but they might instead decide that very deep inequalities between temporal parts of lives could be more important than smaller inequalities between lifetimes. My view itself did not provide an answer.

4. Parfit on Personal Identity and Equality

However, there was a more influential response to the standard egalitarian view which also made room for applying equality to temporal stages in lives. This response came from the work of Derek Parfit (1973, 1984). Parfit did not identify himself as an egalitarian, but he wrote at length about the relationship between egalitarianism and philosophical theories of personal identity.

Parfit defended what he called a 'complex' rather than a 'simple' view of the identity of persons (later he used the name 'reductionist' for his view). He maintained that personal identity consisted in psychological relations of connectedness and continuity holding between the experiences of what we consider to be one and the same person over time. The view gradually changed into the somewhat weaker claim that those psychological relations were what mattered with respect to personal identity—roughly, that the importance for rationality and for morality that was attributed to personal identity itself was better understood as the importance for rationality and morality of these relations themselves.

The implications that Parfit drew for egalitarianism were striking. The view made him question whether there was moral outweighing between benefits and harms inside one life. The psychological relations he describes will hold to varying degrees between the different temporal parts of the same life. The relations holding between my childhood and my old age are attenuated, at least when they are compared to the relations holding between myself today and myself tomorrow. The ordinary understanding of personal identity says that the relation of identity holds between myself as a child and myself as someone very old in exactly the same way that it holds between myself today and myself tomorrow. However, according to Parfit it is the psychological relations themselves that matter, not the relation of identity. We will look to those relations, not to identity, to determine when benefits outweigh harms. So if as a child I consider my old age, it is possible that a larger benefit when I am old will not count as outweighing a smaller harm during my childhood, if the psychological relations between those two temporal parts of my life are sufficiently attenuated.

If we accept this view, it will change what we think about both interpersonal judgments and intrapersonal judgments. In general its effect will be to make intra-personal judgments seem to be more like interpersonal judgments. If we agree with Parfit, we think that harms and benefits might not balance one another out inside the same life. This means that in the intrapersonal case we can believe that there are egalitarian distributional constraints holding inside lives. So inside a life, maximizing might not be the right principle for either morality or rationality.

In one sense Parfit's view challenges the standard egalitarian view. It allows us to apply egalitarianism inside a single life. But in another sense Parfit's view conforms to the standard view. It applies egalitarian constraints inside lives, but only because it maintains that if we think in the right way about personal identity we will realize that intrapersonal judgments are much more like interpersonal judgments than we previously thought them to be. The divisions between the different temporal stages of one life are at least to a certain extent like the divisions between different lives. So we apply egalitarianism inside a life because we have discovered there the same reasons that motivate us to apply egalitarian constraints between lives.[5]

The standard egalitarian view apparently depended on the existence of a contrast between intrapersonal judgments and interpersonal judgments. If we have changed our mind about intrapersonal judgments, it might seem that this will make it harder for us to make interpersonal egalitarian judgments. But this consequence does not follow. We can still maintain that benefits do not always outweigh harms across lives, so that egalitarian distributional constraints apply between different lives. And we could argue that this judgment is even stronger in the interpersonal case than in the intrapersonal case. The psychological connections between a harm in one life and a benefit in another life will be much weaker than the psychological connections between a benefit and a harm located at different times in the same life.

Parfit's view changes what we think about applying egalitarian constraints to temporal parts of lives. The most obvious consequence is that it makes it possible to apply egalitarian constraints to the different temporal parts of a single life. But it also has implications for applying egalitarian constraints to the temporal parts of different lives, as opposed to restricting egalitarian principles to the temporal scope of complete lifetimes. If we are willing to apply the constraints to the temporal parts of the same life, it seems that we should not think that there is an objection in principle to applying them to temporal parts of different lives.

One concern about my own view was that some might doubt whether a temporal part of a life really is an appropriate locus of distribution. If we agree with Parfit, these

---

[5] Parfit also described another consequence of his theory of personal identity for egalitarian distributive principles. He suggested that since the theory holds that the boundaries between different lives are not as deep as they would be on the simple view of identity, adopting the theory might lead us to give less weight to distributive principles. This is one reason why Parfit himself was not clearly committed to egalitarianism. However, it also illustrates his allegiance to the standard egalitarian view. Because egalitarian constraints are strongly linked to interpersonal judgments, a change in our thinking that makes interpersonal judgments out to be more like intrapersonal judgments will inevitably weaken the force of egalitarian constraints.

doubts are removed. His view explains why a temporal unit other than a lifetime can be an appropriate locus of distribution—given his view about personal identity, benefits might not outweigh harms inside a life. Parfit's view also answers the original argument against caring about distribution between temporal parts of different lives. That argument appeals to the fact that if B is worse off than A now B might be compensated for this disadvantage by receiving benefits that A does not receive at earlier or later times. However, Parfit's view applies to B's life in the same way that it applies to A's life. If we agree with Parfit then even if B is benefited at other times those benefits might not actually outweigh the harm that B experiences now. Since Parfit's view can answer the objection in this way it is not forced to maintain that we should care about equality in the special way that I have described in explaining my own view. My view offered a complicated response to the objection that some will find unconvincing; Parfit's response to the same objection is simpler.

Parfit's view may make it easier to think that there are distributional constraints holding between the temporal parts of different lives, but it also has another consequence. If our concern with temporal parts of different lives rests on Parfit's foundation, it will not be exclusively concerned with inequality between the simultaneous parts of different lives. Parfit's ideas support distributional constraints between the non-simultaneous parts of the same life, so they should also make the case for the moral importance of equality holding between the non-simultaneous parts of different lives. Each temporal stage of each life will be an appropriate locus of distribution, so it seems that we should be concerned with minimizing inequality between all of those temporal stages. As I have said, I think that this conclusion has very little intuitive support.

It is the other side of this feature that Parfit's view does not give moral importance to the fact of simultaneity of two temporal stages of lives, as my view did. Some might see this as an advantage of his view, despite my claim that it is intuitive to restrict our concern to equality between the simultaneous parts of different lives.

However, Parfit's view might clash in an even more serious way with our intuitive judgments. It applies equality inside a life. This means that if the view understands the value of equality in a certain way, the view might tell us to 'level down' inside lives. That is, if A is much better off at T_1 than at T_2, we might reduce A's level of welfare at T_1 simply to reduce the inequality between the two temporal stages of A's life even if this does not improve A's level of welfare at any other time. This is extremely counter-intuitive. I find it far more implausible than the suggestion that we should level down across different lives to achieve equality between lifetimes.

Parfit's earlier writing about egalitarianism did not reveal whether he thought it was reasonable to value equality this way. His more recent work on the relationship between equality and priority seems to indicate that he would not wish to value equality in a way that would permit levelling down, so this might be his answer to this objection (Parfit 1995). Someone might also attempt to meet it by arguing that if we were to fully adopt Parfit's way of thinking of personal identity and its consequences then we would no longer be inclined to think that levelling down inside one life was strongly objectionable.

There is also a question about the compatibility of Parfit's view with applying distributional constraints to lifetimes as well as to temporal parts of lives. If the view changes the temporal scope of egalitarian principles, perhaps the change is a matter of replacing the traditional view that we care only about the temporal unit of a lifetime with the view that we should care only about the temporal unit of a temporal stage in a life.

Some views about personal identity would have that consequence. They would claim that we should replace the thought that there is a single person who persists throughout a complete lifetime by the thought that a so-called person is really only a series of distinct selves that stand in psychological relations to one another. If we reduce the person to the sequence of selves we might think that we should only be concerned with inequality between selves—whether the selves are part of the same lifetime or not—and that we should not be concerned about inequality between persons.

However, the view about identity need not take the form of replacing an ontology of persons by an ontology of selves, and in Parfit's work it never did take that form. When he did offer an account of what a person is, the reduction was to relations between experiences, not to selves understood as ontologically basic. Those psychological relations will hold to some extent across a complete lifetime, even if Parfit himself tends to emphasize how the relations can be attenuated over time and what he sees as the important implications of that attenuation. So Parfit's view is compatible with understanding a lifetime as a morally significant unit (although presumably it is not as morally significant as it would have been if the simple view of identity had been correct), and as a significant unit with respect to the application of egalitarian principles. His view gives us a reason to care about temporal parts in lives, but it does not eliminate the reason to care about lifetimes.

The reader will have noticed that Parfit's view avoids the three claims that my own view was committed to: the need to care about equality in a particular way, the claim that time has a certain kind of moral importance, and the claim that a temporal stage in a life counts as a locus of distribution. Nevertheless, I think it faces serious problems. One problem is that it is very difficult to specify what kind of weakening in psychological connections would be needed to trigger the consequences for morality and rationality that Parfit describes. Arguably, even if we agree with Parfit about the potential significance of these psychological relations, the kind of weakening that we find in ordinary human lives over time (as opposed to, for example, a life in which the person is afflicted with severe dementia in old age) would not be enough to make outweighing problematic. This would mean that the consequences that Parfit describes would not actually follow. Also (though this is hardly an argument), some readers feel that Parfit's view gets the order of explanation backwards. Parfit appeals to ideas about personal identity to explain why we are inclined to make judgments about morality and rationality that are concerned with temporal parts of lives rather than with lifetimes. But I think myself that those judgments are a response to the significance we attach to time and the passage of time, or to the special importance of the present, or to important changes in values and character during a person's life. Our explanation of these judgments should come from a moral principle that asserts the importance of those facts themselves, not from a metaphysical theory of personal identity (although the moral principle that I think provides the best explanation does not assert the importance of any of those facts in a simple way). It might be the fact that we make those judgments on the basis of some such moral principle that helps to make Parfit's view about the basis of personal identity seem persuasive, not the other way round.[6]

5. Priority and Time

The final view I will consider was formulated after egalitarians had distinguished between the values of equality and priority. Some have argued that despite its apparent persuasiveness the distinction cannot be clearly drawn, but I will not attempt to answer those objections in this chapter.

The basic idea in the Priority View is that a benefit can be more important, or can have more value, if it is received by someone who is badly off rather than by someone with a higher quality of life or level of well-being. In virtue of this a smaller benefit for someone badly off might be more important than, and so might morally outweigh, a larger benefit for someone better off.

It is striking that the writers who first tried to make this claim plausible tended to focus on examples where our choice was between helping someone who was currently badly off versus helping someone whose present level of well-being was high. A typical

---

[6] McMahan (2002) is work in Parfit's tradition, although McMahan does not discuss equality. McMahan thinks that the strength of the psychological connections holding between the temporal parts of a person's life will have important consequences for moral choices, although on his view these psychological relations do *not* constitute personal identity. McMahan seems to think that the consequences only follow when the psychological relations are extremely weak—for example, the connections holding between a fetus and the adult person the fetus eventually becomes, or the connections between an elderly person and her future self after she has been stricken by a severe form of Alzheimer's disease.

case might involve a contrast between one person who was experiencing agonizing pain and someone else who was also suffering but not nearly so acutely. The suggestion would be that it might be more important to relieve at least some of the first person's pain rather than to relieve a larger amount of the second person's pain. Those writers did not start with cases in which one person has a significantly worse complete life than someone else and then argue that it was the first person who deserved to be helped even if he would receive those benefits at a particular time when he happened to be very well off.

In other words, the examples that were the most effective at persuading people to take priority seriously focused on the current state of people's lives, on their levels of well-being at a particular time. This point was not emphasized in the early discussions of priority, but it raised the possibility that one application of the idea of priority with strong intuitive support was to a person at a particular time, or to a temporal stage of a person's life, rather than to an entire lifetime.

I tried to say more about such an application of the notion, just as I had done with equality (McKerlie 2002). However, it seemed to me that there was a case for making different choices in spelling out the view about priority than the choices I had made for equality. The differences came out in the answers that we gave to the questions about egalitarianism that I have been discussing.

To be more specific, it seemed to me that there was a simple, intuitive, and persuasive way of stating the principle underlying judgments of this kind of priority, the priority that applies to a person at a particular time. We need only say that the value of a benefit depends on the level of well-being of the person who receives the benefit as well as on the size of the benefit. Here the well-being in question is the level of well-being of the person at the time at which the benefit is experienced.

This principle seemed to capture the judgments that I wanted to make about examples involving pain. However, an obvious point to make about the principle is that unless we deliberately choose to restrict its generality it will apply inside lives as well as across lives. That is, the principle will apply when we are choosing between a benefit for A when A is well off and a benefit for B when B is badly off, but it will also apply to choosing between a benefit for A at a time when A is badly off and a benefit for A at some other time when A is better off.

This application of the idea of priority inside a life does not depend on any view about the nature of personal identity. It also does not appeal to a weakening of the psychological connections holding between A when the first benefit would be received and A at the time the second benefit would be experienced. The application is completely explained by the basic claim that the value of a harm or a benefit depends on the current level of well-being of the person who receives the benefit. Consequently, there is no need to argue that the relationship between different temporal stages in the same life is more like the relationship between different lives than we ordinarily think. Supporting the application just requires persuading us that we do make the judgments about an individual's well-being at a time that the principle envisages.[7]

Understood in this way, priority—whether it is applied to the temporal unit of a lifetime or to the temporal unit of a particular temporal stage in a life—is not an essentially comparative notion in the way that equality is. At the most basic level priority judgments are made about a single life, while judgments about equality are made about relations between lives or about relations between temporal stages in different lives or in the same life, if we have decided to extend the application of equality in these ways. If we are choosing between benefits for two different people, and we make priority judgments about both lives, the Priority View will give us an answer as to which person it is more important to help, and in that sense the Priority View makes a comparative judgment. But the priority judgments we make about each life—the judgment that tells us how much value a benefit for the first person would have given that person's level of welfare, and the corresponding judgment about the second person—will be the same whether or not we then go on to compare the two different lives.

Since priority is not essentially comparative, if we apply it to temporal stages in lives there is no need to make an additional case that a temporal stage of a life is an appropriate locus of distribution.[8] If we choose between the two benefits by appealing to priority our thinking is not essentially distributive in the way that it would be if we made the choice using the notion of equality. The conclusion we reach is accounted for by the basic claim about priority, not by the view that there are distributive claims

---

[7] Some will doubt that we do apply priority to temporal parts of lives as well as to lifetimes. A comparison with the ordinary notion of poverty might be persuasive, since there are connections between priority and our response to poverty. We have a special concern with helping those who are living in poverty. In the very worst cases people spend their whole lives in that condition. However, I think we still have a special concern with poverty in a case in which a person lives a significant temporal part of her life in that state. We care in a special way about helping her when she is poor. We would give a kind of priority to benefiting her during that part of her life, and we would not be indifferent between benefiting her at that time and benefiting her at a time when she was not poor. And I think we would still give priority to helping her when she was poor even if her life when viewed as a temporal whole did not rank as one of the worst complete lives. Arguably we have both a special concern with people living in poverty at a particular time and a special concern with people whose lives as a whole are lived in poverty. If so, the application of the notion of poverty would involve the two different temporal units that I am attributing to the notion of priority.

[8] This comment needs further explanation. If we agree that the value of a benefit can depend on the current level of welfare of the person who receives the benefit, then we are already making priority judgments about people at particular times, at least as I understand priority judgments. These judgments will influence the conclusions that we draw about which person it is most important to help, even if we must weigh them against other moral reasons (including, in my opinion, reasons that apply priority to lifetimes).

applying to temporal stages of lives. So this view escapes one of the commitments of my view about equality.

The view also differs from my earlier view about equality with respect to time. I suggested that the earlier view objected specifically to equality between the simultaneous temporal stages in different lives. Restricting the view in that way implies that the temporal fact that the two stages occur at the same time has moral significance. In the case of the view that applies priority to temporal stages of different lives, I think there is no need for a similar restriction. The idea that the value of a benefit can depend on the current level of welfare of the person who receives that benefit applies in the same way to any temporal stage in any life, and it allows us to make judgments about the relative importance of benefits that would be received by different people whether the temporal stages that we are comparing are simultaneous or not. There are no reasons based on intuitive judgments for restricting the application of priority to temporal stages of lives to cases where we are comparing simultaneous stages of different lives.[9] This means that the view escapes another commitment of the view about equality—as well as not having to maintain that a temporal stage in a life is an appropriate locus of distribution, we do not have to believe that a fact about timing has intrinsic moral importance.

I should also add that since the value being applied to temporal stages of lives is the value of priority, not equality, this view would not lead to levelling down when we compare different temporal stages in different lives. For the very same reason it would not lead to levelling down when we apply priority intrapersonally to the different temporal stages inside one life. We have seen that levelling down inside a life was at least a danger in the case of Parfit's view, and in the case of other views that might choose to apply the value of equality both across lives and inside lives.

This application of priority departs from the standard egalitarian view since it applies the same idea of priority both inside lives and across lives. So it differs from my view about equality, which struggled to maintain consistency with the standard view. It is also different from Parfit's view, which broke from the standard view but did so for reasons (Parfit's revisionist ideas about personal identity) which did not challenge the moral claims in the standard view but rather changed their scope.

---

[9] Is this claim compatible with my view that our intuitive judgments do support restricting the application of equality to the simultaneous stages of different lives? I think the difference is that equality, because it is a relative or comparative notion, introduces the question of which comparisons are relevant. I believe that when we think in terms of equality we will find comparisons between lifetimes to be relevant, and comparisons between the simultaneous stages of different lives, but not comparisons between the non-simultaneous stages of different lives. Priority is not a comparative notion, so it does not raise a question about which comparisons are relevant. I would agree that we do sometimes judge that there should be redistribution between non-simultaneous stages in different lives, but I think that these judgments are explained by priority rather than equality.

However, there is an explanation of why the application of priority does disagree with traditional egalitarianism. The traditional view of egalitarianism maintained a fundamental distinction between intrapersonal judgments and interpersonal judgments since it rejected a maximizing principle in the case of interpersonal judgments and it assumed that intrapersonal judgments did depend on a maximizing principle. But if we apply priority to a temporal part of a life in the way I have explained—if we apply it inside a life—then we are supposing that the principle for intrapersonal judgments is not simply a maximizing principle. We might prefer a smaller surplus of benefits over harms in the case of a single life, depending on the level of welfare of the person at the times at which those benefits and harms would be experienced. And once we have rejected maximizing inside a life, we do not have the same reason to insist as traditional egalitarianism does that interpersonal judgments must be fundamentally different from intrapersonal judgments.

It also seemed to me that this view about priority did not inevitably lead to any conclusion about the relative importance of priority applied to lifetimes and priority applied to temporal stages in lives. A might have a worse complete life than B, but B might now be considerably worse off than A is now. In virtue of priority applied to lifetimes a benefit that A would receive now would have special value, but in virtue of priority applied to a person's well-being at a particular time a benefit received by B now would also have special value. Nothing in the foundation of the view seemed to me to imply that one kind of priority would always be stronger than the other. Our conclusions about this question could only be based on the judgments that we found it plausible to make about particular choices.

Because this view makes priority judgments both inside and across lives, and the intrapersonal and interpersonal judgments are made for the same reason and have the same strength, the view is very simple. I think this simplicity should be counted as an advantage, provided that the view is not otherwise objectionable. It was the view's simplicity (and not its avoidance of levelling down) that made me think it was more persuasive than my earlier view about equality.[10] If we agree that egalitarianism does include a concern for how people are faring at particular times, I have come to believe that this concern is best expressed in terms of priority rather than equality.

However, others will see the simplicity as a serious disadvantage. They will think that intrapersonal priority judgments and interpersonal priority judgments should differ in strength. They believe that the degree of priority awarded to the worse-off temporal stage should be greater when the stages we are comparing are stages in different lives than when we are comparing different temporal stages of the same

---

[10] For the view that the Priority View is to be preferred on the basis of the levelling down objection, see Holtug, Ch. 5 in this volume, Sects. 4–6. For the opposite view, see Christiano, Ch. 2 in this volume, Sects. 20–1.

life. If we agree and change the view accordingly it will bring the view back into line to some extent with the standard egalitarian view that there should be a significant difference between intrapersonal and interpersonal judgments, even though we will be applying priority inside lives as well as across lives.

The strongest reason for making this change is that it seems undeniable that a lifetime is a morally significant unit. How can the difference between lives have moral significance if we make exactly the same judgments of priority across two lifetimes and inside one lifetime?

Nevertheless, I am not convinced that we should revise the view. I agree that we must treat human lives as morally significant units. But I think that we can do this by making priority judgments about lifetimes as well as temporal parts of lives. Why is this not sufficient acknowledgement of the moral importance of the difference between one life and another life? Why must we acknowledge it once again when we are considering temporal stages of lives rather than lifetimes, by insisting that the degree of priority is greater in an interpersonal judgment than in an intrapersonal judgment?

An example might help. Suppose that I can prevent a harm from being suffered by a person who is now much worse off than I am. Priority tells me to do it. However, also suppose that refusing to help is necessary to prevent me from experiencing the same degree of harm at some future time when I will be just as badly off as the other person now is. If priority has the same weight inside lives and across lives, the Priority View will be indifferent about which choice I should make. If the degree of the priority is stronger in an interpersonal judgment then I should help the other person and accept the future harm.

I think it is indifferent. In reply someone might point out that I am better off now than the other person is, and ask how it could be right for me to allow him to suffer even more harm to save myself from suffering harm in the future. However, when we reason in this way we have slipped into thinking in terms of lifetimes. If I refuse to help I am allowing the current state of the other person's life to become even more worse than the current state of my life, and I am also making my own life better at the future time at which I would otherwise have suffered the harm. Other things being equal, this will make my complete life better than the other person's life. That is why we find it objectionable. It is not that we think that the other person's present condition has a stronger claim on my help than my own future condition. If we suppose that for other reasons the other person's lifetime would be better than my own in any event, the inclination to think that I must help the other person will vanish.

6. Conclusion

I have discussed three departures from the standard egalitarian view that would allow us to apply egalitarian values to temporal parts of lives. I think we should apply egalitarian values in that way. I also believe that the third view about priority provides the best account of such an application. This view departs from standard egalitarianism in the most radical way. However, I think it gives us good reason to doubt that egalitarianism always does require the existence of a fundamental difference between interpersonal judgments and intrapersonal judgments.

References

BRINK, D. (1993), 'The Separateness of Persons, Distributive Norms, and Moral Theory', in R. Frey and C. Morris (eds.), *Value, Welfare, and Morality* (Cambridge: Cambridge University Press), 252–89.

DANIELS, N. (1988), *Am I My Parents' Keeper?* (Oxford: Oxford University Press).

DWORKIN, R. (1977), 'Justice and Rights', in Dworkin, *Taking Rights Seriously* (Cambridge, Mass.: Harvard University Press), 150–83.

MCKERLIE, D. (1988), 'Egalitarianism and the Separateness of Persons', *Canadian Journal of Philosophy*, 18: 205–25.

_____ (1989), 'Equality and Time', *Ethics*, 99: 475–91.

_____ (2002), 'Justice Between the Young and the Old', *Philosophy & Public Affairs*, 30: 152–77.

MCMAHAN, J. (2002), *The Ethics of Killing* (Oxford: Oxford University Press).

NAGEL, T. (1970), *The Possibility of Altruism* (Oxford: Oxford University Press).

_____ (1979), 'Equality', in Nagel, *Mortal Questions* (Cambridge: Cambridge University Press), 106–27.

PARFIT, D. (1973), 'Later Selves and Moral Principles', in A. Montefiore (ed.), *Philosophy and Personal Relations* (London: Routledge & Kegan Paul), 137–69.

_____ (1984), *Reasons and Persons* (Oxford: Oxford University Press).

_____ (1995), *Equality or Priority*, The Lindley Lecture (Lawrence: University of Kansas).

RAWLS, J. (1971), *A Theory of Justice* (Cambridge, Mass.: Harvard University Press).

SCANLON, T. (1976), 'Nozick on Rights, Liberty, and Property', *Philosophy & Public Affairs*, 5: 3–25.

_____ (1982), 'Contractualism and Utilitarianism', in A. Sen and B. Williams (eds.), *Utilitarianism and Beyond* (Cambridge: Cambridge University Press), 103–28.

TEMKIN, L. (1993), *Inequality* (Oxford: Oxford University Press).

7

Who Are the Least Advantaged?

Bertil Tungodden and Peter Vallentyne

1. Introduction

The difference principle, introduced by Rawls (1971, 1993), states that the basic institutions of society should promote the social and economic interests of the least advantaged members of society. Most writers have contented themselves with the leximin version of the difference principle, saying that we should assign priority to the interests of the worst-off *person* in society (and the second worst off if the worst off is indifferent, and so on).[1] But this is clearly not what Rawls (1971) has in mind. He argues that the persons in the original position should interpret the difference principle as a '*limited aggregative principle* and assess it as such in comparison with other standards. It is not as if they agreed to think of the least advantaged as literally the worst off individual' (1971; 98; our emphasis). In other words, the difference principle accepts a certain trade-off between gains and losses of people that belong to the least advantaged group in society, but assigns absolute priority to the least advantaged in any distributive conflict with the better off members of society.

Rawls (1971: 98) admits that 'The serious difficulty [with the difference principle] is how to define the least fortunate group.' He sketches some possibilities, for example counting the least advantaged as all those with an income less than half of the median income and wealth or less than the average income and wealth of the unskilled

For helpful comments, we thank Nils Holtug, Karsten Klint Jensen, and the participants at the University of Copenhagen Conference on Egalitarianism, 2004.

[1] Pogge (1989) is an exception. He explicitly defines the least advantaged group as those below a certain percentile of the distribution.

worker, but more generally he suggests that a certain arbitrariness is unavoidable in defining the least advantaged group and thus that the exact formulation of the difference principle has to be done on an ad hoc basis.

> In any case we are to aggregate to some degree over the expectations of the worst off, and the figure selected on which to base these computations is to a certain extent ad hoc. Yet we are at some point entitled to plead practical considerations in formulating the difference principle. Sooner or later the capacity of philosophical or other arguments to make finer discriminations is bound to run out. (Rawls 1971: 98)

Even though it is easy to accept that practical constraints will limit the formulation of the difference principle in any particular application, it is hard to accept that the outline of the ideal version of the theory does not need a principled definition of the least advantaged group. The ideal version should guide practical applications of the theory, and thus it is essential to have a clear understanding of the appropriate foundation of the definition of the least advantaged group. Given any particular conception of benefits, should we relate the definition of the least advantaged group to the median benefits, the average benefits, the benefits of the best-off person, an independent norm, or some other notion?

The aim of this chapter is to study the implications of adopting different approaches to the definition of the least advantaged group in society.[2] In particular, we will study what definitions lead to a version of the difference principle that is significantly different from the leximin principle. We start by showing that certain seemingly plausible conditions on the definition of the least advantaged group leave little room for the difference principle to depart significantly from the leximin principle. We then show that the difference principle can take an *aggregative* form (as intended by Rawls) if the least advantaged group is defined as those having fewer benefits than some strictly positive transformation of the lowest benefit level. Finally, we discuss the implications of requiring that, in comparing two alternatives, the cutoff for the least advantaged group of one alternative be the same as that for the other alternative.

2. The General Framework

We shall assume a fixed population of individuals. The variable population case (where who exists depends on what choices are made) is much more complex and we shall not attempt to address it here.

To specify fully an egalitarian theory, one must specify the type of benefits that it seeks to equalize. As is well known, Rawls defends a focus on some notion of primary

---

[2] See also Tungodden (1999).

goods. Throughout the chapter, however, we will leave open the relevant conception of benefit (resources, primary goods, brute luck well-being, etc.). References to a person being worse off than another should be understood in terms of the relevant benefits.

We shall assume, for the sake of argument, that benefits are fully measurable and interpersonally comparable (i.e. there is a natural zero and unit for benefits and these are fully interpersonally comparable). This may seem like a strong assumption, but in the present context it is a very weak assumption. The assumption that benefits are so measurable and comparable does not entail that such information is *relevant* for the moral assessment of options. The assumption is simply that such information is available. This ensures that no definition of the least advantaged group, and hence of the difference principle, is ruled out merely on the grounds that it presupposes that benefits are measurable or comparable in ways that are not possible.

We shall be concerned with the assessment of the justice of alternatives, where alternatives are possible objects of choice (e.g. actions or social policies). Rawls, of course, took the relevant option to be social structures, but, for the sake of generality, we leave open the nature of the options. Alternatives may have all kinds of features: they generate a certain distribution of benefits, satisfy or violate various rights, involve various intentions, and so on. In what follows, we shall assume that the only relevant information for the assessment of justice is the benefit distribution that an alternative generates. More formally, we shall assume

> *Benefitism.* Alternatives can be identified with (and thus their justice assessed solely on the basis of) their benefit distributions.

Benefitism is a generalization of welfarism (the view that justice supervenes on individual welfare). It holds that justice supervenes on individual benefits whatever they are. If two alternatives generate the same distribution of benefits, then they have the same status with respect to justice. Given Benefitism, we can identify an alternative with the benefit distribution that it generates, and in what follows we shall do so for simplicity. The difference principle satisfies Benefitism, since it assesses alternatives solely on the basis of their benefit (e.g. primary good) distributions.

Finally, we assume that the set of distributions generated by the set of possible alternatives is *rich* in the following sense:

> *Domain Richness.* For any logically possible benefit distribution X, there is an alternative that generates that distribution.

This condition rules out, for example, the possibility that, where there are just three people, the distribution ⟨3,7,9⟩ (3 to the first person, 7 to the second, 9 to the third) is not one of the alternatives. All logically possible benefit distributions are among the alternatives. This is not to say that all are part of any given *feasible* set (the alternatives that are open to an agent on a given occasion). Of course, there are lots of logically possible benefit distributions that are not feasible on a given occasion. The claim here is about the range of benefit distributions that can be assessed by justice. The condition holds that such judgements can be made for all logically possible distributions. We believe that this is a highly plausible condition. Benefit distributions here play the role of test cases for the theory of justice. All logically possible test cases—assuming, as we shall, a finite population—are admissible. Benefitism and Domain Richness will be assumed throughout the chapter, and thus we will not state these conditions explicitly when reporting the results.

We will be concerned with the *justice relation* of (one alternative) being-at-least-as-just-as (another). Following the standard definitions, (1) an alternative is *more just* than another if and only if it is at least as just and the other is not at least as just as it; and (2) an alternative is *equally just* as another if and only if it is at least as just and that other is also at least as just as it. We shall assume that the justice relation satisfies the following consistency condition:

> *Acyclicity.* If, for alternatives $X_1, \ldots, X_n$, X_1 is more just than X_2, X_2 is more just than $X_3, \ldots$, and X_{n-1} is more just than X_n, then X_n is not more just than X_1.

Acyclicity is much weaker than the better-known requirement of transitivity. It applies only to chains where each alternative is more just than its successor (as opposed to being at least as just) and allows the possibilities of silence (no ranking) and of the first alternative being judged equally just as the last (whereas transitivity requires that it be judged more just in such cases). It is about as close to being uncontroversial as one can get when it comes to consistency requirements on the justice relation.

For some of the results, we will strengthen this condition slightly in two ways. One is to invoke

> *Strong Acyclicity.* If, for alternatives $X_1, \ldots, X_n$, X_1 is at least as just as X_2, X_2 is at least as just as $X_3, \ldots$, and X_{n-1} is at least as just as X_n, then (1) X_n is not more just than X_1, and (2) if for some i inclusively between 1 and $n-1$, X_i is more just than X_{i+1}, then X_n is not at least as just as X_1.

This strengthens Acyclicity by covering chains where each alternative is at least as just as (as opposed to more just than) its successor. If each of the pairs is equally just, then it concludes that the last alternative is *not more just* than the first (as opposed to the silence of Acyclicity). Moreover, if all the relations in this chain are the relations of being more just, then Strong Acyclicity strengthens Acyclicity by requiring that the last alternative *not be at least as just* as the first (as opposed to Acyclicity's requirement that it not be more just). Like Acyclicity, Strong Acyclicity is accepted by almost everyone.

We will also consider the implications of the further strengthening of Acyclicity:

Transitivity. If, for alternatives X_1, X_2, and X_3, X_1 is at least as just as X_2, X_2 is at least as just as X_3, then X_1 is at least as just as X_3.

Transitivity is much more controversial than Strong Acyclicity. Indeed, one of us would reject it on the ground that sometimes silence is appropriate concerning the ranking of the first and last alternatives. Fortunately, our core results do not depend on this assumption. We shall merely note how they can be strengthened if one assumes Transitivity as opposed to Strong Acyclicity.

For the record, we state one final condition:

Completeness. For any two alternatives X and Y, either X is at least as just as Y or Y is at least as just as X.

Completeness rules out the possibility of silence in the comparison of the relative justice of any two alternatives. For most of our results, we do not assume Completeness. It is only for a final possibility result that we will invoke it.

3. The Least Advantaged Group and the Difference Principle

In order to state precisely the difference principle, we need a definition of the least advantaged group. Formally, we designate, for each alternative X, the least advantaged group as L(X). We assume that this group is defined by a *cutoff function*, c, for which c(X) is the benefit level such that L(X) consists of all and only those individuals with benefits strictly *less* than c(X).[3]

More formally, we have

The Least Advantaged Group, L(X). For any alternative X, an individual *i* belongs to the least advantaged group, L(X), if and only if *i*'s benefits are strictly less than c(X).

---

[3] Notice that the introduction of a cutoff function excludes a definition of the least advantaged group that is common in practice, to wit as the bottom *n*th (e.g. 20th) percentile of the population. To see this, consider ⟨1,1,2,3,4⟩. The bottom 20th percentile here consists of just the first person, but any cutoff function will treat the first person the same as the second (since they have the same benefits). Defining the least advantaged group in terms of percentiles may be useful in practice, but the fact that it treats individuals with the same benefits differently shows that it is theoretically unsound. Note, however, that the appeal to cutoffs does not preclude defining the least advantaged group as those who have lower benefits than those at some percentile. In the above example, setting the cutoff at the benefits of the 60th percentile (i.e. 3 units) has the result that the first two individuals are in the least advantaged group.

In order to focus our discussion, we need to impose some structure on the cutoff function. The following condition should be entirely uncontroversial:

> *Monotonicity.* For any two alternatives X and Y, if the benefits of each individual are at least as great in X as in Y, then $c(X) \geq c(Y)$.

The cutoffs may be either absolute (not dependent on features of the distribution of benefits to which it is applied) or relative (e.g. based on the mean, median, or percentile distribution). If they are absolute, the cutoffs will be the same for all alternatives. and thus Monotonicity will be satisfied. If the cutoffs are relative (e.g. 50 per cent of the average benefits), then they may be different for different alternatives. Where. however, each individual has at least as much benefits in X as in Y, then the cutoffs for X should not be lower than for Y. It would be crazy, for example, for an income cutoff for the least advantaged to be $20,000 in a poor country and $200 in a rich country. If they change, they will be higher for the alternative in which the benefits are higher. Monotonicity is thus highly plausible, and we shall assume it throughout.

We shall show that, if the cutoff functions satisfy Monotonicity and certain other conditions, then the difference principle cannot depart significantly from leximin. To start, consider

> *The Full Difference Principle.* For any two alternatives X and Y, if the least advantaged group is strictly better off in X than Y, X is more just than Y.

This principle, as intended by Rawls, requires some way of aggregating benefits in the least advantaged group (so that it can require that such aggregate benefits be maximized). Because our project is to determine what kinds of aggregation are possible, given certain plausible assumptions, we do not want to presuppose any particular method of aggregation. Our point of departure will therefore be the following weaker principle:

> *The Core Difference Principle.* For any two alternatives X and Y, if (1) each individual who is a member of at least one of L(X) and L(Y) has at least as much benefits in X as in Y, and (2) at least one such member has strictly more benefits in X than Y, then X is more just than Y.

This is entailed by the full difference principle. It says that benefits to those in the least advantaged group (of either X or Y) take absolute priority over benefits to those not in that group. It is silent, however, about how benefits among individuals in the least advantaged group are to be traded off. Our task is to examine what kinds of trade-off are permitted by various plausible background conditions. We shall show that, given certain additional conditions to be identified below, the Core Difference Principle cannot significantly diverge from leximin. More exactly, we will show that it must agree with the following principle:

> *Minimal Maximin.* For any two alternatives X and Y, if there are more benefits in the worst-off position in X than Y, then Y is not more just than X.

This is weaker than leximin in several ways. First, it is silent where the benefits for the worst-off position are the same for two alternatives (e.g. ⟨2,4,9⟩ vs. ⟨2,3,3⟩), whereas leximin makes judgements even in such cases (namely, that ⟨2,4,9⟩ is more just). Second, where the benefits for the worst-off position in X are greater than those in Y (e.g. ⟨2,3,5⟩ vs. ⟨1,4,6⟩), Minimal Maximin allows X to be judged *equally just,* and also allows silence about the ranking, whereas leximin requires X to be *more* just.

Even though Minimal Maximin is weaker than leximin, it nevertheless captures the core of the leximin principle. Like leximin, it gives absolute priority to the benefits of the worst-off individuals in that it never judges that things are made more just by reducing the benefits of the worst off in order to increase benefits of others (e.g. it does not judge ⟨1,99,99⟩ to be more just than ⟨2,3,4⟩). Hence, in showing below that, given certain assumptions, the Core Difference Principle must satisfy Minimal Maximin, we are showing that it cannot significantly diverge from leximin.[4]

4. Some Initial Results

The conditions imposed so far do not require the Core Difference Principle to satisfy Minimal Maximin. Consider an *absolute benefit level cutoff* function that specifies the same benefit level for all alternatives—for example, the minimum level of benefits compatible with a decent life. The least advantaged group consists of those with benefits lower than the stipulated minimum level. Such a cutoff function satisfies Monotonicity. For a given cutoff (absolute or not), we can appeal to the total *restricted benefits* of an alternative, where these are the total benefits *up to the cutoff* (e.g. for a cutoff of 4, the total restricted benefits of ⟨2,3,5⟩ is 9). Note that the total restricted benefits include everyone's benefits up to the cutoff, and not just those of the least advantaged group. This reflects a concern for all benefits below the cutoff. Consider now the following principle scheme:

> *The Modified Total Restricted Benefits Principle (Scheme).* For any two alternatives X and Y: X is at least as just as Y if and only if (1) its total restricted benefits are at least as great, or (2) its total restricted benefits are equal and its total (unrestricted) benefits are at least as great.

---

[4] For a further discussion of the relationship between the leximin principle and the Core Difference Principle, see Tungodden (1999).

We shall appeal to this principle throughout the chapter. It holds that that ranking of alternatives is determined on the basis of the total restricted benefits, except that in cases of ties, further ranking is done on the basis of the total (unrestricted) benefits. This principle judges one alternative as *more* just if and only if it has greater total restricted benefits or if it has the same total restricted benefits but a greater total benefit.[5]

Given an absolute cutoff function, this principle, it is easy to show, satisfies the Core Difference Principle and Transitivity (and indeed even Completeness). Moreover, it is very different from Minimal Maximin. For example, if the cutoff is 10, it judges ⟨1,10,10⟩ as more just than ⟨2,9,9⟩, whereas Minimal Maximin says that the latter is more just. Unlike Minimal Maximin, this principle allows the benefits of the worst-off individual to be significantly traded off against the benefits of other members of the least advantaged group (as opposed to giving absolute priority to the worst-off member). So far, then, our conditions allow radical divergence from leximin.

In what follows, however, we shall limit our attention to *relative* cutoff functions, which are cutoff functions that make the definition of the least advantaged group somehow dependent on the individual benefit levels of that distribution (e.g. 50 per cent of the average benefits or 80 per cent of the median benefits). This is appropriate since, for the purposes of the difference principle, the least advantaged group is almost always understood in relative terms.

A natural relative cutoff condition is the following:

Conditional Best Off Excluded. If not everyone has the same benefits, then no one who is a best-off individual is a member of the least advantaged group.

For distribution ⟨1, 1, 5⟩, Conditional Best Off Excluded entails that the third person is not in the least advantaged group.[6] This condition rules out absolute cutoffs. For example, if the cutoff is set at the absolute level of 10, then ⟨1,2,3⟩ violates Conditional Best Off Excluded.

Consider now one further cutoff condition:

Non-Best Off Includable. For any alternative, it is possible to increase sufficiently the benefits of the best-off individuals so that everyone else becomes a member of the least advantaged group.

This says, for example, that in ⟨1,3,4,n⟩, for some sufficiently high n, everyone but the best-off position is in the least advantaged group. Even the second-best-off person is in

---

[5] Recall that we are assuming a fixed population of individuals. In variable population cases, the Modified Total Restricted Benefits Principle has the usual problems of total principles. For example, it says that adding people with almost no benefits (below the cutoff) makes things more just.

[6] Note that Conditional Best Off Excluded is silent for ⟨1,1,1⟩ and all other cases of perfect equality.

the least advantaged group for some sufficiently great n (e.g. in $\langle 1,3,4,999999999999 \rangle$)). After all, for a sufficiently great n, everyone but the best-off person will be much closer in benefits to the worst-off person than to the best-off person and their share of the overall resources in society will be almost negligible. This condition is satisfied, for example, by any cutoff that is based on some positive percentage of the benefits of the best-off position, or on some positive percentage of the average benefits (which is sensitive to the benefits of the best off).

We are now ready for our first result:

Result 1. Suppose (1) the cutoff function satisfies Monotonicity, Conditional Best Off Excluded, and Non-Best Off Includable, and (2) the justice relation satisfies the Core Difference Principle, and consider any two alternatives X and Y for which the benefits in the worst-off position in X are greater than those in Y. In this case: (*a*) if the justice relation satisfies Acyclicity, then Y is not more just than X, (*b*) if the justice relation satisfies Strong Acyclicity, then Y is not at least as just as X, and (*c*) if the justice relation satisfies Transitivity, then X is more just than Y.

The proofs for all results are in the Appendix, but for each result we shall illustrate the force of the result. Suppose that the least advantaged group for an alternative is defined as those who get less than average benefits in that alternative (which satisfies each of the cutoff conditions). Consider the Modified Total Restricted Benefits Principle, which, recall, holds that, for any two alternatives X and Y: X is at least as just as Y if and only if (1) its total restricted benefits are at least as great, or (2) its total restricted benefits are equal and its total (unrestricted) benefits are at least as great. Compare the alternatives $\langle 1,2,12 \rangle$ (average of 5) and $\langle 1,3,5 \rangle$ (average of 3). The total restricted benefit is 8 in the first alternative and 7 in the second alternative. Thus, the Modified Total Restricted Benefits Principle judges $\langle 1,2,12 \rangle$ as more just than $\langle 1,3,5 \rangle$. However, this violates the Core Difference Principle, and hence this version of the Modified Total Restricted Benefits Principle is not a counterexample to Result 1.

The proof of Result 1 generalizes the intuitions of this illustration. If the conditions of the result are granted, then, the difference principle (which Rawls intended to be aggregative within the least advantaged group) cannot 'radically disagree' with leximin (which involves no aggregation). It cannot 'radically disagree' in the sense that it cannot judge one alternative to be more just if it gives lower benefits to the worst-off individual (i.e. cannot violate Minimal Maximin). The core result does not rule out the possibility that the difference principle judges two alternatives equally good, or is silent about their justice ranking, when one gives more benefits to the worst-off position. Still, the result places severe limitations on the nature of the difference principle. Moreover, if the highly plausible Strong Acyclicity is assumed, then the two alternatives in this case cannot be judged equally good, and if the more controversial Transitivity is assumed, then the alternative with greater benefits for the worst-off individual must be judged more just.

Result 1 depends upon Non-Best Off Includable, but this condition is not entirely uncontroversial. It is violated by relative cutoffs that are based on the benefits obtained at some percentile other than 100 per cent. For example, if the cutoff for the least advantaged group is 90 per cent of the median (i.e. 50th percentile) benefits, then, in $\langle 1,3,5,7,n \rangle$, only those with less than 4.5 (90 per cent of the median of 5) are in the least advantaged group. This cutoff is insensitive to the level of benefits of the best-off position (unlike an average benefits cutoff, which is so sensitive). Hence, there does not exist any n such that everyone in $\langle 1,3,5,7,n \rangle$ except the best-off position be in the least advantaged group, and thus Non-Best Off Includable is violated.

It turns out, however, that a significant result can be obtained without assuming Non-Best Off Includable. Consider the following condition:

> *Conditional Worst Off Included.* If there is some inequality, then all worst-off individuals are in the least advantaged group.

The idea is that, although the least advantaged group may be empty where there is perfect equality, in all other cases the group is not empty and includes at least all worst-off persons. This may seem fairly plausible for a relative approach.

Result 2. Suppose (1) the cutoff function satisfies Conditional Best Off Excluded, and Conditional Worst Off Included, and (2) the justice relation satisfies the Core Difference Principle, and consider any two alternatives X and Y for which the benefits in the worst-off position in X are greater than those in Y. In this case: (*a*) if the justice relation satisfies Acyclicity, then Y is not more just than X, (*b*) if the justice relation satisfies Strong Acyclicity, then Y is not at least as just as X, and (*c*) if the justice relation satisfies Transitivity, then X is more just than Y.

Adding Conditional Worst Off Included ensures that all conflicts involving worst-off individuals take place within the least advantaged group. Given the other conditions, this ensures that absolute priority must be given to the worst-off position. Thus, Non-Best Off Includable is not essential for the Minimal Maximin result.

Conditional Worst Off Included is sufficient for the result in the context of the other conditions. It is not, however, as plausible as it may at first seem. It rules out, for example, a cutoff of 50 per cent of mean, or median benefits. For example, in $\langle 5,6,7 \rangle$ (average and median of 6), the worst-off individual has more than 50 per cent of the average (and median) benefits and is thus excluded from the least advantaged group.

It turns out, however, that a significant—but slightly weaker—result can be obtained without assuming Conditional Worst Off Included (or any replacement). Consider, then,

Result 3. Suppose (1) the cutoff function satisfies Monotonicity and Conditional Best Off Excluded, and (2) the justice relation satisfies the Core Difference Principle, and consider any two alternatives X and Y for which the benefits in the worst-off position in X are greater than those in Y *and, for each of X and Y, their respective worst-off individuals are in their least advantaged group.* In this case: (*a*) if the justice relation satisfies Acyclicity, then Y is not more just than X, (*b*) if the justice relation satisfies Strong Acyclicity, then Y is not at least as just as X, and (*c*) if the justice relation satisfies Transitivity, then X is more just than Y.

This result shows that if the controversial Non-Best Off Includable is dropped (and the uncontroversial Monotonicity invoked), the difference principle must agree with Minimal Maximin in those cases where the worst-off individuals in each alternative are in their respective least advantaged groups. The result may not hold where the worst-off individual is not part of an alternative's least advantaged group. In this case, however, *no one* is a member of that group. The core cases of interest are those where the least advantaged group is not empty. Thus, if the conditions of this result are accepted, there are significant limitations on the form that the difference principle can take.

5. Conditional Best Off Excluded Reconsidered

The previous results have assumed Conditional Best Off Excluded, which is a relatively weak condition and compatible with, to our knowledge, all the relative definitions of the least advantaged group that are used in practice. Consider, for example, where the cutoff is some percentage, between 0 and 100, of the *mean* benefits. This will satisfy the above condition, since, for any unequal distribution, the best-off individuals are above the mean. Conditional Best Off Excluded is also satisfied by any cutoff that is some percentage, between 0 and 100, of the benefits at some specified benefit *percentile* inclusively between 0 and 100. It is satisfied, for example, by the cutoff of 90 per cent of the benefits at the 80th percentile.

Nonetheless, it turns out that Conditional Best Off Excluded is not entirely uncontroversial—even for relative cutoff frameworks (as we assume throughout). Consider, for example, (2,2.1,2.1). Is it obvious that the second and third individuals should be excluded from the least advantaged group? After all, their benefits, we may suppose, are only trivially greater than those of the worst-off person. At least sometimes, it seems, best-off individuals should be considered part of the least advantaged group.

Consider instead the following condition:

Non-Worst Off Excludable. For any alternative and any individual, it is possible to increase sufficiently the benefits of those individuals with greater benefits so that they are not members of the least advantaged group.

This is entailed by Conditional Best Off Excluded since, for any alternative with some inequality (e.g. $\langle 2,3,4 \rangle$), and any given position (e.g. the first person), one can increase the benefits of all the better-off positions (if there are any) to be equal to the benefits of the best-off position (e.g. to $\langle 2,4,4 \rangle$), and then Conditional Best Off Excluded entails that they are not in the least advantaged group. This condition does not, however, entail Conditional Best Off Excluded, since it does not guarantee that the best-off position is excluded from the least advantaged group (even where there is inequality). It can allow, for example, that everyone is in the least advantaged group for $\langle 2,2.1,2.1 \rangle$. It only guarantees that non-worst-off individuals *can be excluded* by sufficiently increasing their benefits. It is thus a much weaker condition than Conditional Best Off Excluded.

If we impose only Monotonicity and Non-Worst Off Excludable (but not Non-Best Off Includable, Worst Off Included, or Conditional Best Off Excluded), then the Core Difference Principle can diverge significantly from leximin. This is because these two cutoff conditions are also satisfied by *absolute* cutoff functions, and, as discussed in Section 3, absolute cutoffs can satisfy the background conditions without satisfying Minimal Maximin. Our concern, however, is to explore the possibility of using a *relative* cutoff that diverges from Minimal Maximin. Some of our earlier conditions ruled out absolute cutoffs, but we have now dropped them because they also controversially ruled out certain seemingly plausible relative cutoff functions. The following condition, however, rules out absolute cutoffs without ruling out any minimally plausible relative cutoffs.

Strict Monotonicity. For any two alternatives X and Y, (1) if the benefits of each individual are at least as great in X as in Y, then $c(X) \geq c(Y)$, and (2) if each individual has more benefits in X as in Y, then $c(X) > c(Y)$.

This is like Monotonicity, except that the second clause has been added. It rules out absolute cutoffs by requiring that the cutoff increase when everyone's benefits increase. All minimally plausible relative cutoffs satisfy this condition.

Result 3 above established that, given Conditional Best Off Excluded and our other conditions, the Core Difference Principle must satisfy Minimal Maximin when the worst-off individuals of X and Y are in their respective least advantaged groups. We have now dropped Conditional Best Off Excluded and replaced it with the weaker Non-Worst Off Excludable and also strengthened Monotonicity to Strict Monotonicity. We shall now examine whether this broader framework opens up the possibility of the Core Difference Principle violating Minimal Maximin.

To start, note that no new possibilities are opened up concerning cutoff functions that set the cutoff: (1) between 0 and 100 per cent of mean benefits, or (2) between 0 and 100 of some percentile benefits (e.g. median benefits). This is because such cutoff functions satisfy Monotonicity and Conditional Best Off Excluded, and thus Result 3 establishes that they cannot significantly diverge from Minimal Maximin.

Weakening Conditional Best Off Excluded to Non-Worst Off Excludable does, however, open up the possibility of a different kind of cutoff function. Consider *worst-off-based cutoff functions*, which are strictly increasing functions of the benefits of the worst-off individuals (e.g. some percentage above 100 per cent of the benefit level of the worst-off person, or some fixed number of units above that benefit level). Such cutoffs violate Conditional Best Off Excluded, since, wherever they set the cutoff above the worst-off position, the best-off person might have less than the cutoff but still be better off than the worst-off person. In this case, the best-off person would be deemed to be in the least advantaged group, and that violates Conditional Best Off Excluded. Moreover, worst-off-based cutoff functions satisfy Strict Monotonicity (trivially) and Non-Worst Off Excludable (since the benefits of all the non-worst off can be increased to be above the specified worst-off-based cutoff).

Of course, it might be that even worst-off-based cutoff functions cannot significantly diverge from Minimal Maximin. Our next result establishes that this is not so. Indeed, it establishes this, even if we add the following standard condition and demand Transitivity:

> *Strong Pareto.* For any two alternatives X and Y, if the benefits of each person are at least as great in X as in Y, then (1) X is as least as just as Y, and (2) if there is at least one person who has more benefits in X than in Y, then X is more just than Y.

Strong Pareto is a weak efficiency condition on the promotion of benefits (much weaker than the utilitarian sum-total conception of efficiency). It requires, for example, that $\langle 2,4,6 \rangle$ be judged more just than $\langle 1,4,6 \rangle$ and also more just than $\langle 2,3,5 \rangle$. It is silent about whether $\langle 2,4,6 \rangle$ is more just than $\langle 99,1,6 \rangle$.

In our results so far we have not needed to assume Completeness or Strong Pareto. The following possibility result, however, holds even if they are assumed.

Result 4. Suppose the cutoff function satisfies Strict Monotonicity and Non-Worst Off Excludable. Under these conditions, there exists a justice relation that (1) satisfies the Core Difference Principle, Transitivity, Completeness, and Strong Pareto, and (2) sometimes judges an alternative Y to be more just than an alternative X, where: (*a*) the benefits in the worst-off position in X are greater than those in Y and (*b*) the worst-off individuals of X and Y are in their respective least advantaged groups.

The proof of this result, which we here outline, is constructive in that we define a cutoff function and a justice relation satisfying all the conditions and which violates Minimal Maximin. The justice relation that we appeal to is Modified Total Restricted Benefits Principle with the cutoff as some positive number of units greater than the benefits of the worst-off individual. This cutoff straightforwardly satisfies both Strict Monotonicity and Non-Worst Off Excludable. The justice relation generated by applying this cutoff on the Modified Total Restricted Benefits Principle is obviously complete and straightforwardly satisfies Strong Pareto. Moreover, it ensures that the Core Difference Principle is satisfied. For example, if the cutoff is 5 units above the lowest benefit level, then $\langle 2,8,9 \rangle$ (cutoff of 7 and total restricted benefits of 16) is judged more just than $\langle 2,3,9 \rangle$ (cutoff of 7 and total restricted benefits of 12), as required by the Core Difference Principle. It also ensures that Minimal Maximin is violated. For example, if the cutoff is 5 units above the lowest level, then $\langle 1,5,10 \rangle$ (cutoff of 6 and total restricted benefits of 12) is judged more just than $\langle 2,2,10 \rangle$ (cutoff of 7 and total restricted benefits of 11). We prove in the Appendix that the relation satisfies Transitivity. Hence, this version of the difference principle constitutes a real alternative to leximin.

Thus, if the cutoff function defining the least advantaged group need only satisfy Strict Monotonicity and Non-Worst Off Excludable, the difference principle can significantly diverge from leximin (violate Minimal Maximin)—even if Transitivity, Completeness, and Strong Pareto are required. Of course, there could be additional plausible cutoff conditions that rule out this possibility. We are, however, reasonably optimistic that worst-off-based cutoff functions are the most promising way for the least advantaged group to be defined, and thus doubtful that there are any additional plausible cutoff conditions that would rule out such functions.

There are, however, other ways that the significance of this result can be challenged, and we address them briefly in the next section.

6. Indeterminate or Comparison-Relative Cutoffs

So far, we have assumed that there is a determinate (sharp, precise) cutoff that defines the least advantaged group and that the cutoff for a given alternative is *comparison-invariant* in the sense that it is the same no matter what alternative it is compared with. Each of these assumptions could, of course, be questioned. We note below that Results 1–3—the results that show that, given certain assumptions about cutoff functions, the difference principle cannot radically disagree with leximin—remain valid even if these two assumptions are each relaxed. Proofs of these claims are given in Tungodden (2004).

First, the cutoff for the least advantaged group may be allowed to be *indeterminate* (i.e. be in some *range of values* with no particular value in the range being uniquely correct). In this case, the results remain valid even if the core difference principle is weakened to apply only when someone who is *determinately* in the least advantaged group benefits and no one who is determinately or indeterminately in the least advantaged group is made worse off.

A second way of relaxing the assumptions is by allowing cutoffs for the least advantaged group to be *comparison-relative*. This would allow, for example, that the cutoff for the least advantaged group in ⟨98,99,100⟩ need not be the same for the purposes of ranking it with ⟨980,990,1000⟩ as it is for the purposes of ranking it with ⟨8,9,10⟩. After all, it seems plausible that everyone is in the least advantaged group of ⟨98,99,100⟩ when it is compared with ⟨980,990,1000⟩, but no one is in the least advantaged group of ⟨98,99,100⟩ when it is compared with ⟨8,9,10⟩. A comparison-relative approach might, for example, set the cutoff as 5 units above the lowest value *in either alternative*. This would say that (1) in comparing ⟨98,99,100⟩ with ⟨980,990,1000⟩, the cutoff is 103, and thus everyone in the former is in its least advantaged group, but (2) in comparing ⟨98,99,100⟩ with ⟨8,9,10⟩, the cutoff is 13 and no one in the former is in its least advantaged group. Even if the nature of cutoff functions is relaxed in this way, however, Results 1–3 remain valid—even if cutoffs are also allowed to be indeterminate.

Consider now Result 4, which establish that the justice relation can radically diverge from leximin, if the assumptions on the cutoff functions are plausibly relaxed in a certain way—even if the justice relation must satisfy Transitivity, Completeness, and Strong Pareto. We shall now discuss whether this result remains valid in the context of comparison-relative framework. For simplicity, we shall assume that cutoffs are determinate, and will not give the needed reformulations of the various conditions in the comparison-relative framework.

To start, note that the comparison-relative framework can be understood *broadly* so that it allows, but does not require, cutoffs to vary with the comparison being made. In this broad sense, the comparison-relative framework includes the comparison-invariant framework, and thus Result 4 remains fully valid. Alternatively, the comparison-relative framework can be understood *narrowly* in the sense that it *requires* cutoffs to vary, at least sometimes, with the comparisons being made. Any comparison-invariant cutoffs—such as the worst-off-based function that we invoked for the proof of Result 4—are ruled out. Hence, our proof of Result 4 is not valid for this narrow framework.

We are inclined to think that the narrow comparison-relative framework is the appropriate framework. To motivate this view, suppose that we use a cutoff of 2 units above the lowest benefit level, focus on the total restricted benefits (i.e. benefits up to the cutoff), and consider $\langle 1,3,3,4,4 \rangle$ and $\langle 2,2,2,4,4 \rangle$. On the comparison-independent approach, the former (with a cutoff of 3) has *lower* total restricted benefits (13) than the latter (with a cutoff of 4 and total restricted benefits of 14). On the narrow comparison-relative approach, however, an opposite conclusion can be reached. Suppose that, for this comparison, the cutoff is 2 units higher than the lowest benefit level *in either alternative*. In this case, $\langle 1,3,3,4,4 \rangle$ still has a cutoff of 3 and total restricted benefits of 13, but $\langle 2,2,2,4,4 \rangle$ now also has a cutoff of 3 (not 4), and total restricted benefits of 12 (not 14). Hence, this comparison-relative version of the total restricted benefits principle favors $\langle 1,3,3,4,4 \rangle$ over $\langle 2,2,2,4,4 \rangle$. This seems more plausible than the opposed judgement reached by the comparison-invariant version. In the context of this comparison, it seems quite implausible to ignore the benefits beyond 3 for the first alternative but count them for the second alternative. The same cutoff, it seems, should be used for both.

Suppose, then, that we assume the narrow comparison-relative framework, and that we take the cutoff to be 2 units higher than the lowest benefit level in either compared alternative. Does the Modified Total Restricted Benefits Principle—thus reinterpreted—still satisfy the conditions of Result 4? Unfortunately it does not. It violates Acyclicity (and hence Transitivity). To see this, note that it judges (1) $\langle 1,3,3,3,3,3 \rangle$ as more just than $\langle 2,2,2,4,4,4 \rangle$ (with a cutoff of 3 and total restricted benefits of 16 and 15 respectively), (2) $\langle 2,2,2,4,4,4 \rangle$ as more just than $\langle 2,3,3,3,3,3 \rangle$ (with a cutoff of 4 and total restricted benefits of 18 and 17 respectively), and (3) $\langle 2,3,3,3,3,3 \rangle$ as more just than $\langle 1,3,3,3,3,3 \rangle$ (with a cutoff of 3 and total restricted benefits of 17 and 16 respectively). In sum $\langle 1,3,3,3,3,3 \rangle$ is more just than $\langle 2,2,2,4,4,4 \rangle$, which is more just than $\langle 2,3,3,3,3,3 \rangle$, which is more just than $\langle 1,3,3,3,3,3 \rangle$, which violates Acyclicity.

In this example, the problem of Acyclicity arises because the cutoff for a given alternative varies with the comparison being made. $\langle 1,3,3,3,3,3 \rangle$ is more just than $\langle 2,2,2,4,4,4 \rangle$ based on a cutoff of 3, and $\langle 2,2,2,4,4,4 \rangle$ is more just than $\langle 2,3,3,3,3,3 \rangle$ based on a cutoff of 4. The first judgement ignores the benefits above 3 in $\langle 2,2,2,4,4,4 \rangle$ whereas the second judgement does not. It is thus not surprising that Acyclicity is violated.

It is, however, possible to satisfy Transitivity (and hence Acyclicity) and all the other conditions of Result 4 if one does not require disagreement with Minimal Maximin. Leximin straightforwardly satisfies Transitivity, Completeness, and Strong Pareto. Moreover, it ensures that the Core Difference Principle is satisfied for any definition of the least advantaged group satisfying Strict Monotonicity and Non-Worst Off Excludable (even though it gives no role to the cutoff and thus gives no special role to the least advantaged group so defined).

Thus, in the narrow comparison-relative framework, the conditions of Result 4 can be satisfied (e.g. by leximin) as long as one does not require that Minimal Maximin be violated. The crucial question is whether they can be satisfied in a way that violates

Minimal Maximin (i.e. in way that significantly diverges from leximin). Unfortunately, we do not know the answer to this question. We have tried to find a justice relation that establishes this possibility, and we have tried to prove that it is not possible, but both attempts have been unsuccessful. We must leave this as an important open question: Is it possible in the narrow comparison-relative framework to satisfy Strict Monotonicity, Non-Worst Off Excludable, Acyclicity, Strong Pareto, and the Core Difference Principle in a way that violates Minimal Maximin (and thus significantly diverges from leximin)?

7. Conclusion

Most interpreters of Rawls's difference principle have interpreted it as leximin, and thus as requiring that any alternative that gives greater benefits to the worst-off position be judged more just. This, however, was not how Rawls intended this principle to be understood. As indicated by the quoted passages at the beginning of the chapter, he intended it to require lexical priority to the *aggregative benefits* (e.g. total or average) to the least advantaged group (as opposed to lexical priority to the worst-off individual). We have explored the possibility of the difference principle significantly diverging from leximin.

As we noted, the difference principle can radically diverge from leximin if the cut-off for the least advantaged group is a *fixed* number (i.e. absolute cutoff function). In that case, for example, all the conditions that we have invoked other than Minimal Maximin are satisfied by the principle that judges one alternative at least as just as another if and only (1) the sum of the total restricted benefits is greater, or (2) the sum of the total restricted benefits is equal and the sum of the total benefits is at least as great. Almost everyone interested in the difference principle, however, is interested in combining it with relative cutoffs (which vary with the level of benefits of individuals and satisfy Strict Monotonicity). Hence, we have focused on this latter approach.

The most common cutoff relative functions specify the cutoff as some percentage, between 0 and 100, of the *mean* benefits, or as some percentage, between 0 and 100, of the benefits at some specified benefit *percentile* inclusively between 0 and 100 (e.g. median benefits). Such cutoff functions satisfy Conditional Best Off Excluded, which requires that the best-off individuals not be part of the least advantaged group when not everyone has the same benefits. Results 1–3, however, established that any justice relation satisfying this cutoff condition and the other background conditions must, when the worst-off individual is in the least advantaged group, also satisfy

Minimal Maximin (which requires that an alternative with lower benefits for the worst-off individual not be judged more just). Consequently, any such approach cannot significantly diverge from leximin.

Conditional Best Off Excluded, however, is not uncontroversial. It rules out the possibility of appealing to a worst-off-based cutoff function that sets the cutoff as some fixed number of units above the benefit level of the worst off. Such a cutoff violates Conditional Best Off Excluded by including the best-off individuals in the least advantaged group when their benefit levels are sufficiently close to those of the worst-off individuals. We believe that such cutoffs are especially plausible and in line with the Rawlsian perspective, since they always include the least well-off individuals in the least advantaged group, typically include some others who are better off, but do not include those who are sufficiently better off than the worst-off individuals.

Conditional Best Off Excluded, we suggested, should be weakened to Non-Worst Off Excludable (which requires that, for any alternative and any individual, it is possible to increase sufficiently the benefits of those individuals with greater benefits so that they are not members of the least advantaged group). Result 4 then establishes that, in a comparison-invariant framework satisfying Strict Monotonicity and Non-Worst Off Excludable, it is possible for the Core Difference Principle, Transitivity, Completeness, and Strong Pareto to be satisfied in a way that violates Minimal Maximin. Indeed, the result is constructive and appeals to a particularly appealing way of satisfying these conditions: the cutoff for the least advantaged group, for a given comparison, is set at some positive number above the lowest benefit level in either alternative, and then one alternative is judged at least as just as another if and only if (1) its total restricted benefits (i.e. benefits up to the cutoff level) are at least as great, or (2) its total restricted benefits are equal and its total (unrestricted) benefits are at least as great. This is indeed a promising version of the difference principle that clearly diverges significantly from leximin.

Finally, we noted that the above comparison-invariant framework (in which the cutoff for a given alternative is the same no matter what alternative it is compared with) seemed somewhat questionable. Suppose, for example, that cutoffs are set at 2 units above the lowest level and consider the comparison of $(1,3,3,4,4)$ and $(2,2,2,4,4)$. The comparison-invariant approach says the cutoff for the former is 3 and the cutoff for the latter is 4. It seems, however, that they should have the same cutoff when they are compared. We therefore briefly discussed what results can be obtained if one moved to a comparison-relative framework in which, for a given comparison, the cutoff is the same for the two alternatives. Unfortunately, we have not been able to determine whether in this framework it is possible to satisfy the basic conditions without entailing Minimal Maximin. This remains an important open question.

Appendix. Proofs of Results

For any alternative X, let x_i refer to the benefits of person i in X and x^i the benefits in position i in X, where $x^1 \leq x^2 \leq \ldots x^i \leq \ldots \leq x^n$. We may now introduce the formal versions of the various conditions imposed on the cutoff function.

Monotonicity. For any two alternatives X and Y, if for all individuals i, $x_i \geq y_i$, then $c(X) \geq c(Y)$.
Conditional Best Off Excluded. For any alternative X such that $x^1 < x^n$, and any individual i, if $x_i = x^n$, then $x_i \geq c(X)$.
Non-Best Off Includable. For any alternative X, there exists another alternative Y such that, for all individuals i, (1) if $x_i = x^n$, then $y_i > x_i$, and (2) if $x_i < x^n$, then $y_i = x_i$ and $y_i < c(Y)$.
Conditional Worst Off Included. For any alternative X such that $x^1 < x^n$, and any individual i, if $x_i = x^1$, then $x_i < c(X)$.
Non-Worst Off Excludable. For any alternative X and individual k, there exists an alternative Y such that for any individual i (1) if $x_i \leq x_k$, then $y_i = x_i$, and (2) if $x_i > x_k$, then $y_i > x_i$ and $y_i \geq c(Y)$.
Strict Monotonicity. For any two alternatives X and Y, (1) if for all individuals i, $x_i \geq y_i$, then $c(X) \geq c(Y)$, and (2) if for all individuals i, $x_i > y_i$, then $c(X) > c(Y)$.

We are now in a position to prove the various results. As in the main text, Benefitism and Domain Richness will not be stated explicitly when reporting the results.

Result 1. Suppose (1) the cutoff function satisfies Monotonicity, Conditional Best Off Excluded, and Non-Best Off Includable, and (2) the justice relation satisfies the Core Difference Principle, and consider any two alternatives X and Y for which the benefits in the worst-off position in X are greater than those in Y. In this case: (*a*) if the justice relation satisfies Acyclicity, then Y is not more just than X, (*b*) if the justice relation satisfies Strong Acyclicity, then Y is not at least as just as X, and (*c*) if the justice relation satisfies Transitivity, then X is more just than Y.

Proof

(1) Consider any two alternatives X and Y and persons j and k, where $x_j = x^1 > y_k = y^1$.

(2) By Domain Richness, there exists an alternative Z, for which $x_k \geq x_j > z_k > y_k$ and $x_j > z_i = z_j > z_k$ for all individuals different from k. From Conditional Best Off Excluded, it follows that (at least) all individuals different from k are not in the least advantaged group $L(Z)$.

(3) By Domain Richness, Non-Best Off Includable, and Monotonicity, there exists an alternative W, where $w_i = w^n > y_i$ for all i different from k, $w^n > z_k > w_k > y_k$, and k is a member of $L(W)$. Moreover, from Conditional Best Off Excluded, it follows that no one else is a member of $L(W)$. Finally, from the Core Difference Principle, it follows that W is more just than Y.

(4) Suppose that $L(X)$ is empty. Then it follows from the Core Difference Principle that X is more just than W (because k is the only member of $L(X)$ and $L(W)$ and $x_k > w_k$). By (3) and Acyclicity, it then follows that Y is not more just than X.

(5) Suppose that $L(X)$ is non-empty. Then it follows from the Core Difference Principle that X is more just than Z. Moreover, in this case, by (2) and (3) and the Core Difference Principle,

it follows that Z is more just than W (because k is the only member of the union of $L(Z)$ and $L(W)$ and $z_k > w_k$). By (3) and Acyclicity, it then follows that Y is not more just than X.

(6) In both cases, replacing Acyclicity with Strong Acyclicity ensures that Y is not at least as just as X, and replacing Acyclicity with Transitivity ensures that X is more just than Y.

Result 2. Suppose (1) the cutoff function satisfies Conditional Best Off Excluded, and Conditional Worst Off Included, and (2) the justice relation satisfies the Core Difference Principle, and consider any two alternatives X and Y for which the benefits in the worst-off position in X are greater than those in Y. In this case: (*a*) if the justice relation satisfies Acyclicity, then Y is not more just than X, (*b*) if the justice relation satisfies Strong Acyclicity, then Y is not at least as just as X, and (*c*) if the justice relation satisfies Transitivity, then X is more just than Y.

Proof

(1) Consider any two alternatives X and Y and persons j and k, where $x_j = x^1 > y_k = y^1$.

(2) By Domain Richness, there exists an alternative Z, where $x_k \geq x_j > z_k > y_k$ and $z_i = x_j$ for all individuals different from k. From Conditional Best Off Excluded, it follows that all individuals different from k are not in the least advantaged group $L(Z)$. From Conditional Worst Off Included, it follows that k is in the least advantaged group $L(Z)$. From the Core Difference Principle, it follows that X is more just than Z.

(3) By Domain Richness and Conditional Worst Off Included, there exists an alternative W, where $w_i = w^n > y_i$ for all i different from k, $w^n > z_k > w_k > y_k$, and k is a member of $L(W)$. Moreover, from Conditional Best Off Excluded, it follows that no one else is a member of $L(W)$. Finally, from the Core Difference Principle, it follows that W is more just than Y.

(4) By (2) and (3) and the Core Difference Principle, it follows that Z is more just than W (because k is the only member of the union of $L(Z)$ and $L(W)$ and $z_k > w_k$). By (2) and (3) and Acyclicity, it then follows that Y is not more just than X. Replacing Acyclicity with Strong Acyclicity ensures that Y is not at least as just as X. Replacing Acyclicity with Transitivity ensures that X is more just than Y.

Result 3. Suppose (1) the cutoff function satisfies Monotonicity and Conditional Best Off Excluded, and (2) the justice relation satisfies the Core Difference Principle, and consider any two alternatives X and Y for which the benefits in the worst-off position in X are greater than those in Y and, *for each of X and Y, their respective worst-off individuals are in their least advantaged group.* In this case: (*a*) if the justice relation satisfies Acyclicity, then Y is not more just than X, (*b*) if the justice relation satisfies Strong Acyclicity, then Y is not at least as just as X, and (*c*) if the justice relation satisfies Transitivity, then X is more just than Y.

Proof

(1) Consider any two alternatives X and Y and persons j and k, where $x_j = x^1 > y_k = y^1$ and j is in $L(X)$ and k in $L(Y)$.

(2) By Domain Richness, there exists an alternative Z, where $x_k \geq x_j > z_k > y_k$ and $x_j > z_i = z_j > z_k$ for all individuals different from k. From Conditional Best Off Excluded, it follows that all individuals different from k are not in the least advantaged group $L(Z)$. From

the Core Difference Principle, taking into account that j is in $L(X)$ (from (1)), it follows that X is more just than Z.

(3) By Domain Richness, Monotonicity, and (1), there exists an alternative W, where $w_i = w^n > y_i$ for all i different from k, $w^n > z_k > w_k > y_k$, and k is a member of $L(W)$. Moreover, from Conditional Best Off Excluded, it follows that no one else is a member of $L(W)$. Finally, from the Core Difference Principle, it follows that W is more just than Y.

(4) By (2) and (3) and the Core Difference Principle, it follows that Z is more just than W (because k is the only member of the union of $L(Z)$ and $L(W)$ and $z_k > w_k$). By (2) and (3) and Acyclicity, it then follows that Y is not more just than X. Replacing Acyclicity with Strong Acyclicity ensures that Y is not at least as just as X. Replacing Acyclicity with Transitivity ensures that X is more just than Y.

Result 4. Suppose the cutoff function satisfies Strict Monotonicity and Non-Worst Off Excludable. Under these conditions, there exists a justice relation that (1) satisfies the Core Difference Principle, Transitivity, Completeness, and Strong Pareto, and (2) sometimes judges an alternative Y to be more just than an alternative X, where: (*a*) the benefits in the worst-off position in X are greater than those in Y and (*b*) the worst-off individuals of X and Y are in their respective least advantaged groups.

Proof

As indicated in the text, the Modified Total Restricted Benefits Principle satisfies the various stated conditions. We here give the proof that it is transitive. The rest of the proof is straightforward and indicated in the test.

Transitivity. We will show that for any three distinct alternatives X, Y, Z, if the Modified Total Restricted Benefits Principle judges X as at least as just as Y and Y as at least as just as Z, then it judges X at least as just as Z. Given that the Modified Total Restricted Benefits Principle judges one alternative at least as just as another if and only if one of two clauses is satisfied, there are four possible cases to consider (two ways that X can be judged at least as just as Y, and two ways that Y can be judge at least as just as Z).

(1) Suppose clause (1) of the Modified Total Restricted Benefits Principle applies both to the comparison of X and Y and to the comparison of Y and Z. It then follows straightforwardly that it also applies to a comparison of X and Z, where the total restricted benefits are at least as great in X as in Z.

(2) Suppose clause (2) of the Modified Total Restricted Benefits Principle applies both to the comparison of X and Y and to the comparison of Y and Z. It then follows straightforwardly that it also applies to a comparison of X and Z, where the total (unrestricted benefits) are at least as great in X as in Z.

(3) Suppose clause (1) of the Modified Total Restricted Benefits Principle applies to the comparison of X and Y and clause (2) to the comparison of Y and Z. It then follows straight-forwardly that clause (1) applies to a comparison of X and Z, where the total restricted benefits are at least as great in X as in Z.

(4) Suppose clause (2) of the Modified Total Restricted Benefits Principle applies to the comparison of X and Y and clause (1) to the comparison of Y and Z. It then follows

straightforwardly that clause (1) applies to a comparison of X and Z, where the total restricted benefits are at least as great in X as in Z.

Given (1)–(4), it follows that Transitivity is satisfied.

References

POGGE, T. (1989), *Realizing Rawls* (Ithaca, NY: Cornell University Press).

RAWLS, J. (1971), *A Theory of Justice* (Cambridge, Mass.: Harvard University Press).

_____ (1993), *Political Liberalism* (New York: Columbia University Press).

TUNGODDEN, B. (1999), 'Rawlsian Reasoning and the Distribution Problem', *Social Choice and Welfare*, 16: 229–45.

_____ (2004), 'The Difference Principle: Is Limited Aggregation Possible?', mimeo, Norwegian School of Economics and Business Administration.

8

Feminist Distributive Justice and the Relevance of Equal Relations

Linda Barclay

1. Introduction

What should feminists expect from a theory of distributive justice? While there are some powerful feminist critiques of distributive justice, there are few well-developed, feminist-inspired alternatives (Fraser 1995; Phillips 2004; Young 1990). Elizabeth Anderson's 'democratic equality' stands as one of the most significant conceptions of distributive justice congenial from, and partly motivated by, a feminist perspective (1999).

Anderson develops her conception of democratic equality partly as a response to what she dubs 'equality of fortune' or luck egalitarianism, the most dominant egalitarian conception of distributive justice in its various versions. Despite its claim to be egalitarian, Anderson persuasively argues that equality of fortune has lost touch with the real value and point of equality, primarily because it fails to respect all people as moral equals. In wrongly supposing that the central egalitarian imperative is to negate the role of luck in determining how well a person does, luck egalitarianism is disrespectful to people and invites us to feel contemptuous pity for the badly off. It also fails to address what Anderson considers the most pressing failure of equality: forms of social and institutional oppression. Most of the things that make people's lives go very badly are forms of oppression, not bad luck.

I wish to thank Elizabeth Anderson, Nils Holtug, and Kasper Lippert-Rasmussen for their very helpful comments on an earlier draft of this chapter.

More specifically, it is patterns of socialisation and social relationship, institutional rules and norms, and forms of cultural and symbolic representation that significantly impede many people's chances of faring well. People's lives can go badly because they are excluded from productive activity and thus lose an important source of self-development and esteem; or because they perform menial and repetitive tasks in a workplace where they have no decision-making power; or because they are powerless to effectively influence political decision-making; or because social expectation and the rules and norms of institutions effectively combine to make it difficult to achieve work success if one is a mother; or because prevailing cultural stereotypes and images and media representation encourage discrimination, violence, and social exclusion even when such things are formally prohibited; and so on.[1]

The feminist complaint is not only that significant forms of oppression are ignored by most discussions of justice, but, more strongly, that most theories of justice are *incapable* of addressing oppression. Most contemporary theories of justice, including the family of equality of fortune views that Anderson discusses, are almost exclusively concerned with the distribution of privately enjoyed divisible goods, such as wealth and income. While the distribution of wealth and income is a substantial part of justice, not least because wealth and income are related in complex ways to oppression, many forms of injustice cannot be dealt with by a redistribution of money. When lack of money is not the problem, or only part of the problem, more money is not the answer.

For the rest of the chapter, I will accept the claim that any credible theory of egalitarian justice must address, must be able to address, the patterns of socialization and social relationship, institutional rules and norms, and forms of cultural and symbolic representation that cause many people to fare badly. This leaves open the question of what role these elements should play in an egalitarian theory of justice. One response might be to argue that many of these factors can be accommodated by the prominent approaches to justice, even if most proponents of those approaches have tended to overemphasise the distribution of material goods. For example, one could argue that equalizing opportunity for welfare allows, indeed, properly demands, including oppressive relationships as among the targets of egalitarian redress. A resourcist theory of justice might plausibly argue that rights, opportunities, and the social bases of self-respect are among the things to be equally distributed, not just income and wealth, and an equal distribution and proper enforcement of rights, opportunities, and the bases of self-respect go a long way towards undermining oppressive relations.[2]

---

[1] For a more detailed discussion of forms of oppression, see Young (1990).
[2] I myself think that both welfarist and resourcist theories of justice can argue along these lines with some plausibility.

Anderson's own solution involves rejecting resourcist and welfare approaches altogether. She argues that the metric of equality, the answer to the 'equality of what?' question, is equal relations among citizens, understood as the absence of oppressive relations and equal participation in civil and political life. Equal relations among citizens are not just an element in securing equality of welfare, nor the effect of equality of resources broadly conceived. Instead, equal relations themselves are the aim of egalitarian justice. I will argue that this is an implausible theory of egalitarian justice. Feminists like Anderson have been right to highlight the significance of certain social and institutional relations for the well-being of citizens, but it is wrong to reduce all plausible claims of justice to the issue of equal standing among citizens.[3] After a short account of Anderson's view, I will defend this claim. First, I will argue that the ideal of equal relations piggybacks on more basic elements of individual well-being, and without further specification of what those elements are, 'relations of equality' is an indiscriminate category, unable to differentiate among the vast range of demands made in the name of justice. Second, I will argue that even with a suitable account of what elements of individual well-being are jeopardised or annulled by unequal relations, relations of equality is far too narrow as a metric of equality: many of those aspects of our well-being which plausibly command collective response have nothing at all to do with the relations in which we stand.

2. Democratic Equality

The primary assertion of all true egalitarian movements, according to Anderson, is the equal moral worth of all persons. The social and political equality egalitarians champion is based on this fact of universal moral equality. Thus, egalitarian movements have sought to abolish oppression, forms of relationship in which some people dominate, marginalise, demean, and inflict violence on others, because of differences in ethnicity, class, national origin, and so on. Such differences between people never justify treatment that negates equal moral worth. Positively, egalitarianism seeks a social order in which people stand in relations of equality, constituted by democratic community understood as collective self-determination by means of open discussion and participation among equals. I take it that there is not much within this very abstract conception of equality to cause disagreement. Everyone working within the liberal egalitarian tradition accepts that ethnic, class, and gender differences between

---

[3] At this stage, I mean to use the notion of well-being in a way neutral with respect to welfare, resources, capabilities, etc. For the purposes of argument, I will later accept Anderson's claim that well-being is measured in terms of capabilities.

people cannot justify oppression. I take it that all egalitarians also accept some form or another of collective or democratic self-determination at the political level. It is the specific principles of distributive justice that Anderson derives from these abstract claims about equal moral worth that are of interest in this chapter.

According to Anderson's specific view of equality, which she calls democratic equality, 'the fundamental obligation of citizens to one another is to secure the social conditions of everyone's freedom' (1999: 314). In fulfilling their obligations to secure the social conditions of everyone's freedom, citizens have an obligation to secure relations of equality because relations of equality are the central social condition of freedom. For example, standing in equal relations with others means we are not subject to oppressive relations, and it is oppressive relationships that negate freedom. Standing equally to one another means no one is subject to arbitrary violence by another, which is a fundamental condition of genuine choice. Equals are not marginalised, so they are free to participate in politics and the major institutions of civil society; they are not dominated, so they do not live at the mercy of others' wills, which means they govern their lives by their own wills, which is freedom, and so on (1999: 315).

Anderson argues that egalitarians should seek equality for all in terms of capabilities, as specified by Amartya Sen (1980, 1993). Negatively, people are entitled to whatever capabilities are necessary to enable them to avoid or escape oppressive relationships. One might, for example, insist that all people be provided with a certain level of material wealth because poverty renders one particularly vulnerable to entanglement in relations of exploitation and domination. Positively, people are entitled to whatever capabilities are necessary for functioning as an equal citizen in a democratic state, understood not only as functioning as a political agent, but also as participating as an equal in civil society, that is, the vast sphere of social life that is open to the general public but is not part of the state bureaucracy. A disabled person's standing as an equal would be jeopardised if we failed to provide a state subsidy for wheelchairs, for example, because the inability to move about in public spaces negates equal participation. Anderson argues that all people are entitled to a certain threshold of capabilities necessary to stand as an equal.[4]

3. Equal Relations and Well-Being

Democratic equality is congenial from a feminist perspective inasmuch as it takes relationships as the central concern from the perspective of justice. As Anderson

---

[4] She argues that this is so irrespective of what level of responsibility an individual bears for falling below the threshold, a position that makes her view unattractive for many luck egalitarians. See e.g. Arneson (2000).

puts it, democratic equality is 'a relational theory of equality: it views equality as a social relationship', and 'democratic egalitarians are fundamentally concerned with the relationships within which goods are distributed, not only with the distribution of goods themselves' (1999: 314).[5] Certain patterns of distribution of divisible goods may well be necessary to realize equal relations, but they are not sufficient in themselves and nor are they the currency of egalitarian justice.

However, the nature of relations of equality and the capabilities supposed to secure them is considerably unclear, as is the connection between the two. We can start by considering oppressive relationships. Anderson claims to follow Iris Marion Young's account of oppression, which identifies five different forms: exploitation, marginalization, powerlessness, cultural imperialism, and (exposure to) violence (1990). In each of the five cases a person's standing in relation to others is identified as oppressive because some or another important aspect of their well-being is jeopardised by those relations. Thus, being exploited means exercising one's capacities 'under the control, according to the purposes, and for the benefit of other people', all of which leads to material deprivation and a loss of control and power, as well as being deprived of important elements of self-realization and self-respect (Young 1990: 49–52). The marginalised are those expelled from participation in social life, and thus subject to material deprivation, demeaning treatment by welfare bureaucracies, a sense of uselessness, and a lack of self-respect. The powerless are those who have little capacity to influence decision-making in areas that directly affect their lives, and thus suffer exposure to disrespectful treatment, an inhibition in the development of important capacities, and a sense of powerlessness. Those subject to cultural imperialism are subject to the dominant group's perspectives and interpretations and are thus marked as deviant, inferior, or just stereotyped in various ways. The oppressed 'group's own experience and interpretation of social life finds little expression that touches the dominant culture' (Young 1990: 60).

In each of the cases of oppression, the claim is made that some important aspect of a person's well-being is jeopardised by the relation in question: the development of certain key human capacities and the ability to decide how they are used, forms of well-being for which material wealth is necessary, being treated with respect by others, being able to influence cultural meanings and images, and so on. That such aspects of a person's condition are jeopardised by the relation is what defines the relation as oppressive. If we accept that these are important elements of a person's well-being, then it can plausibly be argued that justice should be concerned with eliminating oppressive relations, and in so far as these oppressive relations are constituted or maintained by policies,

---

[5] This is slightly misleading as it stands. All egalitarian theories are relational in asmuch as they are concerned with a particular relation between individuals, namely equality. Presumably the force of Anderson's claim that democratic equality is a relational theory of equality is that relations are themselves the currency of distributive justice.

rules, and widespread norms and expectations, then it can be plausibly argued that the state may properly involve itself, *ceteris paribus*, in changing policies, rules, norms, and expectations in a range of institutions and cultural practices. None of this should obscure the fact that the notion of oppression piggybacks on more basic elements of well-being; that a relationship is identified as oppressive and thus becomes the focus of egalitarian concern is because it undermines certain aspects of a person's well-being.

It may indeed follow from all this, as many feminists have argued, that egalitarian justice has to be concerned with more than the distribution of resources (including rights and opportunities) and with something other than welfare, if some people have no preference for those aspects of well-being secured or made possible by non-oppressive relations. However, this still leaves Anderson with the task of spelling out what elements of well-being are at stake: the demand that oppressive relations should be negated is empty without some kind of account of what elements of well-being oppressive relations threaten. The point can be expressed in the language of capabilities, given Anderson's declared allegiance to the capability approach as the best account of well-being. Yet Anderson's use of the capability approach is somewhat confusing. For Sen, capabilities refer to the potentially extremely vast combinations of functionings that people can achieve, where functionings refer to the things a person can do or be. If my analysis is correct, then we can characterise an oppressive relation as one which jeopardises certain important capabilities, that is, opportunities or freedom to do and be certain valuable things. Yet Anderson seems to conflate capabilities with whatever *means*—resources, rights, opportunities, social programmes—secure certain capabilities. When she says that people are entitled to whatever capabilities they need to enjoy equal relations, she gives wheelchairs, access to money, and the like as examples. But a wheelchair is not a capability, it is a means to the attainment of a capability.[6] So when Anderson says people are entitled to whatever capabilities enable them to avoid oppressive relationships, we should properly understand this to mean that they are entitled to whatever means—wealth, policies, laws, social programmes—negate the oppressive relations that undermine important capabilities. Having those capabilities is the negation of oppression. As is obvious when stated this way, one still has to specify what those capabilities and functionings are in order to know what people are entitled to.

Similar questions arise with the more positive aspect of democratic equality: equal participation in society. What kind of participation, or capability to participate, is relevant here? And what kinds of social norms and relations threaten participation?[7] Is one excluded from civil society, and therefore does one fail to achieve equal

---

[6] Sen is critical of this kind of confusion. See Sen (1993: 40).

[7] It is unclear whether Anderson regards participation as itself a capability, or a conglomeration of a number of different capabilities, or something that ensures the attainment of more specific capabilities.

standing only if one is legally prohibited from political participation, or only if the law permits civil institutions as such to discriminate? Along with most feminists, Anderson clearly wants to classify as exclusion cases in which people's subjective feelings play a role: the inability of gays and lesbians to appear in public without shame is taken to justify the collective provision of whatever means would reinstate their equal standing, including, for example, 'significant changes in social relations of contempt and hostility, and changes in norms of gender and sexuality' (1999: 320). Even if some of us share Anderson's intuitions on this score, we need some way of determining which individuals or groups of people who feel shamed and uncertain are truly excluded. Members of odd religious cults also feel the need to hide their commitments when moving about in civil society for fear of ridicule and shame: is the incredulity of their fellow citizens really enough to jeopardize their standing as equals and thus justify the means for a suitable public relations campaign? In discussing the case of the deaf, Anderson says that we use a so-called 'objective test' of unjust disadvantage, which sounds promising in terms of resolving the problem just raised (1999: 333–5). As far as I understand it, an 'objective test' means we do not need to rely on people's subjective preferences or states to determine whether they are denied the opportunity to participate. We conclude that the deaf are excluded from society not because of what they report about their 'subjective states' but by observing that the means of communication are only accessible to those who can hear. Similarly, we conclude that the disabled are excluded from society by observing the way public institutions are only accessible to the walking, which is not based on the 'subjective states' of the disabled. Unfortunately, it seems straightforwardly false to claim that for democratic equality a person's subjective states are irrelevant in determining whether he or she suffers exclusion, otherwise we can make no sense of the claim that feelings of shame are appropriate objects of distributive justice, as are the 'self-abnegation, lack of confidence, and low self-esteem . . . that women often face from internalizing norms of femininity' (1999: 319). Clearly a number of factors can jeopardize equal participation apart from the physical configuration of public space, and Anderson regards these other factors as appropriate targets of state response.

There are other potential sources of disagreement over whether people have the genuine opportunity to participate in civil society which the so-called objective test will not resolve. One of Anderson's own repeated examples demonstrates this point particularly well. She argues that people are unconditionally entitled to whatever capabilities are objectively sufficient to stand as an equal: people's tastes as such are irrelevant. Using Thomas Scanlon's example, she argues that 'the fact that someone would rather have help in building a temple to his god than to be decently fed does not generate a greater claim on others to subsidize his temple than to ensure his access to adequate nutrition' (1999: 329). Or, more fully,

People who can't walk are entitled to accommodation in civil society: to wheelchairs, ramps on public buildings, and so forth. However, these conditions are not sensitive to variations in people's tastes. Everyone has an entitlement to the same package of capabilities, whatever else they may have, and regardless of what they would prefer to have. Thus, if a person who needs a wheelchair to get around has an involuntary expensive taste for engaging in particular religious rituals, and would prefer having this taste satisfied to having a wheelchair, democratic equality does not substitute a subsidy for her rituals for the wheelchair. For individuals need to be able to move around civil society to have equal standing as citizens, but they do not need to be able to worship in particularly expensive ways in order to function as equals. (1999: 331)

This easy assertion stands at odds with claims frequently asserted in the literature on multiculturalism to the affect that the inability to display and practise important aspects of one's religion in public space, whether due to economic or legal restrictions, *is* a form of exclusion from civil society. It has also been argued, for example, that laws that require the wearing of head protection on construction sites or when riding a motorcycle treat Sikh men unequally, excluding them from participation in important places of employment and restricting their ability to move about. Indeed, the range of possible demands made by defenders of multiculturalism almost identically match those made on behalf of women or gays and lesbians, as does the range of complaints. The religious worshipper, it is said, can plausibly contend that opportunity for equal participation in civil society is only genuinely attained when the institutions of civil society are themselves at least partly a reflection of the values and interests of the people who wish to participate. After all, a form of this claim has long been argued by feminists: genuinely equal participation for women at least sometimes requires changes to the values and culture of institutions, not just the ability to enter into and compete within them as they already are. In this vein, a religious group, particularly one whose members have on average fewer resources than others, might claim state subsidy for what Anderson identifies as an 'expensive religious taste'—particular religious rituals. Given all she says about women and gays and lesbians it is hard to understand Anderson's confidence that that kind of religious functioning can just be dismissed as an expensive taste.

The point here is not to defend the religious worshipper's claim to state subsidy of his religious rituals. The foregoing examples raise a general concern for Anderson's focus on relations of equality as the measure of justice: if the state is going to be in the business of securing equal relations, we need a clear account of what counts as oppression and equal participation. To put it again in the language of capabilities, we can say that just as we need a clear account of what valuable capabilities oppressive relations negate, so we also need an account of what particular capabilities to participate people should have. Only then can we embark on the task of assessing whether social practices and relations, the norms and rules of institutions, and forms of cultural representation threaten those capabilities and thus count as oppressive or exclusionary. In other words, this detailed specification of a range of capabilities is needed to evaluate the clamour of claims made about oppression and exclusion. Of course, this process itself will undoubtedly be fraught with disagreement over a vast range of competing views about what particular capabilities are important, or are the compelling duty of the state to secure.[8] Nonetheless, without such a concrete specification we have little way of determining whether people are oppressed or whether they enjoy equal participation, and without any way of determining this, democratic equality can be held hostage by any number of implausible claims: it will at least be very difficult to dismiss claims as expensive tastes without further ado. This would be a particularly unfortunate result for Anderson as she herself is sharply critical of equality of fortune's use of representative examples in discussing contested claims for distribution: namely, 'beach bums, the lazy and irresponsible, people who can't manage to entertain themselves with simple pleasures, religious fanatics' (1999: 288). The use of these examples is related to discussion about the significance of welfare disadvantage to distributive claims. Anderson rejects the relevance of preferences in determining what others owe us at least partly because a focus on preference holds justice hostage to the claims of spoiled brats, religious fanatics, and so on. Without a concrete specification of the capabilities people should have, the concern is that the charge can be volleyed straight back at Anderson.[9]

4. Equal Relations and Non-Equals

None of the preceding discussion shows that democratic equality is fatally flawed; it simply shows that the account of equal standing is as yet undeveloped. Anderson can of course acknowledge that we need a concrete specification of the capabilities that oppression negates, as well as a specification of the capabilities for participation that people should have, and that this is part of the task of filling out the details of the theory. None of this need affect the core claim of the theory—that equal relations among citizens is the currency of justice.

In this section, I wish to pursue a second and more fundamental criticism of democratic equality which does give reason for doubting that equal relations are

---

[8] So much so that one can surely appreciate the appeal of either a resource or a welfare approach, as opposed to a capability approach. See Arneson (1989: 93).

[9] The problem is likely to be less acute for Anderson as she argues that the state has a duty to ensure only a threshold of capabilities whereas luck egalitarians do not stop being concerned with inequalities at any level. This doesn't answer the objection, however: even providing only a threshold level of capabilities can potentially hold democratic equality hostage to a large range of apparently unreasonable demands.

plausibly the aim of distributive justice. Without a list of the concrete capabilities that unequal relations negate, equality of standing is too empty and undiscriminating as a basis for responding to distributive claims. However, limiting the range of capabilities and functioning that should evoke state concern to those related to equal standing is, on the other hand, far too narrow. There is a broad range of important capabilities and actual functionings which are part of our basic well-being and which should be central to distributive justice, but which have little to do with our standing vis-à-vis others.

We can begin by considering whether it is really plausible to suggest that every instance in which amelioration of a disadvantage seems warranted is because a person's standing vis-à-vis others is jeopardised. Recall that Anderson justifies the provision of capabilities because of their role in ensuring people can avoid entanglement in oppressive relations and enjoy equal participation as a citizen.[10] Like Anderson, Samuel Scheffler argues that questions of distribution are important because certain kinds of distribution are incongruous with equality: 'people whose basic needs have not been met—people who lack adequate food, clothing, shelter, education or medical care—cannot participate in political life or civil society on a footing of equality with others, or can do so only with great difficulty' (2002: 23).

This way of putting things strikes me as seriously odd. Why reduce the importance of having adequate food and shelter to their role in ensuring a person's equal participation in political and civil life? Being hungry and sick decidedly makes one extremely vulnerable to co-option into unequal relations in a world where not everyone is equally destitute, thus threatening to make one's already bad situation even worse: one begins with one capability failure—the inability to be well nourished—and ends with many more—the inability to participate in making important decisions over the use of one's capacities, the inability to escape violence and coercion, the inability to secure self-esteem, and so on. The fact that not being able to nourish oneself leads to more capability failures connected to co-option in oppressive relations provides us with another very good reason to ameliorate hunger. But suppose, hypothetically, that in a certain case, or range of given cases, hunger and sickness do not lead to entanglement in oppressive relations, or are neutral with respect to participation. It is surely an implausible egalitarian position to suggest in any way that sickness and hunger do not require amelioration in those cases, as opposed to the cases where they do lead to unequal relations. Take another example. Suppose we could ensure equal standing for malaria patients either by curing them or by ensuring them full participation by other means, in much the same way that participation is ensured for disabled people with the use of wheelchairs, ramps, and the like. In the second possibility, the malaria patients still suffer fever, cramps, and so on, but the

---

[10] I have already noted Anderson's rather confusing use of 'capabilities' in this sense to refer to the means of securing certain capabilities.

negative effects of their illness on equal citizenship are eliminated.[11] From the point of view of democratic equality, the options seem equally good, which is surely wrong.

It is important to emphasize that one doesn't have to imagine unlikely scenarios to cast serious doubt on the idea that equal relations are the currency of justice. It is partly attention to long-standing feminist concerns that motivates Anderson's focus on relations of equality or equal standing. Yet too much focus on equal standing threatens to lead us into another error unacceptable from a feminist perspective: the neglect of the reality of human dependency. Reducing our entitlements to equal citizenship entitlements commits this error. Babies and small children, the terminally sick, and the old and very frail may not be active and equal participants in civil life. They may not be able to exercise even very basic political rights, such as voting. They can surely fare very badly nonetheless, and their faring badly can surely be the basis of distributive claims. Nor is it plausible to say that we have a collective duty to respond to the well-being of the dependent in order to ensure that they do not become entangled in oppressive relationships. The very old and sick *are* especially vulnerable to their well-being interests being neglected, but it is that neglect that distributive justice should first and foremost obviate. It is unacceptable from a feminist perspective that the well-being of the young, the extremely ill or disabled, or the very old does not figure centrally in a theory of distributive justice, yet it is unclear that Anderson's egalitarian theory has the resources for accounting for its importance.[12]

Anderson does classify the capability to function as a human being as commanding state response. But the capability to function as a human being explicitly enters the theory because functioning as a participant in a system of cooperative production, and functioning as a citizen in a democratic state, presuppose functioning as a human being (1999: 317). Similarly, Anderson also recognises that long 'periods of dependency on others' caretaking are a normal and inevitable part of everyone's life cycle' (1991: 311). But acknowledging the reality of dependency appears in Anderson's theory in order to explain why people's moral obligations to care for dependants shouldn't condemn them, the carers, to unequal status. She argues that some luck egalitarians condemn caretakers to poverty, and thus relations of domination and exploitation, because they regard the choice to leave the workplace to look after small children or other dependants as an expensive taste for which no compensation is owed. Anderson's response is twofold. First, she argues that carers should not be rendered vulnerable to

---

[11] I owe the example to Kasper Lippert-Rasmussen.

[12] Anderson does suggest that we have more general 'global humanitarian obligations' to everyone, considered simply as human beings, for which she gives relief for famine and disease and the avoidance of warfare as examples (1999: 321). This doesn't seem satisfactory. We typically consider the state's duties to relieve the hunger and disease of its own citizens as having a different status to its international humanitarian duties. When these duties are local, their fulfilment is regarded as a matter of distributive justice within the state, which is the issue being considered here.

exploitation and domination because they fulfil their moral obligations: egalitarianism shouldn't just be a theory for the egoistic and self-sufficient. Second, she argues that the labour performed by dependent carers contributes to the economy, and thus should be rewarded: in taking care of dependants carers free up other workers to be more productive, they rehabilitate the sick and injured so they can return to the workforce, and, in raising children, they produce the next generation of workers and consumers (1999: 323–5).

I agree with both of these responses. It is absurd to reduce moral obligations to expensive tastes, and domestic labour does contribute to the economy. Thus, these two facts provide a conclusive reason for ensuring that caretakers who fulfil their moral obligations (or, who often fulfil them on behalf of the less conscientious) do not suffer capability failures as a result. But what about the well-being of the dependent themselves? Why don't citizens as such have a duty to secure the well-being of the non-productive, even if it is the case that delegating day-to-day responsibility to close family members is much more effective in securing their well-being?[13] Why dissolve the importance of dependants' needs into the 'moral obligations' of their caretakers? This implies that whilst the state has direct responsibility for securing an independent adult's capabilities, they do not have the same direct responsibility for her dependants, whose needs are, apparently, her individual moral duty to secure. Why individualise responsibility for some citizens' capabilities and functionings in this way? There is no doubt that Anderson, along with other feminists, would want to insist that the needs and interests of children receive direct consideration from the political community. But characterising our duties towards one another as providing whatever means are necessary to negate oppressive relations and enable equal participation seems to offer little hope of giving an account of justice for the dependent.

The source of this problem is Anderson's overarching commitment to freedom: recall that her claim is that the fundamental obligation of citizens to one another is to secure the social conditions of everyone's freedom. Our freedom is indeed essential to any plausible measurement of how we each fare, although specifying the exact relationship between freedom and the capability approach is a difficult and controversial matter (Sen 1993: 38–9, 42–5; Cohen 1993: 16–28). First, the capabilities that oppressive relations negate are themselves types of freedoms or opportunities to do and be certain things. If participating in decision-making in one's work life is an important aspect of well-being, then the capability (the freedom, opportunity) of doing so is important. In this sense, the capabilities are important because we care not only about what people are doing or being, but what they have the opportunity to do and be if they so choose. The freedom to choose among the various possible functionings, in other words, is important when we measure a person's advantage. Similarly, if participating in civil

---

[13] Assume here that the non-productive can in no way be held responsible for their plight.

and political life is an important aspect of well-being, then the freedom to do so is also important: in measuring how well a person is doing on this score we have to look at whether she has the real opportunity or capability of participating, not just whether she happens to be doing so at the moment. Second, as Sen notes, freedom may also be of intrinsic importance for a person's well-being in the sense that ' Acting freely and being able to choose may be directly conducive to well-being, not just because more freedom may make better alternatives available' (1993: 39). If we characterise participating in decision-making, or in civil and political life, as themselves ways of acting freely, and if Sen is right that acting freely may be an intrinsic aspect of well-being, then it is indeed true that participating in political and civil life and decision-making are forms of free activity intrinsically conducive to well-being. Third, the free activity associated with the various forms of participation enabled by equal relations is also instrumentally important: inasmuch as one can participate in civil and political life and in decision-making over those areas of direct relevance to oneself, one also increases the likelihood that one's other well-being needs and interests will be met. For example, the inability to participate in decision-making in the workplace is bad not only because participation is intrinsically connected to well-being, but because it is also instrumentally important for ensuring that other well-being needs of workers are secured.[14]

Having said so much about the importance of freedom, it is still wrong to reduce all aspects of a person's advantage plausibly commanding collective response to that one dimension. Such a reduction entails that a large percentage of citizens in any country have no direct claims of justice. It also gives a quite distorted picture of why the amelioration of suffering and deprivation is a good thing. It's good not to suffer from malaria, and at least a large chunk of the goodness of that has absolutely nothing to do with choice or agency. A person free from malaria is free from something not of her choosing, she is free from something not in accord with her preferences, and she can also subsequently make more choices than someone suffering from the disease. These are all good reasons for being free from malaria. Not experiencing the pain, incapacity, and potential deadliness of malaria are also very good reasons, including for those people for whom questions of choice and agency are otiose. Justice demands the amelioration of malaria for babies, the old, and the very weak and severely disabled, not just for those whose standing vis-à-vis others might be jeopardised by suffering from it. No theory of justice suitable from a feminist perspective should have trouble explaining any of that.[15]

---

[14] Both of these aspects are clearly at play when people claim that powerlessness and exploitation are forms of oppression: both the self-esteem and the dignity of the worker is undermined because he is treated as a tool instead of a free and autonomous being, and his well-being is also undermined as those who have the power to make decisions do not make them in his interests.

[15] It seems unfortunate that Anderson's use of the capability approach is at odds with the advantage Sen believes we gain from it, namely its plurality. According to Sen, measuring advantage is an

5. Conclusion

The feminist criticisms of prominent theories of distributive justice should be taken seriously. The distribution of divisible goods cannot be the only thing distributive justice should concern itself with. Patterns of socialisation and social relationship, institutional rules and norms, and forms of cultural and symbolic representation are among those things that can have a serious detrimental impact on a person's well-being. Justice should therefore be concerned with these things too. Whether addressing these threats to well-being are best handled by welfare, resource, or capability approaches to justice remains to be seen. What does seem correct is that none of the proponents of either welfare or resources approaches seem to have been particularly attentive to these aspects of inequality. Whatever a proper rectification of this failure will in the end involve, it doesn't seem to be elevating relations of equality themselves to the currency of justice. Relations of equality are too narrow a metric of our well-being concerns relevant from the perspective of distributive justice.

References

ANDERSON, E. (1999), 'What Is the Point of Equality?', *Ethics*, 109: 287–337.

ARNESON, R. J. (1989), 'Equality and Equal Opportunity for Welfare', *Philosophical Studies*, 56: 77–93.

_____ (2000), 'Luck Egalitarianism and Prioritarianism', *Ethics*, 110: 339–49.

COHEN, G. A. (1993), 'Equality of What? On Welfare, Goods, and Capabilities', in M. C. Nussbaum and A. Sen (eds.), *The Quality Life* (Oxford: Clarendon Press).

FRASER, N. (1995), 'From Redistribution to Recognition? Dilemmas of Justice in a "Post-Socialist Age" ', *New Left Review*, 212: 68–93.

PHILLIPS, A. (2004), 'Defending Equality of Outcome', *Journal of Political Philosophy*, 12/1: 1–19.

SCHEFFLER, S. (2003), 'What Is Egalitarianism?', *Philosophy & Public Affairs*, 31/1: 5–39.

irreducibly plural affair because there are many different things it may be appropriate to measure in different contexts. We may be interested in measuring a person's very basic level of functioning, her more complex functioning, her basic capabilities or her more complex ones, whether she has achieved her own goals other than her well-being or whether she has the opportunity to achieve her goals. In reducing the claims of distributive justice to securing each other's freedom, Anderson loses this plurality. Of course, according to the critic the very plurality and scope of the capability approach is one of its greatest weaknesses (cf. Richard Arneson 1989: 93).

SEN, A. (1980). 'Equality of What?', in S. McMurrin (ed.), *The Tanner Lectures on Human Values*, 1 (Salt Lake City: University of Utah Press), 139–62.

—— (1993), 'Capability and Well-Being', in M. C. Nussbaum and A. Sen (eds.), *The Quality of Life* (Oxford: Clarendon Press).

YOUNG, I. M. (1990), *Justice and the Politics of Difference* (Princeton: Princeton University Press).

9

Of Mice and Men: Equality and Animals

Peter Vallentyne

1. Introduction

I shall address a problem that can arise for a certain kind of egalitarianism once sentience is recognized as a sufficient condition for moral standing and speciesism is rejected. Consider the following conditions, where well-being is understood to be quality of life in an absolute sense:

> *Moderate Egalitarianism.* Morality requires that, perhaps subject to certain relatively weak constraints, we significantly promote equality of fortune among individuals with moral standing.

This is a slightly revised version of my paper 'Of Mice and Men: Equality and Animals', *Journal of Ethics*, 9 (2005), 403–33, © 2005 by Springer Science and Business Media, reprinted with the kind permission of Springer Science and Business Media. In addition to miscellaneous stylistic revisions, this version of the paper corrects two errors in the original version: n. 13 contained a numerical error and Idea 6 was poorly formulated. For insightful comments, I thank Dick Arneson, Alexander Cappelen, Paula Casal, Matthew Clayton, Roger Crisp, Trent Dougherty, Marc Fleurbaey, Nils Holtug, Brad Hooker, Brian Kierland, Jeff McMahan, Gene Mills, Mike Otsuka, Thomas Pogge, Mathias Risse, Larry Temkin, Bertil Tungodden, Jo Wolff, and the participants in the following colloquiums: the Kline Colloquium on Equality, Poverty, and Global Justice, University of Missouri–Columbia, 2004; the University of Warwick Graduate Student Conference, 2004; the University of Copenhagen Conference on Egalitarianism, 2004; the Lofoten Genes and Justice Conference, 2004; and the James Rachels Memorial Conference at the University of Alabama at Birmingham. I'm especially indebted to Jeff McMahan for his encouragement and help as I struggled with this perplexing problem, and to Nils Holtug for raising several important objections to earlier versions of this chapter.

Fortune as Well-Being. Fortune is well-being (quality of life), opportunity for well-being, or brute luck well-being.

Sufficiency of Well-Being for Moral Standing. The capacity for well-being is sufficient for moral standing.

Mouse Well-Being. Mice have the capacity for well-being (because they are sentient), but most human beings have more well-being (opportunity for well-being, or brute luck well-being) than most mice.

Given certain plausible empirical assumptions, these conditions lead to the following conclusion:

The Problematic Conclusion. Morality requires a massive shift of resources away from most humans—even most of those with significantly diminished human lives—to most mice.

If equality of well-being is what matters, and normal mice have moral standing, then normal mice have a much stronger claim to resources than almost any human. This is because the well-being of normal mice is much lower than that of normal humans. Thus, equality of well-being requires a massive shift of resources away from most humans to most mice. This view, however, seems crazy. It may well be that mice should have much more resources than they currently have. It seems quite implausible, however, that morality requires that almost all mice have more resources than almost all humans. Of course, the same problem arises for any other animal species with the capacity for well-being.

Of course, this apparent implausibility may simply be the result of our failure to rid ourselves fully of speciesist prejudice against non-human animals. In this chapter, however, I shall assume for the sake of argument that the conclusion is indeed wildly implausible and examine ways in which it can be avoided.

Although I shall focus on the problem that arises when egalitarianism covers sentient non-human animals such as mice, it's important to note that a version of the problem can arise even within a given species. Within a given species, such as *Homo sapiens*, there is variability in the capacities and potentials for well-being. Equality of well-being requires a massive shift of resources from normally abled humans to humans with innately limited capacities and potentials. Many people find this implication almost as absurd as the corresponding implication concerning mice. Most egalitarians, however, do not find this implication so absurd. They are quite willing to accept that genuine equality among humans may require very radical redistribution of resources to the disadvantaged. I therefore focus on mice, since most egalitarians will, I believe, find the implication there absurd.

The general problem is not new. Most of the ground-breaking work was done by Jeff McMahan (1996, 2002) and others.[1] My contribution is to give a more general characterization of the problem and to explore some new solutions.

2. The Problem Examined

For simplicity, throughout I shall write as if the only beings with the capacity for well-being are mice and humans. Nothing of substance depends on this. In addition, for simplicity, I will assume a fixed set of individuals, and thus ignore the problems that arise when choices affect who exists.

The problematic conclusion is generated in part from the assumption that mice have the capacity for well-being but typically have lower well-being than most humans. The first part of this premiss is plausible, since mice are sentient (i.e. capable of pleasure and pain), and sentience is sufficient for the capacity for well-being (since pain and pleasure are components of well-being). The second part of the premiss—that mice typically have less well-being (opportunity for well-being, brute luck well-being) than most humans—is plausible for the following reasons. The typical human capacity for well-being is much greater than the typical mouse capacity for well-being. Part of well-being (what makes a life go well) is the presence of pleasure and the absence of pain. The typical human capacity for pain and pleasure is no less than that of mice, and presumably much greater, since we have, it seems plausible, more of the relevant sorts of neurons, neurotransmitters, receptors, etc. In addition, our greater cognitive capacities amplify the magnitude of pain and pleasure. Moreover, well-being does not depend solely on pain and pleasure. It's controversial exactly what else is relevant—accomplishments, relationships, and so on—but all accounts agree that typical humans have greater capacities for whatever the additional relevant items are. In short, typical humans have greater capacities for well-being than typical mice. This leaves open, however, whether typical humans *realize* greater well-being than typical mice. This is an empirical question. For some species, such as chimpanzees, it may be that, although their typical capacity for well-being is somewhat lower than ours, their typical realized well-being (e.g. if living freely in the wild) may be greater than that which we typically realize. For mice, however, this is quite improbable (although still an empirical question). Their capacity for well-being is radically lower than ours, and, as a result, it is quite plausible that most mice realize less well-being than most humans.

[1] McMahan is, of course, building on the work of Singer (1990). See also, Rachels (1990, ch. 5); Persson (1993); Kaufman (1998); Arneson (1999); Crisp (2003).

The problematic conclusion also rests on the claim that the capacity for well-being is sufficient for moral standing. There are two main ways of challenging this assumption. One is to hold that moral standing requires that the individual be rationally autonomous or psychologically sophisticated in related ways. Rational autonomy is clearly relevant and gives possessors a special kind of moral standing (e.g. because their will is morally relevant), but, as is well known, it seems quite arbitrary to limit moral standing to autonomous agents. In addition to sentient animals, this view implausibly excludes infants and severely cognitively impaired persons from moral standing. The second main way to deny that mice have moral standing is to endorse a form of speciesism and to claim that moral standing requires that the individual be a member of a species (such as *Homo Sapiens*) whose 'normal' adult members are rationally autonomous or psychologically sophisticated in related ways. The problem with this view is that it is quite implausible that one individual would have moral standing, while another with the same capacities and potentials does not, merely because of a difference in species-membership (just as it is implausible in the cases of race and sex). In what follows, I shall assume (without any defense) that at least many non-autonomous animals with the capacity for well-being (and mice in particular) have moral standing.[2]

The argument for the problematic conclusion also assumes moderate egalitarianism for all beings with moral standings. Of course, there are many ways of objecting to moderate egalitarianism. Some may completely reject any demands of equality. Others may hold that the demands of equality apply to only *some* beings with moral standing. Many (and probably most) egalitarians, for example, hold that the requirements of equality apply only to rationally autonomous agents. Non-autonomous sentient animals may have moral standing (and thus be protected against certain kinds of harm), but they have no claim to equality of well-being (etc.) with autonomous agents.[3] I see little reason, however, to exclude sentient animals from the domain of equality, and I shall simply assume that they are included.

Moderate egalitarianism holds that morality requires, perhaps subject to some weak constraints, that equality be *significantly* promoted. It does not necessarily require that we maximize equality. It may leave agents with some moral freedom to pursue their own projects (i.e. options). Of course, if the requirement that equality be promoted were very weak, then few significant implications would follow. Moderate egalitarianism, however, requires—plausibly in my view—that equality be significantly promoted. In what follows, I shall tend to illustrate claims by assuming that equality must be

---

[2] Note that, in any case, restricting moral standing to rationally autonomous agents does not avoid the problem. The problem arises, for example, if equality of welfare is required and some rationally autonomous agents have only the capacity for welfare that mice have.

[3] McMahan (1996: 30) suggests such a view.

maximized, but significant implications follow as long as the equality promotion requirement is significant.

Moderate egalitarianism allows that there may be some relatively weak constraints on the promotion of fortune. One constraint that is highly plausible is that options should be *Pareto optimal*, that is, such that no one can be made better off without making someone worse off. The requirement of Pareto optimality is a weak efficiency requirement, and imposing it ensures that equality is not required when this would involve leveling down (i.e. making some worse off and no one better off). Let us now stipulate that a constraint on the promotion of equality of fortune is *relatively weak* just in case it does not typically rule out a high proportion of the Pareto optimal distributions of well-being. This stipulative definition ensures that imposing the constraint of Pareto optimality is relatively weak, and thus permits moderate egalitarianism to avoid the objection that it requires leveling down. This definition of relative weakness also allows that moderate egalitarianism may impose some deontological constraints against killing, harming, and so on—provided that these constraints do not typically rule out a high proportion of the Pareto optimal distributions of well-being.

It's important to note that the requirement that the constraints on equality promotion be relatively weak is crucial to generating the problem of mice. The simple version of the problem can be avoided if the constraints need not be relatively weak. For example, if the constraint of efficiency is strengthened from Pareto optimality to total well-being maximization (i.e. utilitarianism), then the problem need not arise in its simple form. In this case, equality would play the limited role of selecting among those distributions that maximize the total. Given that typical mice are much less efficient than typical humans at generating well-being from resources—at least once their basic needs are met—this view will typically require that mice get some resources, but it will not require that they get as much as humans.

There are other ways that the problem can be avoided by imposing relative strong constraints prior to the demands of equality. For example, there may be an *agent-neutral* constraint requiring that *all rational agents* have (to the extent possible) minimally adequate levels of well-being. Alternatively, there may be an *agent-relative* constraint requiring that *all members of one's species* have minimally adequate levels of well-being. If the minimally adequate level is set high enough, each of these constraints would radically limit the demands of equality (and thus not be relatively weak) and thus avoid the requirement for a massive shift from humans to mice.

Moderate egalitarianism can, as I have indicated, be challenged on several grounds. Nonetheless, many (myself included) find it highly plausible. In what follows, I shall simply assume that it is true and investigate how the problematic conclusion can be avoided for moderate egalitarianism.

It's worth noting, however, that, although we shall focus on egalitarianism, the problematic conclusion can arise for any theory of morality that gives significant concern to providing benefits to those whose *level* of well-being is low in a certain sense. Thus, for example, the problem can arise for sufficientarian theories of morality, which require that each individual's level of well-being be adequate in some specified sense. If the level of adequacy is, for example, set in a species-independent way somewhere between the average level for mice and the average level for humans, sufficientarianism will require a massive shifting of resources from humans to mice. The problem can also arise for leximin prioritarianism and for forms of weighted total prioritarianism that give significantly greater weight to those whose well-being level is lower. For simplicity, however, we shall focus on moderate egalitarianism.

The final assumption in the argument for the problematic conclusion is Fortune as Well-Being. This holds that fortune—that which is to be equalized—is well-being, initial opportunity for well-being, or brute luck well-being (i.e. impact on well-being of events that the individual could not reasonably have influenced). Obviously, the claim that well-being is the sole source of that which is to be equalized is controversial. Alternative possibilities include capabilities (i.e. effective opportunities to function), the competitive value (based on supply and demand) of resources, and primary goods (i.e. resources the possession of which are in an individual's interest, no matter what her conception of the good). Although I shall continue to focus on well-being, the problem arises for these conceptions of fortune as well. The problem is particularly acute for well-being and capabilities, since each assesses the value of resources for an individual in terms of their value for the individual (as opposed to their value in general). Individuals, such as mice, that (beyond some minimal level) are poor converters of resources into what ultimately matters (well-being or capabilities) thus need more resources to achieve the requisite equality. The problem also arises, although in a diminished form, for resources and primary goods. Because these views are not sensitive to what a particular individual can do with resources, they do not require giving mice larger shares to compensate for their more limited abilities to convert resources into well-being or capabilities. Nonetheless, given the other assumptions, these views do require giving mice an equal share of resources or primary goods, and even this seems absurd.

One final point: old-style egalitarianism tended to require that outcome advantage (e.g. well-being) be equalized, but contemporary egalitarianism tends to favor initial opportunity for advantage, or brute luck advantage, on the grounds that they leave greater room for accountability for one's choices. The problem at hand, however, does not depend on this issue, and for brevity I shall therefore use the term 'well-being' to cover well-being, initial opportunity for well-being, and brute luck well-being. For simplicity I shall typically focus on outcome well-being.

Something about Fortune as Well-Being is, we shall assume, right. Nonetheless, in what follows, I shall examine several ways of modifying it so as to avoid the problematic conclusion.

3. Fortune as Well-Being as a Ratio of Species Potential

Fortune as Well-Being holds that fortune (the equalisandum of equality) is well-being, where outcome well-being is understood as the quality of life on some absolute scale. The problematic conclusion arises because the well-being of a typical mouse is much lower than that of almost all humans. The most commonsensical way of avoiding this problem is to hold that fortune must be understood as well-being relativized to the potential of the *species* of the individual. More specifically, fortune can be understood as well-being relativized to the maximum potential well-being level for a member of the individual's species. Consider, then,

> *Fortune as Well-Being as a Ratio of Species Potential.* Fortune for an individual is the ratio of her well-being to the species-maximum well-being.[4]

Suppose, for example, that the maximum well-being for mice is 2, and a particular mouse has well-being of 1. Her fortune, on this conception is .5 ($= \frac{1}{2}$). Suppose that maximum well-being for humans is 200 and that a particular human has well-being of 100. His fortune is also .5 ($= 100/200$). On this conception of fortune, moderate egalitarianism does not require any shift of resources between the two. More generally, although this will require some shifting of resources from some humans to some mice (and from some mice to some humans), it does not require a massive shift of resources from most humans to most mice.

This account of fortune avoids the problematic conclusion, but it is implausible because of its speciesism. Consider a severely cognitively impaired human who has the innate potential (e.g. potential at conception) of a normal mouse. Why would morality be more concerned in principle with the human than with the mouse? Of course, there may be various contingent factors related to species that are relevant (e.g. how much others care about the individual), but there seems little reason to think that there is any principled difference. In any case, although this is controversial, I shall assume that speciesism is untenable.[5] We shall assume, that is:

> *Species Neutrality.* Morality makes no essential reference to the species of individuals.

Fortune as Well-Being as a Ratio of Species Potential violates Species Neutrality, and thus must be rejected. Nonetheless, the idea that fortune is some kind of potential-relative well-being has some plausibility. In what follows, I shall formulate and assess two such approaches that satisfy Species Neutrality.

---

[4] This is roughly a specific version of the species-norm account discussed by McMahan (1996; 2002, ch. 2). Daniels (1990) and Buchanan *et al.* (2000, ch. 4) appeal to a species-relative account but based on capabilities rather than well-being.

[5] McMahan (2002, ch. 2), for example, argues against any kind of species-norm account.

4. Individual Potentiality

In what follows, we shall assume the following:

Fortune as Positively Sensitive to Well-Being. An individual's fortune is positively sensitive to her well-being.

Fortune as Well-Being and Fortune as Well-Being as a Ratio of Species Potential each satisfy this condition, but so do other conceptions. This condition leaves open how inter-individual ('interpersonal') comparisons of fortune are made. It allows, for example, that a mouse with well-being of .8 may have greater fortune than a human with well-being of 10.

If fortune is well-being, then, given the other assumptions, the problematic conclusion follows. If the problem of mice is to be avoided, then fortune must, it seems, be understood as some kind of potential-relative well-being. The species-potential-relative account of fortune avoids the problem of mice, but errs in appealing to the potentials of members of the individual's species. It thus may seem plausible that fortune is well-being relativized to the potential of the individual:

Individual Potential Relativity. Fortune for an individual is somehow relative to her individual potential for well-being.

I shall ultimately argue against this condition, but it will be useful first to explore its implications. We shall explore some ways of avoiding the problematic conclusion, given Moderate Egalitarianism, Sufficiency of Well-Being for Moral Standing, Mouse Well-Being, Species Neutrality, Fortune as Positively Sensitive to Well-Being, and Individual Potential Relativity.

First, however, a few remarks on the notion of individual potential are in order. This is a slippery notion, and I shall not be able to pin it down fully. The one thing that is clear is that the relevant potential is not the *current* one that an individual happens to have at the time of application. It is rather the individual's *innate* potential. This includes at least the full potential that the individual had when she first came into existence. Thus, although the passage of time in general reduces one's current potentials (e.g. from aging, accidents, and/or failure to develop various capacities), and never increases them,[6] this does not affect the relevant potential for the purposes of assessing fortune.

There are, however, several different ways in which innate potential can be understood. On a relatively narrow understanding, one's innate potential is the

---

[6] Of course, one's capacities (i.e. abilities to do things at will) can increase over time (e.g. from practice and education), but this is simply the development of a potential that was present all along.

empirical potential that one had when one first existed. On the broadest under-standing—metaphysical potentiality—one's innate potential also includes all the possibilities that one might have had, given all the ways that one might have come to exist. Suppose, for example, that when I came into existence I had no empirical potential for sight. Suppose, however, that there are many ways that the sperm and egg that produced me might have been altered (e.g. by genetic engineering) prior to my conception while still producing me. On the broad understanding of innate potential, my potential includes these possibilities as well. If on one of these I have sight, then my potential so understood includes sight.

In specifying an individual's potential, it's crucial that the alternative possibilities involved are ones in which that *same individual* comes into existence, and not merely ones in which someone like her comes into existence. Although I'm skeptical that the relevant notion of individual identity is robust enough to apply much beyond the narrow notion of possibility (empirically possible when one comes into existence), I shall assume, for the sake of argument, that we can make sense of individual identity even where individuals come into existence in different ways, in different world histories, and even in different worlds.

A second open issue concerns how well-being is to be relativized to potential well-being. For simplicity, I shall assume that such relativization is based somehow on the individual's maximum potential well-being. One might also invoke minimum potential well-being (since this is variable among individuals), but I shall assume that the relevant minimum is zero, where this represents the point that separates a life worth living from one worth not living. I make this assumption both for simplicity of presentation and because, given that morality is concerned with making lives better, variations in how miserable a being can be do not seem relevant for determination of the relevant minimum level of well-being. Given that all beings will be assumed to have the same relevant minimum of zero, we can effectively ignore the minimum for the issues at hand. In any case, it will be useful to make this assumption for the purposes of simplifying the presentation.

How then is the maximum set? The most natural possibility for the specification of the maximum is as the maximum well-being that is possible *in principle* for the individual given her innate potential. It is possible, however, that there is no maximum: for any given level of well-being, there could be a higher one that is possible for that individual. One way that this can arise is where there is no maximum but there is a lowest bound on the maximum, as in the progression $\frac{1}{2}, \frac{3}{4}, \frac{7}{8}, \ldots$ (which is always smaller than 1). In this case, we can take the maximum to be the least upper bound (1 in this case). More problematic is the case where there is no least upper bound, as in the progression 1, 2, 3, 4, . . . This is an important problem, and I have no solution. As a practical matter, we can deal with this by taking the maximum for such individuals to be (for example) a trillion times the maximum ever achieved by any individual in the past. This leaves the theoretical problem, but eliminates any significant practical problem. In any case, I'm going to ignore this important problem.

These are all important and controversial issues, but I shall not attempt to resolve them. I shall simply assume that we have a plausible and well-defined conception of innate potential and of the maximum individual well-being relative to that potential. (I will, in any case, argue below that fortune should not be understood as well-being relativized to potential.)

5. Fortune as Individual Potential-Relative Well-Being

We shall here consider three different ways of relativizing well-being to individual potential. The first two, I shall argue, are clearly implausible, whereas something like the third approach seems to be the most plausible way of taking fortune to being potential-relative well-being. Nonetheless, in later sections, I will argue that even it is implausible and defend a different kind of approach.

5.1. Fortune as Well-Being as a Ratio of Individual Potential

The most natural way of relativizing well-being to the individual's potential is the following:

> *Fortune as Well-Being as a Ratio of Individual Potential.* The fortune of an individual is the ratio of her well-being to her maximum well-being.

This is just like Fortune as Well-Being as a Ratio of Species Potential, except that the relevant potential is individual potential and not species potential. Consider, for example, (1) a mouse with well-being of 1 and a maximum well-being of 2, and (2) a human with well-being of 100 and a maximum potential well-being of 200. Each has well-being as a ratio of individual potential of .5. Equality of well-being as a ratio of individual potential requires no shift of resources between the two.

This view avoids the problematic conclusion because it does not compare the well-being of mice with the well-being of humans (or any other individual). It only compares well-being as a ratio of individual potential. Equality of fortune so understood thus does not demand that mice have lives equally good with humans.

The main problem with this approach is that it treats some trivial improvements in well-being as just as important as very significant improvements. Suppose that a 1-unit difference in well-being is trivial and that a difference of 100 units is significant. Consider a mouse with maximum well-being of 2 units. Suppose that the only other individual is a human with a maximum well-being of 200 units. Suppose that the only choices are 0 well-being for the mouse and 100 units of well-being for the human, or 1 unit for the mouse and 0 for the human. Equality of well-being as a ratio of individual potential views these as equally acceptable. The first option gives the mouse a .5 ratio of potential and the human a 0 ratio. The second option gives the mouse a 0 ratio and the human a .5 ratio. With respect to equality of well-being as a ratio of individual potential, there is no difference between the two. It is, however, quite implausible to treat the trivial 1-unit improvement for the mouse as equally as important as the significant 100-unit for the human. The objection here is not against equality as such. We are assuming that some sort of equality is indeed required. The objection is simply to taking the ratio of well-being to individual potential as the equalisandum.

In sum, Fortune as Well-Being as a Ratio of Individual Potential avoids the problematic conclusion, but goes overboard and attaches too much importance to providing benefits to mice. (This problem, it's worth noting, also arises for the Fortune as Well-Being as a Ratio of Species Potential, considered above.)

5.2. Fortune as Closeness to Maximum Potential

Let us now consider a second individual potential-relative account of fortune:

Fortune as Closeness to Maximum Potential. Fortune for an individual is the closeness of her well-being to her maximum potential well-being.

Like the preceding view, this relativizes to maximum (individual) potential well-being, but it does so in a different way. Instead of viewing fortune as a ratio of well-being to maximum potential, it views it as the shortfall in well-being from each individual's maximum potential. In the above example, the mouse with 1 unit of well-being is 1 unit short of her maximum of 2, and the human with 100 units is 100 units short of his maximum of 200. Thus, the mouse is much closer to her maximum than the human is to his. Both views hold that fortune increases the closer one gets to one's maximum. The difference concerns whether closeness is viewed in percentage terms or absolute terms. Fortune as Closeness to Maximum Potential views closeness in absolute terms and thus avoids the problem of treating trivial shortfalls as equally significant for fortune as very significant shortfalls.[7]

The closeness to maximum potential account also avoids the problematic conclusion. Like the previous view, it does not require that mice have as much well-being as

[7] Note that, in the example given, the mouse (who is 1 unit short of her maximum of 2) is 1 unit above her minimum, whereas the human (who is 100 units short of his maximum of 200) is 100 units above his minimum. A different view of fortune would take fortune to be the excess over the minimum. If the minima are the same (e.g. zero), this view is equivalent to Fortune as Well-Being. In any case, it generates the problematic conclusion, since mice will typically have a smaller excess.

humans. It only requires that (to the extent possible) the shortfall of mice from their respective maxima be the same as that for humans. Nonetheless, this view, I shall now argue, is also implausible.

The main problem with this view is that it seems to give inadequate attention to mice. It has, for example, significantly less effective concern for mice than utilitarianism. Utilitarianism factors in the benefits to mice along with those to others, but, given that, beyond basic needs, most mice are much less efficient at generating well-being from resources than most humans, they tend to receive much fewer resources than humans. This is not obviously problematic. The closeness to the maximum potential view, however, tends to favor humans for a second reason: even where a given human and a given mouse would reap the same benefit (in absolute terms) from a given resource, the closeness to potential will tend to favor the human on the ground that her shortfall from her maximum potential is greater than that of the mouse. This is because the potential range in well-being for typical humans (e.g. 0–200) is much greater than that for typical mice (e.g. 0–2). As a result, almost all humans have a greater shortfall from their maxima than almost all mice. The closeness to the maximum view thus does not take the interests of mice seriously enough.

5.3. Fortune as Excess Over Relevant Intermediate Well-Being

As we have seen, equality cannot be merely concerned with (absolute) well-being. Otherwise, almost all mice have greater equality claims than almost all humans. We are considering approaches that relativize well-being to individual potential. One view is to take fortune to be well-being as a ratio of individual maximum potential. This is implausible because it treats some trivial improvements for disadvantaged mice as more important than some significant improvements for disadvantaged humans with a normal human range for well-being. This suggests that shortfalls should be understood in absolute terms, but the reference point should be selected in some potential-relative way. Selecting the reference point as the maximum potential, I have suggested, inappropriately disadvantages beings with lower potentials (since their shortfalls will typically be smaller). This suggests that the reference point should be some level of well-being between zero and the maximum.

One possibility is to appeal to the mid-point between zero and a person's maximum potential. This seems, however, rather arbitrary. It seems more plausible to appeal to (something like) the *maximum average potential-relative well-being ratio* at the time of evaluation, where this is understood as follows. The potential-relative well-being ratio is (as defined earlier) the ratio of well-being to the individual's maximum well-being. At a given time, given the total resources in the world, there is a maximum achievable *average* potential-relative well-being ratio for the set of beings with moral standing. For example, if there are just two individuals and one can give them ratios of .7 and

.3 respectively (average of .5) or .4 and .8 respectively (average of .6), the maximum achievable average potential-relative well-being is .6. For a given individual, his/her maximum average potential-relative well-being *point* (at that time) is that level of (absolute) well-being that gives him/her the maximum average potential-relative well-being ratio. Note that the maximum average potential-relative well-being ratio is a number between 0 and 1, whereas the maximum average potential-relative well-being *point* is the level of absolute well-being that, for a given individual, represents the maximum average potential-relative well-being (at that time). For example, if the maximum average potential-relative well-being ratio is .3 (i.e. the best one can do on average is to give individuals 30 per cent of their maximum potential well-being), then for an individual with a maximum of 10, her maximum average potential-relative well-being point is 3.

Fortunately, we don't need to resolve the issue of how an intermediate reference point is selected—since I will argue against more general features of this approach. Let us simply assume that there is some principled basis for selecting each individual's relevant intermediate level of well-being (e.g. as some percentage of his/her maximum). Let us consider, then,

> *Fortune as Excess Over Relevant Intermediate Well-Being.* Fortune, for a given individual, is the excess of well-being over her relevant intermediate level of well-being (where shortfalls are negative excesses, and thus cases of misfortune).

Fortune, on this view—as with the previous view—is concerned with absolute differences of well-being from a reference point, and the reference point is picked out, for each individual, in an individual potential-relative way. The new feature is that the reference point is some level of well-being between zero and the maximum. This reduces (but does not eliminate) the extent to which individuals with great potentials will tend to have greater shortfalls from the reference point. For example, if the reference point were set at the zero point, this tendency would be entirely eliminated.

With an appropriately set reference point, this approach may seem to give the right balance to the well-being of mice and humans. A mouse and a human who are each at their respective reference points are deemed to have equal claims with respect to equality. Furthermore, each has, from the point of view of equality, less priority than any being who has less than her reference point. Thus, there will be some redistribution from humans who are above their reference point to individuals who are below. For individuals below their reference point, however, humans will tend to have a stronger equality claim than mice. This is because their shortfall will typically be larger. Thus, to the extent that there is a shifting of resources from individuals who have more than their reference point to individuals who have less than their reference point, it will tend to be a shift from humans (since human excesses are typically larger than mouse excesses) to humans (since human shortfalls are typically larger than mouse shortfalls).

Fortune as Excess over Relevant Intermediate Well-Being, or something like it, is, I speculate, the most promising individual potential-relative account of fortune for a form of egalitarianism that rejects speciesism and that includes sentient beings in its scope. Of course, it is highly controversial and subject to many objections. The main objection is that it treats differences in innate potential as given and ineligible for egalitarian compensation. For example, consider two individuals with the same level of well-being, and the same current capacities for well-being, but with different potentials for well-being. Suppose that 1 unit of well-being can be given to one of them but not both of them. According to Fortune as Excess over Relevant Intermediate Well-Being, the one with the greater potential has lower fortune (since her potential is greater, and thus her reference point well-being is greater, and thus her shortfall from that point is greater (or her excess is smaller)). It seems implausible, however, that in this case equality requires giving the benefit to the person with the greater potential. This, however, is not a conclusive refutation of the view. The problematic conclusion (that morality requires a radical shift of resources from most humans to most mice) is much more implausible. It may be that, once speciesism is rejected, the troublesome conclusion just mentioned must be accepted. It may be, that is, that all views have troubling conclusions for some cases, and that this is the most promising path to take.

I shall now argue, however, that there is a deeper problem of interspecies equality that this approach does not solve and that an adequate solution does not take fortune to be any form of potential-relative well-being.

6. The Problem of Radical Enhancement

Sometime in the future, it will, it seems, become feasible—through genetic engineering and other means—to enhance the capacities of mice, or other sentient beings, to be roughly equal to those of typical humans.[8] In particular, it will be possible to radically enhance the capacity of mice for well-being. Thus, the maximum potential well-being of most mice for well-being will be, at least roughly, that of most humans. Of course, the potentials of humans will also be radically enhanced, but the difference in the potential for well-being between a typical mouse and a typical human will arguably eventually become quite small. Moreover, the cost of such enhancement will eventually become reasonably small. When this is true, the problematic conclusion

---

[8] McMahan (1996; 2002: 2) insightfully discusses this issue at length.

returns even on the proposed approach. The maximum potential for most mice will be roughly the same as that for most humans, and thus unenhanced mice will have greater shortfalls from their reference points than most unenhanced humans. Hence, equality will require a radical shift in resources from most humans to most mice.

Of course, if the capacities for well-being of mice can be enhanced, then typically their productive capacities can also be enhanced. If the latter can be enhanced enough that they produce enough wealth to provide for the benefits to which there are entitled (and perhaps more!), then, of course, there is little that is problematic about their enhancement. This, however, need not always be possible, and I shall therefore focus on the case where it is not.

The possibility of *radical enhancement* generates the problematic conclusion only if the enhanced mice are the same individuals as the original mice. Otherwise, the original mice (as opposed to different beings) do not have the potential for the enhanced capacities. This places some constraints on the relevant enhancements of mouse potentials, but it seems plausible that there is no barrier in principle to such radical enhancement of the capacity for well-being while maintaining the relevant individual identity. Indeed, for individuals, such as mice, whose moral standing is grounded entirely in their capacity for well-being, it seems plausible that the relevant identity is simply that of being the same center of well-being, and it seems plausible that radical enhancement can preserve this. In any case, in what follows, I shall tentatively assume that this is so.

The possibility of radical enhancement has significant implications for the problematic conclusion. One, just noted, is that even if innate potential is understood narrowly as the *practically achievable* potential that one had when one first came into existence (i.e., roughly, what the then current knowledge, resources, and technology permitted us to achieve reliably at will), someday the potential of mice in this sense will be roughly that of humans (although they do not currently have that potential). A second implication is that this is true *now*, if innate potential is understood more broadly as the *empirically possible* potential that one had when one first came into existence (i.e., roughly, the possibilities left open by the laws of nature given the state of the world then). The mere fact that one day we will be able to implement radical enhancement is enough to show that it is, and always has been, empirically possible, even if we do not know how to bring about these results now. Of course, this is also true if innate potential is understood more broadly still, such as including all metaphysical possibilities compatible with being the same individual.

The lesson seems to be this. Assessing fortune in a potential-relative way makes some difference, since typically at least some individuals have different potentials. Given the possibility of radical enhancement, however, the difference seems not to be as great as we have thought. This is especially so if potential is understood in the broadest metaphysical sense. It seems still to be so (although to a lesser extent) if potential is understood in the sense of empirical possibility. If potential, however, is understood in the relative narrow sense of practical possibility, then there is currently a lot of variation in potential-relative well-being. Even that difference, however, will significantly diminish with the advancement of technology, and the problem of those demanding little mice will eventually return.[9]

Thus, it may seem that, if we are to avoid permanently the problematic conclusion, we need to narrow further the notion of innate potential. I shall suggest, however, that this is not promising.

Jeff McMahan (2002, ch. 2) suggests that we limit the relevant potentials to *intrinsic* potentials, where these are something like the (e.g. empirical) potentials that individuals have, the realization of which do not involve 'direct alteration of their constitution'. The rough idea is that one's intrinsic potential is somehow based solely on one's 'internal' condition and not on 'external' conditions such as the presence or absence of the possibility of adding body parts (e.g. eyeballs, brain cells, or synthetic circuitry). If, for example, given the right training environment, mice could develop the same capacities as humans (which they can't), then their intrinsic potentials would be the same as those of humans. The mere fact that genetic engineering, or other direct physical alterations, would enhance a mouse's potential, however, would not establish that mice have the same *intrinsic* potentials as humans.[10] Hence, if potentials are restricted to intrinsic potentials, the problematic conclusion does not arise—at least not so easily.

There are two problems with this approach—each acknowledged by McMahan. One is that it's not clear that there is much content to the distinction between intrinsic (as here understood) and unrestricted potentials. What one realizes depends on the kind of nourishment one obtains (which is a kind of external contribution), but that is taken not to make the potential for such achievement non-intrinsic. Otherwise no potentials would be intrinsic. Consider then a mental enhancement pill. It would seem also not to make the potential it generates non-intrinsic—even, say, if the pill promotes neural connections. Why then, wouldn't the possibility of surgery

---

[9] It's worth noting that, if radical enhancement is possible, then even total utilitarianism faces the problematic conclusion, once the cost of radical enhancement becomes small. Given decreasing marginal well-being and roughly identical marginal well-being for any two individuals at the same level of well-being, enhancing mice and then transferring resources to them from humans will generally increase total well-being. Indeed, this illustrates the point that there is a close connection between the problems generated by radical enhancement and problems in population policy about adding additional individuals to the world. The latter concerns our duty to add beings to the world with a given level of standing, whereas the former concerns our duty to increase the moral standing of existing individuals to a given level.

[10] Of course, once such 'external enhancements' have taken place, the mouse's intrinsic potential is enhanced. Likewise, the offspring of mice that have been genetically enhanced to produce offspring with enhanced capacities have enhanced intrinsic potentials. The issue here concerns the force of the moral reason to provide such enhancement in the first place.

that establishes various neural connections also enhance one's intrinsic potential? All realizations depend both on internal and on external conditions, and almost all involve enhancing internal constitution by external means. It is thus unclear what the distinction is supposed to be between internal potentials (which do not require direct alteration of one's constitution) and non-internal ones.

The second problem with restricting innate potentials to those that do not require direct alteration of one's constitution (assuming that the intuitive content is capturable) is its plausibility. As McMahan (2002: 153) notes, this view has the implication that an innately blind infant, whose condition is easily and cheaply correctable, has less relevant (i.e. intrinsic) potential than an innately normal infant who acquired the same condition as a result of an accident shortly after coming into existence. In both cases, the needed treatment involves altering their internal constitution. The only difference is that the innately normal infant had the intrinsic potential for sight when she came into existence, whereas the innately blind infant did not. It strikes most of us as wildly implausible to hold that this difference is relevant to assessing their fortune. In a very real sense the innately defective infant has the potential to have normal capacities. It seems quite arbitrary to treat her differently from the other infant. Of course, this is not a knockdown objection. We are dealing with cases where some of our strongly held intuitions must be given up. Nonetheless, I claim that it is more plausible to treat the enhanceable mouse as having the same relevant potential as the normal human being than to treat the two infants differently. Thus, the restriction to intrinsic potential so understood seems unpromising.

Perhaps there is some other relevant way to characterize intrinsic potentials, but I shall not pursue that possibility here.[11] This is because there is a general problem with restricting potential more narrowly than empirical possibility when the individual came into existence (and perhaps even that restriction is problematic). The empirical possibilities open to an individual when she comes into existence are real (as opposed to counterfactual) possibilities for that individual. It therefore seems quite arbitrary to ignore some of them for the purposes of specifying fortune. For example, limiting potential to *practical* potential (potential that is, roughly, reliably realizable) seems arbitrary. Of course, practical limitations are highly relevant for what we should do in practice (e.g. there is no point in trying to accomplish something for which we don't have the know-how). It seems inappropriate, however, to assess fortune in a way that ignores in principle certain empirical possibilities merely because they are

---

[11] For example, one might understand intrinsic potential to be those possibilities that the individual has in his/her statistically normal (e.g. most common) environment. It seems quite arbitrary, however, to limit the relevant potentials to those states that are achievable in statistically normal environments. The mere fact that a child cannot overcome dyslexia in statistically normal environments surely does not mean that the child does not have the relevant potential to overcome the condition.

not now practical possibilities. Likewise, it seems inappropriate to assess fortune solely on the basis of intrinsic empirical potential, however that is understood. Why should differences in real potential be ignored?

If this is right, and if, as we have been assuming, radical enhancement of potential well-being is empirically possible for mice, then taking fortune to be relative to individual potential may somewhat reduce the requirement to shift resources from most normal humans to most normal mice, but it leaves in place a very strong requirement for such transfers. If the problematic conclusion is to be robustly avoided, some additional machinery is, it seems, needed. Before concluding, I shall propose some such machinery.

7. A Possible Solution

So far, we have explored ways of avoiding the problematic conclusion that take fortune to be well-being relativized to individual potential. We have seen two main problems with this approach. First, as just noted, given the possibility of radical enhancement, it does not avoid the problematic conclusion (since the potentials of mice may not be that different from ours). Second, as noted earlier, it implausibly takes brute luck limitations in innate potential (e.g. of a human) as demanding no egalitarian compensation (since fortune is relative to innate potentials).

I believe that we have taken a false turn. Instead of focusing on the *potential* for well-being, we should, I believe, focus on the *capacity* for well-being. A *capacity* is something that can be realized now, whereas a potential can be something that can be realized only at some later time after the capacity is developed. Thus, for example, most normal adults now have the potential to play a simple piece on the piano (i.e. after much practice to develop their capacities), but only a few adults now have the capacity to do so. I shall suggest that fortune should be understood as well-being relativized to the degree of moral standing, where moral standing is grounded in the capacities of the individuals (rather than in their potentials).

The solution that I shall sketch requires several significant departures from the standard way of thinking of things. The best I can do here is to formulate and motivate this approach. I will not attempt anything close to a rigorous defense. Indeed, the following is highly speculative, and should be understood merely as identifying an approach that needs to be developed and assessed more carefully.

I shall introduce six ideas, which taken together offer the promise a plausible way of avoiding the problematic conclusion. Consider, then,

> *Idea 1.* Moral standing is grounded in the capacity for well-being and the capacity for rational choice.

This is a strengthening of Sufficiency of Well-Being for Moral Standing. It recognizes that capacity for rational choice is also relevant for moral standing, and further claims that nothing else is. Of course, this claim is not uncontroversial. Those who hold that moral standing is grounded in the possession of a Cartesian soul or in being a member of certain species would reject it. Most moral theorists, however, would accept this assumption, and I shall not here attempt to defend it.

In what follows, I shall, for simplicity, ignore the capacity for rational choice. This is because, for the problem at hand, that capacity is not relevant. Those with the capacity for rational choice are protected by the *morality of respect*, and this requires, roughly, that their autonomous wills be respected in various ways. Moderate egalitarianism may indeed impose various constraints on respecting the wills of autonomous agents, but such respect does not block the problematic conclusion (e.g. where the issue is simply of how to divide up resources). Thus, for simplicity, I shall focus below solely on the *morality of interests*, and for this purpose we can ignore the capacity for rational choice (except, of course, as it contingently impacts on well-being). Given this simplifying assumption, we shall assume that moral standing is grounded solely in the capacity for well-being.

This leads naturally to

Idea 2. Moral standing (for the morality of interests) comes in degrees, with zero for no moral standing, and, for example, one unit for the current average degree of moral standing for normal humans with normal lives.

If moral standing is grounded solely in the capacity for well-being, then it is natural to think that moral standing comes in degrees, given that the capacity comes in degrees. This does not, however, follow as a matter of logic. Full moral standing may be (and has typically been taken to be) a *threshold concept*: Those who have the grounding features above some specified degree have full moral standing. The concept of being a dollar millionaire is a threshold concept. Everyone who has at least $1 million is a million-aire. A person with just $1 million has the same status in this regard as a billionaire. Full moral standing has typically been taken to be a threshold concept. All normal human beings, for example, are taken to have the same full moral standing (for the morality of interests). When we focus on normal adult human beings, this seems plausible, given that our capacities are all roughly equal. Moreover, it is seemingly natural to extend this idea to sentient fetuses, young children, and severely cognitively disabled people.

Once, however, we start to consider sentient individuals of all the various species, the implausibility of treating moral standing as a threshold concept becomes apparent. Consider two individuals one of whom spends her life just below the threshold capacity for well-being (perhaps a snail) and the other who spends her entire life just above it (perhaps a squid). The former has no moral standing whereas the latter has some moral standing. It would be crazy, however, to think that the individual who just barely has the capacity for well-being (e.g. the squid) has the same moral standing as a normal human adult human (who has a much greater capacity for well-being). Such a small difference in capacities cannot make such an enormous difference in moral standing. This is especially clear in the context of egalitarian theory where full moral standing would generate a claim to equal benefits with all others. It is also true more generally in the context of theories that hold (as I believe plausible) that we have no duty to ensure that individuals who would have good lives acquire moral standing but do have a duty to ensure (to the extent possible) that those with moral standing have good lives. Development of the relevant capacities for moral standing from slightly below to slightly above some threshold does not make a big difference in our duties to make sure that the life goes well (which is not to deny that it does make some difference). It thus seems that we need to recognize degrees of moral standing.[12] Obviously, the issue is complex and highly controversial, but I cannot defend this claim here.

We are finally ready for the core of the solution (although more qualification will be given below):

Idea 3. Fortune is well-being relativized to degree of moral standing, such that (1) zero well-being represents zero fortune, and (2) for a given level of well-being, fortune is inversely related to moral standing (i.e. increasing moral standing reduces fortune, for a given level of well-being).

The idea is that a mouse and a human both have zero fortune if each has zero well-being, and that, for a given level of well-being, the fortune (that which is to be equalized) of the mouse is greater than that of the human. To make this more concrete, I shall make the following assumption:

Working Assumption 1. For non-negative levels of well-being, fortune is divided by degree of moral standing.[13]

---

[12] Degrees of moral standing also seem necessary in order to deal adequately with future people who will come into existence with less than certainty. I shall suggest below that their standing is discounted by the probability of their coming into existence.

[13] I here sidestep the important issue of how fortune is to be calculated when well-being is negative. It would be quite implausible to hold that here too it is well-being divided by degree of moral standing. This would have the result that a mouse with moral standing of .01 and well-being of −1 has worse fortune (−100) than a human with moral standing of 1 and well-being of −99. It would also violate Idea 3's requirement that for a given level of well-being (e.g. −1) fortune is inversely related to degree of moral standing (e.g. that a mouse with well-being of −1 has better fortune than a normal human with −1). One promising way of relativizing negative well-being is to set fortune equal to well-being *multiplied* (cf. divided) by degree of moral standing. This ensures that those with lower degrees of moral standing require less well-being to achieve a given level of fortune (as required by Idea 3). I shall not, however, pursue this important and difficult question.

Suppose that a mouse has moral standing of .01 and a human has moral standing of 1. If the mouse has well-being of 1 and the human well-being of 100, then they each have fortune of 100. The relativization to the degree of moral standing thus seems to avoid the problematic conclusion. Mice have a claim on resources, but, because their moral standing is typically much lower than that of most humans, their claim is much weaker. This idea also seems independently plausible. A being with no moral standing has no claims on us (by definition). Given that moral standing comes in degrees, it seems plausible that a being who has a very low degree of moral standing (e.g. only slightly above no moral standing) has only very weak claims on us.[14]

There are two issues that need to be addressed about how the degree of moral standing is determined. One is that moral standing, I believe, needs to be relative to possible actions, and not independent of what action is performed. This is admittedly a very unusual idea. To motivate it, consider a situation in which there is a (presentient) zygote and one can perform one of three possible actions (where no one else is affected): (1) allow the zygote to die, (2) provide sustenance for the zygote, in which case it goes on to live a very good life with normal human capacities, and (3) provide partial sustenance, in which case it goes on to live a poor life (but worth living) with normal human capacities. If one ensures that the zygote dies, it never acquires moral standing, and is thus not wronged. Even though it could have had a very good life, failure to provide that life does not wrong the zygote because it ensures that the zygote never acquires the relevant capacities for moral standing. (Those who think that a zygote already has moral standing can change the example to one combining a particular sperm and egg, or failing to do so, to produce a particular possible person.) Nonetheless, providing only partial sustenance to the zygote, I claim, wrongs the zygote. In that case, the zygote does acquire the relevant capacities and is needlessly made to live a poor life. I believe that the most plausible way of making sense of this is to say that moral standing is relative to the action performed. The zygote has no moral standing relative to an action that ensures that it dies prior to acquiring the relevant capacities, but has full moral standing relative to an action that ensures that it acquires normal human capacities. It is thus wronged by the action that needlessly deprives it of benefits.

Consider, then,

Idea 4. For a given choice situation of a given agent, the degree of moral standing that an affected individual has is *action-relative* (i.e. depends on which action the agent performs).

---

[14] It's worth mentioning that throughout I am putting aside issues of rectification for past wrongs. A person who has a low degree of moral standing because her capacities were wrongfully thwarted has, I would argue, a claim to have her capacities suitably enhanced, or at least to be compensated so that her well-being is no lower than it would have been had she not been wronged. In any case, this issue is ignored throughout.

This idea is highly controversial, and there are other ways of addressing the problem just raised. Nonetheless, I believe that relativizing moral standing to action performed is independently plausible.[15] My goal here, however, is not to defend it, but simply to identify it and to show how it can help avoid the problematic conclusion.

The final main question that we must address, before I illustrate how this general approach seems to avoid the problematic conclusion, concerns how the degree of moral standing is grounded in past, present (just prior to action), and future capacities for well-being. Clearly, the present capacities are relevant. Moreover, future capacities, I have already suggested above, are also relevant: a being with no past or present capacity for well-being (such as a presentient fetus) has moral standing relative to an action for which she later develops that capacity (and thus can be wronged by that action). Finally, past capacities are also relevant. If they were not, then a normal adult who temporarily lost her capacity for well-being would not be wronged if she were then killed (since she would never have the relevant capacities now or in the future). Hence, the past is somehow relevant. Once, however, an individual has lost all potential for present and future capacities for well-being, she no longer has, I claim, any moral standing (dead people have no moral standing). Hence, the past is relevant only if there is present or future potential for the capacity for well-being.

This leads us to

> Idea 5. The degree of moral standing that an individual has relative to a given action depends positively on (1) the current capacity for well-being, (2) each of the various empirical possibilities for future capacity for well-being if that action is performed, and (3), if there is a least some present or future potential for the capacity for well-being, on past capacity for well-being of at least some past times.

This leaves open exactly how the degree of moral standing is determined, and it seems that any possible function of past, present, and possible future capacities has some problematic implications. I shall not attempt to resolve this issue here. Instead, I shall simply make the following working assumption for illustration:

> Working Assumption 2. The degree of moral standing that an individual has relative to a given action is the expected average capacity for well-being that she has over the course of her life if that action is performed (but zero if the individual has no current or future potential for the capacity for well-being at the time the action is performed).

---

[15] The idea of relativizing moral standing to action performed is similar to the idea, proposed by Elizabeth Harman (1999), that moral standing depends (if I understand correctly) on how the future turns out. However, I reject this claim. Moral standing, I claim, is determined at the time of action. It depends only on what action is performed and the probabilities of future events that it imposes. It does not depend on which of the possible future events contingently ends up occurring.

Implicit in this assumption is the view that future capacities are discounted for their probability. An individual who has no past or present capacities, and only a very small chance of a future high capacity, has a low degree of moral standing. She might, however, have a high degree of moral standing if the future capacities were great and highly likely. Also implicit in this working assumption is the view that all past capacities matter equally. One might, on the contrary, hold that only the recent past matters, or that the past matters more the closer it is to the present. This whole issue is complex and murky, and I fully agree that there is no simple answer.[16] Nonetheless, I believe that the general idea of Idea 5 is plausible. I will invoke Working Assumption 2 simply as a way of illustrating the idea.

Let us now consider an example that illustrates how these ideas help avoid the problematic conclusion. Suppose for simplicity that there is just one mouse (M) with current and past capacities for well-being of .01 and just two humans (H1 and H2) with current and past capacities for well-being of 1. Humans have potential for well-being of 100 and the mouse has the same potential with radical enhancement. For simplicity, I'll assume that radical enhancement of mice costs nothing to implement and that further enhancement of humans is not possible. Here there are three feasible actions (represented in Table 9.1). Doing nothing leaves the mouse with low capacities and moral standing of .01 (normal mouse standing). Although the mouse gets only .5 well-being, its fortune (50) is higher than that of H1 (10). Relative to moral standing of .01, .5 well-being represents greater fortune than 10 units for an individual with moral standing of 1. The second feasible action also involves no enhancement, but it distributes well-being in a way that equalizes fortune. The third feasible action enhances the mouse and then equalizes fortune.

What does moderate egalitarianism require in this case? For simplicity, here and below, I'll assume that it requires maximizing equality rather than simply significantly

Table 9.1

Possible actions	Well-being			Moral standing			Fortune (WB/MS)		
	M	H1	H2	M	H1	H2	M	H1	H2
Do nothing, unequal fortune	.5	10	50	.01	1	1	50	10	50
No enhance, equal fortune	.301	30.1	30.1	.01	1	1	30.1	30.1	30.1
Enhance, equal fortune	18.7	20.9	20.9	.9	1	1	20.9	20.9	20.9

[16] Working Assumption 2 entails that two individuals with the same current capacities, and the same future capacities if a given action is performed, may nonetheless have different degrees of moral standing relative to that action, if their past capacities are different. Admittedly, this seems bizarre. Nonetheless, the past must somehow be relevant. Otherwise, a person who temporarily lost her capacity would not be wronged if she were killed.

but non-maximally promoting it. Nothing of substance depends on this. I also assume that a plausible version of egalitarianism will never require leveling down. Instead, it will require choosing a most equal distribution of fortune from among those that are Pareto optimal in well-being. Pareto optimality is a weak kind of efficiency requirement. It requires that it not be possible to improve one person's well-being without making someone worse off. Thus, for example ⟨2,2,2⟩ is not Pareto optimal when ⟨2,3,4⟩ is also feasible (since the second and third individuals are better off and the first person is not worse off). For simplicity, I'll focus on examples, such as the one above, where all the feasible options are Pareto optimal.

In the above example, all three options are Pareto optimal in well-being, and the second and third options achieve maximum feasible equality of fortune. Moderate egalitarianism thus judges the first option impermissible (since it is less equal than the others) and judges the other two permissible (since they are each Pareto optimal in well-being and each maximally equal in fortune relative to the Pareto optimal set). In this example, then, enhancement of the mice is not required, but it is permitted. Thus the problematic conclusion in its strict form is avoided (since there is no requirement to radically shift resources to mice), but a weaker form remains: it is permissible to radically shift resources to mice (after enhancing them). This is less problematic, but it is still significantly problematic. We have not yet, I believe, fully solved the problem.

If we add one more twist, we can, I believe, avoid even the weak version of the problematic conclusion. The twist (very roughly) is that we strengthen the efficiency requirement to give a certain priority to increasing the well-being of those whose degree of moral standing is not decreased over increasing benefits to those whose degree of moral standing is decreased. Consider, then,

> *Idea 6.* Efficiency requires that an option, X, be Pareto optimal and such that there is no alternative Pareto optimal option, Y, such that:
>
> (1) for all individuals with the *same degree* of moral standing in X and Y, all have at least as much well-being in Y and some have more in Y;
> (2) all individuals with a *higher degree* of moral standing in Y than in X have *maximal well-being* for that feasible set; and
> (3) for all individuals with a *lower degree* of moral standing in Y than in X, their *fortune* is at least as great in Y as it is in X.

This idea strengthens the efficiency requirement that is prior to the equality requirement. It still maintains that Pareto optimality in *well-being* is necessary, but further rules out certain options that are not Pareto optimal in *fortune* relative to the Pareto optimal (in well-being) set. The third option above of enhancing the mice fails this requirement, since the second option provides more well-being to the humans (whose degree of moral standing is not affected) and it provides more fortune (although less

Table 9.2

Possible actions	Well-being			Moral standing			Fortune (WB/MS)		
	M	H1	H2	M	H1	H2	M	H1	H2
Do nothing	.1	10.2	50.2	.01	1	1	10	10.2	50.2
No enhance, equalize humans	.1	30.2	30.2	.01	1	1	10	30.2	30.2
Enhance, equalize all	18.7	20.9	20.9	.9	1	1	20.9	20.9	20.9

well-being) to the mouse (whose degree of moral standing is decreased). The first and second options, however, satisfy this requirement. Given that the first option is less equal in fortune than the second, only the second option is permissible. In particular, radical enhancement is impermissible, and even the weak problematic conclusion is avoided in this case.

This strengthened efficiency requirement creates a presumption against enhancement. Enhancement increases the moral standing of individuals, and if there is a fixed total of well-being, then enhancement must decrease the fortune of at least some individuals (and perhaps increase no one's). The above ideas do not, however, entail that radical enhancement is always impermissible. Indeed, sometimes they require it. Consider the case of Table 9.2. Here each option satisfies the enhanced efficiency requirement of Idea 6. Enhancement is not ruled out in this case, because, although the second option gives more well-being to the two humans (whose degree of moral standing is unaffected), it does this by reducing the fortune of the mouse. Thus, enhancement is not ruled out on efficiency grounds. Moreover, the third option (enhance the mouse and then equalize fortune) is the uniquely most equal in fortune (because for contingent reasons it is not possible to equalize fortune without enhancement). Hence, only it is permissible. Radical enhancement followed by a shift in resources from humans to mice is morally required in this case.

Some may find even this implication deeply troubling, but I do not. If mice have moral standing and are protected by the requirements of equality, then at least sometimes we will be required to shift some resources to them and sometimes this will involve radical enhancement. This is much less problematic than the implication that morality requires a *radical shift* of resources from *most* humans to most mice.

8. Speculative Conclusion

We have been exploring the implications of accepting moderate egalitarianism while holding that sentience, as a capacity for well-being, is sufficient for moral standing and while rejecting all forms of speciesism. We have been seeking a way of avoiding the problematic conclusion that morality requires a massive shift of resources from most humans to most mice. I have sketched a way of avoiding the problematic conclusion. The demands of equality should be understood as something like equality of fortune, relative to the feasible options that are efficient in the enhanced sense of Idea 6. Fortune, for a given action, should be understood as well-being relativized to moral standing if that action is performed—more specifically (for positive well-being), as well-being divided by degree of moral standing. This gives, I suggest, a plausible approach to interspecies equality in the simple case where radical enhancement is not possible and also in the deep case where it is.

Even if the specifics of this approach are mistaken, the following two general features of this approach are, I claim, independently plausible: (1) Moral standing comes in degrees and those who only barely have moral standing have only very weak moral claims. (2) Differences in one's past, present, or future capacities for well-being affect the strength of one's moral claims (because they affect one's degree of moral standing), but mere differences in potential for well-being do not. If two individuals have the same moral standing (grounded in past, present, and future capacities) and would reap the same benefit in well-being, they have an equally strong claim to that benefit—even if their potentials are different.

Admittedly, I have done little more than formulate and motivate this general approach. Further analysis may show that it is deeply flawed in unanticipated ways. My only claim here is that egalitarians should worry about the problem, and that the proposed solution is at least worth considering carefully. Much more analysis is of course needed before we have an adequate sense of what kinds of solution are possible, and which are the most plausible.

References

ARNESON, R. (1999). 'What, If Anything, Renders All Humans Morally Equal?', in D. Jamieson (ed.), *Peter Singer and His Critics* (Oxford: Basil Blackwell), 103–28.

BUCHANAN, A., BROCK, D., DANIELS, N., and WINKLER, D. (2000), *From Chance to Choice: Genetics and Justice* (Cambridge: Cambridge University Press).

CRISP, R. (2003), 'Equality, Priority, and Compassion', *Ethics*, 113: 745–63.

DANIELS, N. (1990), 'Equality of What: Welfare, Resources, or Capabilities?', *Philosophy and Phenomenological Research*, 50 (suppl.), 273–96; repr. in N. Daniels, *Justice and Justification* (New York: Cambridge University Press, 1996), 208–31.

HARMAN, E. (1999), 'Creation Ethics: The Moral Status of Early Fetuses and the Ethics of Abortion', *Philosophy and Public Affairs*, 28: 310–24.

KAUFMAN, F. (1998), 'Speciesism and the Argument from Misfortune', *Journal of Applied Philosophy*, 15: 155–63.

McMAHAN, J. (1996), 'Cognitive Disability, Misfortune, and Justice', *Philosophy and Public Affairs*, 25: 3–35.

_____ (2002), *The Ethics of Killing: Problems at the Margins of Life* (Oxford: Oxford University Press).

PERSSON, I. (1993), 'A Basis for (Interspecies) Equality', in P. Cavalieri and P. Singer (eds.), *The Great Ape Project* (New York: St Martin's Press), 183–93.

RACHELS, J. (1990), *Created from Animals: The Moral Implications of Darwinism* (New York: Oxford University Press).

SINGER, P. (1990), *Animal Liberation*, 2nd edn. (New York: Random House).

Part III
Equality and Other Values

10

Liberty, Liability, and Contractualism

Andrew Williams

1. Introduction

Most egalitarians accept that a just society would not only require its members to share fairly in each other's fortunes and misfortunes but also empower them to decide various aspects of their lives for themselves. Egalitarians face consequent questions about the relevant types of luck as well as the contours of the pertinent decision-making liberties. They also face questions about how to assign liability for the costs and benefits generated when individuals exercise those liberties. For illustration, consider some issues concerning luck, liberty, and liability raised by procreation. Egalitarians need to decide whether treatment for involuntarily infertile individuals should be publicly funded because of its impact on their welfare, or resources, or capabilities. They also need to decide whether there are any limits on parents' rights to decide the size of their families, and the extent to which the costs of reproductive choices should be borne by parents alone (Casal and Williams 2004).

Over the last two decades, we have witnessed real progress in understanding these types of question, thanks in large part to the work of John Rawls (1999, 2001) and

I am greatly indebted to Paula Casal for persistent but constructive criticism of this chapter. For helpful written comments or conversation, I also thank Jeppe Andersen, John Baker, Brian Barry, Akeel Bilgrami, Matthew Clayton, Thomas Christiano, G. A. Cohen, Jon Elster, Marc Fleurbaey, Nils Holtug, Brad Hooker, Rahul Kumar, Andrew Lister, Alistair Macleod, Margaret Moore, Serena Olsaretti, Martin O'Neill, Michael Otsuka, Thomas Pogge, Kasper Lippert-Rasmussen, Michael Rosen, T. M. Scanlon, Houston Smits, Zofia Stemplowska, Philip Stratton-Lake, and Peter Vallentyne.

Ronald Dworkin (2000), as well as various other political philosophers and economists. During the same period in moral philosophy, T. M. Scanlon has developed a powerful version of contractualism, elaborated most fully in his widely discussed treatise *What We Owe to Each Other* (1998). Building on his earlier Tanner Lecture 'The Significance of Choice' (1988), Scanlon devotes the sixth chapter of his book to a contractualist account of the meaning and grounds of judgments about moral responsibility. Scanlon's account is important in its own right, but also is of interest because it addresses questions about choice and responsibility that have become central to contemporary egalitarianism. Unfortunately, however, Scanlon's answers have generated much less discussion than other aspects of his contractualism. This chapter attempts to correct that deficit by clarifying Scanlon's account, and identifying various difficulties that egalitarians contemplating its adoption need to consider.

2. Attributive and Substantive Responsibility

Scanlon's chapter begins by noting that a statement of the form '*P* is morally responsible for *x*' can express two very different judgments (1998: 248). The first is a judgment of *responsibility as attributability*, in which case *x* refers to an action, or attitude, which constitutes a basis of moral appraisal of some person, *P*, as culpable or commendable. One of the chapter's two main ambitions is to defend a compatibilist conception of attributive responsibility, which denies that the purpose of blame is to deter, or sanction, wrongdoing. Instead, Scanlon argues that judging someone blameworthy involves a distinctive type of criticism of her attitudes, forceful because of its implications for her relations with others (1998: 275–6, 287). Furthermore, such a judgment is consistent with the Causal Thesis that 'all our actions have antecedent causes to which they are linked by causal laws of the kind that govern other events in the universe' (1998: 250).

Scanlon also notes the statement '*P* is morally responsible for *x*' can express a judgment of *substantive responsibility* stating how individuals are required, or permitted, to act. In this case, *x* refers either to some outcome that *P* is required to bring about, or to some burden that others are permitted to leave *P* to bear. For illustration, Scanlon mentions an example in which a father must decide whether to arrange his estate to prevent his grown son from making foolish financial decisions. He explains we could speak of substantive responsibility in a broad sense by asking whether it is the father's responsibility to protect his son from his foolishness. Instead, speaking with a narrower sense in mind, we could ask whether the son's choice to squander his inheritance makes the resulting loss his own responsibility rather than one that others are also required to bear.

The second main ambition of Scanlon's chapter concerns substantive responsibility in the narrower sense. Thus, Scanlon proposes what he terms a Value of Choice account of the role an agent's decisions and opportunities should play when deciding whether some burden is his exclusive responsibility (1998: 249). Because of the Value of Choice account's focus on agency-based personal liability the account should be of interest to contemporary egalitarians. Before outlining the account, it is worth noting the role it also plays in Scanlon's defense of contractualism.

To do so, recall the contractualist claim that 'an act is wrong if and only if any principle that permitted it would be one that could reasonably be rejected' (1998: 4). One standard objection to this formula alleges that acts are not wrong because principles permitting them can reasonably be rejected; a principle's rejection is reasonable only because it permits wrongful acts (1998: 4–5, 213–18). The Value of Choice account is one of several attempts to rebut this *circularity charge* by showing there are grounds for reasonable rejection other than wrongness. Thus, Scanlon uses his account to show that the value of having outcomes depend upon an agent's responses is relevant when judging whether she can reasonably reject certain principles conferring liability on her. Similarly, he appeals to the disvalue of arbitrary subjection to inferior treatment to explain why principles permitting certain type of unfairness are also subject to reasonable rejection (1998: 211–13). If Scanlon's appeal to the Value of Choice is successful it not only illuminates an important area of normative ethics and political philosophy but also helps vindicate contractualism.

3. The Value of Choice Account

Describing the purpose of the Value of Choice account, Scanlon writes that

Two things need to be explained. The first is why principles that no one could reasonably reject often must be ones that make outcomes sensitive to individuals' choices, or at least their having had the opportunity to choose. The second is how considerations of responsibility can diminish a person's reasonable grounds for rejecting a principle. How can the fact that a person could have avoided a burden by choosing appropriately make it the case that he cannot reasonably reject a principle that makes him bear that burden? (1998: 251)

Declaring how he will approach these questions, Scanlon then states that his

strategy will be to derive an answer to the second question from an answer to the first. Once we understand the positive reasons that people have for wanting opportunities to make choices that will affect what happens to them, what they owe to others, and what others owe to them, we can see also how their having had such opportunities can play a crucial role in determining what they can reasonably object to. (1998: 251)

To understand how Scanlon pursues this strategy, consider first his explanation of 'why principles that no one could reasonably reject often must be ones that make outcomes sensitive to individuals' choices'.

According to that explanation, there are *instrumental*, *representative*, and *symbolic* reasons 'for wanting to have certain powers and opportunities in our lives' (1998: 253). Illustrating those reasons, Scanlon writes that

in societies in which arranged marriages are not the norm, people have reason to want to choose their own mates rather than have their parents do it for them, not only because they think this will lead to a more satisfactory choice (instrumental value), or because they want their choice to be an expression of their own taste and affections (representative value), but also because having their parents make the choice would be 'demeaning'—that is to say, would suggest that they are not competent, independent adults (symbolic value). (1998: 253)

What I shall term the *positive element* of the Value of Choice account appeals to these three values in order to show that individuals have reasons to reject principles that permit others to deny them, or fail to provide, certain opportunities.[1] As Scanlon explains, these values can 'figure as reasonable grounds for rejecting proposed moral principles' (1998: 253–4). Referring to instrumental, representative, and symbolic considerations, he writes, 'Where these three values are significant (and there are no sufficiently strong countervailing ones), the principles that no one could reasonably reject will forbid paternalistic intervention, thus making it a person's own (substantive) responsibility whether to risk the harms in question' (1998: 254).

Scanlon's inference seems plausible in what I shall term *wrongful protection cases*, which involve a choice between either restricting individuals' opportunities or protecting them from certain burdens. For example, suppose that (i) there are decisive reasons to reject principles permitting others to restrict the foolish son's ability to squander his inheritance, and that (ii) only such restrictions can provide him with protection against financial disaster. If so, then it seems plausible that the son cannot complain that others have wrongfully denied him protection against the relevant disadvantages. On the contrary, for them to provide such protection would wrong him.

Suppose, however, that the example of the foolish son is revised so that condition (i) still holds but (ii) does not: it is now feasible to protect the son from bearing the entire costs of his decisions by requiring his fellow inheritors to offset at least some of

---

[1] The idea that the Value of Choice account contains positive and negative elements is suggested by Scanlon's remark that in 'the case of contracts, the value of control figures both positively and negatively. Positively, it is a central aim of the law of contracts to give effect to the wills of the parties. In order to do this, it must make the legal normative consequences of an act dependent on the beliefs and intentions of the agent. Negatively, this dependence greatly weakens the case of a person who complains about the enforcement of a contract knowingly and voluntarily undertaken: if he or she wished not to be bound, he or she could simply have refrained from consenting' (2003a: 227–8).

the losses he would otherwise incur.[2] Thus, the son can enjoy both the opportunity to decide how to dispose of his inheritance and protection from bearing the disastrous costs of his decision, provided that others are required to share those costs. In such *permissible protection cases*, where the absence of restriction does not preclude protection, the Value of Choice account cannot rely solely on its positive element to justify judgments of substantive responsibility.

Nevertheless, many egalitarians, and others, believe that if the son was capable of making decisions for which he is attributively responsible, received ample financial advice, and had no worse financial opportunities than his fellow inheritors, then the latter are not required to share such costs. They judge that the son possesses not only a power to make such decisions, but also a liability to bear any burdens arising from his decision. To understand how the Value of Choice account can assess whether that judgment is sound, and other claims about substantive responsibility in permissible protection cases, we need to consider its negative element. By doing so, we can better understand Scanlon's answer to his second question, namely, 'How can the fact that a person could have avoided a burden by choosing appropriately make it the case that he cannot reasonably reject a principle that makes him bear that burden?'

The negative element of Scanlon's account is supposed to explain why 'when a person could have avoided a certain result by choosing appropriately, this fact weakens her grounds for rejecting a principle that would make her bear the burden of that result' (1998: 256). Appealing to what I shall term the *protective value of choice*, Scanlon argues that when certain opportunities are in place, individuals lack sufficient reason, or have lesser reason, to make morally compelling demands on others to relieve them of certain burdens. As Scanlon explains, 'what matters [in assigning responsibility to a person] is the value of the opportunity to choose that the person is presented with. If a person has been placed in a sufficiently good position, this can make it the case that he or she has no valid complaint against what results' (1998: 258). By appealing to this element of the account, a contractualist can argue that whether the foolish son's losses are entirely his responsibility depends upon whether his opportunities were sufficiently valuable so that he cannot reasonably reject a moral principle that permits his fellow inheritors to refuse to offset his losses.

Scanlon illustrates the negative element of his account with an example in which officials arrange the removal of hazardous waste that threatens to contaminate a city's water supply (1998: 256–7). During the removal process, the officials take extensive precautions, including fencing off the relevant sites, minimizing the amount of waste

---

[2] Note that the revised example presents us with a choice between three options, namely (i) limiting the son's decision-powers, (ii) requiring others to share the costs of his decisions, or (iii) leaving him to suffer their disastrous consequences alone. For further discussion of the relevance of this type of trilemma to contemporary egalitarianism, see Williams (2006).

released into the air, and warning individuals to keep away. Despite these measures, enough waste will be released into the air to cause lung damage to susceptible individuals who, because they fail either to hear or to heed official warnings, do not keep away. Scanlon stipulates that although some individuals will suffer lung damage during the removal process, no one can reasonably reject a principle permitting the officials' course of action. He then asks what role the fact that the injured individuals 'were warned, and thus given the choice of avoiding exposure, plays in making it the case that they cannot complain of the outcome' (1998: 257).

Explaining how his account answers this question, Scanlon reiterates its key assumption that there are generic reasons for individuals to want outcomes to depend on the way they respond when presented with alternatives. He then assumes that, in the present case, the relevant reasons are instrumental, and purely protective since 'No one has reason to place positive value on having the opportunity to be exposed to hazardous waste' (1998: 257). Thus, he writes that

the moral significance of choice in cases like the hazardous waste removal example lies in its value as a protection. This is a special case of . . . the 'predictive' or 'instrumental' value of choice. 'Having the choice'—having what happens depend on how one responds when presented with certain alternatives—is something we have reason to want because it decreases the likelihood of our suffering certain harms. (1998: 261)

Relying on these assumptions, Scanlon claims the protective value of the opportunity to avoid exposure is sufficiently great that individuals could reasonably reject a principle permitting officials not to warn them about the risks they face from the waste. However, since there are limits on the level of protection individuals can reasonably demand (1998: 258), and officials have gone to such lengths to warn and otherwise protect them, there will come a point when the occurrence of harm becomes a matter of personal liability. Scanlon emphasizes that the Value of Choice account endorses the latter conclusion regardless of whether those harmed in the removal process consciously decided to risk injury (1998: 258). In doing so, he contrasts his account with a rival account of agency-based personal liability, which I now briefly examine.

4. The Forfeiture View

According to the Forfeiture View, when individuals consciously decline to avoid certain harms or risks, they relinquish various rights to protection against such harms. As Scanlon explains, what 'lies behind the Forfeiture View is . . . [t]he idea that . . . a person who could have chosen to avoid a certain outcome, but who knowingly passed up this choice, cannot complain of the result: *volenti non fit iniuria*' (1998: 259).[3] Thus, on the rival account's analysis of the waste removal case, in assessing whether any injured individuals have valid complaints, 'it matters crucially whether an outcome actually resulted from a conscious decision in which the agent intentionally passed up specific alternatives' (1998: 258).

In criticizing the Forfeiture View, Scanlon acknowledges that in some cases, such as those involving the acquisition of contractual obligations, the presence of conscious decision is important in determining an individual's liabilities. Nevertheless, he claims there are at least two reasons to reject the Forfeiture View as an adequate in general, or in the hazardous waste case in particular. (I mention a third below when discussing the case of the *forgetful man*.) First, as mentioned, sometimes the mere fact that an individual 'was placed in conditions in which he had the choice of avoiding the risk may be sufficient' to diminish, or undermine, his complaint (1998: 260). Second, the Forfeiture View's focus on conscious choice overlooks the choice-independent moral significance of the background conditions against which choice takes place (1998: 261). Since conscious choice is not always either necessary or sufficient for assigning liability, Scanlon concludes that forfeiture is 'a creature of particular institutions and relatively specific principles such as those governing promising . . . It is not a moral feature of choice in general' (1998: 265).

Scanlon also acknowledges that the Forfeiture View is appealing because it offers an explanation of the apparent moral difference between injured individuals who 'knew what they were getting into', and those who did not. Illustrating the difference with the waste removal case, he contrasts the case of an *uninformed man*, who failed to hear the official warnings, with the case of an *imprudent risk-taker*, who heard the warnings, but deliberately entered the removal site in order to satisfy her curiosity. Scanlon claims that there 'seems to be a clear difference between the cases' (1998: 258). We can say to the uniformed man that he has no complaint against his injury because the officials had 'done enough' to protect him. We are, however, tempted to respond to the risk-taker by citing the Forfeiture View that

> she is (substantively) responsible for her injury; and it is this fact, rather than the amount that has been done to protect her or the cost to others of doing more, that makes it the case that she cannot blame anyone for what happened. By choosing, in the face of warnings, to go to the excavation site, she laid down her right to complain of the harm she suffered as a result. (1998: 258)

Despite this apparent virtue, Scanlon argues that it does not constitute an advantage for the Forfeiture View since the Value of Choice account also implies that there

---

[3] Referring to Nino (1983), Scanlon notes (1998: 399 n. 4) that the 'idea expressed in the Forfeiture View is stated with particular clarity by Carlos Nino'.

is an important difference between the two victims of waste removal. As Scanlon explains,

> Since it is true in both cases that we did as much as we could be asked to do to protect these people against injury . . . neither could reasonably reject a principle permitting such a project to go forward with the safeguards it involved. But it remains true that only the woman in the second example was put in the position that these safeguards aim at providing for everyone. (1998: 259)

Moreover, the Value of Choice account has at least one advantage over the Forfeiture View, namely that it can explain why a forgetful man, who heard the warnings but then failed to recollect them rather than consciously refrained from heeding them, can be as responsible for any injury he incurs as the imprudent woman (1998: 259).[4]

5. A Strategic Difficulty

So far, I have outlined the Value of Choice account, and claimed that it needs to justify judgments of substantive responsibility in permissible as well as wrongful protection cases. I have also argued that in order to deal with permissible protection cases it is necessary to appeal to the account's negative element. Thus, on Scanlon's view, in such cases an individual's substantive responsibility for her condition depends not on whether 'she asked for it' but on whether others have 'done enough' for her by

---

[4] Although G. A. Cohen has suggested his own conception of *equality of access to advantage* has 'affinities' with the Forfeiture View (1989: 935 n. 640), there are at least two reasons to think that it would be hasty to conclude Cohen's position, or other 'luck egalitarian' positions (Anderson 1999), must rely on the View, and hence also fall prey to Scanlon's persuasive objections to it. First, luck egalitarians hold individuals substantively responsible for negligent as well as conscious decisions. Second, and more importantly, it is arguable that luck egalitarians can attempt to defend their permissive attitude to avoidable inequality from within the Value of Choice framework. Thus, they can assert that it is unreasonable for a political community to expect any of its members to accept less valuable opportunities than their co-members, but then proceed to claim it is not unreasonable to insist that once each member has been given equally valuable opportunities the community has 'done enough' to hold them liable for their responses. Commenting on my second suggested reason, Samuel Scheffler (2005: 27 n. 20) has objected that the 'distinction between choices and circumstances does not have the kind of general justificatory significance on a Value of Choice account that the Forfeiture View assigns to it'. The objection seems to assume that the luck egalitarian attitude to the distinction between choice and circumstances applies to all choices, and then appeals to the plausible assumption that the Value of Choice account would not support so indiscriminate an attitude. It is not clear, however, that luck egalitarians do ascribe such general significance to choice. Instead, to slightly amend Scheffler's earlier illuminating characterization of their position (Scheffler 2005: 6), luck egalitarians may claim only that there is something unjust about unavoidable inequalities but nothing comparably unjust about inequalities deriving from voluntary choices *made against a background of equally valuable circumstances*.

providing sufficiently valuable opportunities for her to choose to avoid that condition. I shall now examine three problematic aspects of the account, the first of which concerns a general feature of Scanlon's explanatory strategy.

Before presenting the initial problem, note that the Value of Choice account could be understood as being more or less ambitious. Understood more ambitiously, the account claims that our reasons to value opportunities are sufficient to ground the verdictive conclusions involved in substantive responsibility judgments. Understood more modestly, the account claims that those reasons make some difference in assigning substantive responsibility.[5] In the hazardous waste case, for example, the account might imply that offering warnings is 'crucial' because a necessary condition for transportation being permissible. The account might allow, however, that identifying the sufficient conditions for permissibility requires reference not only to the opportunities available to individuals harmed during transportation but also to the burdens suffered by individuals if the waste is not transported. Since appealing to the reasons to value opportunity need not suffice to show that enough has been done for individuals, on the second understanding the positive reasons to value opportunities provide at best a partial rather than complete account of substantive responsibility. The essential negative element in the Value of Choice account also requires support from additional considerations.

To consider the first problem suppose we initially adopt the ambitious understanding of the Value of Choice account, and attempt to apply it to the foolish son example, reconstrued as a permissible protection case. Scanlon's own remarks imply that an adequate account of substantive responsibility should answer two questions about the example. First, which powers to dispose of his inheritance can the son justifiably demand? Second, which liabilities can others permissibly assign to the son? Though determining the precise extent of the son's rightful powers is difficult, it is plausible to claim that the son, assuming a certain level of competence, has sound instrumental, representative, and symbolic reasons to reject principles that permit others to deny him any say over his inheritance. So, the Value of Choice account provides some contractualist answer to the first question. However, it is far less clear whether those three considerations also provide reasons to reject different principles for assigning liability. To appreciate their limited role in explaining the son's liabilities, think first how an appeal to them might proceed.

---

[5] Scanlon suggests the more ambitious understanding by describing the Value of Choice account as an answer to the question 'How can the fact that a person could have avoided a burden by choosing appropriately make it the case that he cannot reasonably reject a principle that makes him bear that burden?' (1998: 251). Some of Scanlon's other statements suggest, however, that the account is only part of the answer. For example, he also writes that 'when a person could have avoided a certain result by choosing appropriately, this fact weakens her grounds for rejecting a principle that would make her bear the burden of that result' (1998: 256).

There certainly appear to be instrumental reasons for the son to reject principles that permit others to refuse to share in his losses, especially if those losses become sufficiently grave. Some would deny that these are *reasonable* grounds for such rejection since it is not wrong for others to refuse to bear the costs of the son's choices, but a contractualist cannot employ this type of argument without falling prey to the circularity charge noted earlier. The contractualist can still, however, insist that others are likely to have comparable instrumental grounds for rejecting principles that do not permit them to refuse to share in the son's losses.

Nevertheless, since it is arguable that such a permission enhances the representative value of the son's opportunity to dispose of his inheritance, there may be additional countervailing reasons for the son not to reject such permissive principles. Just as the meaning of a gift, as Scanlon suggests (1998: 252), can depend on whether the giver chose it herself, so the significance of the son's decisions may vary if it is known he will be unable reasonably to demand others' assistance if his project fails. Such knowledge may enable him to display a higher degree of commitment to his project than would otherwise be available. It could also relieve him from the inhibiting thought that others might be required to bear the costs of his project if it fails. (Perhaps these considerations could even support a requirement for others not to share in the son's losses.) Turning to the third consideration, its implications are once again hard to assess. The son may have symbolic reasons to reject principles that do not permit others to decline responsibility for his losses, especially if he was singled out for special protection, and not permitted to decline any offer to share his losses. If the requirement to share in others' losses was general, and demanded only the offer of assistance, it is less clear whether there are weighty symbolic reasons for the son to reject it.

Though more could be said about the implications of instrumental, representative, and symbolic considerations, it is evident those considerations have far clearer implications for questions concerning the son's powers than his liabilities, and may pull in opposite directions when addressing the second type of question. I provisionally conclude that appeal to those reasons alone does not provide an adequate way of assigning liability across individuals. There is also a second, and more basic, reason to accept this conclusion.

Regardless of the specific values under consideration, arguments that address questions of substantive responsibility primarily from the decision-maker's standpoint are unlikely to provide convincing answers across a suitably wide range of cases. For we normally respond to those questions by treating the perspective of agents other than the decision-maker as at least as important in deciding how liability should be assigned. Thus, although a decision-maker sometimes has reason to want others not to feel obliged to bear the costs of his own choices, or even feel obliged to decline those costs, most of us are inclined to suppose that her liabilities are grounded to a large degree in potential benefactors' reasons to reject a prohibition on not offsetting others' self-incurred losses. Those reasons explain why it would be unfair *to them* to endorse such a prohibition. In this respect it seems that we have similar attitudes to self-incurred losses as self-imposed obligations, such as those generated by promises. Thus, we normally assume that in both cases interests other than those of the decision-maker play the primary role in explaining individuals' liabilities. Indeed, Scanlon's own explanation of the duty of fidelity in his book's next chapter gives primary explanatory importance to reasons arising from the standpoint of the promisee rather than promiser.[6] If our assumption is sound, then we should expect to see an important continuity between Scanlon's general account of the significance of choice for substantive responsibility and his more specific account of substantive responsibility in cases involving promises. Basing the Value of Choice account primarily upon the decision-maker's perspective frustrates this expectation, and creates a general difficulty for the account.

Because of the specific and more general worries mentioned, it seems unpromising to appeal primarily to the instrumental, representative, and symbolic reasons for a decision-maker to demand at least a certain level of opportunity in order to establish that she would be unreasonable to demand more. I conclude Scanlon's claim that 'Standards of [substantive] responsibility . . . arise in large part from the importance, for agents themselves, of having their actions and what happens to them depend on and reflect their choices and other responses' (1998: 290) either exaggerates the importance of the decision-maker's perspective, or is somehow misleading.

The latter conclusion, however, raises the possibility that we should adopt the more modest understanding of Scanlon's view. Thus, we might construe the Value of Choice account as granting that an appeal to agents' reasons to value opportunities is insufficient to decide when others have done enough because reference to additional considerations is also necessary in order to reach verdicts about liability. The problem with this response is that Scanlon's actual discussion contains little explanation of how to identify those additional considerations, and integrate them into a complete contractualist account of substantive responsibility. For example, in his discussion of the waste removal case Scanlon offers no explanation for his stipulation that the officials have done enough to protect citizens to avoid responsibility for causing them harm (1998: 257). In contrasting his view with the Forfeiture View, Scanlon implies that the willing risk-taker has no right to complain about her damaged lungs because of 'the amount that has been done to protect her' and 'the cost to others of doing more' (1998: 258), but he provides no indication of how to compare the costs to others

---

[6] Note that Scanlon, having mentioned Joseph Raz's view of the importance of promisers' interests in being able to bind themselves (Raz 1986: 173), writes, 'It seems to me, however, that the interests of promisees are primary here and provide the clearest grounds of obligation. The interests of promisers have real force only when linked to them' (1998: 403 n. 4).

of being required to do yet more with the losses to her of their being permitted to refuse to do more.

Because Scanlon's explanation of why the officials have done enough is under-developed, it is also difficult to determine the implications of his view for other questions of substantive responsibility raised by the hazardous waste case. Most obviously, we might ask whose responsibility it is to finance medical care, or compens-ation, for those harmed by the waste removal program, and, in particular, whether the differences between the informed risk-taker and the uninformed man warrant different assignments of individual and collective responsibility for these tasks. Here Scanlon does make some relevant remarks. He insists, for example, that the informed risk-taker 'does not lay down her right to rescue or treatment' (1998: 265), but he also immediately qualifies his claim by adding, 'unless this has been prescribed and the policy including this prescription is justified' (1998: 265). He does not, however, examine how such a policy might be justified, or criticized. Without such elaboration, the Value of Choice account has a limited capacity to guide our judgments about an agent's substantive responsibilities.

I conclude, then, that the Value of Choice account is problematic because it faces the following dilemma. Construed ambitiously as an explanation of what grounds conclusionary judgments about substantive responsibility, the account fails because we cannot explain when enough has been done for an agent solely by reference to agents' instrumental, representative, and symbolic reasons to value the provision of opportunities.[7] Such an explanation will be inadequate both because of the specific reasons involved, and because any satisfactory explanation must, in large part, also appeal to other individuals' reasons to value certain immunities. Construed more modestly as an explanation only of why certain factors are relevant when arriving at conclusionary judgments, the account is unsatisfactory because so incomplete.

---

[7] This failure resembles one mentioned in H. L. A. Hart's 'Legal Responsibility and Excuses' (1968: 149), an influential paper to which Scanlon expresses his indebtedness (1998: 399 n. 1). Anticipating Scanlon's view of the protective value of opportunity, Hart argued that even if determinism is true, a defensible system of punishment should contain excusing conditions that limit individual liability to punishment. Thus, Hart wrote that on his account of punitive systems, 'Recognition of excusing conditions is . . . seen as a matter of protection of the individual against the claims of society for the highest measure of protection from crime that can be obtained from a system of threats.' It is notable, however, that Hart also clearly conceded that his strategy does not *suffice* to justify such systems rather than a less ambitious conclusion about one feature they should possess. As he put it, 'I cannot . . . claim to have solved everyone's perplexities. I do not know what to say to a critic who urges that I have shown only that the system in which excusing conditions are recognized protects the individual better against the claims of society than one in which no recognition is accorded to those factors . . . I cannot satisfy the complaint . . . that I have not shown that we are justified in punishing anyone *ever*, at all, under any conditions.' I have expressed similar doubts about whether Scanlon's Value of Choice account justifies verdictive claims about substantive responsibility even if it does succeed in grounding requirements to provide certain opportunities.

6. The Disvalue of Choice

The previous section left unquestioned one of the Value of Choice account's key claims, present on both of the readings I distinguished. Thus, it took for granted that an agent's opportunities make a difference to her liabilities because opportunities are valuable, and so relevant when deciding whether others have done enough for the individual to leave her substantively responsible for certain consequences. It is a familiar thought, however, that individuals are sometimes better off with fewer opportunities (G. Dworkin 1988; Elster 1979). My next remarks examine the implications of this possibility.

To understand some of those implications, consider a variation on the waste removal case in which officials have to choose between the original removal policy, involving public warnings and other precautions, and another policy that deprives the public of any knowledge of the risk to which they are being exposed. Suppose that the former *cautionary policy* will result in a larger set of individuals suffering lung damage, but all its members will have heard the warnings and failed, either deliberately or inadvertently, to heed them. The latter *covert policy*, in contrast, will result in a smaller, and only partly coextensive, set suffering lung damage, none of whose members had any opportunity to avoid harm by responding to warnings.

Before discussing the merits of these two policies, note that the example is inspired by, though distinct from, an objection a defender of the Forfeiture View might press. Describing it, Scanlon writes,

> it might be objected that in the case of the imprudent woman who climbed over the fence being warned of the danger and given the choice of avoiding it turned out to have no positive value. The warning only aroused her impetuous curiosity, and she would have been better off if she had never been told at all. Yet we still feel that it is important that she was warned to stay at home, and the fact that she was warned is an important element supporting the conclusion that she cannot complain about what happened to her . . . The objection concludes that since this moral significance cannot be accounted for by the positive value of her being given this choice we need some other explanation. The natural alternative is something like the Forfeiture View. (1998: 261)

Scanlon's two-part reply to this objection first appeals to the distinction between generic and person-specific reasons to reject moral principles.[8] As he explains, 'The reason why it is important that this woman was informed of the danger, and thus given the choice of avoiding it, is not that this was necessarily advantageous to her

---

[8] Scanlon explains that a generic reason 'is one that we can see people have in virtue of certain general characteristics; it is not attributed to specific individuals' (1998: 205), and that generic reasons 'are reasons that we can see that people have in virtue of their situation, characterized in general terms, and such things as their aims and capabilities and the conditions in which they are placed' (1998: 204).

but rather that it is something that people in general have reason to value and hence to demand that an acceptable principle insist on' (1998: 263). In addition, Scanlon also notes that because 'some people are likely to choose unwisely, it is not enough merely to warn people even if they could all protect themselves by taking appropriate precautions' (1998: 263). Thus, as well as invoking the distinction between generic and specific reasons, he emphasizes that 'it was necessary to put fences around the excavations and to wet the hazardous material down and transport it carefully in order to minimize the risk to those who failed to stay indoors'.

Even though it may succeed against the Forfeiture theorist, Scanlon's reply does not apply in the dual policy case previously described. There we can stipulate that impetuous curiosity, or some other disposition with similar effects, is sufficiently widespread that the generic value of warnings as a form of protection is negative: given individuals' decision-making tendencies, the best way to protect them from harm under the circumstances is by denying them the opportunity to choose.

Granted that stipulation, what then are the respective merits of the cautionary and covert removal policies? Scanlon argues that where burdens are comparable, the moral relevance of aggregative considerations can be explained within a contractualist framework (1998: 229–41). Though some contest that conclusion, I shall not do so.[9] Instead I shall assume that the fact that covert removal minimizes the number of individuals who suffer lung damage is a consideration that counts in its favor, and that its status can be explained by the contractualist. Nevertheless, I also conjecture that many will think that there are countervailing considerations of personal responsibility, which support the cautionary policy. The second problem arises because I doubt that Scanlon's Value of Choice account can provide an explanation of that conviction.

To test first the conjecture, suppose that the covert policy has been chosen, and that it is true of a substantial number of its victims that if the alternative cautionary policy had been chosen they, unlike people in general, would have heeded the warnings, remained indoors, and thereby avoided the lung damage from which they now suffer. Suppose too that each of the individuals involved is a responsible agent, whose decision to heed or disregard the warning, even if misguided, can still be taken as the object of an attributive judgment rather than some type of non-rational response. Now consider the possibility that the more prudent individuals complain that they have been treated unfairly by the city officials' choice of the covert policy. They argue that it would have been less unfair to choose the cautionary policy because each individual would then have enjoyed an equal opportunity to avoid harm, and the only individuals harmed would be those who have decided to expose themselves to

---

[9] For further discussion, see Otsuka (2000); Kumar (2001); Parfit (2003); Scanlon (2002: 354–7; 2003b: 430–4).

risk rather than those who, like them, had been involuntarily exposed to risk by others.

Even if they do not think it shows there are decisive reasons against the covert policy, most of those I have asked find this argument quite convincing. Suppose we share this conviction, and are inclined to think that the argument shows there are at least some reasons of fairness in favor of the cautionary policy. If our conviction is sound, then when dealing with individuals whose decisions and attitudes are appropriate objects of attributive judgment, there are reasons to equalize their opportunities to avoid harm rather than merely equalize their prospects of avoiding harm in a way that preempts the exercise of their own decision-making capacities. Since these reasons do not appear to be canceled merely because conforming to them may not minimize the number of individuals who suffer harm, I conclude that there are grounds to favor the cautionary policy over the covert policy.

The question remains whether Scanlon's Value of Choice account can explain this conclusion. To address that question, recall that the account states that the only reasons to want the opportunity to avoid exposure to hazardous waste are instrumental (1998: 257), whilst the revised example stipulates that such an opportunity is not, in general, a reliable means to reduce the likelihood of injury. Given these assumptions, a contractualist who relies on Scanlon's explanation faces a serious difficulty. Because the cautionary policy provides individuals with opportunities having negative protective value, it seems implausible to defend such a policy by arguing that it provides sufficient protection for individuals harmed in the removal process. How can the officials be said to 'do enough' by selecting the policy when, *ex hypothesi*, there are no generic instrumental reasons to want such an unreliable means of protection? Contractualist variants of the Value of Choice account may be able to answer this question by expanding the range of considerations that support the cautionary policy. For example, perhaps we have generic *action reasons* to prefer to avoid danger through our own endeavors rather than to do so fortuitously, or there may be symbolic reasons to portray us as competent judges about danger even if, in fact, we tend to be incompetent.[10] Whatever the likelihood of these suggestions succeeding, Scanlon's own account appears to require revision if it is to provide plausible results in the dual policy case. Without such revisions, I conclude that there is a second respect in which the account is incomplete, namely because we still have some reason to hold individuals substantively responsible for choices they would have been better off not having to make.

---

[10] As defined in Raz (1986: 145), action reasons 'are based on the value of a particular (class of) agent(s) performing a certain action (including the bringing about by those agents of a certain outcome)'.

7. Substantive Compatibilism

Referring to substantive as well as attributive responsibility, Scanlon claims that 'neither form of responsibility is threatened by the general truth of determinism or of the Causal Thesis' (1998: 251). He defends *attributive compatibilism* by appealing to his non-punitive understanding of blame, and a conception of excusing conditions that does not require the withdrawal of blame whenever our attitudes are capable of causal explanation (1998: 277–80). I find Scanlon's account of culpability plausible, but am less confident about his defense of *substantive compatibilism*. This section outlines the latter defense, and airs some final doubts.

As a preliminary, it is worth emphasizing Scanlon's claim that attributive judgments are an insufficient basis for substantive responsibility judgments. As he explains, it is a 'mistaken assumption that taking individuals to be responsible for their conduct in the sense of being open to moral criticism for it requires one also to say that they are responsible for its results in the substantive sense, that is they are not entitled to any assistance in dealing with these problems' (1998: 293). Of the many insights in *What We Owe to Each Other*, this one has especially great political importance. As Scanlon himself notes (1998: 293), the tendency to infer liability from culpability is prevalent, with regrettable effects, on both ends of the political spectrum. Thus, those on the right single out disadvantaged individuals whose antisocial activities are widely regarded as subject to moral criticism. Taking for granted that their culpability renders those individuals liable to various penalties, right-wingers then advocate harsh prison sentences and cuts in welfare payments. Various leftists appear to endorse the right-wing inference as valid, but nevertheless abhor those conclusions. So, turning a conservative *modus ponens* into a progressive *modus tollens*, they try—often unsuccessfully—to convince others that the individuals concerned are not really blameworthy.

In contrast, Scanlon rejects the inference from culpability to liability. Asking us to 'imagine a person who, as result of generally horrible treatment as a child and the lack of proper early training, is both undisciplined and unreliable', he writes,

If this person lies to his employers, fails to do what he has agreed to do, and never exerts himself to get a job done, he is properly criticized for these actions and attitudes. But if they render him unemployable it would not be permissible to deny him welfare support on the ground that his unemployability is due to actions for which he is responsible. He is responsible (that is to say, open to criticism) for these actions, but he cannot simply be left to bear the consequences, since he has not had adequate opportunity to avoid being subject to them. (1998: 292)

Scanlon's use of the important distinction between attributive and substantive responsibility in the chronic shirker case is very attractive, especially to those of us who regard appeals to moral responsibility as often yet another way of adding insult to the injury already suffered by the victims of economic injustice. When it comes to defusing the causal threat, however, his position has a theoretical downside. For, having stressed the distinction between the two types of judgment concerning responsibility, Scanlon cannot simply appeal to attributive compatibilism in order to show that the Causal Thesis does not undermine our judgments about substantive responsibility. Instead he must provide a further argument for substantive compatibilism.

Scanlon attempts to meet this challenge by arguing that 'the instrumental, representative, and symbolic values of choice are not threatened by the Causal Thesis' (1998: 256). As he explains, speaking of our responses 'having causes outside us',

As long as these causes affect our responses only by affecting what we are like, it will remain true that these responses can be good predictors of what will bring us enjoyment or advance our aims. Similarly, in the case of representative value, it is quite plausible to suppose that many of our tastes and capacities for discernment that we want our choices to express have a basis in our causal makeup, but this fact does not make them less part of us and hence does not diminish the value of choices that express them. (1998: 256)

Dealing finally with symbolic considerations, Scanlon adds that so long as causal processes do not prevent us from judging the relative force of competing reasons, 'nor do they affect the fact that being allowed to make these judgments for ourselves is an important form of recognition as competent independent agents' (1998: 256). These remarks are persuasive in so far as they provide compatibilist arguments for granting individuals certain opportunities to exercise their decision-making capacities. Nevertheless, whether they suffice as a successful defense of substantive compatibilism is debatable for reasons I shall now present.

Recall that the Value of Choice account implies that an agent's choices allow others to hold her substantively responsible for certain burdens only if she enjoys a fair opportunity to avoid that liability by choosing otherwise.[11] Scanlon's defense of substantive compatibilism must, therefore, do more than show that opportunities can vary in value even if the Causal Thesis is sound. It must also show that the Thesis does not preclude individuals from having a sufficiently good opportunity to avoid liability. The Causal Thesis, however, entails that the ultimate causes of an agent's response to her opportunities lie outside her, and that this remains true even when those causes operate through her judgment. Scanlon himself seems to accept this

---

[11] Thus, Scanlon claims that 'In order for an action to entail the imposition on the agent of some burden, such as an obligation, two things must be true. First, the action must be attributable to the agent. Second, a principle according to which such an action generates that obligation must be one that could not reasonably be rejected. But, we may suppose, in order for such a principle to be one that could not reasonably be rejected it must hold that such an action generates this obligation only if it is an action that the agent had a fair opportunity not to perform' (1998: 286).

conclusion in his memorable closing remarks about the attitude we should take to individuals who behave badly, or are injured as a result of not heeding warnings. Thus, he recommends that we should

Recognize that what separates us from such people is not just, as we would like to think, that we behave better and choose more wisely, but also *our luck in being the kind of people who respond in these ways*. In this respect our attitude toward those who suffer or are blamed should not be 'You asked for this' but rather 'There but for the grace of God go I'. (1998: 294; italics added)

Such recognition, however, creates an immediate difficulty for any view that appeals to our opportunities to avoid liability in justifying judgments of substantive responsibility. If the Causal Thesis is sound, whether we avoid liability by choosing appropriately is determined by factors over which we have no control, and so ultimately a matter of luck. Pressing this difficulty, we might construct an egalitarian objection to Scanlon's defense of substantive compatibilism as follows.

The objection begins in conciliatory fashion by granting that individuals who could have avoided certain burdens had they chosen differently but who instead brought those burdens on themselves are more likely to have gained some offsetting benefit in the process than if the burdens been randomly imposed. For that reason, if specific burdens are distributed in a way that depends on individuals' responses, the overall magnitude of each individual's burden, and the cost to others of redressing inequality by compensating burdened individuals, may be reduced. So, the objection concedes that response-dependent methods of distributing burdens across individuals might be justifiable despite the truth of the Causal Thesis.

Nevertheless, the objection continues, this concession does not show that inequality can be justified by showing that less advantaged individuals had the same opportunities as everyone, and could have avoided being less advantaged had they chosen to do so. For if the Causal Thesis is true, the ultimate causes of each individual's response to her opportunities, and any relative misfortune she consequently suffers, are factors that lie outside her control. As Scanlon himself recognizes, it is a matter of luck that those factors are present rather than other factors, which might have caused different responses. According to the core egalitarian conviction, however, fairness demands that we share the effects of luck, at least where it is feasible do so without leveling down; moreover, it is unfair for individuals to be disadvantaged relative to others, and to some alternative feasible arrangement, because they have suffered worse luck than others. If these convictions are sound, the fact that an individual had the opportunity to avoid becoming disadvantaged by choosing appropriately but did not exploit that opportunity does not suffice to show that it is fair for him to be less well off than others.

The egalitarian objection expresses a natural reaction to Scanlon's defense of substantive compatibilism. Moreover, the reaction arises even if we assume that there are reasons to value opportunities whether or not the Causal Thesis is true. Like my first objection to Scanlon's explanatory strategy, the critique accepts that assumption, and grants that it may explain why it is wrong to deny an individual certain opportunities. Nonetheless, it disagrees about whether the presence of those opportunities explains an individual's substantive responsibility by rendering certain liabilities sufficiently avoidable. It insists that if the Causal Thesis is sound, then appeal to opportunities cannot play this explanatory role since an individual's response to her opportunities is determined by factors outside her control.

It is also worth noting, however, that such insistence does not rely on the assumption that all unavoidable inequalities are unfair. Instead, it merely rebuts one defense of certain inequalities by arguing that if the Causal Thesis is sound, then individuals' opportunities cannot have enough burden avoidance value to render those inequalities fair. Even if the rebuttal succeeds, there are alternative strategies for showing that individuals can enjoy differential luck without some suffering *worse* luck than others.

To illustrate one strategy, consider a variation on the chronic shirker case, suggested by Ronald Dworkin. Imagine a second individual, just as work-shy as the chronic shirker, who did not grow up 'in a desperately poor urban slum with high and endemic unemployment' but rather was 'an upper class twit raised to think that work was beneath his class' (R. Dworkin 2000: 490 n. 9). It is arguable that even if the attitudes of both shirkers are ultimately outside their control the deprived shirker has lesser liability for his unwillingness to work than the privileged shirker because of his fewer advantages. Yet one need not argue that the deprived shirker is less advantaged because of his lesser opportunity to avoid being a shirker. One might eschew that argument on the grounds that it depends on a contra-causal conception of opportunity, appeal to which is ruled out if the Causal Thesis is sound. Instead, one could argue we should explain the difference by appeal to an alternative standard of interpersonal comparison, according to which the deprived shirker's poor start in life is offset by lesser liability in later life.

To illustrate another strategy, which accords a larger role to individuals' subjective attitudes, suppose that it is a matter of luck that men and women differ not only in their biological endowments but also in their preferences regarding those endowments. Even so, it is arguable that the absence of envy over endowments indicates that neither group has suffered worse luck than the other. Similarly, one might argue that what should make a difference to our response to the prudent risk-taker and the uninformed risk-taker is the fact that only the former regards the chance of harm as a price worth paying to pursue a valuable project, and so does not prefer the reduced risk of harm enjoyed by others.[12]

---

[12] See Williams (2002: 386–9) for further discussion of the importance of distinguishing not only *luck* from *choice* but also *bad* luck from *good* luck, and the relevance of individuals' own convictions in doing so.

8. Conclusion

Scanlon's discussion of substantive responsibility, like the rest of his book, addresses fundamental issues in moral and political philosophy in an exceptionally subtle and illuminating manner. I have described three aspects of the discussion, which, notwithstanding its merits, I find very puzzling. It is possible that the problems I have posed rest on misunderstanding some aspects of the Value of Choice account. It is also likely that a revised version of the Value of Choice account, or some alternative contractualist view, might be able to avoid at least some of these problems. It may be feasible, for example, to diminish the unsatisfying incompleteness in the negative element of Scanlon's the account by describing more fully the standpoint of individuals who might be asked to bear the costs of others' choices. In doing so, we may be able to arrive at a better understanding of the various reasons they have to reject such a request, and explain how those reasons are to be compared with reasons from other standpoints. It may also be feasible to defuse the threat the Causal Thesis poses by diminishing reliance on appeals to the avoidance value of opportunities. All these possibilities merit further discussion. Like everyone interested in practical philosophy, egalitarians have weighty reasons to engage with contractualism.

References

ANDERSON, E. S. (1999), 'What Is the Point of Equality?', *Ethics*, 109: 287–337.

CASAL, P., and WILLIAMS, A. (2004), 'Equality of Resources and Procreative Justice', in J. Burley (ed.), *Dworkin and His Critics* (Oxford: Basil Blackwell), 150–69.

COHEN, G. A. (1989), 'On the Currency of Egalitarian Justice', *Ethics*, 99: 906–44.

DWORKIN, G. (1988), 'Is More Choice Better Than Less?', in G. Dworkin, *The Theory and Practice of Autonomy* (Cambridge: Cambridge University Press), 62–84.

DWORKIN, R. (2000), *Sovereign Virtue* (Cambridge, Mass.: Harvard University Press).

ELSTER, J. (1979), *Ulysses and the Sirens* (Cambridge: Cambridge University Press).

HART, H. L. A. (1968), 'Legal Responsibility and Excuses', in H. L. A. Hart, *Punishment and Responsibility* (Oxford: Clarendon Press), 28–53.

KUMAR, R. (2001), 'Contractualism on Saving the Many', *Analysis*, 61: 165–70.

NINO, C. (1983), 'A Consensual Theory of Punishment', *Philosophy and Public Affairs*, 12: 289–306.

OTSUKA, M. (2000), 'Scanlon and the Claims of the Many Versus the One', *Analysis*, 60: 288–93.

PARFIT, D. (2003), 'Justifiability to Each Person', *Ratio*, 16/4: 368–89.

RAWLS, J. (1999), *A Theory of Justice*, rev. edn. (Cambridge, Mass.: Belknap Press).

―― (2001), *Justice as Fairness: A Restatement* (Cambridge, Mass.: Belknap Press).

RAZ, J. (1986), *The Morality of Freedom* (Oxford: Clarendon Press).

SCANLON, T. M. (1988), 'The Significance of Choice', in S. McMurrin (ed.), *The Tanner Lectures on Human Values*, 8 (Salt Lake City: University of Utah Press), 149–246.

—— (1998), *What We Owe to Each Other* (Cambridge, Mass.: Belknap Press).

—— (2002), 'Replies', *Social Theory and Practice*, 28/2: 337–58.

—— (2003a), 'Punishment and the Rule of Law', in Scanlon, *The Difficulty of Tolerance* (Cambridge: Cambridge University Press), 219–33.

—— (2003b), 'Replies', *Ratio*, 16/4: 424–39.

SCHEFFLER, S. (2005), 'Choice, Circumstance, and the Value of Equality', *Politics, Philosophy and Economics*, 4/1: 5–28.

WILLIAMS, A. (2002), 'Equality for the Ambitious', *Philosophical Quarterly*, 52: 377–89.

—— (2006), 'Liberty, Equality, and Property', in J. Dryzek, B. Honig, and A. Phillips (eds.), *Oxford Handbook of Political Theory* (Oxford: Oxford University Press).

11

Desert and Equality

Richard J. Arneson

1. Introduction

Does justice require, at least in part, that people get what they deserve? The question is whether ideals of desert play a substantial and nonderivative role in establishing the content of social justice principles. Of course, even if the correct answer to this question were negative, once one has determined the requirements of justice independently of substantive considerations of desert, one could always add that the treatment of individuals that justice demands is to be identified with the treatment that they deserve. However, on this way of proceeding, ideals of desert do no real work and could be dropped from the account without any loss.

This first question resonates with a second one. Should egalitarian justice resist or accommodate the idea that desert considerations should be incorporated into the formulation of principles of justice at the ground floor level? Are desert and equality comrades marching together or sworn enemies or what? *Egalitarian justice* here shall be understood as principles that hold that if we are dealing with a fixed population and choosing social arrangements that will not affect the aggregate total of well-being but may affect its distribution across persons, arrangements that would bring about an equal distribution of well-being, if that is obtainable, should be chosen.[1] The class of

Thanks to audiences at the University of Copenhagen and at the Center for Human Values at Princeton University for helpful comments and criticism. Special thanks to Gilbert Harman, Kasper Lippert-Rasmussen, and Ingmar Persson for valuable written comments, and to Larry Temkin for instructive conversation.

[1] The view stated in the text is inclusive in that it counts as an egalitarian one who gives first priority to maximizing aggregate well-being and appeals to equality only as a tie-breaker. A stricter and perhaps

egalitarian justice principles divides into two groups, one that values equality for its own sake, as intrinsically morally valuable, and a second that values equality only as a means to the maximization of weighted well-being, with greater weight assigned to a unit gain in well-being, the less the recipient's lifetime well-being would be without that gain.[2] The latter family of views, which goes by the name *priority*, strikes me as more plausible, so in this chapter egalitarian justice is identified with prioritarian principle.[3] For the purposes of this chapter this espousal of priority is an unargued assumption. The focus of this chapter is the relationship between egalitarian justice so conceived and deservingness.

On the face of it, giving people equal shares will conflict with the policy of giving each individual what she deserves unless it happens to be the case that everyone deserves the same so that the two patterns of distribution coincide. Philosophical advocates of equality sometimes propose principles that look like amalgams of equality and desert. Offering what looks to be a canonical formulation, Larry Temkin states, 'it is bad—unjust and unfair—for some to be worse off than others through no fault [or choice] of their own'.[4] I'm not sure how to understand this ideal of equality, but I'm sympathetic to pluralistic principles of justice that attempt to balance or integrate equality ideals with some norms of responsibility and deservingness. This chapter explores how this might be done, peers down some threatening analytical abysses that lie on the path, and tentatively proposes a type of amalgam.

Section 2 of this essay raises three objections against the idea that justice requires rewarding people according to their deservingness. Section 3 observes that even if rewarding desert is not morally valuable for its own sake, widespread practices of holding people responsible according to contextual norms of desert are undeniably instrumentally valuable. Section 4 explores the attempt to defend rewarding desert as morally valuable for its own sake by rejecting the principle that people should be held responsible only for what lies within their power to control. The attempt does not succeed. Section 5 explores the attempt to defend rewarding desert as morally valuable for its own sake by accepting this control principle and fashioning a norm of desert as conscientiousness that is compatible with it. This avenue looks more

better definition would stipulate that a position qualifies as egalitarian only if it prefers an equal to an unequal distribution even if there would be substantially greater aggregate well-being in the unequal distribution.

[2] The formulation of equality in the text just assumes that the proper measure of people's condition for a theory of justice is their overall well-being. For some defense of the assumption, see Arneson (2000).

[3] The first statements of the prioritarian idea known to me are in Scheffler (1982) and Weirich (1983). A thorough clarification of the idea is in Parfit (1995).

[4] Temkin (1993: 13). In the formulation in the text 'or choice' does not occur, but it is added in a clarificatory footnote on the same page.

promising. Section 6 suggests that the view proposed obviates the circularity objection against introducing deservingness as a constituent in fundamental moral principles. Section 7 argues that desert as conscientiousness can be a constituent in principles of justice without crowding out equality values despite Shelly Kagan's endorsement of desert against equality. Section 8 countenances the possibility that part of the moral goal that morality bids us promote is that people become more deserving rather than less deserving, desert being interpreted as conscientiousness. This line of thought issues in a form of consequentialism that is prioritarian both in the domain of desert and in the domain of well-being and gives extra priority to achieving well-being gains for those who are comparatively more deserving. Section 9 denies that desert as conscientiousness has to be nonadministratable and therefore has no place in fundamental justice principles. Section 10 notes that the position upheld here has a consequentialist flavor that some will find distasteful.

2. Three Objections

The rough idea that the content of principles of justice is partly constituted by considerations of desert confronts three major objections.[5]

2.1. Entanglement

In many social contexts, what an individual is deemed to deserve reflects the quality of her performances that are relevant given the context. In the economic market, the operative notion of desert is individual productive contribution. The question then arises, To what degree is it reasonable to take credit or discredit, praise or blame, for one's choices and conduct? When an individual is praised for an admirable deed and says modestly 'It's nothing', surely sometimes this discounting is correct, but what determines how much discounting is appropriate? To simplify discussion, let us stipulate an assumption favorable to desert: human agents have free will and sometimes choose one alternative when they could have chosen others in exactly the same circumstances. This claim might be interpreted in either a compatibilist or a libertarian sense. If the latter, then prior causes impinging on the agent do not fully explain the choice made either probabilistically or deductively.

Even on this assumption, causal forces impinge differently and with varying force on different choice situations. If one is suffering torture inflicted with the aim of

---

[5] Rawls asserts the first and third objections in his (1999, sect. 48). The second objection seems to me to be implicit in Rawls's account.

inducing one to betray a noble cause, it is both difficult and painful to make the right choice of noncompliance. It will be variously difficult and costly for different persons placed in the same decision problem or a relevantly similar one to make the right choice. At some threshold level of these excuses, it would be unreasonable to blame a person for choosing wrongly, and what level of difficulty and pain that is varies with a host of hard to detect and undetectable factors including the person's genetic endowment and socialization along with myriad other environmental influences.

Even one's subjective experiences of trying to do the right thing and exerting willpower and resisting temptation are evidently an unreliable guide to singling out what one can truly take credit for (discredit if one is not making a good-faith try). Recall John Rawls's comment on the precept of rewarding people according to their conscientious effort. He writes, 'Once again, however, it seems clear that the effort a person is willing to make is influenced by his natural abilities and skills and the alternatives open to him. The better endowed are more likely, other things equal, to strive conscientiously, and there seems to be no way to discount for their greater good fortune' (Rawls 1999: 274; also Barry 1973: 155).

The point is that even on an assumption that appears to be clearly favorable to the idea that we are morally responsible for our choices and conduct and come to be variously deserving according to their quality, the factors that influence choice that are entirely beyond the agent's power to control and for which she cannot reasonably assume responsibility and the residual factors that are reasonably imputable to the agent are inextricably tangled. We do not in principle know how to separate them, but even if we did, in practical terms the extent to which I am genuinely responsible for a given choice I make or inadvertent failure to attend is impossible to measure. Rawls's conclusion following the passage quoted above is that 'The idea of rewarding desert is impracticable' (Rawls 1999: 274). The conclusion is seemingly modest. It's not that the ideal of rewarding genuine desert appropriately makes no sense or is morally defective. Rather the concern is that as we clarify the idea of what it is to be genuinely deserving, the plausible candidates for this conceptual role reveal themselves as for practical purposes impossible to measure, so the ideal is nonoperationalizable.

The entanglement objection obviously applies to the doctrine that justice requires extra rewards for the more deserving that is premised on libertarian free will and moral responsibility. Soft determinist positions are vulnerable to this objection, so long as they allow that the moral responsibility of an individual for her choices can vary by degree according to factors that are impossible or unfeasible to measure. Any nuanced doctrine on moral responsibility will face the entanglement problem, provided the nuances that render one more or less deserving are too subtle to register reliably on any monitoring system we could implement in a satisfactory manner.

2.2 The Economic Market and Desert

The ideal of bringing it about that people get good fortune in life corresponding to their desert loses some of its luster if one tries to envisage how institutions (feasible or not) might achieve the ideal.

Consider economic contexts. In modern times, economic activity is organized by the market framework: Let each person contract with any other on mutually agreeable terms with given endowments. The market over time distributes fruits of economic cooperation to individuals. The market distribution is set by supply and demand conditions, which have no tendency to produce results that are in conformity with any reasonable conception of individual desert. If I offer Spanish lessons for sale, the gain that will accrue to me depends on the extent to which people want Spanish lessons and are willing to pay for them, on the one hand, and on the extent to which other people are offering Spanish lessons (or more or less close substitutes) for sale. And these magnitudes in turn are affected by the ensemble of people's preferences to produce and consume, as modeled in general equilibrium theories. If market activity unfolds in circumstances that satisfy certain constraints, the result will be efficient, and efficiency is attractive[6]—but there is no reason to think that the economic market will shower benefits and costs on people so that each gets what she deserves according to any remotely plausible conception of desert.

So it seems that either the theory of justice, if it requires that individuals should get what they deserve, must be utterly in conflict with the market, or the theory of justice, if it is to be in principle tolerant of the market economy, must not include as a fundamental requirement that each person should get what she deserves. If the idea of abolishing the economic market and organizing economic life as some form of moral meritocracy, to bring it about that individuals tend to get what they deserve, looks unattractive, we have reason to accept a theory of justice that does not attach great intrinsic significance to any ideal of desert.

2.3 Circularity

The third objection is that the search for a plausible standard of desert settles on a notion that renders the idea that justice is (in part) distribution according to desert viciously circular (Rawls 1999: 275).

To avoid basing desert on characteristics of persons and their conduct that are clearly beyond their power to control, stipulate that the relevant desert basis is moral

---

[6] A policy that is efficient induces states of affairs that could not be altered to make anyone better off without making someone else worse off. If 'better off' is interpreted so that one is better off just in case one has more well-being, efficiency in the economist's sense encapsulates a plausible norm of fairness.

desert. But if we then say, as seems sensible, that a person is morally more deserving, the more firmly she is dedicated to bringing about fulfillment of the principles of justice (the fundamental moral principles), we immediately start spinning in circles. If justice in part is rewarding people according to their moral desert, and one becomes morally deserving by bringing about fulfillment of the principles of justice, then one becomes morally deserving (in part) by bringing about the rewarding of people according to their moral desert—which is what? In this way the search for a viable conception of what makes one morally deserving runs into a dead end.

3. Desert: More Than Instrumentally Valuable?

To my mind the most pressing conundrum the arguments expose is that the norm that people cannot reasonably be deemed deserving or undeserving in virtue of what lies beyond their power to control appears massively in conflict with our common-sense understanding of norms of responsibility and desert as they function in many different and significant social settings. The control principle thus appears to be radically at odds with a host of social practices and arrangements that will strike many of us as in fine working order and not at all a fitting target of radical critique.

This conflict will be grossly exaggerated if we fail to notice the extent to which common-sense assignments of responsibility and desert would survive as instruments for achieving uncontroversial goods even if we entirely embraced the control principle and on this basis concluded that no one is ever truly responsible for anything or deserving or undeserving in any respect.[7]

Social life is laced with the regulation of conduct in many practices by ideas of desert and responsibility. We could barely imagine social life without such regulation; nor would any sober person wish to eliminate it. We punish criminals and require those who tortiously injure others to pay compensation. We enforce contracts. We tend to leave individuals for the most part responsible for their own well-being, in the sense that well-being gains and losses that accrue to them in the course of legally permitted interactions with others are allowed to stick. In a wide variety of relations with associates, work mates and colleagues, acquaintances and strangers and friends, kinfolk and lovers, we seek to return good for good and evil for evil, with an emphasis on the former if we are decent. We seek to identify people who will not cooperate in transactions that have the form of single play Prisoner's Dilemmas and avoid interaction with

---

[7] The idea that the usable core of the notion of responsibility is an instrumental notion (holding people responsible can be a means to achieving various valuable goals) is a theme in Smart (1961). For discussion, see Arneson (2003c).

these noncooperators. From the moral point of view, holding people responsible for their conduct in these and many other ways is broadly justifiable on the ground that this practice of responsibility is instrumentally useful in bringing about consequences that are morally far superior to what would come about if we dropped the practice.

It bears emphasis that the good effects of holding people responsible and treating them according to their achieved deservingness are suffused throughout social life. That responsibility and desert serve the purposes of a wide variety of social practices is of course no accident. Sometimes they are designed to be functional in this way and sometimes they emerge by processes that tend at least in part to be shaped by pressures that push in the same direction. Within the various social practices, spheres of justice as they have been called, standards of performance, merit, and worth emerge that serve the practices in the sense that they encourage conduct that helps people achieve the goals that drew them to the practice or the goals that the practice has been established to serve. Since different practices serve different ends, standards of responsibility and desert tend to be heterogeneous across the range of practices. The traits we prize in a lawyer, politician, professional athlete, priest, entrepreneur, employee in a bureaucratic hierarchical agency, artist, unskilled laborer, medical doctor, plumber, cook, shaman, criminal law judge, husband, lover, soldier, fellow crook, clerk, and friend differ in gross and subtle ways that register the different uses of these social roles. A priest becomes deserving by being holy and a sensitive, nurturing minister to his congregation. A defensive cornerback in the National Football League becomes deserving by skillfully preventing pass completions and by viciously tackling pass receivers and running backs. And so on. Instrumental desert correlates with appropriate compensation and reward; the more deserving should get more. Again, the supporting ground is an instrumental consideration. Human nature being what it is, people in any sphere of activity tend to be motivated significantly by the desire for personal advantage. For this reason, the behavior and traits that conduce to the flourishing of the people who have a stake in a social practice and that accordingly get tagged as deserving should be rewarded. In general, the more deserving one is by the standards of the practice, the more it should be the case that one is advantaged by participation in the practice.

This does not mean that whatever the prevailing standards and norms happen to be in a sphere of human activity, they must automatically be judged 'functional' and regarded as normatively appropriate. On the contrary: egalitarian justice will condemn some practices and propose that others should be altered so that they function in ways that do better to achieve egalitarian goals. Prevailing standards of responsibility and desert, assessed by egalitarian standards, may be found instrumentally deficient. I only mean to insist that if one regards practices of holding people responsible according to norms of desert as (possibly deficient) means to the achievement of social justice goals, one will be led to propose not across-the-board uprooting or elimination of these practices, which would drastically and unjustifiably reduce human well-being, but rather their regulation and adjustment at the margins.

4. Relaxing Control

The question for this chapter is whether or not responsibility and desert are intrinsically morally significant, so that it is morally valuable to reward the truly deserving independently of any possible further good effects of doing this. Given the undeniably vast instrumental benefits of holding people responsible in various ways in sundry domains, the dispute regarding the putative intrinsic moral value of rewarding the deserving is a somewhat delicate residual issue. I shall focus on the idea that justice demands that people who are more deserving should enjoy higher lifetime well-being than those who are less deserving.

The thesis that people's getting what they deserve is a per se requirement of justice takes two different forms. One version denies the control principle and appeals against it to the claimed evident rightness of common-sense assignments of desert in various social spheres. These should be taken at face value and not explained away by reconstructing them in thought as means to other goals that have nothing per se to do with desert. The alternative version accepts the control principle and strives to revise ordinary common-sense norms of responsibility and deservingness to bring them into conformity with it.[8]

Political theorists who champion desert as a principle of justice typically reject the control principle, which they believe is subversive of the project of taking desert seriously. David Miller has vigorously pursued this approach (1999, ch. 7).

One generic difficulty that anyone who rejects the control principle faces is where to draw the line: in what ways and to what degree are people reasonably held responsible for what lies beyond their power to control, so that these uncontrollable factors legitimately render them truly deserving and undeserving? Once the control principle is rejected, why not say that children born into wealthy families deserve to inherit their elders' great wealth? A principled stopping point, a boundary where true desert peters out, is difficult to locate.[9]

---

[8] The control principle holds that one should not be held responsible for what lies beyond one's power to control. This implies that one should not be deemed deserving or undeserving in virtue of the quality of one's choice, if the choice's manifesting that quality lies beyond one's power to control. For all that I say in this chapter, a compatibilist account of moral responsibility might yield the result that the control principle can be satisfied sometimes and agents can be more or less deserving in virtue of the quality of their choices even if determinism holds.

[9] One possibility is that to be deserving or undeserving, one must have the opportunity to do an act, of variable quality. One can then be variously deserving depending on further effects of the agent's act,

If justice requires rewarding the truly deserving, true desert tracks common-sense norms that vary from sphere to sphere, and rewarding desert in this way is intrinsically and not merely instrumentally morally valuable, it should be possible to find unambiguous cases in which rewarding the deserving serves no useful purpose but should be upheld anyway as valuable for its own sake. Such cases are hard to find. Perhaps the retributive theory of criminal punishment is the best source of plausible instances in which it might with some plausibility be held that rewarding the deserving and punishing the undeserving are morally valuable for their own sakes even if doing so serves no further valuable goal. Even here, controversy abounds (retributive justice is discussed briefly later in this chapter).

The relaxation of the control principle and the challenge to desert when its instrumental advantages give out create a pincer movement. What becomes pinched and maybe broken is the thought that it is morally valuable to uphold common-sense ideals of desert as significant for their own sake even when they are not serving as means to any other valuable ends. At any rate, my suggestion is that the lackluster appeal of common-sense desert stripped of its instrumental advantages calls into serious question the relaxation of the control principle.

David Miller's position on desert and justice looks to be squeezed by the pincers just described. He holds that justice requires that human performances that are perceived as socially valuable should be recognized in some way, by some benefit-conferring institution or practice, and that in that setting those individuals who perform better deserve proportionally greater benefit. What happens if individuals' performances are affected by factors beyond their power to control? Miller distinguishes integral luck (luck that occurs during performance and influences its outcome) and circumstantial luck (luck that influences whether someone has the opportunity to perform), and both of these from luck in endowments and socialization that render some more talented than others at the type of performance in question. Integral luck nullifies desert, circumstantial luck reduces but does not eliminate it, and luck in possession of native talent does not subvert desert arising from performance.

Consider the economic marketplace, where Miller identifies the extent of one's socially valuable contribution with what others are willing to pay for it.[10] Miller then

which may vary owing to factors beyond the agent's power to control. But opportunity for choice is a prerequisite. But if how the agent responds to the opportunity for choice is caused, the grounds for taking opportunity for choice to establish responsibility are doubtful. Moreover, if luck in the effects of one's choices belongs properly to the agent, it would seem this should be so even when the effects are very surprising, as when my sincere and heartfelt attempts to murder my wife result in saving her life, or my sincere and heartfelt attempts to protect my wife from a remote danger actually cause her death.

[10] This identification of economic desert with the extent to which one produces what people are willing to pay for is already problematic. Consider the manufacture and sale of cigarettes, or the provision of items that people want to purchase just because they are fashionable at the moment.

holds that markets should be reformed so that each individual's economic benefit is proportionate to her economic contribution. Nothing in the nature of an unregulated market would tend to cause it to function so that the payoffs individuals receive reflect their economic contribution with adjustments that undo their integral luck and discount somewhat for their circumstantial luck. A well-functioning market, that operates so as to achieve efficiency, will then deviate systematically from what justice as desert according to Miller's interpretation would demand.

But the notion of desert that Miller is deploying here is already so thoroughly shaped to reflect the workings of the economic market that I do not see that the notion has any critical edge that provides any reason at all for regulating or rearranging market practices. In effect, Miller urges that some things that happen beyond my power to control that affect the quality of my performance really do not make any difference to what I truly deserve and should get in virtue of my economic contribution, whereas other factors that happen beyond my power to control and affect the quality of my performance do legitimately play a role in fixing what I truly deserve. I can make sense of this if one is making a case that the goals that should lead us to establish and preserve the market economy would be better served if the reward structure were altered somewhat. If efficiency required eliminating the impact of integral luck on economic payoffs, we should perhaps restructure the market reward structure. But a market operating efficiently does not distinguish integral luck, circumstantial luck, and luck in talent possession. Why should we care about these matters if the market does not? Miller's idea of economic deservingness appears to fall between two stools. It is not anchored in any normative ideal, conceived independently of considerations of how markets function, that can command our allegiance in conflict with efficient market functioning. But nor is it closely enough anchored to considerations of how markets function and the purposes they serve to capture the normativity that inheres in the limited but important ideal of the competitive economic market.

The point readily generalizes. Suppose one takes at face value the different ordinary norms of desert that operate in practices that are uncontroversially valuable. One says, these norms fix what people truly deserve, and since they allow that people can become deserving due to factors beyond their power to control, so should we allow desert and control to be severed. Then imagine circumstances altered so that the instrumental advantages of rewarding and punishing people according to these common-sense norms cease to accrue. We assume that the practices continue to generate results that people value and within practices people continue to perform in socially valuable ways, but proportioning payoffs in the practice to these individual performances ceases to be in any respect useful. One would then be committed, improbably in my view, to holding that it is morally valuable to at least some degree to continue rewarding people according to these common-sense norms of desert even though doing so no longer serves any goals except bringing about a closer fit between people's good fortune and their 'true' desert.

5. Deservingness as Conscientiousness

The focus now shifts to the alternative strategy of devising an account of what makes people deserving that accommodates the constraint that people cannot become more or less deserving due to factors that are beyond their power to control.

Whether or not an agent's noble goals issue in admirable actions and excellent achievements depends in part on factors beyond her power to control, such as the opportunities she faces and the native talent potential she possesses. Moreover, whether or not the agent's intentions and aims are oriented toward what is noble and fine also depends at least in part on sheer luck. One agent is mistrained in early childhood and seeks under the guise of good what is not really good as a consequence. Another agent lacks the intelligence to think through a difficult evaluative exercise to the proper conclusion concerning what is truly choiceworthy in her circumstances. Another agent through no fault of her own lacks crucial information needed to orient her will toward what is genuinely right and good.

So here is a proposal: what renders agents deserving or undeserving is the degree to which they are steadily disposed to pursue what they believe to be right and good, provided that they have made good-faith efforts to discover what is genuinely right and good and are not culpable for embracing false beliefs. If one conscientiously strives to live as one ought, according to this proposal, one qualifies as virtuous. For simplicity, I drop the reference to what is good and speak only about seeking to orient oneself to what is right.

To avoid confusion, given that one might suppose a person who is virtuous really does achieve wisdom, courage, temperance, and so on, I shall call a person who satisfies the proposed criterion of deservingness *subjectively virtuous*. In *Middlemarch*, George Eliot observes that for every St Teresa of Ávila, who has the opportunity to lead a grand, noble life of great accomplishments and rises magnificently to this challenge, there are many shadow Teresas who never get such opportunities.[11] They might face only choices of little consequence through no fault of their own, or (I would add) they might lack the great talents needed for heroic deeds. On the proposal I am advancing,

---

[11] In the 'Prelude' to *Middlemarch*, George Eliot observes, 'Many Theresas have been born who found for themselves no epic life wherein there was a constant unfolding of far-resonant action; perhaps only a life of mistakes, the offspring of a certain spiritual grandeur ill-matched with the meanness of opportunity; perhaps a tragic failure which found no sacred poet and sank unwept into oblivion.' Next page: 'Here and there is born a Saint Theresa, foundress of nothing.'

all of the shadow Teresas who are just as disposed firmly and steadily to the good and the right as St Teresa are deemed equally deserving as the saint herself.

Objection. According to this proposal, conscientious Nazis become ever more deserving as they remain steadily disposed to harm their victims.

Reply. It would be consistent with acceptance of the proposal that what makes a person truly deserving is conscientiousness (subjective virtue) to hold that the person who makes good-faith efforts to detect correct moral principles will always succeed, so in fact there can never be nonculpable belief in false moral principles. Or one might hold that there is a gray area of candidate principles all of which are sufficiently reasonable that good-faith efforts might lead a person to accept any of them, even a false one. But some putative moral principles, including those that exalt racial purity and approve slavery, are beyond the pale, and will never be approved by a conscientious agent.

The reply implicitly assumes that the fundamental moral principles must be intellectually simple and easy to recognize (or at least that some principles are so bad that no complex argument can make them appear good). It also denies that bad socialization can place evil fundamental principles in a sufficiently attractive light that a person who has undergone the socialization might then innocently and without blameworthy fault affirm evil as right and good. I doubt that these assumptions are correct. There is no a priori reason to suppose that correct moral principles must be simple and easy to detect, or to suppose that socialization is a weak force that cannot mislead any agent who sincerely seeks to form correct ethical beliefs. The conclusion then should be that if the reply is correct, there cannot be conscientious Nazis, and if the reply fails, we should not deny that conscientious Nazis can be genuinely deserving.

Objection. A person who seeks to discover correct morality and conform to its requirements must be motivated by some desire or equivalent psychological state. This initial desire is either present in the agent or absent. Either way, the individual cannot be responsible for having it (on this theme, see Persson, Chapter 3 in this volume).

Reply. The objection might be understood as invoking hard determinism, the doctrine that determinism is true and incompatible with moral responsibility. So understood, it is irrelevant to this chapter's project, which is to explore the moral status of desert on assumptions that are favorable to the claim that desert matters and do not rule it out of court from the outset.[12] The objection becomes pertinent if understood as the assertion that even if we have free will and exercise it in ways for which we

---

[12] To clarify: in this chapter I speak of an agent having 'free will'. But the idea that agents possess freedom of the will construed in some way that leaves room for agents to be genuinely deserving and

bear responsibility, still, different individuals find themselves with desires and given psychological traits that make it more difficult or easy and more painful or pleasant to dispose their wills conscientiously. In a metaphor, the individual is not responsible for the hand she is dealt by genetic endowment and environmental influences. She is responsible for how well she plays the hand she is dealt. Promoral and antimoral dispositions are part of the hand she is dealt, so their influence must be subtracted to find the residue of conscientious effort for which she can take credit.

One might be concerned that the proposal as stated does not after all succeed in drawing the line between what does and does not lie within the individual's control, so far as what might be thought to render her deserving is concerned. Compare two individuals, of whom one makes good-faith efforts to discover the right and the good and goes on to become subjectively virtuous, whereas the other one does not make such good-faith efforts and does not become subjectively virtuous. The difference might be that one is socialized to perceive and value conscientiousness and the other is not.

Still another objection that the proposal invites challenges the claim that one is more or less deserving to the degree that one is more or less subjectively virtuous. Consider the conundrums described by Gregory Kavka (1978). An individual might correctly foresee that she will do enormous good for the world if she brings it about that her character is corrupted, so that her will is not steadily disposed to the right and the good but instead harbors an evil conditional intention such as to retaliate with indiscriminate massive violence to nuclear attack. Suppose the individual does act to corrupt her own character and thereby does enormous good for the world, say by contributing to a stalemate of great power nuclear threats. Surely the person does not thereby render herself undeserving? There will be further cases. Corruption of character might be a foreseen or unforeseen by-product of pursuing a course of character that is itself morally justified all things considered. Also, we might vary these cases by imagining that the agent either deliberately seeks or courts corruption of character as part of her engagement in a course of conduct that is not objectively morally right but that seems right according to her nonculpable conscientious judgment. On the flip side, increases in an agent's conscientiousness or subjective virtue might come about as deliberately cultivated by the agent or as foreseen or unforeseen by-products of the agent's pursuit of other goals.

for rewarding the deserving to be intrinsically valuable admits of many interpretations. Some affirm free will understood as ruling out determinism, but there are also compatibilist doctrines that hold that determinism is consistent with genuine moral responsibility and deservingness. For purposes of this chapter only hard determinism and the 'hard soft determinism' along lines developed by J. J. C. Smart rule out the idea that responsibility and deservingness have standing at the level of fundamental principles of justice. See the references to Smart and to Arneson in n. 8.

Once again the reply will be to separate what one can reasonably be held responsible for in the face of complexity, in this case alteration of character over time for which the agent is to some degree responsible. The first pass at estimating an agent's desert is to note the extent to which she is disposed to pursue what she believes to be right and good over the course of her life. One then adjusts this figure to acknowledge that to some degree the individual may fail to be steadily disposed over the course of her life to make good-faith efforts to form correct beliefs about what is right and good, in general and in her particular circumstances. One then makes a further adjustment to reflect the fact that at any given time in her life, the agent's degree of conscientiousness at that time may be given a motivational boost or reduction brought about by past acts that themselves are variously conscientious. The agent may then be indirectly responsible for the current promoral or antimoral motivations she has, and deserve credit or discredit for their current impact.

The line of thought sketched in the previous paragraph must be mistaken. A simple way to see this is to note that whether an agent's conscientious or unconscientious choices bring it about that she later comes to have increased promoral or antimoral motivation will depend on contingencies beyond the agent's power to control, or luck. Also, a desire qualifies as 'promoral' or 'antimoral' on the ground that, averaging over all the possible circumstances in which one might choose multiplied by their probability, having the desire either increases or lowers the expectation that one will choose rightly. But in unusual or unexpected circumstances a promoral desire may press one toward an immoral choice and an antimoral desire may press one toward a moral choice. Again, whether one's choice at a moment that deliberately or as a foreseeable byproduct induces a certain desire will thereby in the end inhibit or facilitate moral choice in the future depends on contingencies that lie beyond the agent's power to control. What we should say instead is that, moment by moment, what an agent is strictly responsible for is the degree to which the quality of her agency is due to her conscientiousness or lack of it at that time.

Here is a simple picture of how the elusive conscientiousness might manifest itself in choice. Suppose that by virtue of having free will, I can spontaneously bring about a desire to do what I take to be right that varies in strength within a given range depending on my conscientious effort expended on that occasion. The size of the desire within this range is what I can be held responsible for.[13] This desire then simply is added to my other desires at the moment, and my choice depends on the

---

[13] In the special case in which it is held that any agent on every occasion of choice has the ability to will the act that she takes to be is best supported by rational considerations, whatever the constellation of her desires might be, one would be holding, in the terminology suggested in the text, that any agent always can spontaneously bring about a desire to do what she takes to be required by reasons that is sufficiently large to overbalance any contrary desires she might have. On this view no agent ever acts against her conscientious judgment without being responsible for such action.

resultant force of the aggregation of these desires. Some of these desires other than the conscientious desire will have been causally produced by factors that include past choices of the agent. But what really places credit and discredit on an agent, what she is truly responsible for, what renders her genuinely deserving and undeserving, is the degree to which she strives to be for the good and the right on each occasion of choice.[14]

One might worry that an element of contingency beyond the agent's power to control is still present in this account of responsibility and desert. Whether one is faced with a decision problem (as well as what sort of decision problem one then faces) depends on contingency, sheer luck in another guise. One may face temptation or the opportunity for heroism, another not. We are back to George Eliot's point. But this contingency now seems benign. I may face difficult or easy decision problems, but what I am responsible for is responding as best I can within the limit of my conscientious ability to the problems I face. My task as I strive to be conscientious is always adjusted to the ease or difficulty of the choice I face, so everyone has the same opportunity to gain a good score for deserving conscientious performance no matter what choices one faces. So to speak, one's handicap adjusts perfectly to the difficulty of the golf course one is playing, so all golfers' scores achieved on no matter what course are fully comparable.

Another complication is that if free will is understood as an uncaused contribution that the agent can make to the nexus of causal factors that determines choice, there may be situations in which the agent can foresee that the difference she could make by her utmost exertion of will could not overbalance other causal forces that will be decisive in any case. In that case, conscientious striving would seem pointless, so it would be odd to blame a person for not making a futile conscientious effort. If I foresee that the next application of torture will push me to confess and betray my comrades no matter how stridently I exert my will to resist, and on this ground I do not resist, it does not make sense to assign me credit for resisting or discredit for failing to resist. The same goes for controlling my tendency to explosive irrational outbursts of anger or fighting any other evil tendency of my nature (and, *mutatis mutandis*, the same point holds for acts of will that would pointlessly augment the forces of my personality that are carrying me to a good choice in some setting). Epistemic considerations may mute the force of this line of thought. If I cannot tell whether exertion of will would be consequential for choice or not, I should make whatever conscientious effort I am capable of. Still, the difficulty remains.

---

[14] The claim in the text recalls Nagel's observation that the perception that human actions are caused by events is incompatible with continuing to regard human actions as genuine actions: 'The area of genuine agency, and therefore of legitimate moral judgment, seems to shrink under this scrutiny to an extensionless point.' See Nagel (1979a: 35). On the picture of responsible agency I am sketching, it shrinks, beset by the pressure of causes and unchosen circumstances, to a small circle but does not disappear.

What should be said is that conscientious striving, what renders me deserving, is not an act that I perform on a particular occasion, but a disposition I steadily maintain. Whether I face many or few decision problems that call for action on my part is beyond my power to control, a matter of luck, so should not affect my deservingness. Whether the decision problems I face are hard or easy is also part of the situation I face, rather than what is due to me, that renders me deserving. I dispose myself, to a greater or lesser extent, to pursue what is right and good, and thus I am more or less deserving. What is up to me is the character of the disposition, not whether or not it happens to manifest on this or that occasion. Or better perhaps: my deservingness score is calculated moment by moment by the quality of my disposition at that moment, the score being continuously adjusted by the extent to which this quality now is due to factors either entirely beyond my power to control or that are difficult or painful to control.

6. Circularity

Desert as conscientiousness can be included as a constituent element in the fundamental principles of morality without introducing a vicious circularity into the account, such as John Rawls warned us was a trap for the unwary. At least, so I shall claim.

Suppose one says, what constitutes a person as morally deserving is that she seeks to bring about what justice requires. If one adds that what social justice requires is that people are rewarded according to the degree to which they are deserving, one is then asserting that what constitutes a person as morally deserving is that she seeks to bring it about that people are rewarded according to the degree to which they are deserving. A bad circularity vitiates the proposed account. What it is to be deserving has not been successfully characterized.

If being deserving is identified with conscientiousness, the problem does not arise, because the content of what morality requires is not being included in the characterization of deservingness. Deservingness is a subjective orientation of the will. To be deserving is to orient one's will toward what one takes to be morally right. That is to say, the deserving individual is one who makes sincere efforts to discover what is morally right and makes good-faith efforts to act according to whatever she discovers. Her will is decisively oriented toward a blank check: she aims to do whatever it is that is morally right, and she tries to fill in the content of this aim by thinking through as best she can where the balance of moral reasons points, all relevant considerations being taken into account. In this project the object of her will is not really whatever she happens to take to be morally right at the moment, because she recognizes her current opinion, whatever it is, might be wrong. However, in striving to conform her will to what is morally right, the best she can do is to conform her will to what by her lights now seems morally right.

If we aimed to discover to what extent a person is deserving, we would not need to know anything at all about the true content of morality, about what is really morally right. We would look for evidence that the person is conscientiously striving to lead her life according to her conception of what morality requires, and evidence that she acquires her conception by honest seeking. That we can in principle determine the degree to which a person is deserving without knowing anything ourselves about the true and proper content of morality indicates that the substance of what morality requires is not appearing as an element in what it is to be deserving. Hence, we can include this notion of deservingness as conscientiousness as a constituent element in the fundamental principles that fix what morality requires.

There is a residual puzzle. One might wonder what is the content of a person's intentions, when she happens to discover correctly what morality does require. In this case, which can hardly be regarded as a marginal case, won't the content of morality become included in the object that the person strives to achieve, if she is to qualify as deserving? Circularity then appears to emerge again. I have to say that even when the person has justified correct beliefs about what morality requires, these justified beliefs will not enter into the considerations that qualify her as deserving. The person would be just as deserving (provided she sincerely seeks to find out the moral truth and conform to it), whether her beliefs were true or false. What matters is just that she orients her will toward whatever she happens to believe, after good-faith efforts on her part to come to believe the truth about moral requirements. And of course the person herself can be aware of this: she can be aware that the question, whether or not she is deserving, does not hinge at all on the quality of her beliefs about what morality requires. They could be perfectly true or utter malarkey; no matter.

7. No Peaks

Suppose that we have determined that subjective virtue or some suitable modification of it is what constitutes the desert basis for the desert component of distributive justice. The more conscientious one is, the more deserving one is. The next question is how deservingness modifies the distributive share that the individual at that level of deservingness ought to get (on this issue, see Feldman 1999).

The core of this question has been subjected to instructive analysis in recent essays by Shelly Kagan (1999, 2003; see also Olsaretti 2002 and Feldman 2003). He considers equality and desert as values that might be thought to affect the value of outcomes.

Other things equal, one might suppose, more equal distributions are morally better, and other things equal, one might suppose, distributions in which people get what they deserve are morally better. Kagan disagrees. He argues that when desert values are properly understood, they completely crowd out equality values, which should probably have no influence at all in determining the moral value of the outcomes that action and public policy can shape. In my contrary view, in the framework that Kagan sets it becomes clear that equality values do have independent weight and one can discern how equality and desert might sensibly be integrated at the level of fundamental moral principle.

Distinguishing noncomparative and comparative desert, Kagan asserts that more deserving people deserve to have more well-being than less deserving people and that for each person there is some absolute amount of well-being that the person deserves. Getting less well-being than that deserved amount is less good or bad (from the standpoint of desert) and getting more well-being than that deserved amount is also less good or bad. For each person, the amount of well-being that she deserves fixes her peak — the level of well-being for her, having which would be best from the standpoint of desert.[15] This is the idea of noncomparative desert. Comparative desert is defined in terms of it. The idea is that people who are equally absolutely deserving should be equally well off and people who are more deserving in absolute terms than others should be better off than others. Kagan also stipulates that one person is specifically more deserving than another if one suffers a greater shortfall from the well-being level she absolutely deserves (or a lesser surplus of well-being beyond what she absolutely deserves) than the other, so that from the standpoint of desert it is better to confer a one-unit gain of well-being on the specifically more deserving.

The thought experiment that is supposed to induce the judgment that desert supplants equality is this: suppose that one can provide a well-being gain either to a saint who enjoys a high level of well-being, but far less than she deserves, or to a sinner who enjoys a much lower level of well-being, that level being far greater than he deserves. An egalitarian view that holds that if a one-unit gain can go either to a better-off or worse-off person, it should go to the worse off, must hold that (so far as equality values are concerned) it is better that the worse-off sinner get the benefit in the offing rather than the better-off saint. Kagan notes that both noncomparative desert and comparative desert agree that (so far as desert values are concerned) it is

---

[15] The term *peak* is suggested by a graph that Kagan describes. The location of points along the horizontal axis indicates various amounts of well-being that a person might have and the location of points along the vertical axis indicates the value, so far as desert is concerned, of a given individual's having that much welfare. If each person noncomparatively deserves a certain amount of well-being, and if getting more or less than that is less than ideal from the standpoint of desert, then the line that charts the value from the standpoint of desert of that person having gradually increasing well-being will have a highest point, a peak.

better that the benefit go to the saint who is far worse off than she deserves rather than to the sinner who is already far better off than he deserves. Moreover, his response to the example is that not only is it the case that desert values and not equality values have greater weight in determining which outcome would be better all things considered, it is also the case that in no respect would it be better that the worse-off sinner should get the benefit as equality values would dictate. No faint shadow of equality considerations shades the judgment in these circumstances in any respect. (He adduces other examples to explore and strengthen the judgment that equality values have not just less weight than desert values but no weight at all.)

A first clue that this dismissal of equality values proceeds too quickly emerges if one imagines a world in which everyone has exactly what she deserves according to Kagan-style noncomparative desert. Then a windfall gain in resources that can improve people's well-being appears.[16] Perhaps huge oil fields are discovered. The upshot is that we can distribute resources that will bring about a tripling of everyone's well-being level. If everyone initially enjoys as much well-being as she noncomparatively (and comparatively) deserves, then multiplying each person's well-being by three does not worsen the situation as it would be assessed by the standard of comparative justice. But from the standpoint of noncomparative desert, we must say that tripling everyone's well-being level is a disastrous change. We would move from a world of perfect correspondence between desert and well-being levels to a world in which everyone has grossly more well-being than she deserves. Saying this is compatible with holding that all things considered, tripling the well-being of humanity is morally desirable, in view of the aggregate well-being gains thereby realized. But my own judgment is that there is nothing undesirable from the standpoint of desert that occurs in the transition to the world where everyone enjoys huge well-being gains proportionate to their deservingness (their virtue or desert basis). This is the judgment that there is no such thing as noncomparative desert as Kagan conceives it—a peak of well-being suited to one's desert such that to have more or less well-being than that amount would be undesirable from the standpoint of desert. Even if there is no doubt whatsoever that the person has earned a particular desert score, to my mind desert merely amplifies or reduces the moral value of channeling well-being gains to one or another person. One way to accommodate these points is to affirm that all desert is comparative.[17] That is to say, even if the standard for measuring that which qualifies a person as

---

[16] Brad Hooker suggested this example and the point I use the example to make.

[17] This is not the only alternative. One might alternatively hold that the moral value of obtaining a gain in well-being for a person is greater, the greater the person's lifetime desert score, with the stipulation that everybody's desert score is positive. On this view, how one's desert score compares with that of others does not matter at the fundamental level of principle, though it will matter derivatively, in practice. This proposal extends the basic prioritarian idea. I owe this suggestion to Kasper Lippert-Rasmussen.

deserving admits of cardinal interpersonal comparison with a nonarbitrary zero, the desert score that accrues to a person on this basis establishes only comparative desert: other things being equal, it is desirable that those who are more deserving should enjoy more well-being than those who are less deserving.

Another useful thought experiment for exploring the relative weight of comparative desert and aggregate well-being considers whether it is desirable that an extremely undeserving person should get a benefit if the only alternative to his getting the benefit is that the benefit is lost—spoils without advancing anyone's well-being. Suppose Hitler is very undeserving, compared to Mother Teresa and everybody else, so that by comparative desert standards he is the least fitting person to receive a benefit. Either the benefit goes to Hitler, rendering him better off, or it goes to no one. The view that I urge recommends that in such a circumstance it is better that Hitler get the benefit than that no one get it.

This judgment sweeps together distributive and retributive justice considerations that might be implicated. Suppose Hitler has committed crimes that merit punishment. Or suppose Hitler is one of the undeserving poor, to whom a desert-oriented distributive justice policy might be expected to be stingy. Nonetheless, if the only options are really a status quo or an alternative in which Hitler is slightly better off and no one else is worse off, the alternative is morally preferred. On this view, a constraint on the influence of comparative desert on the evaluation of outcomes and actions is the Pareto norm.

For retributive justice, acceptance of a Pareto constraint implies that the imposition of punishment on a person—deliberately aiming to reduce the guilty person's well-being—cannot be justified unless punishment produces some benefit for other people either by deterrence or in some other way.

Taken by itself, comparative desert can recommend reducing one person's well-being when no gain to anyone else results. Imposition of a Pareto constraint rules out leveling down of this sort. The position thus taken is that it is morally desirable that everyone, even Hitler (the least deserving person on earth, let's say), should have a good life, more rather than less well-being. The role of comparative desert is limited to amplifying or reducing the moral value of obtaining a benefit for a person depending on how comparatively deserving the person is.

The reader might well be puzzled that on the one hand I objected that Kagan's position on desert implied that it is in one way good to reduce one person's well-being when no gain to anyone else results, yet on the other hand I accept comparative desert, which also upholds this same thought that leveling down can be in some respect desirable even if never acceptable all things considered. In reply: my claim is that once we see that comparative desert can be understood as a free-standing doctrine independent of any notion of noncomparative desert, the appeal of the former crowds out the attraction of the latter.

More needs to be said to clarify how comparative desert affects the moral value of outcomes and how this desert value interacts with equality and aggregation of well-being. Aggregation holds that an outcome with more aggregate well-being is morally better than an outcome with less. Equality holds that if the total of well-being for a given number of persons is fixed, the state of affairs in which all persons have the same amount of well-being is morally preferred. I believe that the least controversial doctrine in the family of egalitarian views that is consistent with this construal of equality is prioritarianism: one ought always to choose an action among the available options that induces no less moral value than any other option, the moral value of obtaining a well-being gain or avoiding a loss for a person being greater, the larger the well-being gain, and greater, the lower the person's lifetime well-being would be in the absence of this benefit. Priority so characterized is an act-consequentialist doctrine that takes the value of consequences to be set by some function of aggregate well-being and priority for the worse off. It should be noted that this characterization is not mandatory. Priority might on an alternative view be construed as the consequentialist component of morality, which includes other components such as deontological constraints and options. However, the promise of the project is that by introducing distributional considerations that qualify the principle of well-being maximization one ends up with a principle that is not vulnerable to the most damaging counterexamples that tempt one to abandon the consequentialist faith. I tentatively want to explore how one might keep the faith (see also Arneson 2003*a*, *b*).

To consider how aggregation and equality (melded into priority) and comparative desert interact, consider a two-person world consisting of a very deserving person, a saint, and a very undeserving person, a sinner. Suppose that it is possible to obtain a small well-being gain for either the saint or the sinner but not both in four situations: (*a*) the saint and the sinner are both already very well off and each has the same amount of well-being, (*b*) the saint and the sinner are both very badly off, and each has the same amount of well-being, (*c*) the saint is very badly off and the sinner is very well off, and (*d*) the saint is very well off and the sinner is very badly off. In (*a*) and (*b*), whatever relative weight comparative desert should have against priority, the morally preferred outcome should be the one in which the more deserving saint gets the benefit. In (*c*), priority and desert both favor the outcome in which the worse-off and more deserving person gets the benefit. In (*d*), the two considerations of comparative desert and priority pull in opposite directions. Considering a somewhat similar example, Kagan holds that the putative value of equality is entirely eclipsed by desert. I do not share this judgment and want to explore views according to which either desert or priority might determine right conduct when they conflict.

Up to now comparative desert has been thinly described. Consider situations in which one can bring about a one-unit increase in well-being for only one of a number of persons who are unequally deserving (they vary in virtue, or in whatever is the applicable desert basis) and also are at various well-being levels.

Here is a familiar proposal. So far as comparative desert is concerned, the ideal state of affairs is one in which each person enjoys well-being proportionate to her deservingness, so that if Smith's deservingness score is 3, Jones's is 2, and Ben's is 1, the ideal distribution of well-being among them would be in that same patterned proportion 3: 2: 1.

The picture then is that increasing human well-being and preventing reductions of it is always morally a good thing, but the moral goal is not to maximize the sum total of well-being but to maximize the total of well-being weighted by distributional factors. One factor is priority as already described. A second is that it is better to obtain a gain for a person who is specifically more deserving than others to whom the same-sized gain might be given. One is specifically more deserving than others who might be accorded the benefit in question if channeling the benefit to one rather than to any of the others would do most to bring it about that the well-being levels these people are at are proportional to their level of desert. Other things being equal, it is better to get a benefit to someone who is more deserving in this sense, and, other things being equal, it is better to get a benefit to someone, the lower her lifetime well-being without this benefit, and no other matters affect the moral value of the state of affairs in which a benefit is obtained for a person other than the size of the benefit. Everyone is deserving but some are more deserving than others. It is intrinsically desirable that any person's well-being be increased, but it is more desirable to increase the well-being of the worse off.

Distributive justice can be regarded as setting criteria that establish queues of persons standing in line to receive various benefits that are in the offing. Comparative desert and prior well-being level affect one's place in the queue, but no one is deemed intrinsically unfitting to receive any benefit. If there is some good that might be obtained for me, getting which would increase my overall lifetime well-being, the only morally acceptable reason not to obtain the good for me is that someone else stands in front of me in the queue.

This standing-in-the-queue amalgam of comparative desert and priority is controversial along many dimensions, including its denial of noncomparative desert. Perhaps the area of social life in which the denial of noncomparative desert looks most incongruous is criminal justice. Many of us have the belief that a given crime of given culpability, taken by itself, deserves a specific penalty—or, perhaps better, a penalty within a certain range. Comparative desert yields the judgment that if several individuals commit equally heinous crimes and are equally blameworthy, they ought to receive the same punishment. Comparative desert applied to retributive justice, justice in the punishment of crime, holds that people who commit legal offenses of varying wrongfulness ought to be punished in proportion to their culpability—the evil of their crime adjusted to reflect their degree of responsibility for its commission.

But most retributivists hold that 'for every offense there is an ideally deserved punishment', and that being punished by a lesser or greater amount is less than ideal and if the gap between what one noncomparatively deserves and the punishment meted out is too great, this is positively evil. Thomas Hurka observes, 'It is also plausible that failing to punish an offense is not just not good but evil' (2003: 53). David Miller also affirms the noncomparative element in retributive justice: 'When we say that no one deserves to be hanged for stealing a sheep, we are saying not merely that this penalty is disproportionate to others, but that there is an absolute lack of fit between the wrong committed and the proposed penalty' (1999: 154).

People do affirm strict retributive justice, but others find the doctrine appalling, so it cannot be argued by invocation of retributive justice that common sense decisively rejects the standing-in-the-queue approach. This approach applied to criminal justice issues holds that inflicting suffering on a criminal is never morally right unless doing so improves the world by depriving the criminal of the opportunity to commit further crimes or by deterring the criminal or others from perpetrating crimes. Many who are not consequentialists at all approve this judgment. Pointing out under what conditions punishment of one who violates the law of nature is morally acceptable in a state of nature, John Locke asserts that anyone 'may bring such evil on any one, who hath transgressed that law, as may make him repent the doing of it, and thereby deter him, and by his example others, from doing the like mischief' (1980: 10). I suppose Locke means that if punishing an offender would not do good—beyond the alleged intrinsic value of bringing suffering upon one who deserves it—it would be unjustified. Locke's position so understood is still compatible with belief in noncomparative desert in the criminal justice context. For example, one might hold that it is intrinsically morally valuable to bring it about that an offender receives the exact punishment that his offense merits, but that this intrinsic value is always outweighed by the disvalue of the suffering thus brought about, so is never justified all things considered unless some extrinsic benefit is added that tips the scale. But even so interpreted, the view would radically downgrade the supposed intrinsic moral value of making those who are negatively deserving worse off. The view is just a whisker away from the denial of negative noncomparative desert altogether.

8. Desert Prioritarianism?

The previous section stitches together considerations of desert, priority, and well-being, but further thought threatens to pull this patchwork apart at the seams.[18]

---

[18] The problem described in the next paragraph was brought to my attention by Ingmar Persson. It's a good objection, which my replies in the text may not fully resolve.

Suppose that we can by action now affect the extent to which people, ourselves or others, are deserving in the future. Then if morality requires, *inter alia*, that one bring it about that people achieve good fortune proportionate to their desert, it will sometimes be right to bring it about that a well-being gain should go to a (now) less deserving rather than to a more deserving person, just because this (as it seems) deliberate maldistribution will bring it about that those who are now more deserving will become less deserving. Maybe the mistreated will become inappropriately resentful or envious. This apparent implication of my view is weird and counterintuitive.

Maybe the initial supposition that generates the problem makes no sense. The question arises whether the idea of acting in a way that causes a person, oneself or another, to become more or less deserving at a later time makes any sense if deservingness is interpreted as conscientiousness as this chapter proposes. What it is to qualify as deserving on any occasion for any person adjusts to the ensemble of the person's circumstances, so that changing a person's circumstances may render it easier and more pleasant for the person to choose the right course of action, but cannot render it easier or more pleasant for the person to orient her will in a way that qualifies as deserving. This must be so on pain of violating the condition that what one deserves at any given time is not due to luck in one's circumstances. Thus it may be wrong for me to enter a bar, because that act increases the probability that I will indulge excessively in alcohol. But once I am in the bar, the level of orientation of my will toward the right and the good that qualifies me as deserving on that occasion must adjust to my circumstances, so that it is no harder or easier for me to qualify as deserving in the bar than it would be to qualify as deserving if I were outside it. The same is true if my choice is to encourage or discourage another person from entering a bar, when entering would incur the same excessive risk of later wrongdoing.

The condition that how deserving a person is cannot be due to moral luck rules out the possibility that one can cause any person, oneself or another, to be deserving. Nor can one cause it to be more difficult or easier for a person to be deserving. Can one cause the probability that a person will be deserving to increase? I'm unsure. A disposition that it is always equally within my power to sustain or create, whatever my circumstances, will suffice in any circumstances to qualify me as deserving. (In some circumstances the orientation of will that qualifies me as deserving will not suffice to bring it about that I pursue the morally right rather than the morally wrong course of action.) Still, this perhaps leaves it open that one person can act in a way that will foreseeably bring about circumstances in which, as a matter of fact, a person, oneself or another, will conduct herself in a way that is more deserving than the course of conduct she would have pursued absent the circumstance altering intervention. Although one cannot cause it to be more difficult or easy for any person to qualify as deserving on any occasion, still, perhaps it is predictable that in circumstance X, the person will in fact not be deserving, whereas in Y, she would, and one can bring about either X or Y. The alternative view would be that the formation of will that renders people more or less deserving is in principle unpredictable. I take no stand on that issue in this chapter.

If one can as a matter of fact never act in a way that predictably brings it about that a person becomes more or less deserving, then the problem raised at the beginning of this section dissolves. But if one can, it does not dissolve. What then?

Suppose our actions can increase or decrease the aggregate amount of desert as well as the aggregate amount of well-being and its distribution across the better and worse off and the more and less deserving. For example, suppose we could revise the educational curriculum in a way that would bring it about that people are on the whole more conscientious but have less well-being. Perhaps, other things being equal, we should prefer a population of saints all at well-being level 99 than a population of sinners all at well-being level 100. (One should notice that the Pareto constraint introduced earlier will now be reinterpreted, so that it judges unacceptable a state of affairs that can be altered by making someone better off (in virtue and welfare combined) without making anyone else worse off (in virtue and welfare combined)). The idea would be, not that there is some absolute amount of well-being that any person, given her deservingness, deserves, but rather that it is better from the moral point of view that persons be more deserving rather than less deserving. At the very least, surely it is the case that, other things being equal, it is better that a given population at a given well-being level should be more deserving rather than less deserving. Moreover, it is not the case that well-being increases take lexical priority over deservingness increases (so that the greatest possible increase in desert would not outweigh the slightest increase in well-being if the two values are in conflict in given circumstances).

If our acts can affect the total quantity of deservingness in the world, they can no doubt also affect the distribution of deservingness across persons. To stick with a simple-minded example, suppose one can either bring it about that a very deserving saint becomes slightly more deserving or instead that a very undeserving sinner becomes just that same degree more deserving. Which to choose? Or does morality hold that the distribution of virtue across persons is a 'don't care'?

I tentatively propose a prioritarianism of desert. That is to say, it is an intrinsically better state of affairs when persons are more deserving rather than less deserving, and the moral value of bringing about a one-unit increase in desert is greater, the lower the person's lifetime desert level would be absent this increment. Bringing about a one-unit gain in the deservingness of a sinner is more valuable than bringing about an identical one-unit gain in the deservingness of a saint.

The Christian New Testament contains the comment, 'There is more joy in heaven over one sinner who repents than over ninety-nine [nonsinners] who have no need of repentance' (Luke 15: 7). This statement is ambiguous, but does seem to convey a concern for the distribution of deservingness. On its face, the statement is perhaps most naturally read as asserting a sufficientarianism of desert: it is more important morally to get people to the good enough level of virtue than to bring about additional gains in people's virtue above this good enough threshold. The sufficientarianism makes sense given the background view that a certain level of deservingness gets one to the threshold of salvation. In my nontheist world view, there is no salvation, so there is no nonarbitrary 'good enough' threshold level, so sufficientarianism loses its appeal. With perhaps some strain, one could interpret the passage as asserting a priority view in the domain of desert: It is better that the sinner repents a bit, gaining one unit of deservingness, than that ninety-nine saints, already at a high level of deservingness, repent of some small sin and in this way increase their deservingness by one unit for each yielding a total gain of ninety-nine units. I accept the basic prioritarian view that a gain in virtue that accrues to a sinner is intrinsically more valuable than the same gain that accrues to a saint. I doubt that the moral intuition supporting desert prioritarianism is as strong as the moral intuition that supports well-being prioritarianism, but if this is so, this thought could be captured by the idea that the extent to which extra moral value is gained when gains go to those who are worse off rather than better off is less in the domain of deservingness than in the domain of well-being.

The position we then arrive at is desert and well-being prioritarianism with extra priority to well-being gains for the comparatively more deserving. One ought always to choose the act that maximizes moral value. Increasing people's desert as conscientiousness is morally valuable, and the moral value of bringing it about that a person becomes more deserving by a unit is greater, the lower the person's lifetime desert would be absent that increase. Increasing people's well-being is morally valuable, and the moral value of bringing it about that a person gains a unit of well-being is greater, the lower the person's lifetime well-being would be absent that gain, and also greater, the more that gain brings it about that people have good fortune (well-being) in proportion to their desert. Desert is scaled so that everyone always has positive desert, in order to register the judgment that it is intrinsically good for anyone, no matter how low his virtue or desert level, to enjoy more rather than less well-being. *Mutatis mutandis*, what is true of well-being and desert increases is also true of avoidance of well-being and desert losses.

The position as described might seem to magnify the value of increasing saintliness and rewarding saintliness beyond their true value. But nothing said so far specifies the comparative weight that well-being and desert should have in the determination of what should be done, so it is compatible with well-being and desert prioritarianism that desert should count for comparatively little. Well-being does not rule the roost but may be the first among equals.

In this section a difficulty was raised for simple desert-weighted prioritarianism. The view seems to countenance deliberately acting to bring it about that people become less deserving, in order to bring about greater correspondence between people's good fortune and their desert. One reply to the objection is that desert as conscientiousness might be such that one cannot act to increase or decrease anyone's future deservingness. The second reply to the objection is that if people's desert can be altered in this way, then one should acknowledge that it is desirable, other things being equal, that people in the aggregate be more deserving rather than less, and also that the distribution of desert matters, and we should be desert prioritarians. Although I have not tried to show that the resultant more complex combination of desert and priority considerations will not be vulnerable to counterexample, my sense is that appropriate weighting will usually rule out the unappealing implication that sometimes we should deliberately act to bring it about that people become less deserving rather than more deserving just to bring about greater satisfaction of the ideal that people's good fortune should be proportionate to their desert. People's becoming less deserving will itself register as a disvalue on the revised view proposed in this section. Of course, this disvalue can be outweighed, for example, by the conflicting consideration that we ought to increase the extent to which people get priority-weighted well-being increases. But my sense is that this balancing of moral costs and benefits is not counterintuitive. Recall also that, on the view being suggested, one who acts with a view to bringing about a more just outcome by bringing it about that some come to be less deserving cannot be lessening anyone's fair opportunity to qualify as deserving. One is simply providing a perfectly fair test that one expects some to flunk.

9. Azdak

So far in this chapter, I have defended the idea that there is at least one conception of desert that is in principle compatible with the norm that one can become deserving or undeserving only by virtue of matters that lie within one's power to control. Desert as conscientious striving satisfies this norm. Desert so construed can be accommodated as a constituent element in the fundamental moral principles that fix what is just and unjust. I hasten to add that I have not argued against the possibility that some conceptions of desert that find people deserving in ways that are incompatible with the control principle will in the end turn out to be morally justifiable.

It is intrinsically morally desirable, I submit, that the level of well-being that people enjoy is proportionate to their desert and that aggregate well-being be greater rather than smaller. Moreover, bringing about a gain in well-being for a person is intrinsically morally better, the lower the person's lifetime well-being would be absent this gain. Of course, saying just this much does not fully specify a principle that enables us to assess the outcomes of candidate policies—such a specification would have to stipulate the relative weights to be attached to the three elements of well-being aggregate increase, well-being to the deserving, and well-being to the worse off. Of course, the weighting issue is the $64,000 question. However, even in the absence of a proposal as to how properly to set these weights, enough has been said to render plausible the idea that desert and equality can cohabit peacefully in a pluralist conception of justice. The reasons it might make sense to value desert do not subvert the legitimate appeal of equality.

The alert and sympathetic reader may feel sadly compelled to report that I have painted myself into a corner. In the rush to accommodate the constraint that one cannot become deserving or the reverse by virtue of what lies beyond one's power to control I have embraced an ideal of deservingness that could not conceivably be put into practice. Since we cannot see into people's souls, we cannot tell who is truly deserving and who is not. Hence, it cannot be fundamentally morally important to bring about a world in which people's well-being levels are, to any extent, proportional to their desert. This is just to reiterate the entanglement objection against incorporating desert into justice at the level of fundamental principle.

In closing I wish to register a dissent from this proposal to scratch desert from justice. A fundamental principle of justice should be conceived as a regulative ideal that guides the selection and reform of practices and institutions. Even if we cannot see into people's souls, we may be able to fashion administrable, operationalizable proxies for the values that we really care about but perhaps cannot directly implement.

My sketch of how responsibility and desert might be constituents in a fundamental egalitarian justice principle accepts the control principle and singles out exertions of free will as the basis of genuine desert. Even setting aside the likelihood that human actions are entirely caused events so no such exertions of free will ever occur, it might seem that in principle there could be no way to pick out an empirically detectable proxy for the quality of choice that is supposed to render people differentially deserving. It could not then make sense for the theory of justice to require that people's good fortune be made proportionate to their true desert in this undetectable sense.

I make no brief here for the coherence of the libertarian free will hypothesis or for the claim that free will understood in a sense that is compatible with determinism is worthy of the name. Consider just libertarian free will. Accepting the hypothesis for the sake of the argument, in order to explore how responsibility and desert might plausibly be viewed as intrinsically morally important, I do not see why it must be so that public policies could never to any degree bring about by design a state of affairs in which good fortune becomes distributed across people in a way that approximates more rather than less closely to their true desert. Free will has to be ultimately an empirical issue, so if the hypothesis is true, it would be vindicated by a future biologically informed scientific psychology. If free will is an empirical phenomenon with empirical effects, in principle there could be measurement of its quality and reward according to desert. Why not? Improbability is not impossibility.

There is all the difference in the world between upholding a norm as a good practical guide, following which will produce pretty good results so far as we can tell in circumstances as we know them, and upholding a norm as fundamentally morally significant and valuable in itself. For one thing, the world may change, or our knowledge may increase, especially our knowledge of technologies of administration, such that values that were at one time utterly unfeasible to implement become feasibly implementable. So it is always a worthwhile exercise to try to think through what we really care about without letting that question become conflated with the quite different question, Which of the things that we reasonably care about is it reasonable to try and achieve here and now taking into account all morally relevant costs and benefits of the attempt.

For an example of how the social planner might devise policies that work well enough, here and now, as rough and ready instruments to try to achieve our values to the greatest feasible extent, consider the story of the judge Azdak as told by Bertolt Brecht in *The Caucasian Chalk Circle* (1966). The judge must decide a dispute between two women, each of whom claims to be the mother of a child and hence the rightful guardian. In the setting it is just given that the relevant standard of justice that determines in principle the correct decision is that the woman who is more disposed to love and care for the child for his own sake deserves to be awarded custody. (The morality that the play endorses appears to be that things belong to people who are good for them.) Nobody can see into the women's characters, certainly not Azdak, who has just been introduced to them by hearing their conflicting testimony. Azdak institutes a procedure that brings it about that the women's character is revealed by their responses to a decision problem set by the court. The child is placed in the center of a chalk circle and the women are told that whoever pulls the child outside the circle will be awarded custody. The woman who is more disposed to love and care for the child for his own sake yields immediately rather than participate in a determined tug of war that might well break the child's body. Azdak summarily awards this woman custody.

Notice that Azdak's trick fails to satisfy the norm that a just society's basic structure of institutional arrangements be public. The rules of institutions are public just in case 'individuals are able to attain common knowledge of the rules' (i) general applicability, (ii) their particular requirements, and (iii) the extent to which individuals conform to those requirements' (Williams 1998: 233). Azdak's rule cannot fit within a stable system of rules that is public in this sense.[19] For one thing, the rule can be exploited by the clever. If I foresee that losing the tug of war gains me custody of the child and I want custody, I will make haste to be the first to lose the tug of war and gain custody. Azdak's trick works in a particular setting; in other settings, with other agents, different measures would be needed.

The general point is that it is an open question, given that we embrace values that cannot directly be embodied in practices, to what extent we can find good enough proxies that are implementable. These proxies might be ephemeral, like Azdak's trick, and hence could not satisfy the publicity norm. So much the worse for publicity, I would hold. Publicity is a generally good tool for achieving important values, but does not matter morally for its own sake. If we can get more justice by sacrificing publicity, we should always prefer more justice.

10. Conclusion

The lesson I want to take from Brecht's story might provoke unease. In sketching an account of egalitarian justice that caters to desert, I presuppose a background consequentialism.[20] This ethic might seem to license manipulation and duplicity and even exploitation of others rather than reciprocity and a fair-minded disposition to treat each person on whom our actions impinge with respect and consideration. One recalls Thomas Nagel's characterization of the underlying mentality of purely outcome-oriented ethics: 'Utilitarianism is associated with a view of oneself as a benevolent bureaucrat distributing such benefits as one can control to countless other beings, with whom one may have various relations or none. The justifications it requires are primarily administrative' (Nagel 1979b: 68). The description that Nagel applies to utilitarianism applies so far as I can see to any consequentialist ethic, including the prioritarian family of principles with a proviso catering to true desert. The term 'bureaucrat' is perhaps misleading, since the ethic is concerned to specify

[19] Publicity as Williams, following Rawls, understands it is a demanding requirement. Notice that a social norm that requires hikers and campers in remote wilderness areas to exit with their garbage and not permanently deface the landscape will likely fail to satisfy publicity. There likely will be no reliable enforcement mechanism imposing fines or the like on violators that is feasible to implement, so the norm can only be enforced by the sanction of conscience, which will weigh lightly on scofflaws and variably heavier on others, depending on the sensitivity of their conscience in this domain. Still, it seems to me a society with the social norm in place might succeed in keeping the wilderness reasonably usable for present and future generations, and might thereby qualify as more just than another society that fully satisfies publicity but lacks the social norm in question.

[20] For an interpretation of one form of egalitarianism, a revolutionary communist ethic, as brutally consequentialist and utterly in conflict with common-sense norms of decency, see Brecht (1965).

what anyone occupying any social role ought to do, and in particular speaks to the natural mother and to the would-be guardian in the story just as much as to the judge. Nagel of course might be suggesting that consequentialisms go astray in ceding to everyone anywhere a moral authority that only some public officials and others in circumscribed social roles possess, and then only in limited respects. Another quibble one might have with Nagel's characterization is that once we bring into the account a realistically sophisticated understanding of human well-being or 'utility', what benefits and harms any agent can produce for herself or others depends in complicated ways on the special relations she has with some of them, and they with each other—friend to friend, parent to child, teacher to student, colleague to colleague, promisor to promisee, and so on. But allowing for nuances of tone, Nagel's characterization is broadly correct. I don't regard it as an indictment—quite the contrary—but others will disagree.[21]

References

ARNESON, R. (2000), 'Welfare Should Be the Currency of Justice', *Canadian Journal of Philosophy*, 30/4: 497–524.

——— (2003a), 'Moral Limits on the Demands of Beneficence?', in D. Chatterjee (ed.), *The Ethics of Assistance: Morality, Affluence, and the Distant Needy* (Cambridge: Cambridge University Press), 33–58.

——— (2003b), 'Consequentialism Versus Special-Ties Partiality', *The Monist*, 86/3: 382–401.

——— (2003c), 'The Smart Theory of Moral Responsibility and Desert', in S. Olsaretti (ed.), *Desert and Justice* (New York: Oxford University Press), 233–58.

BARRY, B. (1973), *The Liberal Theory of Justice* (Oxford: Oxford University Press).

——— (1966), *The Caucasian Chalk Circle*, trans. E. Bentley (New York: Grove Press).

BRECHT, B. (1965), 'The Measures Taken', in Brecht, *The Jewish Wife and Other Short Plays*, trans. E. Bentley (New York: Grove Press), 75–108.

ELIOT, G. (1994), *Middlemarch* (1872), ed. R. Ashton (London: Penguin Books).

FELDMAN, F. (1999), 'Adjusting Utility for Justice: A Consequentialist Reply to the Objection from Justice', in L. Pojman and O. McLeod (eds.), *What Do We Deserve? A Reader on Desert and Justice* (New York: Oxford University Press), 259–70.

——— (2003), 'Return to Twin Peaks: On the Intrinsic Moral Significance of Equality', in S. Olsaretti (ed.), *Desert and Justice* (New York: Oxford University Press), 145–68.

---

[21] For a broadly similar expression of misgiving, see T. M. Scanlon's comment that certain notions of equality of opportunity seem to presuppose 'what might be called the "parental" conception of the state' (2000: 45). See also Scheffler (2003), in which he contrasts the ideal of a society of equals with an 'administrative conception of equality' that he finds less attractive.

HURKA, T. (2003), 'Desert: Individualistic and Holistic', in S. Olsaretti (ed.), *Desert and Justice* (New York: Oxford University Press), 45–68.

KAGAN, S. (1999), 'Equality and Desert', in L. Pojman and O. McLeod (eds.), *What Do We Deserve? A Reader on Justice and Desert* (New York: Oxford University Press), 298–314.

—— (2003), 'Comparative Desert', in S. Olsaretti (ed.), *Desert and Justice* (New York: Oxford University Press), 93–122.

KAVKA, G. (1978), 'Some Paradoxes of Deterrence', *Journal of Philosophy*, 75/6: 285–302.

LOCKE, J. (1980), *Second Treatise on Government* (1690), ed. C. Macpherson (Indianapolis: Hackett).

MILLER, D. (1999), *Principles of Social Justice* (Cambridge, Mass.: Harvard University Press).

NAGEL, T. (1979a), 'Moral Luck', in Nagel, *Mortal Questions* (Cambridge: Cambridge University Press), 24–38.

—— (1979b), 'War and Massacre', in Nagel, *Mortal Questions* (Cambridge: Cambridge University Press), 53–74.

OLSARETTI, S. (2002), 'Unmasking Equality? Kagan on Equality and Desert', *Utilitas*, 14/2: 387–400.

PARFIT, D. (1995), *Equality or Priority?* (Lawrence: Department of Philosophy, University of Kansas).

RAWLS, J. (1999), *A Theory of Justice*, rev. edn. (Cambridge, Mass.: Harvard University Press).

SCANLON, T. (2000), 'The Diversity of Objections to Inequality', in M. Clayton and A. Williams (eds.), *The Ideal of Equality* (New York: St Martin's Press).

SCHEFFLER, S. (1982), *The Rejection of Consequentialism* (Oxford: Oxford University Press).

—— (2003), 'What Is Egalitarianism?', *Philosophy and Public Affairs*, 31/1: 5–39.

SMART, J. (1961), 'Free-Will, Praise, and Blame', *Mind*, 70/279: 291–306.

TEMKIN. L. (1993), *Inequality* (New York: Oxford University Press).

WEIRICH, P. (1983), 'Utility Tempered with Equality', *Noûs*, 17: 423–39.

WILLIAMS, A. (1998), 'Incentives, Inequality, and Publicity', *Philosophy and Public Affairs*, 27/3: 225–47.

Part IV

Applications

12

Market Failure, Common Interests, and the Titanic Puzzle

Jonathan Wolff

1. Incentives, Public Benefits, and the Free Market

Defenders of the free market often argue that in a free market it is possible to make a profit in a sustainable way only by giving people what they want. One inspiration for this argument is Adams Smith's famous observation that 'It is not from the benevolence of the butcher, the brewer, or the baker, that we expect our dinner, but from their regard to their own self-interest. We address ourselves, not to their humanity but to their self-love, and never talk to them of our own necessities but of their advantages' (Smith 1904, bk. 1, ch. 2).

Now, it is true that over a very wide range of cases Smith's argument holds. Free competition and profit-seeking behaviour should drive out poor-quality goods, and so it can be an excellent way of providing value for money for consumers. However, there is a question of how far this argument generalises. Opponents of the free market allege that consumers are likely to be tricked and cheated by ruthless capitalists in an insufficiently regulated market. The mis-selling of financial products is a particular recent bugbear, but the concern is much older. For example, it seems that it took the

I am very grateful to the participants in the Copenhagen Conference on Egalitarianism, 2004, and in the Lisbon workshop on philosophy and public policy, 2005, for extremely useful discussion of this chapter. In particular I would like to thank Nils Holtug for his written comments, which have led to a number of improvements, and to Shepley Orr for numerous discussions of related issues in economics. I am also grateful to the Arts and Humanities Research Council for their support during the final writing up of this chapter.

Adulteration of Food and Act of 1860 to stop publicans putting salt in beer and bakers chalk dust in bread in the United Kingdom.

Both defenders and critics of the free market assume that capitalists on the whole pursue their self-interest to a high degree. Where they differ is in their claims concerning the likely effects of such behaviour: the invisible hand, or the slap in the face. Here I want to argue that although individual capitalists may differ in respect of their motivations, there is a more significant difference of which we should take note. The nature of some goods is such that the market for those goods will tend to drive up quality and drive down prices, but there are other goods where the market provides no such inbuilt tendencies, and, indeed, the incentives of profit-seekers will not further the interests of consumers, especially those who are worst off. In such cases we will need to explore alternative ways of pursuing the interests of the poor, such as common provision or highly regulated markets, rather than the free market of classical economics.

2. A Market for Safety?

To illustrate the general issue I want to start by considering a remarkable passage from Thomas Schelling, which concerns the sinking of the *Titanic* and begins: 'There were enough lifeboats for first class; steerage was expected to go down with the ship. We do not tolerate that any more' (Schelling 1984: 115–16).

One reading of this passage is that it appeals to what we could call 'the equality of safety' principle: that whatever else is true, inequalities in safety are not to be tolerated. Many people may find this appealing. But why? No doubt the first-class passengers had access to bars and restaurants which were not open to steerage passengers. Some may object to this, or, at least, a society in which this is possible, and maybe with good reason. But a significant group of people, I conjecture, would be untroubled by inequalities in access to gourmet food, but troubled by inequality in access to lifeboats. Why?

Is there something special about safety as a good, or, perhaps, anything special about markets for safety? Let us explore this through another example. In 1996 I met a man in Beijing who told me that his wife and mother-in-law jointly owned a factory in southern China where they manufactured 'low-standard car parts'. Many people in China, he said, drive old cars and when parts wear out they don't want to be forced to spend good money on something that may well outlive the car. They know low-standard parts are less safe but they take this into account when they buy them, and, perhaps, in their driving habits. Everyone knows the situation. The factory next door made 'one-week shoes': they look great on a big night out, but you throw them away when you get home. The only trouble is that, in both cases, middlemen buy in bulk, rebox them as the genuine article, and sell them abroad. At the time there had been a scandal in the UK about counterfeit car parts, and I had to wonder whether this man's wife was the not entirely innocent source of the problem.

While the idea of producing and selling low-standard car parts may seem scandalous in these safety-conscious times, it is as well to pause and ask why. What is wrong with allowing the sale of low-standard car parts? There is, after all, some room for variation in standards even in highly regulated societies. There would seem to be no bar to a manufacturer offering 'deluxe standard' parts, and so, by implication, suggest that others are relatively low standard. So it is possible to offer different levels of safety performance. In fact we see this with tyres, where expensive tyres are sold on the basis of the safety improvements they offer. And indeed it is possible—or at least used to be—to buy retreads or recuts. Variation in safety standards is accepted and understood, and we do allow people to purchase different levels of safety. Hence any grand claim along the lines that 'safety has no price' or 'safety should never be for sale' flies in the face of accepted commercial practice.[1] Nevertheless, we do insist on minimum safety standards in this, as in so many areas.

One obvious reason for not allowing the sale of low-standard parts is that, as we saw, they may be passed off as high-standard. Another is that cars are a danger not only to the driver but to third parties who need protection. But to concentrate on the central issues let us assume away such market failures. Let us assume, first, that everyone has the same knowledge and no one can be deceived. This is not the assumption of perfect knowledge of classical economics, but rather an assumption of common knowledge, which I will put in terms of 'no asymmetries of knowledge', which allows symmetries of ignorance. Second, imagine there are no third-party effects. Risks are taken only for oneself. Would there remain any reason for regulating safety if people knew that their choices affected only themselves, and they knew exactly the risks they were taking?[2]

A practical problem is that often we do not have a choice. Think about rail safety. If there were ten completely independent operators running routes between London and Manchester, offering differing levels of safety at different prices, then each of us could choose our own price–safety trade-off. But there is only one system and so no chance of setting a price–safety trade-off for yourself. Where there is a monopoly, there is a monopoly safety level too. It seems that regulation is our only sensible option under such circumstances.

We have identified three ways in which real markets may fail to live up to the textbook fiction of the perfect market: asymmetries of knowledge, externalities, and

---

[1] This should be sufficient to rule out any simple version of an argument, inspired by Walzer (1983), that safety constitutes a 'separate sphere', and so safety should never be exchangeable for money.

[2] For discussion of the question of whether people should bear the costs of their own choices, see Chs. 3, 11, and 10 in this volume, by Ingmar Persson, Richard Arneson, and Andrew Williams.

monopoly. If we didn't regulate safety, there could be disastrous outcomes in which traders exploited asymmetries of knowledge and monopoly positions, and everyone ignored third-party effects. I understand China is experiencing a major breakdown in road safety. Perhaps a little more regulation of the standard of car parts wouldn't be a bad thing.

Do any of these arguments apply to safety aboard the *Titanic*? First, there is no obvious sense in which there are third-party effects. Second, the suppliers of the good did not know more about the safety of the *Titanic* than the passengers: all were equally deluded. This delusion, is, of course, a concern, but it is not clear that it is salient here. After all, even if everyone believed the *Titanic* to be unsinkable, this does not rule out the possibility of the vessel becoming ravaged by fire, and so safe exit should always have been a consideration. Finally, as different safety standards could in principle be offered, there are no monopoly effects to concern us. The source of our concern does not appear to stem from one of three standard forms of market failure.

In response, it could be said that there is something which could be called a third-party effect which may be highly disturbing. In this particular case we are offering not purely a different level of safety, but, in the case of the ship sinking, a different form of treatment by other human beings. Differential entitlement to access to lifeboats would be horrible to implement and to police in an emergency. The ship's officers would effectively be sending people to their deaths. Perhaps it is the horror of that situation, and not differential safety per se, which determines our thoughts about the case. So let us change the case. No doubt there is empirical evidence about which cabins would be safer than others, given risks of explosion, fire, and other hazards, as well as sinking. Would it be wrong for the owners of the *Titanic* to place the first-class cabins in the safest spots, and advertise that, say, they are 50 per cent safer than the steerage cabins, as well as much larger, better appointed, and so on? Does this strike us as 'off-colour'? Or suppose a train-operating company advertised that they were putting the first-class carriages in statistically the safest part of the train (at the moment they are often at the front, the most dangerous part). I predict that the press would attempt to manufacture an 'outcry' about this, and may have some success, whereas other differences are accepted without comment. I am not suggesting that the outcry is obviously correct, but there seems more resistance to market pricing of safety than to other issues of consumer choice.

The source of this resistance may be clarified by considering a modification of the *Titanic* example, in which each comfort class came with two possible levels of safety. People could pay a supplement for a higher level of safety within any class of travel. Perhaps the inequality in safety between first-class passengers would not trouble us. Those who decide to save what for them is a little money, we might think, should be entitled to make their own decisions. If this is right, then the problem is not inequality in safety per se, but rather the inevitability that the poor will suffer reduced safety if safety is left to market pricing. The concern, then, is that the inequality that will inevitably follow market pricing will, most likely, adversely affect the poor.[3]

3. Further Arguments for Regulation

We have seen a number of arguments for regulating safety based on the idea of market failure. Yet we have also noted that there is some intuition that the market for safety should be regulated to protect the poor, who inevitably will find themselves subject to higher risks, at least on average, if safety is market-priced. What lies behind this intuition?

Perhaps this is best explored by considering its denial: the argument that 'if the poor wanted better safety, then they can purchase it'. This counter rings hollow. Safety is rarely perceived as urgent as buying food or paying a utility bill. Importance and perceived urgency can easily come apart.[4] People can be tempted to skimp on safety when this is against their interests, values, or true preferences. Mandating equal safety, so it could be argued, is required in order to protect people from themselves. There are many ways in which such an argument could be developed, and there is little to be gained by going through the possible variations. The important question is whether such arguments prove too much. If an argument along these lines can be constructed to support equal safety standards, can it be stopped from spreading to equal food standards, or levels of cabin comfort? After all, better food and a better bed may also lead to a healthier, longer life. Yet many who argue for equal safety standards would not object to market provision of food of varying nutritional value, and cabins of different comfort levels.

Perhaps the answer is that while any inequality will, in some degree, undermine the idea that we are all equals, some inequalities appear to do this in a more devastating way than others. Accordingly some inequalities will be thought to be relatively trivial, and permissible as a way of allowing greater individual choice, and a richer texture of opportunities and variations within society, while others bite too deep and do too much violence to the idea of a society of equals. Arguably inequalities in health and safety are, in some cases at least, on the intolerable side, while inequalities in comfort are, on the whole, tolerable in this respect.

But why? One argument is that certain inequalities can take on a particular symbolic value. Inequalities in access to particular goods can have an enormous social

---

[3] I am grateful to Nils Holtug for clarification on this point.

[4] Anyone who has rushed to meet an urgent deadline on a trivial matter should be familiar with this distinction.

importance, even if the goods themselves are not very important. For example, racial or religious exclusion from a golf club has been used deliberately as an instrument for sending the message that the races or religions are not equal. Here, though, context is all, and the main issue is whether a group which has previously suffered from discrimination is also excluded from access to the good in question. Indeed I have argued elsewhere that in such cases levelling down can be justified (Wolff 2001, drawing on arguments from Phillips 1999).

I accept, then, the argument that differential access to goods symbolizes and encourages inequality among citizens when it correlates with a salient social distinction involving previous discrimination. Does this help in this case? I doubt it. Most thinkers within the broad egalitarian tradition accept that even in a just society some people will have more money than others. But if those who are richer than others are not permitted to purchase things that the poor cannot also buy, then this is a way of saying that inequalities in holdings of wealth or income are not permitted after all. Excluding access to goods on grounds of relative poverty is a natural consequence of differential wealth and income and not a form of arbitrary discrimination.

The only other 'symbolic' argument I can think of is that certain goods are considered so important that differential access to them is considered unacceptable, even if the consequences would be reasonably favourable. This may well explain why John Stuart Mill's proposal for plural votes for the wealthy or educated, to save the poor from their own lack of understanding of economics, has attracted no support. Having the same say as others in the electoral process is considered of extreme symbolic significance. Yet to say that safety has such a precious status seems to me in need of justification both conceptually (what is the argument?) and empirically (what is the evidence?). I do not wish to assert that there is nothing to the case, for it may have some plausibility. Yet to rest with such an assertion would be an unsatisfying end point.

4. Difficulties with Regulation

We have been considering the proposition that equality of safety is required to protect the poor. Yet some will argue that this gets things backwards. In general, refusing to allow people to make their own consumption decisions about safety is irrational, and against everyone's interests. Insisting that everyone purchases the same level can be argued to be especially unfair to those who put a lower price on safety—again most likely the poor—who may generally prefer to take greater risks in order to have more to spend on other things. And, equally, it may be unfair to those who would want to pay more. Like all averaging strategies, it will exactly satisfy only a very few. Consequently, from an egalitarian point of view it seems possible to argue that while regulation is a strategy designed to help the poor, in the sense of protecting their safety, it may, in one important sense, actually make them worse off. Hence, unless regulation is backed by subsidy, it looks far less attractive from an egalitarian point of view.

5. The Plot Thickens

It seems hard, then, to find arguments to support the 'equality of safety' principle which appeared to underlie Schelling's argument. However, appearances can be deceptive, as we see when we read how Schelling continues the passage: 'Those who want to risk their lives at sea and cannot afford a safe ship should perhaps not be denied the opportunity to entrust themselves to a cheaper ship without lifeboats; but if some people cannot afford the price of passage with lifeboats, and some people can, they should not travel on the same ship' (Schelling 1984: 115–16).

Amazingly, then, the concern Schelling is reporting seems not to be with minimum safety standards, or equal safety standards within society, but simply equal safety standards within a tightly defined group. And remember that in the particular case Schelling describes we are talking about equality within one of the most status conscious sub-populations there has ever been; the passengers on the *Titanic* on its maiden journey.

What arguments can be made to support the idea that equality should obtain within a group but that equality between groups is less important? One argument appeals to the instrumental benefits of a uniform safety standard. One version of this points to the negative effects of differential standards: the bitterness and resentment it may cause. This is rather like the policy that children on a school trip should all have the same amount of spending money. Furthermore, it doesn't seem to matter if children on a different trip all have more: equality within the group is the thing. The idea, presumably, is that if some children within the group have more to spend than others, this could cause jealousy, arguments, bitterness, division, and resentment, all of which are undesirable in a school trip, part of the point of which is to encourage solidarity and a sense of a group ethos. Perhaps as adults we become used to the idea of differential spending power, but differential provision for our safety may well stir up a host of undesirable side-effects.

Now although there may be truth in these psychological claims, arguments from envy, and social division, need to be handled carefully. Although I would not agree with those who say that issues of envy should always be irrelevant to questions of justice, I would suggest that unless the envy is justified on the grounds of independent injustice, the proper response may well be therapy rather than levelling down.

Psychological arguments against inequality seem not to take us very far. Rather, a positive argument for equality is what we seek.

6. Risk and Common Interests

A second instrumental argument for equality, however, seems to me far stronger. Here it is argued that uniform safety standards are required for the sake of the worst off in a much more direct way. The argument is that the poor will be safer in a vessel in which no one has access to a lifeboat than in a vessel in which only some have access. The general point can be made by means of John Adams's theory of risk compensation, which says that as an individual's environment becomes known to be safer, that individual will tend to change her behaviour, maintaining a relatively constant rate of risk, consuming safety improvements as performance benefits (Adams 1995). Hence, if the environment becomes safer for those in control, and their decisions impose risks on others for whom the environment has not changed, then these others will find themselves facing bigger risks. Consider Adams's example of seatbelts in cars. Adams claims that the initial effect of making seatbelts compulsory for car drivers was to increase the number of passenger deaths (1995: 121 ff.). Hence, with respect to cars, there is good reason to insist that all should wear seatbelts or none, or all but the driver, but certainly not the driver and no one else. In the case of the *Titanic*, if the captain was assured of a place in the lifeboat, or even that the people he most cared about were assured of their place, then he may well have steered a riskier course than otherwise. This is an analogue to the familiar problem of 'moral hazard' in insurance, reducing people's incentives to take care. This may well be why the captain is supposed to go down with the ship, or, at least, be the last one off.

There are, thus, cases, where one person's fate is intrinsically connected with another person's decisions. Could it be that the only way to ensure that everyone's interests are properly taken into account is to give everyone the same interests? Sometimes we need to make it the case that, either literally or metaphorically, we are all in the same boat: and we so will all be affected in the same way by the decisions of some. Accordingly, the underlying idea that some inequalities do more than others to undermine the idea of society as an association of equals receives a straightforward interpretation. It is that in some cases inequality will lead to the interests of some being undervalued or even ignored. In general these will include cases where a single, central decision needs to be made which will impact on all the members of a group.

It has often been noted that societies, like the United Kingdom, which allow private health and private schooling in the name of freedom of choice have not paid proper attention to the importance of creating common interests: setting up structures which force decision-makers to take account of everyone's interests if they take account of anyone's. If decision-makers and the rich are not using public services, then those who do must rely on the goodwill and beneficence of the wealthy and powerful. As many commentators have noticed, these are fragile motivations. It would be much better for the poor if the pursuit of the self-interest of the rich benefited the poor too. Hence, there is a Rawlsian argument for what might look like levelling down but what, in certain cases, actually improves the situation of the worst off: the abolition of private schooling and health care.

If, however, this 'common interests' argument is to do the work we need, explaining why our attitude to lifeboats on the *Titanic* is different from our attitude to its restaurants, then it must also be the case that variation in food standards will not lead to a significant falling off in nutrition for the poor. Here, I think, it could be argued that variation in food standards is better for the poor, as it allows them to tailor their provision to their preferences, rather than being forced to purchase better, and so probably more expensive, food when they would rather spend the money on something else. However, we have already encountered this argument before, as a defence of allowing a diversity of safety standards. What is the difference?

7. The Problem of 'Slow-Release' Goods

To understand the difference it is important to contrast two different decision-making contexts. In one there is a single decision to be made, which may be of huge consequence, with only limited possibility of correction, or recovery, if any. In the other there are many small decisions, none of them disastrous if they go wrong, and a bad strategy—within limits—is fairly easily reversed by changing one's policy for the future. In this latter case freedom of choice may well help the worse off. Recall a remark made earlier: that the poor do better when the rich have an incentive to make decisions that also help the poor. This, we noted, is the classic defence of the free market: one can only enrich oneself by providing things that others want to buy. Hence a market, at least one with proper information flows (which in this context means the possibility of learning by experience and acting on that knowledge), no third-party effects, and no entry barriers, will help the poor, as many libertarians have argued, trying to snatch the Rawlsian ground from the interventionists. But, if so, then, once again, why not a market in safety?

Here we must notice that the market for safety—and for health and schools—fails to meet the conditions just set out for where the market works best: numerous small decisions, little potential for disaster, and the possibility of learning by experience and changing strategy without cost. These are the conditions of the ideal markets of the 'private vices public virtues' textbook; what we can call fluid markets. By contrast, where one is purchasing schooling, or health or safety, or, indeed, many financial products such as pension schemes, markets are quite different. In fluid markets even relatively impoverished consumers have the power to harness the rich's self-interest, for they can defect if they don't like what is on offer, and the possibility of learning by experience and defection is a good remedy for asymmetries in knowledge. By contrast, where you are purchasing what we could call a 'slow-release' good, this is much less the case. A standard slow-release good is here understood as a good where consumption is deferred over time, where payment is either upfront or legally binding over time, and where to change one's decision is costly. A 'high-fidelity slow-release good' has one additional feature: that the quality of the good remains under the influence of the supplier between the time it is purchased and the time it is consumed.[5] A savings plan, your safety on a voyage, and an education for your children, are all of this nature. In this case, once your decision is made, you are stuck with it for some time, unless you are prepared to pay various types of penalty, and if it goes badly you might not have a second chance. And it might go badly because of the action or inaction of the supplier. You can end up with something you did not think you were buying. Regulation then becomes very much a live issue.

To see the importance of context, consider two possibilities aboard the *Titanic* for providing food. First, a complete 'meal plan' is purchased with one's ticket, with no possibility for change, and you are simply provided with whatever is chosen as the dish of the day. Here food is treated as a high-fidelity slow-release good. Second, numerous restaurants operate, all run as competing, profit-maximising, private concerns in a fluid market. In the first case there may be reasons for wanting there to be only one meal plan, and therefore for finding oneself eating the same food as those who are deciding what food is to be made available, or at least eating the same food as those they wish to impress. Otherwise, leaving aside long-term reputational effects, which may or may not be effective, what incentive is there for the food suppliers to keep up the standards? Yet it would be odd to want to move to such a situation if one was in the genuine free market, with competition for one's business and a wide range of food choices. Here those who supply the food have an incentive to make sure it is of a good standard if they want to be able to sell you anything tomorrow. It seems clear, then, that market pricing suits some contexts of delivery, while generating common interests suits others. Generally, safety falls on the latter side, as it is hard to see how to arrange fluid markets in safety, and food, at least above a threshold, falls on the former (keeping in mind the importance of information flows).

---

[5] The term 'high fidelity' is inspired by the slogan of the Lloyd's of London insurance market: 'utmost good faith'; something, as it turned out, many insiders exploited ruthlessly.

Suppose we are convinced that there are times when consumers need producers and suppliers to be consumers of their own products, as the only way of ensuring that quality standards are maintained. Is it not the case that the market can supply this itself? Why shouldn't a firm advertise that all its executives use its products. Indeed this is a familiar tactic. However, first, we don't know for sure that they are, even if they say they are. Second, we don't know whether they rely on the product in the way others might. A director of a pension company may well spread risk in a way no other customer could afford, for example. Hence, at a minimum, high regulation seems appropriate. In essence my argument is that those who want the best for the worse off should, in some cases at least, be libertarians if it is appropriate to create fluid markets and old-fashioned socialists when high-fidelity slow-release goods are in question.

8. Conclusion

The *Titanic* puzzle allows us to bring out a distinctive type of market failure: where the supplier's pursuit of self-interest may, contrary to orthodoxy, harm the interests of consumers. This will particularly be the case with regard to what have here been called 'high-fidelity slow-release goods' which are reasonably common and familiar, if rarely isolated as a special category. The solution suggested here is, in effect, to create common interests by forcing suppliers to consume their own products. Of course, this is not going to suit all cases. But where it does apply, then we can have greater assurance that private vices will bring about public virtues over a wider range of goods.

References

ADAMS, J. (1995), *Risk* (London: UCL Press).

PHILLIPS, A. (1999), *Which Equalities Matter?* (Oxford: Polity Press).

SCHELLING, T. C. (1984), 'The Life You Save May Be Your Own', in Schelling, *Choice and Consequence* (Cambridge, Mass.: Harvard University Press), 113–46.

SMITH, A. (1904), *The Wealth of Nations*, 5th edn. (London: Methuen).

WALZER, M. (1983), *Spheres of Justice* (New York: Basic Books).

WOLFF, J. (2001), 'Levelling Down', in K. Dowding, J. Hughes, and H. Margetts (eds.), *Challenges to Democracy: The PSA Yearbook 2000* (London: Palgrave), 18–32.

13

The 'What' and the 'How' of Distributive Justice and Health

Susan Hurley

1. Introduction

How does health figure into distributive justice? Is health special among the goods relevant to justice? Does it have a special status or require special treatment, or should it be factored into a general theory of distributive justice in the same way as many other goods? Are differences between people with respect to health and access to health care on a par with differences in other goods? Do the same distributive requirements apply to health and health care as to other goods?

Theories of distributive justice tell us *what* goods justice is concerned with the distribution of, and *how* justice requires them to be distributed. On the 'what' question, we can distinguish concern with distribution of welfare (or utility) from concern with distribution of resources (such as income). We usually think of individual welfare as increasing with the level of resources commanded, reflecting preferences about those resources. On the 'how' question, we can distinguish the aim to distribute relevant goods equally from the aim to distribute them so as to give priority to improving the position of the worse off. If the worse off are better off in a situation of inequality than they'd be in a situation of equality, which would be more just?

Together, the welfare—resources distinction and the equality—priority distinction generate a framework of four broad ways of understanding distributive justice: in terms of equality of welfare or resources, or in terms of giving priority to improving the welfare levels or the resource levels of worse-off members of society. I use this framework to survey and analyze issues about the role of health in distributive justice, considering the relationships of health to welfare and to resources, and to the rationales for being concerned with equality and with priority.[1] Is health fungible in relation to other goods that are the concern of distributive justice? Does distributive justice require the same pattern of distribution of health as of other goods? My main aim is not to argue for a substantive thesis, but to provide part of an analytical framework for addressing these questions. I conclude that stronger reasons for treating health as special emerge from considering how we should distribute than from considering what we should distribute.

2. The 'What' Question

2.1. Welfare and Health

Begin with the 'what' question. On one view, distributive justice is ultimately concerned with welfare. It's an attractive thought that each person's welfare matters just as much as any other's, the peasant's as much as the aristocrat's. There should be no favoritism: we shouldn't treat a given benefit to one person as more important than an equal or greater benefit to another.

This thought is one motivation for utilitarianism. According to utilitarianism, you should allocate each unit of resource to the person who will get the most welfare from it. To allocate a unit of resource to someone who will get less additional welfare from it than someone else would have treats the former's welfare as more important than the latter's. Allocating each unit of resource to the person who gets the most welfare from it maximizes total welfare. In this way the nonfavoritism ideal can motivate the aim to maximize welfare.

However, this way of thinking has unattractive implications concerning some unhealthy or disabled persons. Consider someone who is blind and, to be mobile, maintains a guide dog. Or someone who needs regular dialysis. It seems that many such persons would get less welfare from any given allocation of income than would someone bursting with health. A substantial part of a resource allocation to an unwell or disabled person may have to be spent raising her to a minimal level of welfare, which healthy persons take for granted: on buying food for the guide dog, or on dialysis. If so, a healthy person will get more extra welfare from each additional unit of income allocated to her than would an unhealthy or disabled person. It seems that health usually generates welfare out of resources more efficiently than lack of health.

---

[1] This survey and analysis are partial, since there are many other answers to the 'what' and 'how' questions, and other views about justice, such as libertarian views and views that urge the maximization of welfare or of resources, which are not included in this schema.

But utilitarianism treats health conditions, along with others, merely as means to more or less welfare. Thus the utilitarian aim, to allocate each unit of resource where it will produce the most welfare, will direct resources away from the unhealthy and disabled in favor of the healthy, to the extent the healthy are more efficient generators of welfare. As a result, the unhealthy and disabled achieve lower total levels of both resources and welfare than do the healthy (Sen 1982).

This result conflicts with prevalent intuitions about just resource allocations. If the welfare benefits in question are small, or if a much greater welfare benefit could be provided to the healthy than to the unwell, many people do favor allocations that benefit the healthy and maximize welfare. However, where substantial benefits are in question and equal welfare benefits could be provided to the healthy and the unwell, many think we should allocate resources to the unwell. Many would favor the unwell even if a somewhat greater welfare benefit could be provided to the better off (Daniels and Sabin 1997: 320). Allocations that increase the welfare of the unwell or disabled are in some cases regarded as more important or urgent than allocations that increase the welfare of the healthy, even if the former do not maximize welfare.

If in some cases we give extra weight to the welfare of the unwell, does this suggest that there is something special about welfare derived from health, or about lack of welfare derived from lack of health? So far, no. Health considerations merely illustrate a general conflict between welfare maximization and equity. As far as anything said so far goes, lack of health per se is not of special concern for justice, but rather illustrates a feature that is of special concern: the fact that some persons generate welfare less efficiently than others, so that welfare maximization does not treat them equitably. There is no reason yet to suppose that justice cares about the distribution of health or health care per se, rather than of welfare and/or resources more generally.

2.2. Nonfavoritism and Adaptability

We can think about the conflict between welfare maximizing and justice in terms of different types of resource. Instead of allocations of income, consider allocations of time, or life-years. Suppose a healthy person is living at a higher level of welfare than a disabled person of the same age whose condition is stable but incurable; we face a choice between extending the life of the healthy person or that of the disabled person by a given amount. It would maximize welfare to allocate life-years to the healthy rather than the disabled. Yet to allocate life-years to the healthy purely on this basis again seems unjust. Why?

One answer adheres to the nonfavoritism ideal and the aim to maximize welfare, but disputes the assumption that disability results in lower welfare levels. Perhaps this assumption reflects disparaging prejudices about disability that we should challenge, prejudices in tension with the attractive nonfavoritism ideal that motivates the aim to maximize welfare. On this view, the nonfavoritism ideal requires us to take account of the creditable adaptability of preferences and not simply to assume that the unhealthy and disabled don't have as much capacity for welfare as the healthy.

People who actually live with health conditions tend to regard them as less bad than do members of the public, their own families, or the health care professions (Murray 1996: 29 ff.). While at first a disability may reduce someone's welfare dramatically, over time attitudes to disability may adapt. Someone's preference for his pre-disabled state may become less intense; his welfare level and capacity for further welfare may rise although his disability is still present (Brock 1993: 125–6). People can learn to cope with adversity and even to take pride in and identify with their special condition, the community of others who share it, and their accomplishments and insights in adapting to it.

The point about adaptability can be connected with the nonfavoritism ideal as follows: it is inequitable to allocate life-years to the healthy, not for reasons of equality that presuppose that the disabled are worse off, but because of the disparaging and prejudiced way it presupposes that the disabled must have a reduced capacity for welfare per unit of resource. The well-adapted disabled person may rightly believe that additional life years would produce as much extra welfare for him as for his nondisabled counterpart. A policy for distributing medical resources that assumes otherwise fails to give disabled people in general the credit and respect they deserve and treats the welfare of the disabled as substandard. This view does not reject the aim to maximize welfare. Rather, it reasserts the nonfavoritism ideal that motivates the aim to maximize welfare, with a new twist. It insists that welfare of disabled persons matters as much as that of healthy persons, and that to respect this point we must take account of the general adaptability of preferences. The disabled and unhealthy should not generally be regarded as inefficient generators of utility who subsist at lower levels of welfare for any given level of resources allocated to them. The point is not simply that there will be individual exceptions to the generalization that healthy people have more welfare than disabled. Rather, the generalization is false, given adaptability. The truth of this claim is entirely compatible with utility maximization.

This perspective is attractive when we are thinking about welfare that would result from extending the life of a permanently disabled person, under a welfare-maximizing aim. But consider how it would apply when we think also about welfare that would result from improving life, in cases where it is possible to remove or reduce a disability. Suppose it is possible for a disabled person to adapt so that he is at the same level of welfare as nondisabled persons, and would gain as much welfare from a given life extension as a nondisabled person would. But now suppose it becomes possible to remove his disability. Surely we want to allow that there is some reason to do so. Is this a reason of welfare? If his welfare is improved by removing his disability, then he must now be at a higher level of welfare than the nondisabled person. But if so, then welfare maximization will now favor extending the life of the restored, formerly disabled person over extending the life of the continuously healthy person. The ideal of nonfavoritism is now compromised in the other direction, on the assumption that removing a disability increases welfare.

Perhaps the formerly disabled person will likely readapt to his restored state and return to a 'normal' level of welfare. Then the welfare-maximizing reason to favor life extensions for him rather than the continuously healthy will be short-lived, and the compromise to the nonfavoritism ideal only transient. However, now the assumption that removing a disability increases welfare is compromised. Owing to readaptation, the increase in welfare resulting from removing the disability will be similarly short-lived. Thus the welfare-maximizing reason to remove the disability is weakened.

Intuitively, we recognize a strong reason to reduce or remove a disability, and we adhere to the nonfavoritism ideal for life extensions. But we have seen that it is difficult to combine these two positions if we stick to a welfare-maximizing aim that treats health conditions merely as means to more or less welfare.

2.3. Equality of Welfare and Adaptability

Return to this question: Why is it unjust automatically to favor life extensions for the healthy as opposed to the unhealthy or disabled? The first answer adhered to the nonfavoritism ideal that motivates the welfare-maximizing aim, but it insisted it should be understood so as to take account of the adaptability of preferences. A second, different answer rejects the aim to maximize welfare and appeals instead to equality: by allocating life-years to the disabled instead, we would move toward greater equality of welfare levels between the disabled and the healthy. This is an application of a more general view, which holds that justice requires us to try to equalize the welfare levels of different people.

This view corrects one defect of the aim to maximize welfare. It does not shift resources away from inefficient generators of welfare, but toward them. To equalize welfare levels, we should allocate enough extra resources to people who generate welfare inefficiently to bring them up to the same welfare level as others. If many unhealthy or disabled people fall into this category, we should compensate them with extra resources, for purposes of both extending life and improving life.

However, this assumption can again be disputed on grounds of adaptability. We should not assume that the unhealthy or disabled generally subsist at lower levels of welfare, given the widespread tendency to adapt to adversity. How does this point affect the welfare-equalizing reason to favor the unhealthy or disabled? To the extent the well-adapted disabled person's welfare approaches the 'normal' levels of welfare of a nondisabled person, the welfare-equalizing rationale for directing extra resources to the disabled is weakened or limited. If a well-adapted disabled person is at the same welfare level as a nondisabled person, then equality of welfare does not allocate extra resources to removing his disability.[2] If he is no worse off than others as a result of adapting, any preference for treatment he may nevertheless have won't especially concern welfare egalitarianism, even if satisfying it would raise his welfare.

It may be replied that there is still inequality of welfare over whole lifetimes, taking into account the initial, low-welfare period of disability, prior to adaptation. If this lifetime inequality demands remedy, even after adaptation, then there may still be a welfare-equalizing reason to allocate extra resources to removing disability.

Nevertheless, adaptation to disability at least limits the welfare-equalizing rationale for removing disabilities. This is enough to generate a powerful objection to the view that justice requires us to equalize the welfare levels of different people. The objection is that, intuitively, justice requires us to allocate extra resources to the disabled to make it possible to reduce or remove their disabilities, *regardless* of whether their preferences have adapted to their disabilities and their welfare increased to normal levels. (*Not*, of course, to force such treatment on them regardless of their own preferences about it!) On this view, justice requires we offer treatment and let the disabled person choose whether to accept it; this requirement is not weakened or limited by adaptation that raises their welfare levels to those of nondisabled persons. Therefore, this requirement of justice is not captured by the aim to equalize welfare.

Arguments against understanding justice in terms of equality of welfare invoke related examples, such as the case of Tiny Tim from Dickens's *A Christmas Carol*. The aim to equalize welfare would supposedly give more resources to the disabled, to raise them to the same level of welfare as others. But Tiny Tim has such a positive outlook and cheerful disposition that he is already at a higher level of welfare than most people, despite being disabled. If justice requires that we equalize welfare, it would not require us to compensate Tiny Tim for his disability by giving him more resources. Since Tiny Tim is already so well off, the aim to equalize welfare will regard his disability per se as irrelevant to justice. But surely it is not irrelevant. And Tiny Tim's good cheer does not dilute the requirement of just compensation for disability at all. Therefore, justice cannot be understood in terms of equality of welfare (Dworkin 1981*b*).

How can proper respect for the adaptability of people to their health conditions be combined with recognition that in many cases there are obligations of justice to allocate extra resources to the disabled and the unwell, which are not weakened or limited by adaptation? One general response to this question moves away from welfare-based views of distributive justice altogether. The difficulties adaptability presents,

---

[2] I assume a preference-based account of welfare. Including health in an objective list account of welfare would limit the extent to which welfare adaptation occurs and hence the relevance of the point in the text.

whether on a welfare-maximizing or a welfare-equalizing approach, stem from the assumption that what matters is merely how a health condition, or its treatment, affects someone's welfare, that health is merely a means to the end of welfare, which is what really concerns distributive justice. But on reflection, adaptability itself calls this assumption into question.

When someone adapts to her health condition, the function that describes her capacity to generate welfare from resources changes. Is this general information about relations between welfare and resources adequate to address questions about distributive justice and health? In the cases we have considered, such changes do not, intuitively, demand changes in the just allocation of resources available to reduce or remove disabilities. This point could be strengthened into the general claim that, if someone adapts to her disability, she should not receive either more resources or fewer resources just on account of her adapted welfare levels. (However, a resultant depression might count as a further disability to which resources should be addressed.) On this view, the ways someone's welfare levels change as a result of adaptation to a health condition are in an important sense down to her. If she cannot pull herself out of self-pity even with our help, that does not dilute our obligation to help. But if she can do so and find new ways of flourishing even without our help, like Tiny Tim, the more power to her; we are not let off the hook by her success either. She is responsible for what she makes of her condition. Our obligation is to address her condition, not what she makes of it.

Compare the first *nonfavoritism reading* of the importance of adaptability with this second reading. The first reading says: the assumption that the disabled or unhealthy have a lower capacity for welfare is a prejudice, just as was the assumption that peasants have a lower capacity for welfare. The second, *responsibility reading* says: someone's preferences and hence his capacities for welfare in various possible conditions, including health conditions, are her own responsibility. Such capacities vary among the disabled and the unhealthy just as they do among the healthy. Out of proper respect for the disabled and unhealthy as responsible persons, justice should be concerned not with how much welfare someone can generate from her health condition, whatever it is, but rather with that condition itself. The disabled and unhealthy have a call on us, as a matter of justice, for help addressed to their condition rather than to their levels of welfare.

If we accept the second view, does this support the view that health is special? Not yet. If we reject welfare-based approaches, then we will not treat health as merely a means to welfare, a fungible source of welfare on a par with any other potential source, to be factored into a general theory of justice along with other sources of welfare. But we still have various options. Here are some signposts to what follows.

One possibility is that justice should be understood in terms of resources rather than welfare, where health conditions are included under an extended sense of 'resources'. For example, we could adopt a general view of justice as requiring equality of resources rather than welfare (Dworkin 1981a). We could then treat *health as a kind of internal resource*, and factor it in with other resources in an appropriate way, but still not give health any special status or role in that account. Health and health care would not be insulated from competition with other goods (Dworkin 1993).

A second possibility is that health conditions are indeed special, and demand a special status or role within a theory of justice. For example, health may be regarded not as a resource in principle on a par with other resources, but as playing a *special role in establishing fair equality of opportunity* (Daniels 1985; cf. Walzer 1983 on the role of health in complex equality).

A third possibility is that justice should be understood in terms of luck and responsibility. For example, we could adopt a general view of justice as tolerating only inequalities for which people are responsible, not inequalities that are a matter of luck, regardless of whether they are inequalities of welfare or resources (Cohen 1989; Roemer 1996). This view would be concerned not just with the ways in which health conditions affect people's opportunities for other goods, but also with how people choose to respond to their opportunities for health itself. On this view, it is unjust for someone to be poor because he was born blind and so had many fewer opportunities for reasonably paid employment, but it is not unjust if someone is ill because he freely chose to ruin his health for the sake of ephemeral pleasures (though of course there may be other reasons than reasons of justice to help such a person). On such a view, *health conditions, like other advantages and disadvantages, would be of concern to distributive justice only to the extent that people are not responsible for them* (Roemer 1993, 1995, 1996). Again, health and health care per se would not have any special status.

I'll consider these possibilities in turn (there are other possibilities as well, but I'll stick to these). For the time being let's continue to think about justice in egalitarian rather than prioritarian terms. Later I'll shift from the 'what' to the 'how' question, and consider the issue of whether we should think about justice in terms of equality, or rather in terms of giving priority to benefits to those who are worse off, even if that involves inequality.

2.4. Health Conditions Versus Expensive Tastes

The welfare-equalizing approach solves one problem with welfare-maximizing approaches, but gives rise to other problems. Equalizing welfare does compensate those who generate welfare inefficiently, including any unhealthy or disabled persons in this category. However, the distinction between efficiency and inefficiency at generating welfare cuts across the distinction between good and poor health conditions.

On the one hand, as we've seen, many people who are unhealthy or disabled generate welfare efficiently despite their health conditions, to their credit. Equality of welfare fails to compensate such persons for their poor health conditions. Thus, for example, the well-adapted disabled person is penalized relative to the poorly adapted one.

On the other hand, many persons in good health conditions nevertheless generate welfare inefficiently: consider someone with expensive tastes who is miserable without champagne and caviar every day. Equality of welfare will not distinguish such persons from those whose welfare-inefficiency is due to disability or ill health.[3] It will compensate both. But surely it is reasonable to regard ourselves as obliged by justice to provide a blind person with extra resources to feed his guide dog, but not similarly obliged to provide someone with expensive tastes with extra resources for champagne and caviar. Intuitively, someone's tastes are his own business, and do not make a call on justice.

Because the welfare-equalizing approach looks only at welfare, it distinguishes cases that should not be distinguished and fails to distinguish those that should be. Health conditions are special at least in the sense that they should not be conceived merely as sources of more or less welfare, on a par with other determinants of welfare such as tastes. What alternative approach will draw the right distinctions between health conditions and mere tastes? The three positions I shall now proceed to canvass, those of Ronald Dworkin, Norman Daniels, and John Roemer, can be regarded as different ways of answering this question.

2.5. Equality of Resources and Disabilities

One prominent answer draws a fundamental distinction between welfare and resources, and claims that *what* justice requires us to equalize is resources, not welfare (Dworkin 1981a, b). The welfare–resources distinction generalizes some contrasts I have already drawn.

Welfare is a matter of the satisfaction of an individual's preferences and ambitions. These are down to the person herself, and do not make a call on justice. The difference between someone whose preferences and ambitions are well adapted to his disability and someone whose preferences and ambitions are not so adapted to his similar disability does not make it just to compensate only the poorly adapted person. Each person should be treated as responsible for his preferences and ambitions, as free to make what he will from his circumstances, against a background of fair equality of resources.

Resources, by contrast, are a matter of someone's endowments and the circumstances she finds herself in. Someone born into a rich and prominent family or

---

[3] This point does not apply to equality of opportunity for welfare views (see below), but I regard the 'what' these views aim to equalize as luck, not welfare.

highly gifted has to that extent valuable endowments, which someone born into poor and obscure circumstances, or without any special gifts, lacks. The former person has on this account greater resources than the latter. Similarly, someone born with normal vision and good health has a valuable endowment and to that extent has greater resources than someone born blind or susceptible to major health problems. Such endowments are like different internal circumstances people find themselves in. They are not down to the people themselves, the way their different preferences and ambitions are.

Dworkin distinguishes inequalities of welfare that result from people's different preferences or tastes or ambitions, from inequalities of resources, or from differences in circumstances or endowments. He conceives justice as requiring equality of resources, but not equality of welfare. For example, to have expensive tastes is to have a welfare deficit relative to someone with less expensive tastes, other things equal. Nevertheless, someone's expensive tastes are down to him and do not in themselves make a call on justice. Similarly, if people who have the same endowments have different preferences and ambitions and accordingly make different choices in life that lead to their being better or worse off, the Dworkinian aim to equalize resources will leave such inequalities alone. Some people may choose to work hard and get rich, while others take lots of leisure and don't get rich. Some may assiduously avoid risks and insure heavily against risk, while others may blithely run risks and fail to insure. To the extent the resulting differences reflect differing preferences and ambitions, they are not unjust.

Another way to express the aim of equality of resources is in terms of the distinction between brute luck and option luck. Some people choose to take risks. Dworkin regards the outcome of a gamble you chose to take, against a background of a fair initial distribution of resources, as down to you. Suppose you risk a large portion of your fair share of resources by backing an innovative new business. If it had succeeded, you would have been rich. But it fails. Or suppose you decide not to bother to take out household insurance because you'd rather put the money into a new sound system, and your house burns down. Or suppose the risk you run in choosing to climb dangerous mountains on your holidays without adequate medical insurance turns out badly, and you fall and end up seriously disabled. These are examples of bad luck of a kind, but it flows at least partly from your choices, not from your endowments. To that extent, it is bad option luck. This should be distinguished from bad brute luck, like being born blind. In principle, Dworkin's equality of resources does not aim to compensate for bad option luck, only for bad brute luck. Equality is judged from an *ex ante* rather than an *ex post* perspective. How well off you turn out to be as a result of your own preferences and choices, including your choices to gamble, is your own business. In practice, of course, it is difficult to disentangle brute luck and option luck.

Dworkin develops the idea of internal resources and incorporates it into his conception of equality of resources. His theoretical conception of resources includes not just external goods like income, which can be redistributed, but also natural endowments like talents and normal mobility and vision, which may not be possible to redistribute per se. Disabilities and talents are treated symmetrically, as opposites: disabilities count as negative internal resources, while talents count as positive internal resources. To be born disabled or susceptible to major health problems is to have an internal resource deficit that does make a call on justice. External health care resources may be able to reduce this internal resource deficit, to cure or alleviate the poor health condition. But even if no reduction in an internal health-related resource deficit is possible, external resources can be redistributed to compensate for it. However, internal resources do not include people's tastes, ambitions, or preferences. Nor should they strictly include health conditions or disabilities that represent option luck: that are the clear result of freely chosen risks.

What would it be to neutralize inequalities that result from brute luck in internal endowments, such as being born disabled or talented? Dworkin models what equality of resources requires in terms of an imaginary insurance market, in which people who do not know the market value of their own personal internal resources could buy insurance against turning out to be under-endowed with internal resources. The question then becomes: At what levels would people insure? Presumably, they would insure against very bad brute luck, but not against the lack of very good brute luck. It would be irrational to insure against lacking the talent of a Maria Callas; the premiums would be prohibitive and would preempt too many other opportunities in life. But it probably would be rational to insure against bad brute luck in being disabled in various ways. Dworkin suggests that the hypothetical insurance premiums people would pay to insure against being disabled to various degrees can be thought of as modeling the tax payments people make under a progressive tax system.

2.6. Health: One Resource Among Others?

The conception of health as a kind of internal resource can be seen as emerging from criticism of resource-based approaches to justice that include only external, not internal, resources. However, once this conception is in place, and disabilities are seen as at one end of a spectrum with talents at the other end, it becomes difficult to defend the view that health is special. Indeed, Dworkin argues that health and health care cannot rationally be insulated from other resources in a separate sphere of justice, but rather must be integrated into competition with other goods (Dworkin 1993). By contrast, Daniels resists factoring health-related resources into a resource-based theory of justice along with other resources, and argues that they are indeed special (Daniels 1985).

Consider the pressures on resource-based conceptions of justice to 'go internal'. John Rawls (1971) frames his resource-based theory of justice in terms of primary goods, such as income and wealth, liberty, and the social bases of self-respect. He understands primary goods as universal means to whatever your ends may be, the resources that everyone needs to satisfy her own preferences and ambitions. The primary goods framework treats it as my own business, not the business of justice, if my preferences and ambitions are cheap or expensive to satisfy. However, it ignores disabilities and poor health along with expensive tastes (Sen 1982). It would not, for example, compensate a blind person for being unable to do the same things as a sighted person with the same income by giving him extra income.[4]

The idea of internal resources emerges naturally in response to this objection. After all, primary goods are understood to be universal means to whatever your ends happen to be. Normal vision and mobility and good health, as well as external resources such as health care, meet this description. As we have seen, if we allow the concept of resources to extend in this way to internal resources, then disease and disability count as negative resources. Then the aim to equalize resources now directs us to direct further resources to those with diseases and disabilities, regardless of whether their preferences have adapted to their health conditions, but not to compensate those with expensive tastes. External health care resources may either reduce the internal deficit or compensate for it, or both.

Daniels considers but rejects this way of incorporating a concern with health into Rawls's theory of distributive justice. Rawls's theory is, as Daniel notes, idealized to apply to 'normal, active' persons: 'In effect, there is no distributive theory for health care because no one is sick' (Daniels 1985: 43). How should Rawls's theory be extended to cover justice in health care? If this is done by extending the understanding of primary goods to include health-related resources, several related problems arise. There are difficult questions about how to weight specifically health-related primary goods against others, such as income, wealth, and various freedoms and powers. In the context of Rawls's theory in particular, which gives priority to benefiting the worst off, the potentially bottomless pit of health care costs creates a danger that excessive resources might be drained into caring for or compensating those with extreme health problems, to an extent that would reduce society at large to poverty (Daniels 1985: 44; Arrow 1973: 251).

In more general terms, resource-based theories of distributive justice face questions about whether health-related resources are fungible in relation to resources of other kinds, or instead raise special issues of justice. Dworkin argues that the ancient view that treated health as the most important of all goods, to be given priority and insulated from competition with other goods, is no longer credible. In the past, there

---

[4] These remarks apply to Rawls's position in *A Theory of Justice*, not his later position.

was not much of a gap between this ideal and medical possibility. But modern medical technology, which produces more and more ways to spend large sums on health care, puts this ideal to the test and reveals it as preposterous. Any community that really gave health priority over other values might give people marginally longer lives, but the opportunity cost of doing so in terms of all other resources would reduce these lives to a level barely worth living (Dworkin 1993: 886).

Dworkin denies that health-related resources should be insulated in a separate sphere of justice or given priority over other goods. Rather, they should be integrated into competition with other goods. He proposes to extend his resource-based theory of distributive justice explicitly to health-related resources in accordance with his general conception of social justice, which assigns to 'individuals responsibility for making ethical choices for their own lives against a background of competent information and a fair initial distribution of resources' (Dworkin 1993: 893). More specifically, social decisions about the total quantity and the distribution of health care should aim to match the hypothetical choices people would make for themselves, under certain idealized conditions, about which risks to run and which to insure against, and how risks of one kind trade off against risks of another.

The idealized conditions Dworkin proposes are three. First, the economic structure provides fair equality in the initial distribution of resources. What this requires is open to different interpretations. On Dworkin's own conception of equality of resources, as we have seen, this means that resources are divided equally and then each person is free in principle to spend those resources designing a life that he or she believes appropriate. The resulting inequalities of money or goods are compatible with equality of resources in his theoretical sense, since they will flow from the choices people have made as to how to use their fair allocation of resources in pursuing a life that is right for them. Second, the general public has state-of-the-art medical knowledge. Third, no one, including insurance companies, knows anything about how likely any particular person is to contract any particular disease or infirmity. Under these idealized conditions, suppose that health care decisions are simply left to individual market decisions, in a free market.

Dworkin's conception of justice in relation to health defers to hypothetical choices made under these conditions (Dworkin 1993). He claims that whatever *total* such a society would choose to spend on health care would be a just and appropriate total health care expense for that society, and that whatever *distribution* of health care would result in such a society would be a just distribution. He speculates that private insurance would develop into large collective insurance arrangements, which might result in something close to a single comprehensive public health insurance scheme for a basic level of provision, probably supplemented by a secondary insurance market for additional coverage. The basic package that would be chosen, he argues, would not include insurance to provide expensive life-extending care for those in persistent vegetative states or in the late stages of Alzheimer's disease. This is because most would agree that, whether or not they fell victim to these health conditions, the large amount of money that would have to be spent on premiums for such insurance would be prohibitive, and would have been better spent making their preceding lives more worthwhile: on education or travel or family projects. Similar trade-offs might argue against including expensive and/or speculative medical techniques in the basic package, thus avoiding bottomless pit worries (cf. Daniels 1985: 20–1). Practical reform aiming for justice in health care could thus be guided by this kind of exercise: by trying to imagine what people would choose for themselves under these idealized conditions.

However, in Daniels's view, 'we cannot just finesse the question of whether there are special issues of justice in the distribution of health care by assuming that fair shares of primary goods will be used in part to buy reasonable health insurance' (Daniels 1985: 45). This is because a share of resources is fair only if it is enough to cover reasonable health insurance. A share that is too small to do this is inadequate, and it is unfair that someone who has it cannot buy reasonable coverage. To know whether a share is fair, we already have to know if it can buy reasonable coverage. Justice with respect to health and health care cannot be reduced or assimilated to justice with respect to resources in general, because the latter presupposes resources adequate to meet reasonable needs.

To the counterobjection that there is no one level of insurance that is prudent and therefore reasonable for everyone, Daniels replies that our notion of prudence has a structure that reflects a concern to meet basic needs, including health care needs. There is a sense in which to be excluded by resource limitations from participating in a market that meets certain basic needs is to be denied the opportunity to be prudent. Health care needs are not just one preference among many, with no special claim on resources. Health and health care may be objectively more important than individual choices reflect (Daniels 1985: 21–4).

2.7. Health and Equal Opportunity

To develop these points, Daniels appeals to the idea that some needs relate not merely to specific contingent projects, but to the course of a normal human life, in abstraction from particular choices and preferences. He explains the importance or priority of health-related goods in terms of their necessity to achieve or maintain species-typical normal functioning. In particular, impairments of normal functioning through disease and disability reduce the range of opportunity open to the individual, within which he may pursue the life that is right for him, relative to that portion of the normal range of opportunity his skills and talents would have made available to him were he healthy. The normal opportunity range for a given society is the array of life plans reasonable persons in it are likely to pursue. The share of the normal range open to an individual is determined in a fundamental way by his talents and skill. Disease and disability render us ineligible for life plans for which we would otherwise be suited and might find attractive. Maintaining normal species functioning is thus necessary to maintain one's share of the normal range of opportunities and to preserve the possibility of revising one's conception of a good life through time. 'If an individual's fair share of the normal range is the array of life plans he may reasonably choose, given his talents and skills, then disease and disability shrink his share from what is fair.' Health needs are special because 'people have a fundamental interest in protecting their share of the normal range of opportunities' (Daniels 1985: 27, 33–6).

Notice that Daniels's account of why health is special does not treat disease and disability as negative internal resources, at the opposite end of a spectrum from positive internal resources such as talents. Rather, it treats disabilities and talents asymmetrically. Daniels does not presume that a fair share of the normal range of opportunity requires that the effects of normal variation in individual talents and skills are to be eliminated. He is concerned rather with the effects of disease and disability on the share of the normal range of opportunities that an individual's skills and talents would otherwise open to him. In his view, the principle of fair equality of opportunity per se requires only that opportunity be equal for those with similar skills and talents (although *other* principles within a general theory of justice may require compensation for unequal talents). Daniels's position is thus open to the challenge to justify its asymmetrical treatment of talent and health. Why should we respond differently to disability or ill health than we do to lack of talent?

We are now in a position to understand the central point of Daniels's alternative way of extending a resource-based theory of justice, in particular, Rawls's theory, explicitly to health concerns. He proposes that health care institutions and practices are basic to providing fair equality of opportunity, by eliminating or reducing a specific type of impairment to normal functioning. Moreover, in Rawls's theory, the requirement of fair equality of opportunity is given priority over the difference principle, which otherwise governs the distribution of primary goods. The difference principle permits inequalities to the extent that they benefit the worst off, but only subject to the prior requirement that competition for positions in society must be fair, which requires not just the elimination of formal or legal barriers based on race, sex, etc., but also that positive, enabling steps be taken to enhance the opportunities of the disadvantaged (Daniels 1985: 40, 45). Thus, Daniels explains why health is not merely one resource among many, but is indeed special, in a sense that reflects the priority accorded to the requirement of fair equality of opportunity and the fundamentally important role of health in promoting fair equality of opportunity.

In this respect, health care is comparable to education: both are strategically important to enabling fair equality of opportunity and both address needs which are unequally distributed among individuals. Everyone needs food and clothing to more or less the same degree, but health care and learning needs differ greatly between people. Thus, health care, like education, is in a separate category from other basic needs, such as needs for food and shelter, which we can expect people to meet out of their fair income shares (Daniels 1985: 46–7). But despite the specialness of health care needs, Daniels does not regard his view as threatened by the 'bugaboo' of bottomless pit worries about health care costs: health care institutions capable of protecting fair opportunities can only be provided and maintained in a society whose productive capacities they do not undermine (1985: 54).

However, health care also differs from education in an important respect, which generates a limitation on Daniels's argument: the need for education is focused on the young, while the need for health care is not. If the underlying motivation of Daniels's view concerns fair competition for positions, then his view does not seem to speak to the distribution of health care among people who have retired and, thus, no longer compete for positions, i.e. jobs. Yet, presumably we want our theory of just health care to address this issue.[5]

2.8. Responsibility and Health

Time again to take stock of arguments so far and observe signposts to arguments that follow. So far, we've seen that welfare-maximizing views make it difficult to combine reasons to remove disabilities with the non-favoritism ideal applied to life extensions. We then reviewed the defects of welfare egalitarianism in dealing with health-related issues, and considered two responses. One response is to move to a resource-egalitarian framework that extends to include health-related resources, internal as well as external, along with other resources. A second response does not treat health resources as on a par with others. Rather, it treats health as similar to education in playing a critical role in enabling fair equality of opportunity and therefore as inheriting the special priority attributed to equality of opportunity.

Neither of these responses has focused, however, on one important feature of health: that individuals have a degree of control over and responsibility for their own health. Individuals who face equal opportunities for health itself may choose differently: for example, one may choose to smoke or mountain climb, another not. A thoroughgoing concern with equality of opportunity would not only regard health as an important condition of fair opportunities for other goods in life, but would also be concerned with the opportunity for health itself, and how people respond to it. Dworkin wishes to hold people responsible for gambles they choose to take in deciding whether or not to take out insurance. By the same token, it might be

---

[5] Thanks to the editors for this point.

argued, they should be held responsible for gambles they choose to take directly with their health itself, say, by smoking or mountain climbing (see Dworkin 1993: 889 n.; Daniels 1985: 56). On this view we are led to ask: Does justice require society to try to restore the health of those who put their own health at risk? Why should the relatively more risk-averse general public pay for the risky habits of others?[6] Should health insurance schemes charge significantly higher premiums to those who choose to put their health at risk?

One reaction to this line of thought is that some risky activities, such as smoking, are not really freely chosen. Rather, they are in the first instance the result of social pressures and influences on the impressionable young and thereafter the result of addiction. But how compatible is this view with the common antipaternalist view that people should be free to make their own autonomous choices about what health risks to run and that healthy behavior should not be legislated in a free society? For example, there appears to be a tension between maintaining, on the one hand, that the state should not legislate against the marketing of cigarettes, that people's choices to smoke or not must be respected—presumably on grounds of antipaternalism and personal autonomy—and, on the other hand, that people are not really responsible for such choices. If the social and physiological factors that lead people to take up and continue to smoke do so in a way that undermines their autonomy and their responsibility for their behavior, can such factors be protected from paternalistic legislation on grounds of personal autonomy?

A third way of responding to the defects of welfare egalitarianism takes on these thorny issues about responsibility—indeed, makes them central to a general theory of distributive justice in a way that has direct application to health-related issues. This response is made by the luck-egalitarian view of justice developed by Cohen, Roemer, and Arneson.[7] On this general view, it is not quite right to shift from a concern with the distribution of welfare to a concern with the distribution of resources. What really matters, rather, is whether people are responsible for their disadvantages or whether these are a matter of brute luck. And this distinction cuts across the distinction between welfare and resources. *What* justice requires we compensate people for is disadvantages of either resources or welfare to the extent these are a matter of luck. But inequalities in either resources or welfare for which people are responsible are not unjust. Moreover, on this view, people only really have equal opportunities when any relevant differences between them are the result of choice and they are equal in respect of matters of brute luck.

---

[6] See Williams, Ch. 10 in this volume.

[7] Their views differ in detail, but I will ignore these differences here and simply convey the gist of the luck-egalitarian approach. For more details, see Hurley (2003).

We can revisit some of the cases that made trouble for welfare-based views with the responsibility–luck distinction in hand. We can explain the intuition that we should compensate someone for disease or disability but not for expensive tastes in these terms. We normally assume that people are not responsible for being, say, blind—that disabilities are bad brute luck. But we do normally hold people with expensive tastes responsible for their own choices; we don't regard someone's expensive tastes as a matter of bad brute luck for her. However, if someone's disease or disability is the clear result of his own informed and autonomous choices to take gambles, then his claim to compensation as a matter of justice would indeed be weakened. Moreover, if someone's expensive tastes really were involuntary cravings for which he bears no responsibility, then they would be a matter of bad brute luck and would make a call on justice. Disadvantages with respect either to resources or to welfare can make a call on justice for compensation, but only to the extent that they are a matter of bad brute luck.

One of the central problems such luck-egalitarian views face is how to apply the responsibility–luck distinction, given that people are partly but not wholly responsible for many of their advantages and disadvantages. Disease resulting from smoking, for example, might be partly a matter of bad brute luck—the result of, say, peer pressure, but also partly the result of choices for which the individual bears responsibility. John Roemer has made an ingenious proposal for how to operationalize the ideal of equality of opportunity, which he applies to issues of equity in health care. True, we should recognize how brute luck with respect to health may undermine equality of opportunity with respect to other goods. But we should also consider whether people have equal opportunities for health itself. If they do have, but have made different choices resulting in different health outcomes, then equality of opportunity may not treat health needs as special after all. Roemer aims to explain what it would be for people to have equal opportunities for health, among other things, so that differences in health reflect freely chosen risks rather than brute luck (Roemer 1993, 1995, 1996). To the extent that health needs result from freely chosen risks rather than brute luck, Roemer's scheme treats them as on a par with other resource deficits that result from freely chosen risks rather than brute luck.

Consider some type of health-damaging behavior, such as smoking. Roemer asks us to consider all the factors that influence whether and how much people smoke: class, education, sex, family background, degree of self-discipline, etc. We divide these factors into those for which people are responsible and those that are a matter of luck. Roemer himself does not presume to tell us how to make this division. We make it according to our own judgments or best theory about what people are responsible for. Now take all the factors for which people are not responsible, and use them to assign people to types. People who are members of the same type will be similar in respect of all those factors for which we deem them not to be responsible. Roemer suggests, for example, that members of one type might be black male steelworkers, while members of another type might be white female professors.

Between types, there will be differences in average smoking behavior: black male steelworkers might smoke on average considerably more than white female professors. People are not responsible for such intertype differences. Thus such differences do make a call on justice: more health care resources are justly allocated to black male steelworkers as a type than to white female professors as a type, in order to cope with the former's higher overall incidence of smoking-related diseases.

But within each type, there will also be variation in smoking behavior: some black male steelworkers will smoke much less than others, some white female professors will smoke much more than others. People are responsible for such intratype differences. Roemer proposes that we should aim to deliver health care so that people at the median degree of smoking within each type are restored to the same level of health. He views those at the median within each type as having exerted the same degree of effort not to smoke, and therefore as equally deserving. Within a type, people who smoke at the median level for that type should receive the same quantity of health care resources as people who smoke at the median level in other types. As a result, on this view justice and equality of opportunity with respect to health care may require allocations of health care resources that restore someone at the median in a less 'lucky', more smoking-prone, type to a higher level of health than someone who actually smokes less but who is below the median in a 'luckier', more smoking-resistant, type.[8]

This result conflicts with standard views about horizontal equity, which require giving two patients with equal health care needs the same treatment. But Roemer argues for a different understanding of horizontal equity, which incorporates responsibility and requires that two patients who have made the same degree of effort not to damage their health be restored to equal levels of health, even if they belong to very different types.

Let's take stock and observe signposts once more, before shifting from 'what' questions to 'how' questions. We've considered several different answers to the question of what distributive justice is concerned with the distribution of.

We saw that welfare-based answers failed even to distinguish disease and disability from expensive tastes. Such views do not see health as playing a special role in distributive justice; disease and disability are just more ways in which some people fail to generate as much welfare from given resources as others do. By contrast, Dworkin's conception of equality of resources includes health-related resources among the relevant resources and regards disease and disability as negative internal

---

[8] I criticize this proposal in comments following Roemer (1995) and in Hurley (2003), but do not here expound the difficulties I see for Roemer's view.

resources. This view avoids conflating disability and expensive tastes, and it allows us to compensate for disability as a resource deficit per se, regardless of how well adapted the disabled person may be. But it does not treat health as special, either. Rather, it puts health-related resources into competition with other resources and defers to the (idealized) choices people make about whether to spend their fair resource shares on health insurance or other goods.

We've also considered two different views of equality of opportunity, which have different implications for the issue of whether health is special. Daniels takes issue with a view of health as one resource among others. He argues that it is special because of its importance as a condition of fair equality of opportunity for many other goods and because the fair distribution of opportunity takes priority over the fair distribution of other goods. Roemer, by contrast, applies the concept of equal opportunity to health itself, as well as other goods. With health disadvantages as with other kinds of disadvantage: they are unjust only to the extent they are a matter of bad brute luck. Bad health outcomes that result from autonomous choices no more compromise equality of opportunity than bad outcomes of any other kind do when they result from autonomous choices.

A partial answer to our central question is shaping up: consideration of the 'what' question about distributive justice has revealed no decisive reason to regard health as special. Welfare- and resource-based arguments provide no such reason. While Daniels provides an opportunity-based argument that health is special, it may not apply to the retired and it does not take account of the opportunity for health itself, as Roemer's argument does. The weight of argument is on the other side.

However, it is possible to imagine a reply on behalf of the view that health makes special demands of justice, which draws on Daniels's view that *normal* species functioning is necessary for equal opportunity for various social and economic goods. It might be argued that even if we accept that considerations of responsibility apply in principle to health as well as to other goods, there is nevertheless an asymmetry. There are two ways in which health is a condition of opportunities for other, socioeconomic goods. Absolute health is a condition of opportunity for socioeconomic goods, but so also is relative health, in the way Daniels suggests. When we consider the reverse relations, we should allow that absolute socioeconomic standing is a condition of opportunity for health. But *relative socio*economic standing is not a condition of opportunity for health. Merely relative ill health or disability can make other goods unavailable, whereas merely relatively poor socioeconomic standing does not similarly make health unavailable. This asymmetry gives us a reason to be especially concerned with the distribution of health, whether or not people are responsible for their health conditions.

This reply depends on an empirical claim: that while relative health has causal influence on socioeconomic position, relative socioeconomic position does not have a causal influence on health. This claim may have a certain superficial plausibility; it may be natural to think that in so far as socioeconomic position is a condition of health, it is absolute socioeconomic position that matters, not relative socioeconomic position. It is interesting therefore to note that this empirical supposition is challenged by Wilkinson (1996), who argues that health levels within a society are largely a function of the distribution, as opposed to the absolute level, of economic and social goods within that society.[9] In other words, he claims that people's absolute level of health is strongly influenced by their relative economic and social position within their society. It is the more egalitarian rather than the richer societies that have the best health, even when many other factors are controlled for (such as race, smoking, quality of medical services, etc.) (see Wilkinson 1996: 66, 75, 80–2, 213, etc.).[10]

If Wilkinson is right, then someone's share of economic and social goods may in fact be a condition of the opportunity for health, as well as vice versa. If the suggested asymmetry does not hold, we cannot argue from it for the view that health makes special demands of justice because it has an asymmetrically fundamental causal role as a condition of opportunity for other goods. Wilkinson's view reinforces the view that answers to 'what' questions do not give health a special role in relation to other goods that are the concern of distributive justice.

3. The 'How' Question

3.1. Equality Versus Priority: Leveling Down and Trickling Down

Let's now turn, more briefly, to the 'how' question about distributive justice. Can we find a reason to give health a special role here? Perhaps surprisingly, this looks more likely, in relation to arguments about both 'trickling down' and 'leveling down'.

The 'how' question is brought into focus by Parfit's (1995) important distinction between equality and priority. Egalitarianism proper is concerned with whether certain people are actually worse off than other people, and the relations between the actual states of different people. By contrast, priority views are rather concerned with

[9] At least for societies that have gone through the epidemiological transition from infectious to degenerative disease; see Wilkinson (1996, ch. 3, and pp. 75, 83, etc.) For a parallel with respect to the attainment of educational standards, see (1996: 161).

[10] An analysis of data from seventy rich and poor countries found that 'if the absolute incomes of the poorest 20 per cent in each society are held constant, rises in the incomes of the top 5 per cent are associated with *rises* in infant mortality. Given that one might have expected that rises in the incomes of the richest would, other things being held equal, have led to a reduction in their infant mortality, this is a particularly powerful demonstration of the importance of relative income' (Wilkinson 1996: 78; see Waldmann 1992).

the relations between individuals' actual states and other possible states they might have been in, with whether people are worse off than they might have been, and with absolute levels of well-being. According to priority views, benefits to the worse off matter more, not because of the relationship of the worse off to other people, but because of the absolute level of the worse off. The maximin principle, which requires that the worst off be made as well off as possible, can be regarded as an extreme form of priority view, according to which benefits to the worst off matter most. On a priority view, equality between people can, under certain assumptions, be a means to making the worse off better off, but the relation of equality between people per se is not an essential concern. Equality between people is of merely instrumental value on the priority view.

Note that while priority views use absolute levels of goods to weight benefits, they still involve comparisons. The shift from equality to priority involves a shift from one type of comparison to another: from relations between the positions of different persons (whether in well-being, resources, moral status, or whatever) to relations between the actual position of a person and other possible positions he might have been in. This is a shift from interpersonal to counterfactual comparisons. As Parfit puts the priority view, 'what is bad is not that these people are worse off than others. It is rather than they are worse off than they might have been' (Parfit 1995: 22).

Different answers to the 'what?' question cut across the distinction between equality and priority. For example, just as the aim to distribute equally can be applied to welfare or to resources, so various prioritarian principles of distribution can be applied to welfare or to resources. Moreover, there are other answers to the 'how' question, in addition to equality and priority views. For example, Frankfurt (1987) argues that what matters is not whether people are equal, but whether everyone has *enough*. The question then arises whether the relevant threshold for sufficiency should be understood in absolute or interpersonally relative terms. Although sufficiency views raise interesting questions in relation to health, I don't pursue them here but focus on equality and priority answers to the 'how?' question.

Debate between equality and priority views raises issues of trickling down and leveling down. Suppose we start from a position of interpersonal equality of income; we then allow people to receive more income than this initial level, if they do extra or more valuable forms of work. By creating additional incentives to work, such inequality might have trickle-down benefits for everyone, including those at the bottom. Some of the additional product would go to those who do the extra work, but the extra work could also have the effect of making everyone else better off than they would be under strict equality. It is an empirical question whether this would in fact happen in various circumstances.

According to priority views, *if* in fact certain forms of inequality do make everyone as well off as possible, and better off than they would be under equality, then they are not objectionable. To insist on equality in such a case would be to level everyone down. This seems especially hard to justify if it makes even the worst off worse off than they could be. However, leveling down is controversial even if it doesn't lower the level of the worst off, but merely brings the better off all down to the same level as the worst off. And some forms of priority view would permit inequalities even if they don't make everyone, including the worst off, better off, but just make some people better off and no one worse off. Many people are attracted to priority views because they wish to allow that *if* trickle-down effects do occur, inequality is acceptable, and, more generally, because they find leveling down for the sake of equality objectionable.

3.2. Trickle-Down Effects and Health

These issues about trickling down and leveling down can be played out in terms of various different answers to the 'what' question. We can ask whether inequalities of income have trickle-down benefits in terms of income, or in terms of welfare—or in terms of health. The answers to these different questions may not line up. For example, suppose it is true that, as a matter of empirical fact, certain inequalities of income have significant trickle-down benefits in terms of income: that as a result, everyone, including the worst off, has more income than they would under egalitarianism. It would not follow that these income inequalities also have trickle-down health benefits. This is a further empirical question. Even where there are trickle-down income benefits from income inequality in a given society, and people are richer across the board, there may not be trickle-down health benefits. If not, then this may provide one sense in which health may indeed be special among the goods relevant to justice, and may require special treatment rather than assimilation to other goods.

It may seem natural to overlook this empirical possibility, for two reasons. It may be natural simply to assume that health will increase with absolute income levels. And it may also be thought that medical advances and technologies driven by demand from those at the highest income levels in a given society will in due course trickle down to improve medical care for those at lower levels. Perhaps these medical advances and technologies would not be developed and realized in the first place if there weren't rich people and/or private medical insurance to pay for them. However, once established, their costs may fall or they may have spin-off benefits for the quality of medical care across the board.

However, we should not lose sight of the fact that this is an empirical issue; the facts may be counterintuitive. Health levels may not go in step with income levels. Recall that Wilkinson claims that 'the most egalitarian rather than the richest developed countries . . . have the best health' (Wilkinson 1996: 75). If he is right, in developed societies relative income has more of an effect on absolute health levels than absolute income levels do, even when other factors, including quality of medical care, are controlled for. Therefore, even on the empirical assumption that income inequality raises income levels for many of the worse-off members of society, it is possible that it nevertheless worsens their health levels. Prioritarians may thus face a conflict in considering the effects of income inequality, between improving income levels and improving health levels. They may need to give health special treatment by factoring health levels out from the levels of other goods in assessing trickle-down effects.

3.3. Leveling Down and Health

So far, our consideration of the 'how' question about distributive justice has provided one sense in which health may require special treatment, related to trickle-down effects. I now set aside issues about trickle-down effects of income inequality on absolute levels of health. I next want to consider how equality and priority views might apply to health itself, as opposed to other goods.

Recall that priority views gain appeal in part from the unattractiveness of leveling down for the sake of equality. Suppose that in Society A there an inequality with respect to health: half the people in A have some bearable but unpleasant and inconvenient illness, while the other half do not. Suppose it is not possible to cure the illness, but it is possible to induce the illness in the healthy. In Society B the illness is induced in all those who don't already have it. In B but not A there is equality with respect to health; in other respects, A and B are relevantly similar. Equality would favor moving from A to B, or leveling down, though priority views would not. If we deny that there is any reason at all to level down, we should reject equality. Priority views offer an alternative that avoids implying that there is any reason to level down.

Temkin (1993; compare Christiano, Chapter 2 in this volume) defends equality by defending leveling down. He argues that the objection to leveling down is motivated by a 'person-affecting requirement', which Temkin sums up in the 'Slogan' that one situation cannot be worse or better than another in any way if there's no one for whom it is worse or better in any way. For example, how could B be better than A in any way, when no one is better off in B than in A, and indeed half are worse off? Temkin responds to this challenge in two ways. First, he attacks the person-affecting requirement expressed by the Slogan. Second, he invokes pluralism: equality provides some reason, of fairness, for leveling down even if all things considered leveling down is not justified. I will not consider his second, pluralist response here. Nor do I take issue with his attack on the Slogan, with which I largely agree. Rather, I want to take issue with his diagnosis of the objection to leveling down as primarily motivated by the person-affecting requirement.

I suggest that the most basic motivation for the aversion to leveling down is not the person-affecting requirement but simply impersonal perfectionism and the value of excellence. Leveling down wastefully throws away the higher reaches of good in some dimension: welfare, health, or whatever is in question. This is the strongest and most immediate intuitive basis for resistance to leveling down. It is not undermined in any way by attacks on the Slogan. Indeed, perfectionism is strengthened by, and can contribute to, attacks on the Slogan.

The Slogan may lead one to ask: How could equality be better in any way if there is no one for who it is better in any way? This question implies that the same people exist in the equal and unequal scenarios, and that their positions are being compared across the scenarios, as in the comparison of Society A and Society B. But impersonal perfectionism leads one to ask: How could equality be better if it wastes excellence? This question does not imply that the same people exist in the equal and unequal scenarios. The unequal scenario is regarded as better just to the extent that it involves more excellence. The identities of the people involved could change, and the point would still hold. The extra excellence need not count as better for anyone. It is just better in itself for there to be more excellence rather than less, no matter to whom it attaches.

Temkin thinks that the Slogan motivates anti-egalitarianism, while I think that the more fundamental motivation may be perfectionism. How does this disagreement look applied to health? The Slogan is at its weakest applied to the kind of flourishing that good health involves, which is an excellence with strong perfectionist appeal. The perfectionist can plausibly claim that it is simply worse, other things equal, for there to be a unhealthy person than for there to be a healthy person, even if they are different people so that it is not worse for either of them (as when a woman chooses to delay attempting to conceive for a month in order to avoid the damaging side-effects of medication). Of course, this only provides one consideration among many, and may be outweighed within a pluralistic scheme. And it certainly does not license us to do away with the unhealthy in order to make way for the healthy. But it does express why leveling down seems such a very aversive thing to do, regardless of the identities of the persons involved. If leveling down would be aversive even across changes in identity, it does not become any less aversive when identities are held constant![11]

While a parallel perfectionist argument could be made against leveling down for various other goods, it has more force for some goods than others. If we abstract from issues about conflict between the interests of different persons, it is hard for liberals to deny someone's prerogative to make trade-offs freely among goods that are just goods for her. But goods that are not just goods for people, but also good in themselves, may not be available for trade-offs on the same terms. Health is a distinctive kind of flourishing, with a specific natural character and basis, which seems to be a good in itself, in addition to being good for people. It is not just good for people to be healthy rather than unhealthy; it is also good in itself for there to be healthy people rather

---

[11] See and cf. Holtug, Ch. 5 in this volume.

than unhealthy people. Compare: Can we also claim that it is not just good for people to have higher income levels, but also that it is good for there to be people with higher income levels rather than people with lower income levels? The latter claim seems to be only derivatively true, in so far as there are other things that are good in themselves that high income levels are a means to.

Perfectionism and the Slogan seem to be inversely related, in that the goods for which impersonal perfectionism is strongest, such as health, are by the same token goods for which the Slogan is implausible. Thus, the perfectionist objection to leveling down is not in any way undermined by attacks on the Slogan. Rather, perfectionism contributes to undermining the Slogan, as well as to resisting leveling down in arguments about the 'how' question.

At this point Temkin can invoke pluralism on behalf of equality and leveling down. On this view, there is something to be said for equality, namely, its avoidance of unfairness, even if this reason for leveling down is outweighed all things considered. The perfectionist could in principle agree with the egalitarian that there is *something* to be said for leveling down, namely, that it avoids unfairness, even though she holds that this reason is heavily outweighed by perfectionism reasons against leveling down. The pluralism point is surely correct, although I have worries about applying it to fairness in this way. But I will not pursue this issue here.

So, this is another respect in which health may require special treatment and may not properly be assimilated to other goods or to a general measure of resources within a theory of distributive justice. As an excellence which is good in itself, as well as good for those who are healthy, health may be especially resistant to leveling down and hence to strict equality, for perfectionist reasons that do not depend on the Slogan. However, to the extent that perfectionism about health embodies an answer we've not yet considered to the 'what' question, perhaps the 'what' and 'how' issues interact here in giving health a special role in distributive justice.

4. Conclusion

Various answers to the 'what' and the 'how' questions about distributive justice have been canvassed, in search of ways in which health may require special treatment rather than assimilation to other goods. Perhaps surprisingly, stronger reasons for treating health as special have emerged from consideration of *how* we should distribute than from consideration of *what* we should distribute. We do not find strong reasons for treating health as special in 'what' arguments about welfare, resources, or luck. Such reasons are suggested by 'how' arguments about both trickling down and leveling down. The contribution of perfectionism about health to opposition to leveling down for health indicates a way in which 'what' and 'how' considerations may interact in supporting a special role for health in distributive justice.

References

ARNESON, R. (1989), 'Equality of Opportunity for Welfare', *Philosophical Studies*, 56/1: 77–93.

ARROW, K. (1973), 'Uncertainty and the Welfare Economics of Medical Care', *American Economic Review*, 53/5: 941–73.

BROCK, D. (1993), 'Quality of Life Measures in Health Care and Medical Ethics', in M. C. Nussbaum and A. Sen (eds.), *The Quality of Life* (Oxford: Clarendon Press), 94–132.

COHEN, G. A. (1989), 'On the Currency of Egalitarian Justice', *Ethics*, 99/4: 906–44.

DANIELS, N. (1985), *Just Health Care* (Cambridge: Cambridge University Press).

―――― and Sabin, J. (1997), 'Limits to Health Care', *Philosophy and Public Affairs*, 26/4: 303–50.

DWORKIN, R. (1981a), 'What Is Equality? Part 2: Equality of Resources', *Philosophy and Public Affairs*, 10/4: 283–345.

―――― (1981b), 'What is Equality? Part 1: Equality of Welfare', *Philosophy and Public Affairs*, 10/3: 185–246.

―――― (1993), 'Justice in the Distribution of Health Care', *McGill Law Journal*, 38/4: 883–98; repr. in M. Clayton and A. Williams (eds.), *The Ideal of Equality* (London: Macmillan, 2000), 203–22.

FRANKFURT, H. (1987), 'Equality as a Moral Ideal', *Ethics*, 98/1: 21–43.

HURLEY, S. L. (2003), *Justice, Luck, and Knowledge* (Cambridge, Mass.: Harvard University Press).

MURRAY, C. J. L. (1996), 'Rethinking DALY's', in C. J. L. Murray and A. D. Lopez (eds.), *The Global Burden of Disease* (Cambridge, Mass.: Harvard University Press, for the World Health Organization and the World Bank), 1–98.

PARFIT, D. (1995), 'Equality or Priority?', The Lindley Lecture, 1991 (Lawrence: University of Kansas); repr. in M. Clayton and A. Williams (eds.), *Some Questions for Egalitarians* (London: Macmillan, 2000), 81–125.

RAWLS, J. (1971), *A Theory of Justice* (Cambridge, Mass.: Harvard University Press).

ROEMER, J. (1993), 'A Pragmatic Theory of Responsibility for the Egalitarian Planner', *Philosophy and Public Affairs*, 22: 146–66.

―――― (1995), 'Equality and Responsibility', *Boston Review*, 20/2: 3–7, 15–16.

―――― (1996), *Theories of Distributive Justice* (Cambridge, Mass.: Harvard University Press).

SEN, A. (1982), 'Equality of What?', in Sen, *Choice, Welfare and Measurement* (Oxford: Basil Blackwell), 353–69.

TEMKIN, L. S. (1993), *Inequality* (New York: Oxford University Press).

WALDMANN, R. J. (1992), 'Income Distribution and Infant Mortality', *Quarterly Journal of Economics*, 107/4: 1283–1302.

WALZER, M. (1983), *Spheres of Justice* (New York: Basic Books).

WILKINSON, R. G. (1996), *Unhealthy Societies: The Afflictions of Inequality* (London: Routledge).

INDEX